BETWEEN THE DEVIL AND THE DEEP

BETWEEN THE DEVIL AND THE DEEP

One Man's Battle to Beat the Bends

Mark Cowan and Martin Robson

unbound

First published in 2021

Unbound

Level 1, Devonshire House, One Mayfair Place, London W1J 8AJ

www.unbound.com

Text design by Ellipsis, Glasgow

A CIP record for this book is available from the British Library

ISBN 978-1-80018-029-1 (hardback)
ISBN 978-1-80018-030-7 (ebook)

Printed in Great Britain by CPI Group (UK)

1 3 5 7 9 8 6 4 2

For Edik, Guardian of the Blue Lake

Посвящается Эдику, Хранителю Голубого озера

With special thanks to Otter Drysuits

CONTENTS

A NOTE FOR READERS

Between the Devil and the Deep is, in the truest sense, the product of collaboration between Mark Cowan as the writer and the people whose story it tells. From the outset, Mark's approach was to write as factual an account as he could, bearing in mind he was not present for the events described, one that would stand on its own as a piece of journalism. For that, he needed the trust and participation of the people involved. This narrative is based on his interviews with them, on their memoirs, diaries, on contemporaneous reports, online accounts, photographs and videos, and on simply hanging around with people, eating with them, sharing their space, moving with the rhythms of their life and observing them going about their business.

Recreating that period of January 2012 in such detail would not have been possible without the involvement of Martin Robson and his willingness to relive in great detail his experiences in Russia. Mark spent many hours speaking with him about the events. Martin answered his questions candidly and gave him access to files, notes, photographs and dive logs to support his answers. Martin allowed Mark, someone he barely knew at the outset, to intrude into an extremely personal period of his life and accepted his tireless questioning with good grace and humour. In that way, he became an active participant in the storytelling process, helping to recreate the scenes by dredging the recesses of his memory for the tiniest pieces of information. Martin also helped open the doors to a number of the people involved in the expedition and patiently guided Mark's understanding of what it is like to dive well beyond the limits of one's comfort level. This book is the result of that collaboration, which is why both of their names adorn the front cover.

While Martin was, obviously, an active participant in the events being recounted, *Between the Devil and the Deep* is written in third person. This was a narrative choice to allow the book to take the reader to as many places as possible – particularly as the rescue mission got under way – including events that Martin was not party to. As Dr Gennady Sokolov was such a key figure in Martin's rescue, treatment and recovery, the use of third person gave Mark the freedom to write about those events from the doctor's point of view.

In August 2018, Mark accompanied Martin on his return to Russia and his reunion with Dr Sokolov. The doctor and his colleagues warmly welcomed the two men into their Institute. They took great pride in showing Mark and Martin around and talking about the groundbreaking research that had been conducted there. Dr Sokolov was gracious with his time and answered as many questions as Mark could ask. They also got to see the doctor run the chamber for a team of divers on a deep dry dive to one hundred metres. The visits to the Institute bookended the trip in which Mark and Martin followed as closely as possible Martin's original route to Kabardino-Balkaria and Blue Lake. Many people there looked after their welfare, made travel arrangements, interpreted conversations and facilitated a dive in Blue Lake. If one person should be singled out it is Eduard Khuazhev for his hospitality as he took care of them in his hometown of Nalchik.

For the writer, being immersed in the world about which they are reporting can reveal important insights that may not otherwise be available. In some respects, Mark was lucky because he had been a diver for a decade when he first met Martin and started to report his story. To understand the allure of cave diving, he went to Mexico to learn. The hours spent underwater in the middle of the jungle with experienced cave diving instructor Christine Loew opened his eyes to a world beneath his feet, and a subculture of fascinating people. To gain an insight into the work of the technicians who operate recompression chambers, Mark spent time with a friend and recompression chamber technician, Robbie Renalson, and his team in Rugby, UK. Watching them treat a diver suffering the effects of decompression sickness following a holiday dive was particularly helpful.

Even with this understanding, recreating the events of an expedition presented the writer with some obvious problems, among them the conversations people shared. Mark had originally considered dramatising dialogue but feared it might devalue the efforts of reporting. Therefore, no dialogue is invented. Anything that appears in direct quotes was captured by Mark during interviews, is quoted from published material or from personal correspondence. Where this is the case, it has been made clear in the text or in the Notes on Sources.

To research the history of decompression sickness Mark relied on the British Library and the National Archives, Kew, which hold a wealth of books and documents dealing with this long-forgotten story that proved crucial in his research. For records of depths that divers reached during the early days he chose to use the language they used in the spirit of adding authenticity to the text. Where necessary, a conversion to more recognised measurements has been added in parentheses. While the writer acknowledges this choice does not provide a uniform approach throughout the book, it does highlight the changing language of diving.

These historical accounts highlight the painstaking work done by some brilliant minds who set out in search of a solution to the problems of decompression sickness, and to develop safe diving procedures. In telling their stories, Mark would not want any mention of the difficulties they faced to be misconstrued as criticism. The aim was to show how much time and effort they expended on the Herculean task of creating and validating workable diving tables that all divers rely on, and many take for granted. Divers will forever be indebted to the huge number of people whose research over the years has allowed them to explore underwater. Decompression sickness will inevitably remain part of diving, particularly for those mounting significant dives in terms of depth or duration underwater, but those who feature in the pages of this book, along with those who don't, have all made lasting contributions to improving the safety of the sport.

Perhaps the most challenging part of the book was capturing what was going on inside Martin's body at the time. Even with current thinking, those details are something that is not fully known. It is exactly that unknowable element, though, that made the book so compelling to research, report and write. Guided by the thoughts, opinions and academic research from some leading experts in the field, Mark chose to include several possible explanations to drive the narrative without drowning readers under the vast weight of technical theories. Having used those hypotheses to tell an interesting story, he fully acknowledges that new research could throw up other possibilities in the future. He didn't set out to write a treatise on decompression sickness – the subject is too big and there are many people more qualified and better placed to do that.

Finally, Mark also acknowledges that the phrase 'the bends' is not perfectly synonymous with decompression sickness, despite its use as such by laypeople. Originally, the term was a descriptive one to highlight joint or limb pain. With time, it has come to be used as a generic term for decompression disorders. Within the medical profession a classification system has been established to help better recognise the signs and symptoms of the illness. While the writer has tried not to rely overly on the term 'the bends', it has sometimes been used it in its more colloquial meaning for brevity, rhythm and to recognise its everyday usage.

Now the book is finished, the writer can't help but cast a sentimental eye back to when it all started. In the autumn of 2012, Mark was at a diving conference, in Birmingham, when he heard Martin speak about the incident. Afterwards, Mark went to speak with him. Ahead of him was a diver who said to Martin that he should write a book. When Martin replied that he wouldn't know where to start, Mark said: I do. It's been a long journey to get here, but what you hold in your hands is a product of that journey. Martin's story, Mark's writing, their book.

PROLOGUE

He lay there, incapacitated on the stretcher, in the grip of something he had brought back from the deep. A universal tremor had seized control of all his joints, and every part of him convulsed with pain and strangeness: his arms, his legs, his hands, elbows, knees. Even his jaw shook uncontrollably. He had never known anything like it before, might never see anything like it again, and he couldn't do much of anything beyond lying there, hurting.

Around him, gathered in the medical bay on board the Soviet salvage vessel *Spasatel'noye Sudno 87*, were members of the ship's diving team, a group of men who understood the risks of voyaging deep beneath the sea's surface. He knew their faces well. These men were like brothers to him. They had lived, trained and sailed together. They had dived into the cold depths of the sea together, gone beyond the limits of what was thought humanly possible, and reached places where no one else had set foot. As a doctor, he had schooled his comrades on the dangers down there in the darkness and he had told them what to do if they surfaced with pains in their joints. Now they looked at him with painful uncertainty, and he stared back at them. But his eyes did not plead for their help.

Gennady Mikhailovich Sokolov had a plan. A plan that broke all the rules.

I have no right to ask you to do this, he said to the medic at his side.

I know, replied junior doctor Vitaly Kushnir.

But Kushnir knew – they all knew – the gravity of what had to be done to help Sokolov even if they couldn't quite believe what was happening.

Ten hours had passed since Sokolov had been down to the black seabed, 374 feet (114 m) below sea level. Working under pressure, he and a fellow diver attached air hoses to the inlet valves of a submarine lying on the bottom. Reaching such depths was no mean feat back in the mid-1960s, even for men wearing the bubble-shaped copper helmet and lead-soled boots every schoolchild associated with deep-sea divers.

Two men had gone down in the diving bell together as part of the training exercise to test equipment for submarine rescue and worked alongside each other in an alien world on the seabed. Two men had come up from the cold depths, side by side. Two men had jumped from the spherical craft, splashing into seawater that pooled on the deck beneath the skids, and two men had walked into the mess for something to eat. But only one man had gone to bed and woken two hours later to find his body falling apart.

Sitting outside the cylindrical recompression chamber that would be used to treat him, Sokolov could only wonder what the hell had happened down in the dark to spare his comrade but leave him in the gravest struggle for life. He felt anxiety twist his gut and tried to convince himself he would pull

2

through. But even he wasn't sure he would survive the next few hours. The deep was calling in a debt that Sokolov had amassed on the bottom. It had flooded his body with bubbles of gas smaller than the full stop at the end of this sentence. The bubbles attacked his body from the inside. He was suffering from a condition known as decompression sickness.

Decompression sickness is a barotrauma, defined as an injury to a person breathing compressed gas who experiences a rapid decrease in the pressure of water or air that surrounds them. It is, in the words of one scientist, a 'man-made disease, a product of the Industrial Revolution and a consequence of the vacuum pump and air compressor'. For 200 years, decompression sickness has plagued divers, miners and engineers in the most disturbing of ways. Even pilots of America's high-altitude U-2 spy planes had fallen victim to the disorder. One stricken pilot had to be coaxed down by ground controllers and came within five feet of slamming into the runway. The incident left him with persistent headaches, joint pain and a different personality. He couldn't remember how to shave.

The disorder has gone by many names over the years: caisson sickness, tunnel disease, compressed air illness, dysbarism, the chokes. The Germans called it *Luftdruckerkrankungen*. The wives of Greek sponge divers christened it Satan's Disease. Everybody else knows it as 'the bends'. To non-divers, the vast majority of people that is, the bends is the one sure thing they know about diving. To them, it is the devil lurking in the deep, scary enough to dissuade them from strapping on a tank and jumping into the water. To deep divers, the bends is the Damoclean sword hanging over them whenever they push the limits, and they do everything they can to avoid it because they know what it can do to them.

Decompression sickness can screw your joints in pain, mess with your brain, it can choke you to death, or paralyse you so that you end up crippled for life. The worst affected come into the emergency room, as one doctor says, 'bent like a pretzel'. The list of symptoms reads like a doctor's worst nightmare: pain, vertigo, laboured breathing, impaired coordination, confusion, strange skin sensations known as paraesthesia. Worse still is how the effects pile up, one on top of the other, in a systemic attack that devastates the body from the inside out.

The vessels of destruction are commonly believed to be microscopic bubbles of gas which are created on the ascent and grow slowly as the surrounding pressure falls. Imperceptible at first, they lodge in the nooks and crannies of the body and sit there, waiting for the pressure to fall. Then they explode, sudden detonations on a quiet front, obliterating cells, crushing neurons, and sandpapering their way through blood vessels. The bubbles are only one half of the story, though. Bubbles are probably only the gateway to a complex array of consequences and effects that are not yet fully understood, but they can trigger a cascade of biochemical responses that make disturbing reading.

When, in 1912, physiologist Leonard Erskine Hill catalogued fifteen years of research into the affliction, he found all kinds of disturbing abnormalities: giant bubbles swelling the skin; spontaneous flexing of muscles; epileptic fits; raging pulses; blocked and distended bladders; burning eyes; and bedsores sloughing from the body, exposing bone. Within Hill's grue-

4

some archive, three cases from doctors in different parts of the world underline the protean nature of the illness:

> The patient was doubled over and his arms were bent against the front of his body. The pain was so great it made him weep; as great as if someone were tearing open his belly and his chest.
>
> His head swelled and lost shape. In particular, his eyelids grew to the size of eggs, which frightened his comrades. His right eye was black, so that cornea and sclera were indistinguishable.
>
> Japanese, aged about thirty. His condition was of great emaciation. He was suffering complete paraplegia with the loss of control of bladder and rectum, and loss of sensation to the level of the navel.

And on and on. What presented itself unsettled doctors. A Royal Navy pathologist who examined one victim saw black liquid oozing from the incisions made by the scalpel. Veins at the surface of the casualty's brain were engorged with the same sludge. The pathologist found the liver so full of foam he thought it might float in water. The heart was beaded with so much air that, when lifted, it gurgled loudly.

Doctors also noticed the disorder had a strange effect on the spinal column. Some sufferers were permanently paralysed, but others recovered mobility after a few days or months. Between 1900 and 1908, Dr Graham Blick, district medical officer of Broome, Western Australia, recorded an extraordinarily grim series of cases among pearl fishermen. The strange malady took the legs before the arms, he noted. Some men died within an hour, others clung on for a day or two. Examining the body of each man afterwards, Blick was particularly drawn to the effects on the spinal cord: it looked as if it had been stippled with a knife.

In the 1950s, the US Navy produced an educational film showing the effects of the bends on a hard-hat diver. The black and white footage shows the crewcut man chasing his bubbles to the surface. The next shot is a close-up of the bloodstream of a frog which had been rapidly decompressed. Gleaming with a silver sheen, bubbles race across the screen, first in ones, then twos, then more until they coalesce and swell. Soon, the bubbles look like peas in the withered pod of a vein. The film cuts back to the diver sitting on the deck, attendants helping him out of his equipment. He is in visible discomfort. Then he collapses. The narrator soberly announces that decompression sickness is a most serious condition which requires immediate care to prevent permanent damage and perhaps death. The last few frames show five sailors hurrying across the deck, the diver in their arms, and then passing him through the narrow circular doorway into the recompression chamber.

For those suffering decompression sickness, the standard treatment is to be sealed inside a recompression chamber and placed back under pressure. The initial compression will, according to the laws of physics, crush the bubbles and bring some relief. Then the diver is slowly decompressed for an hour or more to allow the gas to leave the body, and everyone hopes the bubbles haven't caused irreparable damage.

This, Sokolov knew, was what was expected of him: to be bundled onto a stretcher by his comrades; to be placed inside the chamber; to lie there powerless; to wait for the medics to save him. To be utterly dependent.

Only Sokolov had no intention of doing what was expected.

As the fleet's chief diving doctor, he knew what all the text-books said about recompression therapy. He also understood the implications of his condition. According to the rules of the Baltic Sea War Fleet, he had to be pressurised to the equivalent of 300 feet (91 m) and wait for his condition to improve. Such a treatment would have to be reported up the chain of command. Diving would be halted because the chief of medicine was injured and locked away under pressure. The whole exercise and all that went with it could be cancelled. Sokolov wasn't paralysed by fear of such things when he spoke with his deputy Kushnir.

Behind his grey eyes, Sokolov's bright mind had been thinking through a new treatment regimen for the bends. Instead of using air, he would breathe pure oxygen. As a result, the treatment time would be shorter and would require less pressure. It was a radical departure from the standard. Sokolov was willing to experiment on himself and direct the treatment from inside the chamber. He had no authority to give Kushnir orders in such circumstances, and his deputy was not com-pelled to follow them; if anything went wrong, Kushnir would be the one to carry the can.

But who was anyone to argue with the doctor? Those on board knew Sokolov as a man with a boyish smile that said all you needed to know about his love for diving. Only thirty, Sokolov's exploits in the team were legendary. He had trained to be a diving physiologist and then joined the diving salvage team to know first-hand what the men who might become his patients were up against. He had earned a reputation on board for pushing the limits. He had worked with Valery Rozhdest-vensky (the future cosmonaut and hero of the Soviet Union), carrying out secret experiments hundreds of feet below the surface; Sokolov had himself reached a depth of 525 feet (160 m).

Sharing his plan, Sokolov was outwardly convincing, and Kushnir agreed to follow his prescription.

Inside the recompression chamber, Sokolov prepared for the experiment to begin. There's no guarantee I'll survive this, he thought. But nor was there any guarantee that the traditional treatment would cure him. Either way, this could be the end, and every one of the divers on the ship must have feared it. Sokolov heard the heavy metal door clang shut. He breathed in deep and readied himself for pressurisation to begin with the first hiss of air.

Poyekhali!

Let's go!

NOT STRANGE, JUST A LITTLE DIFFERENT

Once a man has been bitten by the diving bug he's done for. For there's nothing that can be done against this mania, either by fair means or foul. No nook or cranny seems safe from manfish, no cleft, no cave too deep or too dark. He seems to have a close affinity with the members of the mountaineering fraternity. The latter also risk their lives for an experience of a special kind . . . For them too, it is not really the rock face or the mountain that has to be overcome, but their own selves.

Hans Hass, *Men Beneath the Sea*

A gentle wind came in off the distant snow-capped mountains, between the trees and across the mirrored surface of Blue Lake towards the dive centre on the northern shore. The muffled whirr of a compressor engine groaned in the background and divers with unfastened dry suits hanging at their waists carried aluminium diving cylinders which clanked when stacked on the ground. Air hissed in staccato bursts as divers checked the contents of their tanks. Two men in matching red dry suits and woolly hats stood on the concrete jump platform, taking a moment as they planned to herald a new year of exploration. A cameraman from the Russian television news and cultural channel МИР 24 (MIR 24) towed a reporter with a microphone,

9

and possibility, like the smell of neoprene, was so thick in the air it could almost be brushed away with the hand.

On through the double doors, where rubber hoods and gloves hung from pegs, and along the corridor, past a white-board covered in unintelligible squiggles, beyond the storage boxes and duffel bags filled with butyl, Cordura and nickel-plated brass, and towards the drone of the compressor, British explorer Martin Robson crouched over a bench examining his rebreather, lost in the percussion of diving.

The compressor groaned on. The building was carved, like an underground bunker, into the banks of the lake. The corridor, walls tiled white like a sterile cave, was the main line for the centre's operations. Along one wall stood benches used by divers to prepare and don their gear. Various rooms jumped from the passage, a sparse kitchen-cum-briefing room, a cramped store-room for equipment, a workshop and a filling station. At the very end, a spiral staircase went up to a whitewashed apse with a mortarboard roof, and out to a tree-lined courtyard that over-looked the lake. Wrapped with floor-to-ceiling windows and decorated with a panoramic mountain frieze, the building had been completed in 2005. It was designed as a scientific centre but now stood as an empty edifice to a long-forgotten dream.

The place was a second home to Robson's new friend Eduard Khuazhev. For the past six years, he'd been working as a diving instructor, guide and general manager at the centre.

Martin, Martin. Ty gotov k pogruzheniyu? His bass voice echoed along the corridor. Are you ready to go diving?

Da, Robson replied. Yes. He'd only been in the mountains of the distant Russian republic of Kabardino-Balkaria for a day and already Robson was the star attraction. Journalists from the region's newspapers and television news programmes lined up to interview him, and they described him as a 'champion deep diver', 'famous expert in salvaging', and the 'world's best diving trainer and instructor'.

He was there, in the North Caucasus borderlands, somewhere between Georgia and Chechnya, to lead a multinational diving expedition on a quest to find a submerged cave system hidden somewhere in the lake outside. He might come back from the depths with nothing more than a long immersion on his dive computer, or he might come back with tales of a place not seen since the dawn of time. If he found the cave, it would be nothing more to the world than a footnote in history; but it would be his footnote.

The diving promised to be extreme; it would take him close to the physiological limits of underwater human exploration, and beyond the crush depth of a Second World War U-boat. Yet an inventory of Robson's life suggested a man who lived at the limits: military childhood. Special forces operative. Falklands War veteran. Commando diver. Boxer. Climber. Cave explorer. No one's pushover. Robson stood six feet tall, had brown eyes, cropped brown hair, and packed 160 pounds of wiry muscle. He was a private man with a demanding gaze and a mouth that could take its time to warm into a smile. His hard-bitten exterior, weathered at the edges by years of exposure to the cold, the dark and the deep, did not invite admiration on its own. He shied away from small talk – he didn't need to fill the silence, but when he did speak it was rarely without consequence, says one friend – yet a persona polished hard by experience drew people into his orbit.

The compressor hummed on, and Khuazhev watched Robson assemble his rebreather. Closed-circuit rebreathers are a complex piece of military-grade hardware. Unlike conventional scuba equipment, the unit recycles a diver's exhaled breath, which is contained in a closed loop, scrubbing the carbon dioxide from it and periodically adding a squirt of fresh oxygen so it can be breathed again. Efficient and economical, the bubble-free machines allow divers to venture deeper and longer than logistically acceptable on traditional scuba, known as open circuit, where the gas is breathed from a pressurised cylinder and then exhaled into the water.

Robson finished preparing his rebreather and looked around at his fellow expedition members. Nearby, a man named Roman Dunaev was assembling his gear. Dunaev had been taught how to dive with a rebreather by Robson and, after hearing his friend was coming to Russia, he had talked his way onto the expedition. Slightly taller than Robson, Dunaev was huge – and hugely gentle – with an easy-going nature and a disarming smile. He was from the industrial port of Rostov-on-Don, on the Sea of Azov, in south-west Russia. He was thirty-seven years old, although his blue eyes and dimpled chin made him look five years younger. The two men were joined by Sergei Gorpinyuk, another expedition diver whom Robson had met for the first time only two days before.

Gorpinyuk, forty-three, was a big man from Moscow. He had agreed to accompany Robson and Dunaev underwater. Gorpinyuk and Dunaev were old friends who had dived together over the years. They had plenty of stories of where they had been, how deep they had gone, what they had seen and done. They could pass the time with ease, talking about diving together. But then, who else understood their strange dreams and even stranger language of decompression schedules, run times, set points and oxygen toxicity?

Anna Kozlova, a friend of Robson's from Moscow, was also there taking photographs and video of the group. She longed to make a career out of underwater videography and a few years earlier Robson had taught her to dive on a rebreather, which would make it easier to get up close to marine animals without disturbing them.

Robson smiled to himself. Every dive centre he'd ever known had been occupied by a mix of pragmatists and dreamers who had been presented with opportunity, packed with breathing gas and sent on their way. There were always those who wanted to see mysterious creatures, seated next to those who saw diving as a spiritual journey, next to those who wanted to prove something to themselves. He savoured the comradely tone. He'd been here before, many times over the years, ever since diving had chosen him, or more accurately Commando training officers had chosen it for him, and he'd been happy because it came with the privilege of wearing the coveted green beret. On his first dive, at nineteen, he'd crawled through the murk of a dank, dark pool, alone, with just his breathing for company, unable to see a hand in front of his face. And he loved it.

When everything was ready, the three men zipped themselves into their protective waterproof diving dry suits and smoothed out the seal around their necks to prevent water leaking inside. Bulked out by chunky thermal undergarments worn next to their bodies, the men began to cook as relative humidity inside the suits rocketed. Robson shouldered his rebreather and pulled the breathing loop over his head as he'd done countless times before. He connected the pressure inflation hose to his suit as he always did, held his light in the same hand, the separate battery pack placed in the same spot on his webbing, clipped his secondary light to the same harness ring, put his back-up mask in the same pocket, lined his gauges in the exact same order – compass, computer, back-up computer – on his right wrist. He had back-ups for everything, the writing slates, waterproof notepads, finger spools, strobes, which would be stuffed into a pocket or clipped onto his harness before he went underwater.

Then he heaved himself to his feet. The rebreather hung heavily from his shoulders as Robson headed outside, ready to see what was so special about the lake. Dunaev and Gorpinyuk followed. They all wore thick waterproof gloves, neoprene hoods, like a balaclava, over their heads and black face masks. With emergency cylinders hanging from their harnesses and just a flash of skin showing behind their lenses, they looked like aliens. On the surface, the men could barely move under the burden of their equipment; underwater they would be weightless.

'I think my next job should be an international tiddlywinks referee,' Robson joked in such circumstances. 'The gear will fit into my pocket, and it'll be warm and dry. It's still going to be dangerous, though, one of those counters could have my eye out.'

At the water's edge, each man performed the little personal rituals, checking computers, or whatever else it took to focus their minds. Then they donned their fins and stepped off the platform into the lake. As the first droplets of water wrapped around them, everything changed.

Blue Lake is, depending on one's particular point of view, a divine example of the earth's beauty or an inconsequential mountain puddle. Barely 240 metres long and 140 metres wide, the lake's proportions are too small to impress. Simply trying to locate the blank smudge of water on a satellite image of the mountains is a test of patient examination. With a highway cut alongside the eastern flank, it is not remote enough from human interference to be genuinely tranquil. It is not even the deepest lake in Russia, not by a long shot. The locals call the lake Cherek-köl, an amusing play on a Balkar phrase which roughly translates into 'rotten waters'. That's because of the presence of hydrogen sulphide which sometimes laces the water with a stench of rotten eggs so strong it hangs in the air and announces to visitors on the main road that they are nearing the lake before they can even see it.

While it may lack a certain grace, the lake has an allure which seduces the eye and teases the mind. Found in the Cherek Valley, the eastern side, behind a grove of alder shielding the road, is occupied by a wooded bank rising steeply to a precipitous cliff of the Rocky Range. To the west there is oak and hornbeam. In the sunlight of a windless day, the lake's surface shimmers supernatural cobalt, a 26,000-square-metre oval mirror to the unpolluted skies above. Struck by this scenery, Russian writer Vladimir Gilyarovsky described the unforgettable beauty of the lake as 'blue as sapphire in the sun'. Those words captured Cherek-köl's unofficial name: Blue Lake, or Goluboye ozero to Russian speakers.

At the lake's north-western side is an outflowing river. It meanders beneath a bridge, under a single whitewashed building that serves as a restaurant of sorts, through some trees and into the first of two sump pools before eventually flowing into the Cherek Balkarskiy River. And the discharge is enormous. Flowing out of the lake each day, researchers found, is almost 70 million cubic litres of water. Yet the depth of Blue Lake remains constant. It is like an endlessly overflowing basin. That means there must be an equally large, 70-million-cubic-litre inflow. Only there is no river carrying water to the lake. Well, not on the surface anyway.

The origins of the lake have baffled scientists since 1926 when a professor from the St Petersburg Mine Institute first identified the body of water as a freshwater spring, shaft and lake, all wrapped in one. The fact the lake is found within a region defined by geologists as karstic provides the first clue as to how it is fed. A porous landscape, karst terrain holds little water on its surface. Instead, it's hidden in underground passageways, the earth's unseen plumbing, created by the corrosive action of millions of years' worth of acidic rainwater eating away at the rock, hell-bent on finding its way to the sea. Over time, trickles became streams and streams became rivers. Wherever it finds cracks, water surges to the surface as springs.

'Karstic rocks can contain big caves.' Caves. The word tumbles from the mouth of Perm State University geologist and mineralogist Ulyana Zhakova, who was at the time an authority on Blue Lake. 'The walls are made of limestone and gypsum,' Zhakova explains, 'like layers of a cake.' Highly soluble, the gypsum dissolves at a faster rate than the limestone which sandwiches it.

This creates voids in the rock, and these cavities could be substantial: the outflow carries with it each day fifty cubic metres of dissolved gypsum rock crystal suspended within the water.

'The freshwater is dissolving the gypsum rock, but there are also a lot of tectonic cracks bringing water into this lake,' Zhakova says. 'I'm almost sure there are caves.'

Caves. That word again.

'Like the majority of very deep lakes,' she says, 'Blue Lake has the reputation of being unfathomable. There are stories of people and animals who have fallen in and reappeared in the Caspian Sea.'

Some scientific papers refer to the lake as Lower Blue Lake because in the mountains above Cherek Gorge are a handful of pools known as the blue necklace of the Caucasus. The furthest away is Upper Blue Lake, a gently sloping bowl of water eighteen metres deep. A little closer is Secret Lake. Then there is Kel-Ketchchen: the lake that leaked. Hidden among the trees, Kel-Ketchchen is a karst sinkhole with limestone cliffs that drop 200 metres to the bottom where there is a small lake.

According to local folklore, water lapped at the banks of Kel-Ketchchen until a cataclysmic earthquake shook the mountains. The water vanished into the earth, then down in the valley a new lake, Blue Lake, was said to have been born.

'The Balkar people do not write down their stories,' says Zhakova. 'They tell stories from one mouth to another, from grandfather to grandson. When we speak with people, they say, [she adopts the accent of an old lady] "Oh, I remember many, many years ago there was water in the lake. There was an earthquake, and the water disappeared. . ."'

Did an earthquake really open up a hole in the ground, draining one lake to create another? Could all three lakes be linked by tunnels? 'Who knows,' says Zhakova. 'There is much we don't know.'

Zhakova has a collection of archive photographs of the area. Among them is a black and white image, thought to date back to sometime in the 1960s, of a metal sign which once stood on the banks of the lake. The sign states: 'Blue Lake. Located on the northern slopes of the Rocky Range, at an elevation of 809 metres above sea level, with a depth of 180–258m, ranks sixth among lakes in USSR. Resulting from the gradual dissolution of unconsolidated carbonate rocks by artesian waters. Waters contains significant quantities of hydrogen sulphide. Bathing is not recommended.'

Cave diving was the maypole around which Martin Robson weaved his adult life. In a world with which Robson would readily admit to sometimes feeling at odds, a submerged cave system deep underground was the one place he truly felt comfortable. While most people looked into caves and saw darkness and claustrophobia, he looked into a cave and wanted to know what was around the next corner.

To the uninitiated, cave diving is one of the world's most dangerous endeavours, far removed from the cocktail diving of scuba's single-tank recreational reef tours. The sport is akin to high-altitude mountaineering. Where climbers must contend with vertigo-inducing death drops, cave divers have claustrophobic passageways dominated by primordial counterparts: dark, light; lost, found; poise, panic. Preventing panic is paramount for a cave diver. There are more than enough ways to dispatch yourself underground and underwater, getting lost and running out of air being the most obvious, without letting raw emotion take over. That's because, when it comes to surviving, there's no bolting for the surface. The only thing there is a rock ceiling. The only way out is to retrace the route along serpentine tunnels with dead ends and false leads.

The ever-present possibility of disaster is enough to keep most people on the sidelines. But some are just wired differently. Cave divers are, according to an old psychological profile anyway, white-collar professionals, intellectually inclined and, unlike other adventure athletes, introverted. They hold themselves to a higher standard than everyday divers. With their particular equipment and training drills, they see themselves as practitioners of the sport in its purest form. In the hierarchy of the diving world, they are the ones perched on the topmost rung of the diving ladder. There is the difference between a cave diver and someone who simply dives in caves and only the very best go on to explore. They are the ones with nerves of ice and a heart rate which barely blips when, in the dark, one hundred metres down and a mile underground, they spy a thin trail of bubbles streaming from their precious gas supply. That's because they have already rehearsed every possible fix to save their skin. The sport demands it of them; it demands everything they have and more because being unprepared is just a short step away from the hereafter. That's not to say cave divers don't have close calls. Many have had their epics, as in: 'I was ridin' my scooter, out in the lead, deep inside, when a piece of limestone sliced my buoyancy wing. Boom. I hit the floor. Cloud o' silt. Couldn' see for shit. Gettin' out was epic.'

In return for the risks, caves offer explorers a place to prove themselves, and arguably the last opportunity on the planet to find somewhere new and unseen in a world photographed, mapped and shrunk to the size of a computer screen. Robson had been around long enough to have the memories of adventure, but he still had dreams washing through him. He had ambitions to map the Marble Caves of Chile and to explore the underground lake at Planagrèze, in France.

In a sport which is defined, as much as it has been defined, by technological progress, Robson's status as a cave diving explorer was matched by his mastery of the rebreather. In the first decade of the millennium, rebreathers had transformed underwater exploration, taking the power of the possible and charging it with electric anticipation, and Robson had become a sought-after instructor for wealthy divers around the world. Teaching cave diving was a living. Not one that was going to make him rich, but it paid the bills even if he didn't always share the same tax bracket as his students.

In November 2011, Robson was nearing the end of a month-long assignment in the caves of Florida. It had been a busy year teaching in far-flung places, lodged in one low-rent hotel or another for so long the discount wallpaper, unfamiliar beds and questionable food merged into one. Robson was desperate to get home to the United Kingdom for Christmas and to the woman he loved, Vikki Batten.

Home and Vikki were still another week away, though. Robson had extended his trip to present a paper for sponsor Analox at the Diving Equipment & Marketing Association expo, in Orlando, on the dangers of carbon monoxide poisoning. The subject was close to his heart. Robson's friend Clément Pouillot had died in Mexico's Dos Ojos cave, in March 2004, after breathing from a tank contaminated with carbon monoxide.

After his presentation, Robson walked the crowded halls where equipment manufacturers greeted him by name and plugged their latest must-have, and tour operators claimed their untouched dive spots were the Red Sea of twenty years ago, or the next Indonesia, perfect if he had a couple of thousand bucks to spare. Among the sales patter, Robson chanced upon a small stand promoting a book on an expedition to Orda cave, in the Russian Western Urals. Flicking through its glossy pages filled with photographs of startling white crystal cathedrals set against dark passages, he was fascinated. On the stand was the author, Bogdana Vashchenko. Now in her mid-thirties, she had studied theoretical and mathematical physics before coming to the sport.

This place looks amazing, Robson told her. If you have any more projects like this, I'd like to join your team if you think I could be of any help.

Thank you. But we don't know who you are, he recalled her saying.

While Vashchenko's response appeared casually dismissive, Robson put it down to the differences in culture and language. We're not strange, a Russian friend had told him once, just a little different. Robson handed back the book, thanked her and walked off.

Something about Robson piqued Vashchenko's interest, though, and she did need a diver for her upcoming expedition. After the conversation, she contacted an experienced Russian technical diver named Andrei Bykov. Bykov knew Robson personally, had dived with him on an archaeological expedition in the Black Sea, and he vouched for him. So much, in fact, that Vashchenko ended the conversation thinking Robson had been far too modest about his abilities. To be sure, she spoke to others about the upcoming project and about Robson, and one leading deep diver told her: You have the one you are looking for and he is a good diver.

That was the best recommendation she could possibly get. The following day Vashchenko sought Robson out.

We think you can help us, she said.

'Us' was Vashchenko and her partner, photographer Viktor Lyagushkin. The couple had been the toast of the Moscow diving community, briefly, following their publication of the Orda cave book. They'd presented their findings at a diving exposition in the city and Lyagushkin had seen his images published in the Russian edition of *National Geographic*. Buoyed by its success, they searched for another idea, another book, another exhibition about another unique, little-known beauty spot. They found it at Blue Lake. Only Vashchenko and Lyagushkin had a problem. They needed an experienced deep diver to chart the waters but their first choice, a Russian, had declined their invitation.

Vashchenko pitched the Blue Lake Awareness Project to Robson like a good saleswoman. One version of her press release would later stress the existence of a very deep and significant cave system in the lake. 'One of the objectives is to locate and explore this cave,' it read. Some of the best technical divers in Russia were signed up to the project, the release stated. And then there was mention of treasures waiting to be found at the bottom. She sold the issue hard. The press release told of 'historically significant objects on the bottom' from antiquity, of ancient peoples moving from Africa to Europe and tossing all manner of valuables into the lake. 'It is difficult to imagine what discoveries await the inquisitive explorer of the lake, from the precious weapons of Tamerlane's troops to Second World War Romanian army equipment, from the oldest evidence of human history to the trucks laden with Georgian port wine circa 1920 which has probably matured nicely over the years.'

Historically significant artefacts. Precious weapons. One-hundred-year-old port. Robson wasn't interested in a Boy's Own treasure hunt for such things. No, he was energised by the idea of searching for a virgin cave system. Finding some hitherto unseen and untouched piece of the planet was the holy grail of cave diving, and Robson couldn't shake the idea from his mind. The expedition's start date was January 2012. Robson consulted his diary. He had a three-week window before he was due in the Philippines for a pre-planned assignment. The time-frame was tight. But for those looking for virgin caves the dreams of exploration die hard.

It's not easy being the partner of an underwater explorer. Someone committed to pushing into the dark corners of the globe underwater will spend long stretches away from home, doing perilous things that can leave them out of touch for hours or days on end. And while the diver deep in a cave knows they are okay, their partner at home doesn't. Inevitably then, part-ners live a life of latent tension concerning an uncertain future. That emotional strain is even harder if the partner is also a diver. They know everything that can go wrong because they have already trained to recognise the hazards lying in wait for them underwater.

As soon as Vikki Batten heard about Blue Lake and the search for a virgin cave system, she knew Robson wouldn't be able to resist because a passion for cave exploration was something they shared. Vikki had known the desire of underwater exploration since her first dive while holidaying with her parents, in Kenya, in the early 1990s. Then it was the exceptional something she needed to replace her precarious living as a professional dancer. Exiting the water, she knew scuba diving would become her life.

She found a job in the small town of Newhaven, in Sussex, on the south coast of England, working at the counter in a dive centre. It wasn't perfect, but it beat selling tickets from a theatre box office in London while dreaming of a place on the stage. One day, a new part-time instructor called Martin Robson arrived at the centre.

'He walked in to fill some cylinders,' Vikki says. 'We had a security camera and my boss, a woman, calls another woman and me to the office to look at his bottom on the CCTV. She gave him a ten. That was the very first thing that struck me. After that, it was his deep penetrating eyes, his Scorpio eyes.'

Vikki already had a boyfriend and was planning to tour Australia and work on dive boats serving the Great Barrier Reef. Only she couldn't stop thinking about this man with Scorpio eyes. Soon they started working together, and then they were spending their free time diving.

'We were both in other relationships, but we unravelled it all to be together. Martin walked out of everything he'd worked for his whole life to be with me, and I binned Australia. We both threw everything away to go and live together in a flat with no furniture and no belongings,' she says.

For ten years they ran a successful diver training business in Egham, Surrey, based at an industrial unit which would later become a bathroom showroom. Then, in 2009, Vikki joined the staff at PADI (Professional Association of Diving Instructors), where she managed the company's technical diving portfolio across the UK, Europe and the Middle East. Robson, meanwhile, established himself as a freelance cave, rebreather and deep-diving instructor. With such careers, it was inevitable they would spend extended periods away from home, but their relationship weathered the time spent apart.

Every time Robson discussed Blue Lake, it was clear to Vikki that he was electrified by the prospect of searching for a virgin cave.

It was too great an opportunity to miss, he told her. Vikki understood his desire, but the dates of the expedition meant he would have to jet off immediately after New Year. The timing couldn't have been worse. She'd been looking forward to spending time with him, just the two of them, in January, before work commitments took him to the Philippines.

Vikki bottled the hurt until long after driving Robson to London's Heathrow airport for his flight to Russia. She kissed him goodbye and was back on the road before he'd even reached the check-in desks. Robson didn't see anything wrong; the airport drop-off had been shorn of sentiment long ago. Only there was more to it for Vikki, something she didn't realise until much later. In the days before departure, she had begun, unconsciously, to distance herself from him emotionally. 'I put on a happy face and told him to go and have fun. But I knew the risks were high. I had to consider what I'd do if he didn't come back. Having a plan of action helps to manage stress: I guess it is a way of avoiding the worry and pain,' she says.

In truth, Vikki would have relished the opportunity to join him at Blue Lake, but time didn't allow. Time – and money. After years of living in rented accommodation, they were saving to buy a cottage in the English countryside. In the meantime, they made do with a small house in the village of Clutton, in Somerset, filled with Russian language tapes, diving souvenirs and seashells.

With Robson gone, the place felt empty, and Vikki slipped back into her routine of being temporarily single with just a cat called Honey for company. She tried hard not to notice the remaining signs of his life, the dive guides, cave maps, a profile of Salvador Dalí on the bookcase in the lounge; his slippers in the hallway; the Bialetti coffee pot that he typically took with him on trips, in the kitchen cupboard; the pile of T-shirts in the wardrobe, ironed and folded to the size of *Globe & Laurel*, the official, bimonthly journal of the Royal Marines.

And there was a photograph of the couple, one of only a handful on display at home. The snapshot was from a holiday in August 2001 to celebrate their anniversary. It shows Robson and Vikki floating side by side in the head pool of Gourneyras, in Hérault, France, smiling their best camera smiles. Surrounding them is a vibrant splash of emerald waters, pale green leaves floating near grey rock boulders in the background. The photograph was taken by a young Frenchman who had spotted them as he strolled through the forest. It dropped onto their doormat two years later. Vikki loved the picture for its memories: of passing the red sign emblazoned with the words 'Danger de Mort'; of clambering the steep muddy bank with her equipment, hand over hand down a rope tied to a tree at the top; of the refreshing water holding her on a hot summer's day; and of four hours exploring together, in the darkness underground. Just the two of them.

Robson landed in Moscow on the evening of 3 January 2012, three hours late due to winter gales battering Britain. The border official didn't seem to appreciate the late arrival of the flight and really did accuse him of loitering around the airport like a spy. Then Robson watched as the customs officials, three of them standing shoulder to shoulder like an unpacked matryoshka doll, with their peaked caps increasing in size according to rank, really did individually scrutinise his official invitation before passing it along the chain of command to a superior officer with an even bigger peaked cap. The most senior officer at the end of the line, the one with the biggest cap of them all, really did salute Robson before passing the letter back to his second in command, who in turn handed it to the junior officer, who finally handed it back to Robson and waved him off without a word.

Robson stepped out of the airport and into the car of fellow expedition diver Sergei Gorpinyuk who drove him directly into the gridlock of Moscow traffic, all honking horns and glaring brake-lights. They were bound for a dinner reservation. From the snow-covered parking space, the men stepped behind an anonymous metal door, through a swanky nightclub with thumping bass, past scantily clad women dancing for men in black leather jackets, and into a diner where they enjoyed borsch and fine poached salmon.

They managed to get a few hours of sleep before the early-morning departure to Blue Lake. Robson and Gorpinyuk were stuffed inside the sleeper carriage of a train with dive gear stacked on the floor and piled on bunk beds above their heads as the locomotive dragged its carriages across the country for a day and a half. The sun rose twice yet there was no brilliant dawn, just shades of grey either side of the blackness of night. Beyond the bright lights of Moscow, the pale sweep of the Russian plain rose up to the window and then receded. Robson and Gorpinyuk talked diving, Russia and the world as the wheels turned and the train passed power stations belching smoke into the air, lumbered through austere stations serving leaden towns, and paused in sidings next to crumbling railway sheds and train car after train car after train car shrouded in dust and rust.

But the carriage attendant, the provodnitsa in her sky-blue uniform and epaulettes, did make a welcome cup of black tea for Robson. And the enterprising food sellers waiting at each station offered hearty fare with each stall complementing the one before and the one after. One sold dried fish or meat pies, the next offered potatoes kept warm in a pot, the third fruit, and the fourth a drink.

Finally, they disembarked in a town called Mineral Water, Mineralnye Vody in Russian, and piled into a pick-up truck bound for Blue Lake. Planes, trains and automobiles, literally. The truck eased out of the city and between the patchwork of fields towards the snow-capped barricade of the Caucasus Mountains, a 600-mile scar of jagged rock raking the landscape from the Black Sea to the Caspian. The engine grumbled as the truck slogged higher, and then it exhaled as the road dropped into the Cherek Valley, where hundreds of apple trees stood in formation, row upon row lining the terraced slopes next to a river which thundered from the mountains and fed the hydro-electric power stations in the hill, lighting a small patch of civilisation further down the road.

Babugent in the early-morning light is not quite the edge of the world, but it feels like you might be able to see it from here. For thirteen years the village stood empty after its Balkarian inhabitants, together with those from neighbouring communities, were forcibly deported, in 1944, falsely accused by Stalin of collaborating with Nazi Germany. They were dumped in Kazakhstan and Siberia and eked out an existence until being allowed to return in the late 1950s. Some places were abandoned altogether such as the village of Kunlyum, although the stone walls of the houses and Abaev's Tower still clung to the mountainside. The resentment which flows from that kind of treatment is hard to shake. This is probably why some people looked more towards their Asian neighbours to the south-east than to Moscow; the area is closer, as the crow flies, to Baghdad than the Russian capital. Chechnya is not too far away, nor is Beslan, two names linked with separatist extremism. The British Foreign Office still advises against all but essential travel to the region, and, at the time, the US Department of State warned that its ability to assist American citizens there was extremely limited.

As the pick-up trundled along the P291, the main road through the town reflected in the window next to Robson's seat. Beige-stone buildings with red or green-tiled roofs fronted the main road. There was a school, nursery, cottage hospital and a solitary pharmacy, and the two minarets of the mosque towered over everything. An old man, wearing a check shirt, jogging bottoms, boots and orange beanie hat, stood under a corrugated roof at what looked like a bus stop. There was the occasional bark of a dog. When a herd of cows ambled down the middle of the road, no one really seemed surprised.

In the closest thing Babugent had to a square, a monument poked skyward, between the telephone poles leaning at odd angles, and through a spaghetti junction of power cables. The five symbols fixed to it, a horseshoe, an axe, railway tracks, a circular saw blade and a trophy, captured the heart of the region.

Outside the village, a mile or two south, past the two young boys riding horses bareback, was the industry of Blue Lake. The hamlet emerged from the wilderness, a few mountain chalets and a café nicknamed 'Dive Rite' because of a tarpaulin sign of the equipment manufacturer which hung outside. There was a restaurant which at the weekend turned into a discotheque playing drum and bass. Outside, Ladas being nursed through old age were parked alongside a shiny Lexus. The raw-boned remnants of scrub trees and bare rock crags encircled the faded buildings, and weeds grew right up to the brickwork as if allowing the place just enough room to breathe.

At the southern end of the lake were two imposing buildings. One was a faux castle with the modelled jaws of a bear surrounding its front door. A monstrous statue of an eagle, all outstretched wings and screeching beak, stood off to the right. This was the Baron von Münchhausen Museum built by a man claiming to be a descendant. Hidden among the trees was the other, a stone-clad hotel nicknamed The Castle which served as a base for the expedition and where luxury rooms cost 1,700 roubles (about £35) a night.

The area had developed since the ribbon had been cut at the dive centre, in September 2005, despite the question mark about whether the lake was a realistic draw to attract scuba divers. Yet a steady stream of divers did come; they were the one group of sporting hobbyists not dissuaded by the troubles. They came to experience the brilliant blue waters; they came to set depth records; they came to dive deep. Now they came to find caves.

The water in Blue Lake is so clear you can see the features five, maybe ten metres down, past the point you could reach duck-diving as a kid. Underwater, the bank slopes steeply to a plateau, fifteen or so metres down. Charophytes, more commonly known as stoneworts, form a silk-like fabric of algae draped over the sloping rock face and the petrified trees which have fallen into the lake. In the sunlight, they are like a verdant summer meadow. Their magic is one of the reasons the water in Blue Lake is so clear that it looks like it could be bottled and sold for £5 a pop. Stoneworts filter the water by capturing nutrients and stabilising sediment.

It's bright in the robin's egg blue of the water, and you can see twenty or thirty metres in every direction. Looking back up towards the surface from a few metres underwater, you can still see what's going on. People look like dappled silhouettes, and the trees lining the bank appear like a distant hilltop shimmering in the haze of dawn. The movement of the clouds reveals itself in shadows slinking across the bottom; underwater, the sun still throws your shadow, and the surroundings go from light to dark and back again. Everything is recognisable but. . . not real, rather like a dream, a secret world off-limits to all but those willing to go looking for it. And rational people aren't willing. To them, everything about diving screams 'No!' They see a world devoid of air, one that needs life-support machines to keep them safe. They see, or instead imagine, something lurking in the dark. But they don't see what divers see and don't have in their lives what divers have. . . freedom.

It's not noiseless underwater; on a rebreather you can hear it all. On the coral reefs, you can listen to the fish feeding. It sounds like popping candy in your mouth. In the lake, one sound dominates: breathing. Breathing in, breathing out. Life returned to its most basic. The freedom of just being. A tender *shhh!* as you inhale your breathing gas and a hum as it murmurs along the corrugated hose on exhalation. Periodically, there is a click followed by a spritz as the solenoid opens and oxygen is added to the breathing loop. *Shhh! Ummm! Shhh! Ummm! Click! Spritz! Shhh! Ummm! Shhh! Ummm! Click! Spritz!* The tick-tock of life underwater, the metronome of adventure.

The shallows of the north shore are best described as a lip to the lake's decanter-shaped body. Everything slopes down towards the mine shaft on the eastern side. As you move above the bottom, the slope on your left shoulder, you soon find yourself staring into an abyss of black nothingness. At your side, the rock wall plummets vertically downwards, a mixture of jagged out-crops, smooth faces and rock buttresses. Like the magic of the Eiger's north face at dusk, the features are preternaturally alluring in the smoky sunlight penetrating the surface. Those same wavelets of sun point a way on into the depths. They come from behind your head and converge before your eyes some-where below. No matter how hard you strain, there's no way to see what lies at their end.

A weighted guideline of braided nylon leads you into the beckoning darkness. Following it is an eerie slow-motion slide into a seductive void. Falling through the water column, you squirt blasts of air into the buoyancy wing connected to the rebreather on your back. This controls your descent. The fur-ther you slip from the surface, the darker it gets. It's not quite total blackness, more a trance-like dusk separating the shallow blue void above from the vast, unending black beneath.

You are sixty metres down now. With little sunlight pene-trating the depths, the lake is cold. In the warmest summer months, it just about holds nine degrees Celsius; in January it's six degrees in the shallows, as cold as the milk in your fridge. This is not the kind of place visited purely for pleasure. You've got to love diving to come here. And you do. They all do. Because down here you can shrug off the confines of a life spent in deference to gravity. With the upward pull of air in your buoyancy device matching precisely the earth's downward pull, you are the human equivalent of a hummingbird, without the flapping. Hovering neutrally buoyant is as close to pure weight-lessness as it is possible to get without blasting into orbit. 'I'm

not smart enough to go into space,' one diver said, 'but underwater exploration is something I can actually do.'

Martin Robson revelled in exploring underwater. It was only
a five-minute drop to reach sixty metres for him, Roman
Dunaev and Sergei Gorpinyuk. Arriving at the target depth, the
men stopped. Touching the tips of his index finger and thumb
to make a circle and extending the remaining fingers to make a
reverse '6' shape, Robson flashed the universal sign for 'okay'
to the two men. The sign acted as both question and answer,
and both responded with the same sign. I'm okay. I'm okay.

Powering up their torpedo-like underwater scooters which
they had carried with them from the surface, the men slipped
into formation and began to tour the lake walls. Robson instinctively took the lead, the light on the front of his scooter blazing
forward. Dunaev and Gorpinyuk followed in his slipstream,
slightly off to one side. Tucked into position, Robson rarely
glanced at those behind him. He wasn't negligent of their
safety; he could read the feelings of anyone behind him without
the need to see them. It was hidden in the way they used their
torches. From the corner of his eye, he monitored the sweep of
their lights on the wall. If the halo of light traced along the wall
in a gentle fashion, all was okay. If the beams jerked erratically
from side to side, the accepted action for getting someone's
attention, or if it disappeared altogether, Robson would know
someone was in trouble.

The next hour drifted by in a dreamlike blur as the trio
glided past monolithic rock faces, around jagged outcrops and
across the angled slope of limestone and gypsum seams. Occasionally, Robson would grab the odd crumble of rock lying on

34

an outcrop and stuff it into the hip pocket of his dry suit. He then used his dive computer to take a temperature reading of the water for the scientists. Yet most of the time, he was caught up in the unfettered joy of discovery: a tiny dot of life next to a teetering skyscraper of rock which disappeared into the void in all directions.

But Robson's silent reverie could not avoid one reality of his time in the depths; it was displayed on his dive computer. Time was rationed down here and every minute he spent beyond the allotted dive time added to his decompression obligation. It didn't take long at that depth for a direct ascent to the surface to be off the table. The nitrogen and helium in his breathing mix had been forced into his tissues under pressure during the dive. It needed to be flushed out safely, and that meant spending time on the ascent, sitting at scheduled depths for carefully calculated periods of decompression to allow the gases to escape. If you want to do the depth, you have to be prepared to do the time, as they say. Doing anything else would be to invite one thing divers feared: decompression sickness.

Almost as soon as the diving helmet was invented, men started falling victim to a mysterious illness. Developed by brothers Charles and John Deane in the 1820s, the copper casque was placed over the diver's head and rested on his shoulders. A one-piece, waterproof 'Macintosh' diving suit protected him against the elements. On the surface, men worked a hand-wheel which cranked cylinder pumps to supply the diver with air down a hose. The Deane helmet provided men with access to the seabed as never before and offered a potentially lucrative career salvaging sunken cargo. Divers could descend ten or twenty fathoms, as was the measure back then, and remain down for an hour or more.

Impressed by the merits of the diving helmet, Colonel Charles William Pasley, an officer with the Corps of Royal Engineers, convinced the Admiralty his men could clear the wreck of the *Royal George* from an anchorage in Spithead, Portsmouth, if he were granted salvage rights to the ship. The 108-gun man-o-war was preparing to sail with Admiral Howe's fleet to relieve Gibraltar, in August 1782, when, before the eyes of everyone in the harbour, she keeled over and sank. There were some 1,200 people on board that day, including women and children visiting their men before the ship sailed from British shores. Only 300 escaped.

Pasley was a remarkable man in a corps famous for its ingenuity, and his enterprise was arguably the first significant salvage operation involving divers. He planned to have miners and sappers dressed in the Deane helmet descend to the wreck and place charges of gunpowder around the deck, ready to blast her to pieces. The timbers, pigs of iron ballast and cannons could then be hauled to the surface and shipped to shore. There was no training for underwater operations like this, and the only manual was a pamphlet written by the Deane brothers three years earlier. So, his men just jumped in and found their way.

The corps was courageous and close-knit, mad, married or Methodist, as the saying went, and each spring between 1839 and 1843, they boarded Her Majesty's frigate *Success* and took up a position above the *Royal George*. Divers descended thirteen fathoms (24 m, 78 ft) four, five or six times a day to place their demolition charges. The 2,400-pound blasts threw geysers of white water fifty feet into the air and left dead fish bobbing in the swell. Then the men went back down and began clearing the wreckage. Each diver's haul was measured and logged in the Journal of Operations, which was used to reckon their pay. A diver on a good run could earn the equivalent of two days' pay each tide. It was enough to spark envy among the crew and rivalries saw men pushing the clock underwater.

Spending hours slinging a ship's worth of timbers off the seafloor was punishing work, but men began succumbing to something far worse than fatigue. The first signs were so subtle that they were easily missed. After surfacing, some divers suffered a 'depression of spirits'. Then, there were the niggling pains in the joints that came on after the diver surfaced and would linger for days. Each case was recorded in the neat columns of the ship's sick book, in between sailors diagnosed with colica, diarrhoea and ulcers. On 4 May 1840, a twenty-eight-year-old diver named Fullegard was diagnosed with acute pains and had to be taken ashore. Three months later, diver George Hall was put on the sick list with the same complaint. He was only allowed back on duty when the pain had eased. During the rest of the season, divers Skelton and Symonds were also struck down. Corporal David Harris, so ambitious to earn fame as a diver, was twice laid low by the illness. Baffled by the strange malady, the ship's surgeon recorded it as rheumatism.

The condition may have been considered of little medical interest to the doctor, but no diver on the operation escaped an attack of acute rheumatism. Every year brought another sorry tale of suffering. In August 1841, Hall was forced to quit the job after suffering a bout of rheumatism so debilitating that he was rendered unfit for the strenuous work. Divers John Rae and John Williams were martyrs in suffering, and the two men often returned to work before the pains had gone.

By then, German-born inventor Augustus Siebe had begun to manufacture an updated design of the diving helmet, which would become the standard dress that many associate with deep-sea diving. The diver's tinned copper helmet, with three windows, was attached with a dozen studs to a watertight suit made of rubber and tanned twill. For an air hose, they used tubes smeared with Jenkin Jones's waterproof compound. Staying on the seabed for hours was now a reality for men impatient to add to their account. It was also sheer madness; divers like Private Philip Trevail just didn't know that at the time.

A miner by trade, Trevail was considered one of the strongest and most active men during the salvage season of 1843. Late in the year, with only twenty cannons left on the seabed and eleven days of the season remaining, the twenty-six-year-old Cornishman surfaced after a long and exhausting dive. With the rolling deck of the surface ship wallowing in his stomach, Trevail stomped towards the bench. Weighed down by his lead-soled boots, he might have missed the unusual rubbery feeling in his ankles. Within minutes his left leg had gone numb. A deathlike pallor crossed his face as the paralysis spread, and he most likely passed out from the pain. When he came to, Trevail was in Haslar Hospital.

Pasley asked the Admiralty to waive Trevail's medical expenses because he had been 'severely injured whilst diving, not by any accident, but from his extraordinary zeal, which induced him to over-exert himself and remain too long under-water, which caused him a sort of paralysis of one side'. While Pasley couldn't have known it at the time, his letter was arguably the first reliable reference to decompression sickness. Trevail remained in hospital for thirty-six days, but never fully recov-ered from his injuries. Three years later, he was discharged from the service with a distended left knee and weakness in the lower legs.

That's how it usually went in those early days; the lure of what lay on the seabed was greater than concerns anyone had about the mystery illness. American farm boy turned salvager John B. Green saw the seabed as his bank, one offering a better percentage than those on terra firma. Equipped with a standard diver's dress, he found himself among salt sea divers and their gigantic boasts, searching for shipwrecks laden with riches. One sunny August day in 1855, Green discovered a safe said to contain $36,000 on the steamship *Atlantic*, resting at the bottom of Lake Erie, 152 feet (46 m) down. He bounced to the surface for a grappling hook and rope when he was shot through with excruciating pain. The incident left him quadri-plegic, and a doctor in nearby Port Dover said he would not live. The celebrated diver refused to die, but it was five months before he took his first step and another three before he walked with the aid of crutches.

The star diver of the time was a pocket Hercules named Alex-ander Lambert. He had the barrel chest and moustache of a circus strongman, but the softest voice, and he had done all there was in diving. In 1885, Lambert was sent to Grand Canaria to salvage gold from the wreck of the *Alfonso XII*, which sank in 162 feet (50 m) of water. The operation was said to be the most remarkable deep-sea diving effort on record. Having blasted the hull, Lambert crawled through three deck spaces to reach the strongroom and 10,000 newly minted Spanish gold pieces. According to the records, Lambert made sixty-two dips, being submerged 903 minutes altogether, his longest immersion lasting twenty-six minutes. On his last, he stayed on the bottom for forty-five minutes. Shortly after surfacing, he collapsed. The kindliest and cheeriest man one could meet was paralysed. Although the worst of the symptoms disappeared over time, his legs and urinary organs were affected for the rest of his life.

Dreadful to be sure; only there was worse to come when the diving helmets arrived in the Aegean. For years, natural sponges had been plucked from the seabed by athletic Greek men who could reach more than a hundred feet (30 m) on a single lungful of air and stay down for two or three minutes. The best sponges went to London, Paris and Moscow where they fetched the highest prices. Merchants got rich and mansions stacked up around the harbours of picture-postcard islands such as Symi and Kalymnos in the Dodecanese. If the natural sponges were a blessing to the brokers, the diving helmet was a godsend to productivity, and the Gold Rush for sponges was on.

By 1865, hard-hat divers (the Greeks called them scaphandro) filled dozens of boats. They'd leave port after Easter and spend six months raking the seabed for a good percentage. When the shallow sites were stripped bare, the divers went deeper and stayed down longer. Soon men were being 'hit by the machine', suffering pains in their joints and paralysed limbs. Of the twenty-four divers on one cruise, in 1867, ten died after quickly coming up from depths of 150 feet (45 m). Three died immediately upon surfacing, as if shot; the others languished for three months, paralysed in the lower limbs. The deck reeked of the liniment applied against rheumatism, and of urine which leaked from the bladders of the injured divers.

One summer's day in August 1869, a diver named Nicholas Theodoros, diving off the coast of Crete, descended 121 feet (37 m) and spent more than thirty minutes harvesting sponges. Once finished, Theodoros was blown up to the surface in three or four seconds, as was the habit of the sponge divers back then. He managed to take off his diving gear when he felt queasy. Fifteen minutes after surfacing, he slumped on the deck, unable to move his legs. His captain pulled anchor and sailed for the nearest port of Sitia, but the Italian physician there did not recognise the symptoms and Theodoros went untreated. He died nine days later after suffering terrible abdominal pains. His death certificate stated that Theodoros had died from intestinal strangulation and constipation. It turned out he'd suffered a urinary infection after his bladder had become paralysed.

For the wives and girlfriends back home, the scaphandro brought with it a whole different kind of torment. They hated the infernal diving suit; they called it Satan's Machine, the Tool of the Devil. While their men were away, they spent the summer praying before Saint Nikolas and the Archangel Michael. When the boats appeared on the distant horizon at the end of the summer, lookouts in the bell towers rang furiously. Women and children dropped what they were doing and ran down to the harbour to welcome them home; some women clutched a black shawl just in case.

On the sponge-fishing islands of the Dodecanese, it was said, a third of men of marriageable age were paralysed or dead by this mystery disease. It was not uncommon to see young men on crutches dragging their legs along the coast roads. Yet men still went out to sea. They understood the odds, but they had taken advances on the wages to get through the season. The debt only served to increase the pressure to go down beyond fifty metres and stay longer than the doctor had permitted.

The same was true of the poor Japanese and European pearl divers aboard luggers in Australia. They worked up to two hours at a time at depths up to forty-five metres (148 ft), and cases of paralysis were common. So were deaths among those tempted by the fertile banks of shellfish in the deep. One Japanese man was left paralysed from the navel down. Emaciated, he had a large, deep bedsore, extending from the lower back around the pelvis, which had eaten through the buttocks to expose the bone. He clung on for three weeks before septicaemia ended his life. The mate assigned to look after the wretched fellow said he had suffered as much himself for eight months and had been left with a limp. He told the doctors that swelling of the abdomen was a bad sign and if it got under the ribs death was certain. Men would do anything to hold down the swelling, even sitting on the chest of their stricken friends. The root cause of the disorder still mystified divers and doctors, but a catheter would soon become as much a part of a diver's gear as a copper helmet. No one wanted to contemplate a miserable death caused by septicaemia because they couldn't pass urine.

Being a hard-hat diver, it seemed, presented a man with more ways to kill himself than his wife or children could imagine. Perhaps no case was more completely investigated and recorded than that of a Petty Officer First Class James Deasy. Thirty-three years old and of exceptional physique, the Royal Navy man was employed, in November 1900, diving for a torpedo lost in forty-five metres of water at Lamlash Bay, Scotland. Deasy took forty minutes to reach the bottom and spent an equal amount of time searching the pitch-black seabed before starting his ascent.

Twenty minutes later, he bobbed to the surface. Waves rolled the dive tender, and the air hose slapped against the hull as he grasped the rungs of the ladder and heaved himself to the deck under the burden of his diving helmet and boots. Assistants guided Deasy to his seat and helped remove his helmet. They said they had never seen him, or any other man, come up in better condition. Eight minutes after surfacing, Deasy turned to them and complained of stomach pains. Seconds after calling for the doctor, he fell limp and unconscious into the well of the boat. Fleet-Surgeon A. M. McKinlay found him comatose, his skin cyanosed, his lips covered with froth and his breathing laboured. Six minutes after the first symptoms struck, Deasy was gone. He died so quickly that he didn't even make it to the sickbay.

Down in the ship's medical quarters, Dr McKinlay conducted a post-mortem with the assistance of two surgeons. Slicing into the dead man, he found bubbles everywhere, including large beads of air choking the choroid plexus and veins of the brain. The heart was healthy in size, but veins on the outer wall were blistered with air. When lifted, the heart felt like a bladder half

43

full of water and gurgled loudly. The right ventricle puffed when opened with a scalpel. The intestines were filled with air, as was the layer of fat in the abdomen, and the liver seeped with frothy blood. The autopsy concluded that the main abnormal condition was the presence of large quantities of air in the right side of the heart and throughout the venous system. No one had seen anything quite like it before, and, even for the three medical men, it must have been an unearthly discovery. It was as if Deasy's body had been shaken like a bottle of champagne and then uncorked.

Those early years had been an extraordinary gruesome stretch for divers, one that was being replicated in miners working in compressed air. Pneumatic caissons had become widespread across northern France in the 1830s, allowing access to the coalbeds hidden under quicksand silt and mud. Sealed with an airlock and filled with air pumped by leather bellows, the caissons provided men with a dry working chamber. Miners began shovelling coal by the bucketload and soon they were being struck by a mystery illness.

At a pit in Lourches, northern France, the disease struck with the efficiency of a viral epidemic. Of the sixty-four miners who went into the caisson, all robust and healthy men, half experienced pains; one lost control of all his limbs for twelve hours. Engineers sent for two physicians to examine the men and the symptoms recorded by B. Pol and T. J. J. Watelle were bizarre indeed. A miner, referred to as XX, collapsed minutes after walking out of the lock-chamber. He looked like a corpse. His face was pallid, eyes dull, pupils enormously dilated, ice cold to the touch and struggling to breathe. His

44

heart quivered, his pulse was barely there, and he'd gone blind as well as deaf.

Around the world, more injuries appeared as soon as caissons were sunk deep into riverbeds to build bridge footings. During construction of the Saltash Bridge, over the Tamar, in England, all twenty-five workers suffered joint pains, two were paralysed and one died. Across the Channel in France, sixteen men were injured and another died of cerebral congestion and asphyxia while working on a viaduct over the Lorient. Work on a bridge over the Rhine, at Kehl, Germany, left thirteen men injured. At Kaffre-Azzyat, in Egypt, five men died, and at the Londonderry New Bridge, in Ireland, a twenty-eight-year-old digger collapsed after four hours in the caisson. His blood was black, very black, and treacly, and his heartbeat was almost inaudible. He survived for just a day. Another man, aged eighteen, was paralysed from the fourth rib down and couldn't pass urine. He eked out life for 160 days before succumbing to bedsores. During the construction of the Eads Bridge spanning the Mississippi, in St Louis, in 1869, a twenty-year-old suffered paralysis in both legs, the left arm and the bladder after taking a hot bath at the end of his shift. Four months later, he was no better. The following year, when work began on the Brooklyn Bridge in New York City, six men died and scarcely a worker escaped without suffering some form of pain.

The reports were the same; workers emerged from the caisson only to become doubled with pain, paralysed in the legs, unable to pass urine, senseless below the waist. One case was so severe a twenty-three-year-old man burned his toes on a fire without realising. Men must have wondered what evil had invaded their body and the only treatment for a paralysed diver was forlorn hope and a wistful prayer for a spontaneous recovery.

The phenomenon soon became known in medical circles as 'caisson's disease', but diggers had their own distinct language for what attacked them, slang that soon passed over to divers. The most severe condition, when the blood frothed and swamped the lungs, was referred to as 'the chokes'. Someone with the chokes felt a burning sensation in the chest and gasped for breath. Then there was 'the staggers', which were characterised by dizziness or vertigo, and could lead to permanent damage in the central nervous system, and even death. Minor symptoms, such as fatigue, itching skin and aches, were referred to as 'the niggles'. Getting struck by 'the screws' could refer to any number of ailments. Someone suffering from acute pains in the joints, the most prevalent form of the sickness, was said to have been attacked by 'the bends'. The euphemistic term emerged from the black humour of diggers; sufferers were said to mimic the distinctive posture favoured by ladies who wore a combination of corset, crinolette and bustle and known as the Grecian Bend.

The Chokes. The Staggers. The Niggles. The Bends. These were all fearful manifestations of a devil lurking in the deep; a good many deities and demons had started their mythological lives in such a manner.

They'd been underwater in Blue Lake for sixty minutes and had taken almost twice as long to come to the surface. Close to half of that time was spent floating horizontally just six metres down. The water was so clear, Robson, Gorpinyuk and Dunaev could see people moving about in the fresh air above them. Their way up was blocked by an artificial ceiling positioned above their heads for their very wellbeing. Invisible to a layperson, the ceiling was the theoretical barrier beyond which they could not pass while the clock counted down, not if they wanted to avoid the bends. After the excitement of the dive, their experience had become a mind-numbing act of submersion. Every deep diver understands the price to be paid for going deep. Short periods of exploration have to be followed by long stretches of tedium, time just hanging about in the shallows.

When they had served their time, the three men climbed out of the water and trudged into the dive centre. The dive was over, but the work was not. Robson stripped out of his dry suit and placed it on a hanger; he hung up the gloves and hood he wore to protect his head, set the batteries for underwater torches on charge and placed all the other equipment back into his gear box. After that was done, Robson still had to break down his rebreather and clean it. He rinsed out the breathing hoses and counterlung to prevent the build-up of mould, and set the components to one side to dry. Next, he emptied the scrubber unit which cleaned the carbon dioxide from the unit's breathing loop, and then repacked it with fresh absorbent. Then he put the cylinders to one side, ready to be filled for the following day's dive. The whole process could add an hour or two to his day, and, by then, it was time for someone to make a cup of tea or some soup. After that, it was time to start planning for the following day.

Later that night, while the other divers headed out to dinner, Robson joined the expedition organisers for a media event. He crawled into bed late and was out early the next morning to prepare more equipment for the expedition. In the early hours, a truck had arrived from Moscow filled with safety equipment, surface-supplied oxygen masks, power converters and diving cylinders. The dive centre had finally taken on the raw intoxication of an expedition. Someone lugged the cylinders from the courtyard above down the steps to the compressor room. Next, they stacked boxes, bags and crates along the corridor and began examining everything inside. The building looked like an expensive church bring-and-buy sale, with first stages, demand valves, pressure gauges, hoses, piles of lead and retaining bands spilled across work surfaces. It was hard to believe this crude collection of metal, rubber and plastic served the grand purpose of keeping someone alive in the deep.

Inspecting the gear could take Robson anything from a few minutes to an hour. If a hose showed signs of wear, it was replaced; if a rubber diaphragm looked perished, it had to go. Robson was just so particular about their life-support equipment. Crying out for a regulator in an out-of-air emergency was not the time to discover a malfunctioning mouthpiece made the act of breathing feel like sucking a milkshake through a straw.

Finally, there was the task of filling cylinders with breathing gas. The expedition simply wouldn't be possible without the cylinders. They were conventional scuba units, identical to the ones used by holiday divers the world over. Each diver wearing a rebreather carried at least one. They were called bailout cylinders because they were designed to be used in the event of a rebreather failure. There was no safe way of getting to the surface in an emergency without them. In the shallows, one might suffice; in the deep, Robson would clip six to his body and still need access to more. In total, there were thirty-odd cylinders to prepare for him alone.

The divers used deep-dive gas mixes, an exotic cocktail of oxygen, nitrogen and helium known as trimix, because breathing air at depth presented them with all kinds of hazards. Under pressure, the chief components of air, nitrogen and oxygen, behave in freakish ways. In short, they become dangerous to the body and mind. Nitrogen at depth has a narcotic influence on the brain some compare to drinking alcohol. It's why many divers refer to nitrogen narcosis as the Martini Effect because descending every ten metres is like knocking back a martini on an empty stomach. The greater the depth below thirty metres (100 ft), the more martinis you feel you've downed. Narcosis affects everyone differently. You might become euphoric, or you might become overly anxious, but you will definitely show signs of impaired mental processing and decreased manual dexterity. A niggling problem can take on monumental significance while a serious one can be dismissed as trivial. Confused, you might find yourself bombing into the depths, mistakenly believing the surface lies that way.

Likewise, oxygen has a schizophrenic side. Your lifeblood on the surface, it changes quickly from Jekyll to Hyde under pressure. High concentrations attack your central nervous system like a virulent poison and send you into convulsions. Convulsions are the unequivocal end point of an oxygen toxicity hit. On the surface, they are not in and of themselves too serious, but underwater the threat of drowning becomes a real possibility. That's because a convulsing diver could lose their access to breathing gas. As a result, a depth of sixty-five metres (213 ft), where the amount of oxygen in each breath is seven-and-a-half times greater than in that air on the surface, is the accepted boundary of air use underwater. People have dived deeper, much deeper, than that breathing air, but these days divers use trimix. They reduce the oxygen content in the breathing mix to counter the problem of toxicity, and they swap as much nitrogen for helium as possible to deal with the narcosis.

There's little room for error when using trimix, and the gas has to be pumped using precise formulae. Once settled, the contents must be carefully verified using an electronic analyser and the percentage of air and helium noted on a sticker fixed to the side of the tank for all to see. Breathing from an improperly labelled cylinder can kill a diver.

The quickest way for Robson to get the cylinders filled each day was to invest time teaching Eduard Khuazhev to blend trimix. Khuazhev was built like a rugby prop, with massive shoulders hewn in the coal mines of Tula, and he looked like he'd have no trouble taking a whole front row out. His head was shaven, a mountain man's beard reached down from his chin, hiding a shark's tooth necklace around his neck, and his voice growled like a bear. He carried the grandiose title of President of the Federation of Underwater Sports for Kabardino-Balkaria, but most just knew him as Edik. To many, he was the one constant of the dive centre.

The centre's official name was the Scientific and Research Submarine Center 'Blue Lake'. It had opened in 2005 with the support of the local government which had one eye on attracting scientists to the area, and the other on boosting tourism.

Hooking researchers was considered easy. The Caucasus had long been a focus for archaeologists tracing the migration of the human race across the planet, and geographers had been drawn to the region to study plate-tectonics. Luring tourism money through diving was not thought to be too realistic. Yet a steady stream of divers did come. They came from Moscow, from St Petersburg and Rostov, they came from Ukraine. They came to the lake to experience the brilliant blue waters. They came to dive in the mountains, and to dive deep. Divers came to Blue Lake and stayed anywhere from a few days to a few weeks and left as friends. Rates back then were 1,200 roubles (about £24) for a dive, more if you were headed into the depths, and the centre had all the gas and gear if you turned up empty-handed.

Khuazhev, who went by the name Mountain Diver online, was there at the beginning. He was there when the politician Mahdi Temirzhanova, the man who had questioned if scuba diving was a big enough tourist attraction, learned to dive. And he was there when the head of the republic's Presidential Administration, Oleg Shandirov, went diving in the lake.

Khuazhev knew these people, and that mattered in a place where connections were crucial. He was born in the regional capital of Nalchik and went to school in Tula, an industrial centre 120 miles south of Moscow known for metalworking. He worked for a time as a miner before returning home when his father fell ill. He learned to dive in 2000 and, having found his passion, he looked for a place to live it. He and his wife, Angela, had two children; the lake was like another, she joked. He'd spent more than 3,500 hours underwater there, more hours than most divers accumulate in their lives, and he smiled at the delight of divers emerging from their first time in the lake. His lake.

He arrived at 8 a.m. every day and stayed until after 9 p.m. He did that six days a week, seven during the summer. He made cups of hot black tea for divers when they surfaced, and he would cook up a plate of khychin, a thin flatbread of unleavened dough filled with potato, cheese and fresh herbs, and smothered in butter. Served in a stack and cut into four sections, the dish would sit there, and he'd encourage divers to go over and roll a slice with their fingers and eat it in three or four bites. 'Martin, Martin. Eat, eat.'

To blend gas for the expedition divers, Khuazhev spent three or four hours of his day, every day, behind the closed door of the pump room filling cylinders for the divers. A collection of spanners, pliers and gauges hung from screws in the wall above banks of red and blue tanks containing oxygen and helium. The compressor hammered away in his head, and he wore a 60-rouble pair of yellow ear defenders to protect his hearing. Occasionally, he would have to come out into the corridor to escape the noise and find daylight while he waited for the freshly mixed contents in each cylinder to settle.

If the day was laborious, it was what exploration diving was to Robson. Advancing into the wild was the art of the logistically feasible and maintaining equipment on the fly was nothing more than he expected; he was used to exploring on a shoestring. After all, only a handful of people were still organising large-scale cave expeditions, the kind which attracted corporate sponsors and documentary crews from National Geographic or the Discovery Channel. The rest were doing this for the love of it, for the challenge. They really needed a corporate job as a financial advisor or to own their own business to fund their quests. Unless, of course, they could align their efforts, say, testing the limits of human endurance or searching for microbial life in hostile places, with the quest to send man to Mars. Then, governments might be interested. That's where the big money was. To some, that seemed skewed. More than five hundred people had been into space, and a dozen of them had set foot on another world. In contrast, only a handful had been to the deepest point of the world's oceans, and some caves had only been seen by a single pair of eyes.

PAY ONLY WHEN LEAVING

Naturally, like any explorer, I have been asked what I intended
to find and whether it made any sense to take unavoidable risks
. . . I did not expect to find pirates' gold in brass bound boxes,
it's more the feeling of adventure, the great feeling of putting
your foot where no other has been before.

Dr George Benjamin, *Deep Diving*

The stark reality of the challenge that lay ahead emerged when
Robson sat down with the project's chief scientist, Professor
Nikolai Maksimovich. It was late in the evening when the two
men met at the dive centre. The building had all but been abandoned for the day, and preparations for the expedition were
going well: the bailout cylinders had been pumped and analysed,
regulators had been overhauled, safety lines laid, rebreathers
prepared, and chargers blinked their multicoloured lights as
they juiced the torch batteries. All that remained was to decide
where to begin the search.

The professor had been at the lake with his fellow researchers
since late December conducting a series of experiments.
Encouraged by the expedition organisers, he had agreed to meet
Robson and provide some scientific guidance to his search.
Head of geology at Perm State University, he was an authority

54

on hydrology and engineering geology and had furthered research into areas as diverse as the safe destruction of chemical weapons stockpiles and dealing with underground pollution. In his mid-seventies, he was tall and broad-shouldered. Wearing a blue plaid shirt, brown zip-up jumper and trousers, he was the best-dressed person in the room.

Outside the temperature was already below freezing, and Robson huddled into his winter coat. The two men sat side by side on a wooden bench, hunched over a table littered with empty cups, open jars and a polystyrene tray of food. Gorpinyuk was at the head of the table, there to translate the conversation. Above their heads, affixed to the wall, was a sign in Cyrillic script. It read: Alcoholic drinks are banned by the authorities. That meant no drinking and diving. Well, as long as the authorities ignored the vodka bottle which materialised at the end of each day.

Open on the table before them was a scientific report. Professor Maksimovich had placed a handful of pebbles on one page to hold the document open. Holding a blank piece of paper and pen, Robson listened as the professor summarised his ideas of where the cave might be. The search should start at the north-east corner of the lake, Robson noted.

And depth? he asked.

At least 120 metres, the academic suggested. Possibly deeper. Professor Maksimovich asked Robson if it was safe for him to dive so deep. Robson told him not to worry.

And if I find nothing there? Robson asked.

Maksimovich offered Robson several other possible areas to search. To help advance his hypotheses the professor drew on two previous scientific studies of the lake. There were also the findings of tests which showed the temperature of the water dropped by approximately 1.9 degrees Celsius at depths between 100 and 120 metres. Also, a fall in salinity in deep water had been documented, and invisible up-streams were recorded along the western edges. All of this suggested a significant sub-surface movement of water.

Professor Maksimovich didn't think the search would be easy. Robson didn't disagree. He was trying to find a crack in a cliff face the size of forty football fields, by torchlight, in frigid water that leached the heat from his body, at a depth three times greater than most scuba divers ever venture.

Outside, the black lake glistened in the full moon. The deep dive, they decided, would be held on the 10th. By then, Robson's body would have acclimatised to the mountain altitude which he needed to account for when planning his dives. Further searches would be conducted on alternate days, until the 16th. Having listened to the professor's analysis, Robson agreed to set the target depth for the first scientific search at 120 metres. All dives after that would be no deeper than 170 metres, it was decided.

One hundred and twenty metres. One hundred and seventy. These were skyscraper numbers which Robson soaked up with the workaday approach of examining a grocery list: bread, milk, cheese, 120 metres. The target depth was less than a tenth of a mile below the lake surface. In physical terms, it wasn't far at all – little more than the length of a standard football pitch – but down there, deep down there, Robson would find an environment so alien to human life it might as well have been the dark side of the moon. Diving that deep was no joke, and everybody in the room knew it. The divers would spend hours in the water decompressing. Robson, though, was not troubled by anything he heard. Even so, he sensed anxiety among the scientists. It's okay; I've done this before, Robson said.

He'd already discussed with the professor's Perm University colleague Ulyana Zhakova about bottling water so she could analyse its chemical composition. No problem, he said. She talked him through sketching the angled interchange between limestone and gypsum strata, measuring how thick the layers were and at what angle they lay. No problem. She asked him to take temperature readings and note water movement. No problem. Zhakova also asked for specimens of rock.

I won't prise rock from the face, Robson told her, I'll only collect samples that are already lying loose.

Zhakova was impressed by his input. 'When he started to discuss how to draw the walls of the lake and how to take samples, it was absolutely clear he understood what he was going to do,' she says. 'When I told him that I needed rocks he said: "I will take them from levels this, this, this." He had no problem understanding what we needed.'

When the meeting wrapped up, those in the room were intoxicated with the details of their plan. Finding a part of the world not seen by another human was a mesmerising gamble, but Professor Maksimovich remained reticent.

'He was worried by the risks of diving so deep,' Zhakova says. 'Martin said he had been to such depths many times and would plan everything out. He said the team of divers would be there to help him, but the depth was still an issue of serious concern.'

*

57

At the turn of the twentieth century, men had been diving for Her Majesty for sixty years, yet conditions had barely moved on from the days of Colonel Pasley's first salvage operation. The standard three-light, twelve-bolt dress had hardly changed, and navy men needed to be tenacious. They were not easily broken, but, under pressure, the divers felt as if nails were being driven into their ears, and their noses haemorrhaged. The air that reached their helmets blew hot and reeked of oil, and the hoses leaked so much the men believed they were being throttled. Or they would rebreathe their own toxic carbon dioxide, and feel it pummelling inside their heads. Then there was the infernal illness that twisted their joints at the surface.

The prospect of disability and death from the bends or screws or chokes or whatever they called it still stalked those early divers, and if they had any hope of warding off such evil, they needed to understand what was behind the attacks. There was no shortage of finger-pointing to explain away the illness. Physicians involved in the diving and mining industries blamed it on the age of the victims or their physique. Those in their early twenties were considered low risk, but if you were over forty-five, or with short necks, or had what doctors called a languid circulation, you were not to be employed. Doctors blamed it on the exercise the men did after returning to the surface. Those who walked home after work were more likely to get hit. Industrialists from London to New York City to Angers, in France, blamed it on the drink, on the humidity inside the caissons in which miners worked, or on the rapid cooling in the airlock when they clocked off.

In Great Britain, the death of Petty Officer James Deasy,

whose body appeared to have been uncorked in Scotland, was tragic, but it hadn't roused the fleet to conduct any serious investigation into the causes of what killed him. Instead, divers were told to take it slow and ascend at a steady two feet per second, the slow bleed approach, as prescribed by the *Manual for Divers*. When that didn't stop the suffering, the Royal Navy simply ordered that, unless necessary, no diver was to go deeper than twenty fathoms (36 m, 120 ft) and spend no more than thirty minutes there. To the men in the hard hats that seemed quite deep enough; it was hard for them to think of a reason to go any deeper than to scrape barnacles from a ship's hull, to salvage anchors, or search the seabed for whatever was lost overboard.

By early 1905, the situation changed when the Admiralty started losing its submarines to the sea and found itself staring into an abyss. The first British-designed subs, the Vickers-built A-Class vessels, were plagued by accidents and failures. HMS *A1* sank off the Isle of Wight in March 1904 with the loss of all hands. The tragedy engulfed the naval city of Portsmouth. Hundreds of mourners in black coats lined the streets, ten deep, as the coffins of the eleven crewmen made their way to church. Then, HMS *A8* disappeared in Plymouth Sound the following year with another fourteen officers and bluejackets. Politicians and newspapermen urged the government to consider how those brave fellows had suffered and equip dockyards with rescue apparatus necessary to lift submariners from the seabed. The Civil Lord of the Admiralty, Arthur Lee, told the House of Lords the crucial work of the salvage operations would be done by specially trained divers. Suddenly, the safety of hard-hat divers became a preoccupation of the Admiralty, and in July 1905 it appointed a committee to consider how men could dive safely and do valuable work in thirty fathoms (55 m, 180 ft).

Named to the Admiralty Committee on Deep Diving was a prominent Oxford Fellow named John Scott Haldane. A forty-five-year-old Scot from an affluent and influential family, he had deep eyes, an untamed moustache and a brilliantly eccentric mind occupied by big questions. In his case, it was the influence of foul air on people in the slums, factories and mines. Travelling on the London Underground, he collected smoky air in a jar held from a train window to calculate the levels of carbon monoxide in the tunnels. To measure its effects, Haldane made detailed notes while inhaling gas until he almost passed out. To investigate air quality in mines, he locked himself inside an airtight chamber in his attic and filled it with all sorts of noxious gases. When he thumped, unconscious, to the floor, his young daughter, Naomi, was on hand to drag him clear.

Academically concerned by the strange palsy affecting divers, Haldane was convinced, by pure reason alone, he already had the answers. That he knew where to seek the solution to the riddle before him was thanks, in part, to two physicians who studied the strange malady encountered by miners excavating at Avaleresse-la-Naville, at Lourches, in northern France, in 1854. At the time, it was being suggested that the complaints were related to exposure to compressed air. B. Pol and T. J. J. Watelle made keen observations about the health of the sixty-four workers as the shaft sank deeper and the pressure inside the caisson increased. The danger, they concluded, was not going into a pressurised atmosphere, it was coming out of the caisson that was to be feared. In short: one only pays when leaving.

The culprit for much that was going wrong with miners and divers was discovered by distinguished Frenchman Paul Bert twenty years later. The physiologist was concerned by the effects of air pressure on the human body and sought explanations by experimenting on animals. One was tagged Canine DXXVIII. Locked inside a cylindrical steel pressure chamber, the small animal drew its last, whimpering breath on 18 June 1875. For an hour the animal had been bound to an iron frame under the pressure of ten atmospheres, equivalent to a depth of forty-nine fathoms (90 m, 295 ft). Then Bert cranked open a valve and let the air spill out of the chamber in three short minutes. The effects of sudden decompression on the dog were startling, and it had died shortly afterwards.

When Bert cut open the dog, he observed the right side of the heart and the veins were full of gas, and its blood had turned to foam. An analysis found the bubbles contained nitrogen. In his 1878 publication *La Pression Barométrique*, Bert lay the blame for the illness firmly on the liberation of bubbles of nitrogen in the blood.

Nitrogen is found in large amounts in the air we breathe. Unlike oxygen, though, it serves no purpose in the functioning of the body. It just passes through, breathed in and breathed out. That is why it is known as an inert gas. But under pressure, nitrogen becomes a problem. Under the crushing weight of water, air is compressed. The density of nitrogen and oxygen increases in proportion to the rising pressure. The deeper a diver goes, the greater the amount of air is needed to fully inflate the lungs. In simple terms, we take in more nitrogen and oxygen molecules with each breath.

Nature, so the theory goes, desires balance, and under the Second Law of Thermodynamics the tissues in the body of air-breathing organisms are obliged to seek equilibrium with the gases they respire. In other words, air migrates from the area of high gas pressure inside the lungs to the regions of lower gas pressure around the body. Blood leaves the lungs charged with oxygen and nitrogen, which are held in solution like sugar in tea. The gases are carried around the arteries, move through tiny capillaries and into the tissues – the skin, muscle, fat and brain of the body. There, oxygen is metabolised to provide energy. Nitrogen, on the other hand, has nothing to do and skulks unnoticed in the shadows.

Logically, if nitrogen flows into the body under increasing pressure, the opposite applies when the pressure falls, such as when a diver ascends. The tissues enter a state of over-pressurisation, and the flow of nitrogen is reversed; it streams back into solution in the bloodstream bound for the lungs where it is expelled with each exhalation. This process is known as off-gassing. The human body can tolerate a certain amount of over-pressurisation; indeed, it is necessary to encourage the outward flow of nitrogen. The key then, as Bert discovered, is to regulate the flow, to maintain a controlled transfer, because the body only stretches so far from the norm. Get it wrong, come up too quickly, and gas is liberated from solution. Bubbles form in the tissues and the blood, and your body begins to fizz like champagne, or an uncorked bottle of soda-water. Bert concluded that the symptoms of the disorder varied in severity depending upon the degree of compression and the speed of the decompression.

Taking Bert's discovery, Haldane believed that diver's palsy, as decompression sickness was referred to at the time, was deterministically predictable and that he could establish the absolute limits of safety. He just had to find them. Haldane believed the injuries suffered by divers were the function of pressure – in this case, depth – and time. Men, he suggested, could stay without serious risk for a short period at a pressure which would become dangerous if they remained for several hours. Haldane was aware rapid decompression after brief exposures to two atmospheres of pressure produced no symptoms of the disorder and decompressing from two-and-a-half atmospheres resulted in occasional slight injuries. He deduced that the human body could tolerate an over-pressurisation of nitrogen twice the level of normal atmospheric pressure without risk of illness. If the body was immune to the effects of decompression from two atmospheres to one, it seemed probable, to Haldane at least, that it would be equally safe to decompress immediately from four atmospheres to two, from six to three.

Haldane also believed the human body did not soak up nitrogen in a uniform manner. Rather, the grey matter of the central nervous system, the muscles and glands, had a far greater blood supply than fat, skin and joints, and they would charge and discharge nitrogen at different rates. Haldane assumed the body had five separate tissue types – he called them compartments – which absorbed and released inert gas at different rates. Each hypothetical compartment was assigned a time, from five to seventy-five minutes, for it to half saturate with nitrogen under pressure. He also calculated they would desaturate in the same half-time when the pressure was released. The theory made it possible for Haldane to mathematically map the flow of nitrogen in and out of the body.

To test Haldane's theories, the Committee recruited one of his former students, Dr Arthur Edwin Boycott, and a herd of goats. In the summer of 1906, the scientists and veterinarians moved into the Lister Institute of Preventative Medicine with the animals, eighty-five in number. They picked the five-storey building on London's Chelsea Embankment because, located in a brick structure at the back of the complex, was a steel pressure chamber. The chamber was a section of a boiler with dished steel plates riveted at both ends. When filled with air from a mechanical pump, the steel pot was capable of simulating the pressure of dives as deep as thirty fathoms. The plan was to use the pressure chamber to test how ordinary English goats stood up to the strain of decompression.

Goats had been chosen as much for their insensitivity to pain as their size. They were dumb, for sure, but they still had enough about them to reveal abnormalities caused by rapid pressure changes. Their handlers could predict with a fair degree of certainty what was wrong with them. For two months the veterinarians put the herd of goats through the conditions experienced by divers. Inside the chamber they went, up to eight at a time. They were placed under pressure and left there for a while before being decompressed. Down and up the goats went, 700 times in total. Men in white laboratory coats stared at them through stout glass windows and made notes in their ledgers. At the end of each trial, the men opened the chamber door, and the goats escaped to the yard which reeked of hay feed and urine. The men in their white coats glanced at their watches and made more notes. And they waited for the goats to drop.

They didn't have to wait long. Symptoms typically declared themselves in the first thirty minutes. The creatures bleated and bawled as their blood bubbled. They whimpered as they stood in the yard petrified, one lame leg held aloft. They wailed as they staggered about, hind legs strung out behind them, disabled. They mewled as they collapsed in the hay, turned their nose up at corn and gnawed at paralysed limbs. There was Pa, the largest, oldest and fattest. He was particularly immune to injury, but others suffered permanent paralysis soon after decompression. One of them, Little Billy, smaller and thinner than the others, was quickly prostrate with paralysis. Laboured breathing, known to doctors as dyspnoea, was a precursor to death. Few goats survived once they began gasping for air. Some succumbed in five or ten minutes; others lasted thirty. Three survived for forty hours. The sound of their cries was like the worst kind of slaughterhouse. In the most severe cases, the animals had to be put down. Post-mortem examinations revealed a shocking toll of damage. The white matter of the animals' spinal cords was frothed with bubbles, and tissues had already started to soften. They had died from the inside out.

All this was invaluable research, but Haldane's ideas still needed to be tested on men at sea, and he went in search of volunteers. The professor didn't want any publicity-seeking human guinea pigs. He wanted experienced divers with brains, courage and patience. Two men stood out. As the Royal Navy's

Inspector of Diving, Lieutenant Guybon Damant was an ideal candidate. He'd had fourteen days' diving instruction while training as a gunnery officer, and he found the whole experience delightful, infinitely preferable to the study of ballistics and field gun drill. The second man was Warrant Officer Andrew Yale Catto, the chief instructor of diving at Whale Island, in Portsmouth. The two men had the brains and courage Haldane wanted. Neither courted publicity, but the men knew they were human guinea pigs all the same.

That August, Haldane, Damant and Catto relocated to western Scotland to conduct a series of deep-water trials from the torpedo gunboat HMS *Spanker*. Haldane didn't stay on board; he returned to shore every night to a hotel in Colintraive and would sit at a table in the drawing-room to make decompression calculations. He kept the bottom time of each dive short and then added a margin of safety. He was under pledge to the Lords not to risk the officers.

The flame-haired Damant had never ventured beyond nineteen fathoms (35 m, 114 ft) before the trials started. On the second test dive, off Rothesay, the twenty-four-year-old was dispatched to twenty-three fathoms (42 m, 138 ft), as was written in the log. He and Catto reached twenty-five fathoms (45 m, 150 ft) the following day, and the day after that they went to twenty-seven fathoms (49 m, 174 ft).

On the morning of Friday 31 August, Damant descended the ladder over the side of *Spanker* and vanished into Loch Striven, five lengths of India rubber hose unspooling behind him. It was precisely 11:08 a.m. and fifteen seconds. Three air pumps worked in unison to give a mechanical advantage over the immense pressure waiting for Damant on the bottom. On deck, six sailors turned the double flywheels on each pump. Thirty revolutions a minute was backbreaking work. The men huffed for five minutes because five minutes was as much as they could do before needing to be relieved. A naval officer on the patented electric telephone listened in to Damant as he descended. Two minutes in, his earpiece crackled with the elongated vowels of Damant's Isle of Wight lilt coming from somewhere unseen.

On the bottom.

Someone looked at the needle on the pump's pressure gauge: 216 feet with the pumps stopped, 220 feet while turning.

The human guinea pig was at the maximum limit of the pump's meter.

The depth measured by the shot line, a weighted rope which extended from the boat to the seabed, was a little over 210 feet, 64 metres, or 35 fathoms. Damant was deeper underwater than any man had been in recorded history. More than one hundred pounds of pressure were pressing down on every square inch of his body, but there was no sensation of depth. He was at the end of the line and his boots sank into the mud. His bare hands, the only part exposed to the elements, were cold. He took a glass vial, attached it to a valve on his helmet and filled it with air, a sample for Haldane.

Damant stayed on the bottom for five minutes and forty-five seconds. He couldn't see anything, there was no light, but he still sucked in water through the spitcock to wash away moisture condensing on the inside of the windows. Above him, six sailors were panting hard at thirty revolutions a minute, gasping for air so the man at the end of the hose didn't need to.

At 11:16 a.m. and fifteen seconds, Damant valved off some air and began his ascent. Under the old ways, he would have been hauled slowly to the surface at a uniform speed of five feet a minute. Following Haldane's theory of staged decompression, he was required to pause his ascent at carefully calculated depths for long, cold minutes. Hanging there, he was alive to the slightest changes in his body.

His first stop came at 11:20 a.m. and thirty seconds. He was at ninety feet (27 m), and the outside pressure had halved during his climb to the surface. As a consequence, the pressure of nitrogen inside him was now about twice that of the surrounding water. For three minutes, Damant hung at the end of the line and waited. His next stop came at seventy feet (21 m) and lasted for five minutes. And so on, all the way from the darkness of the deep to the sunshine at the surface. Finally, he spent ten minutes at eleven feet, swaying on his lifeline in the gentle current doing gymnastics to keep his circulation brisk until it was deemed he had breathed off enough nitrogen.

At 12:04 p.m., Damant was finally called up. *Spanker* rolled in the waves and his air hose slapped against the hull.

Damant grasped the ladder just as Petty Officer James Deasy had done six years before. Just like Deasy, he heaved himself up each rung, one sixteen-pound boot after the other. On deck, his tenders guided Damant to his seat, and they removed his helmet. The recompression chamber on board was ready, mechanical pump idling, in case the symptoms of diver's disease showed themselves. They didn't. Nor did any symptoms show when Catto repeated the same dive that afternoon.

Professor Haldane's plan worked, as he knew it would. He'd managed to send a diver deeper than ever before and bring him back safely to the surface. Great Britain, Haldane would declare two years later, now possessed a means of carrying out her diving operations in a way unmatched by any other country.

Members of the public, if they were so interested, were able to purchase Haldane's report for sixpence. At the back were two decompression tables drawn up for divers. The eleven columns headed 'Table I: Stoppages during the ascent of a diver after ordinary limits of time from surface' offered divers precise instructions on how to ascend from any depth up to the stated limit of 204 feet (62 m). The table detailed how many staged decompression stops would be needed, where to pause in the water column and how long to hang there. It could, for example, be used to put a man down to twenty-six fathoms (48 m, 156 ft) for twenty minutes and have them back on the surface, injury-free by all accounts, after four stops totalling thirty-two minutes. The second table provided the ascent numbers for exceptionally long stays underwater. These were dives below the black line, that is dives for which it was too long for men to tolerate. Under Table II, decompression took up to four hours. Haldane acknowledged he had deliberately shortened the time for each stop so that serious injury might be avoided at the cost of some liability to less severe symptoms, such as a pain-only bend in a joint.

In quantifying the absolute limits, Haldane was effectively saying: here's the line for divers to stay on the right side of. Everything on my side represents safety. Everything on the other represents a great risk of injury. The results of his tables were electrifying. He was so certain of the marked superiority of his methods that he stated the risks to life and health of caisson's disease would practically disappear if his procedures were rigorously applied. In the next few years, decompression sickness became almost unknown in the Royal Navy. The first table virtually eliminated caisson's disease for short dives. The second table was not as successful; the schedule only managed to blunt the razor's edge of the diver's disease, but as far as the Admiralty was concerned the causes of compressed air illness had been identified. And because a cure for the anomaly had been found and classified, people believed they finally understood it.

Few modern divers use decompression tables like the two drawn up by Haldane, but they still rely on his research to get them out of the water safely. They plan their decompression schedules by punching numbers into a computer programme which has taken one hundred years of scientific study into the bends and boiled it down into a simple-to-use mathematical algorithm. And they use wrist-mounted devices to monitor their depth and give them real-time readouts during their dive. Computers mean divers can stay down for longer because they eliminate the unnecessary rounding-up that using tables requires. Even so, decompression is still a game of short climbs and long pauses, where there's no cheating the computer's piezoelectric pressure sensor and crystal oscillator.

People think following a decompression schedule to the surface is about patience, as if it's about hanging around and waiting until it's time to move. But adherents know it's all about restraint, restraint measured in half seconds and quarter inches.

On the ascent, the diver doesn't care about what they saw on the bottom; they don't care about what it might mean to them as individuals. They know that the most exciting part of the dive is behind them, and the only thing that matters now is that they travel all the way to the surface safely as dictated by their decompression calculations. And ascending from the deep is a long, tedious process, much like crawling in stop-start traffic towards the bottleneck responsible for the hold-up. The first few stops last a minute or two and go by quickly, but by the time you are in the shallows the experience becomes a trial of patience. That's why divers use words such as penalty and burden, obligation and hang-time. In the shallows you are trying to hang motionless, hunkered against the freezing cold pricking away at you, the surface so close you can see the wind rippling the water. Here everything is about control.

When the final decompression stop is going to be lengthy, divers look for ways of making it safer. For the expedition, Robson planned on using a submerged chamber known as a habitat, and he spent the first few days at Blue Lake ensuring the underwater refuge was in working order. The basics of Robson's habitat are not too dissimilar to an upturned glass plunged into a bucket of water. The vessel doesn't fill with water but contains a pocket of compressed air. On a grander scale, this bubble can provide somewhere dry for a diver to rest while decompressing.

American cave explorer Bill Stone first hit upon the idea of a habitat in 1987 when planning an expedition at Florida's Wakulla Springs. The cave was deep, and he knew exploring the passages would push his dive team into decompression.

Taking inspiration from the Sealab underwater living quarters trialled by the US Navy in the 1960s, Stone scribbled an idea on a piece of paper. The decompression dome was funded by Rolex and fabricated by the Sippel Company, Pittsburgh, from the same fabric as bulletproof vests and looked like an opened parachute. Journalists labelled it an underwater hotel where decompressing divers could relax at the end of a long day diving. They could even call for room service: freshly cooked dinner packed in an airtight tube and delivered to them underwater. A photograph showed divers sitting in beach chairs reading magazines, diving suits folded around their waists and oxygen regulators hanging from their mouths.

Robson would like to have followed Stone's example, but the habitat he'd asked for, a tarpaulin cube around a collapsible metal frame, had proved too costly to get at short notice. The Russians, though, improvised with a makeshift mix of cast-offs that were bolted, welded and tied together. The habitat was fashioned from an intermediate bulk container, the kind used to transport liquids and powders. The rigid polyethylene cube was about fifty inches in dimension and surrounded on five sides by a cage of galvanised tubular steel. Long before Robson arrived, staff at the dive centre had taken a saw and cut a hole in the bottom of the box for an entrance. Then they welded steel bars together to make a platform for a diver to use when climbing in and out. Green fabric ratchet straps, the kind used to secure loads on heavy goods trailers, held the platform in place, leaving a clearance of about twenty-five inches.

Once completed the whole thing was rolled into the water and secured, 4.5 metres from the surface, with rope tied to hooks bolted into an outcrop about twenty metres from the surface. As soon as everyone was happy it was stable, divers took a tank of air inside and cranked open the valve. The entire contents of the cylinder were needed to displace the water and create an air pocket that could provide sanctuary. As the container settled, the plastic bubble flexed under the stress of two thousand-odd litres of gas straining for the surface.

To enter, Robson approached the platform, flipped himself over so that he was looking up at his reflection in the mirrored surface of the moon pool, or wet porch, that marked the opening in the base of the habitat. He wrapped his fingers around the edge of the container and in one swift motion pulled his upper body up through the porch. With his feet now over the platform, he could stand up, his legs still submerged but his upper body out of the water. Robson then folded out a small wooden bench made from two pieces of wood buckled together with what looked like fabric from a car seat belt. With a bit of wiggling, he could lift his legs clear of the water to rest while his decompression clock ticked downwards.

A tangled web of wiring and gas hoses, umbilicals to the surface world above, had been retrofitted to the habitat to make it operational. Three provided electric power to the heated undergarments Robson wore under his dry suit, another was linked to a headset to allow communication between the habitat and the surface. Further hoses supplied oxygen to regulators and a full-face mask for use in an emergency.

The habitat fully functional, Robson now had somewhere to shelter at the end of each dive where he could eat, drink and sleep. If someone cared to bring him a book in a waterproof container he could also read. And he could get warm. Within an hour, the temperature inside could climb as much as four degrees higher than the surrounding water. Writing in his online diary, Robson said the habitat's primary function was to increase diver safety while decompressing and possibly act as a refuge for help should something not go according to plan.

'It took a number of dives to get everything set,' he added, 'and a few more dives with some of the support divers to make sure everyone understood what would happen in the transition from open water and into the habitat, out again at the end, and while inside decompressing. Once this was all done my home from home was ready for some of the deeper dives.'

Thought then turned to the group of divers who had agreed to support Robson's push into the deep. Bogdana Vashchenko had promised Robson the best Russian technical divers, yet their skill and experience were still mostly unknown to him.

Support divers are like Himalayan Sherpas. Their job is to haul tanks of gas. They haul them on land, two at a time, from the filling station to the water's edge, and clip them onto the deep diver before the dive begins. They haul more tanks into the depths, three or four clipped to their bodies, when they go to provide cover for their diver. And they haul tanks back to the surface again. They haul them around so their deep diver can make it to the bottom and back again. They haul tanks to ensure their diver has got something to breathe if a rebreather goes *bang!* underwater.

A catastrophic failure of a rebreather can ruin the deep diver's day, but it doesn't necessarily have to be a killer, not as long as they can switch to a conventional scuba tank. That's why deep divers carry what are known as bailout cylinders. Bailout cylinders are an insurance policy. Ideally, they hold a mix of breathing gas containing a percentage of oxygen suitable for the maximum depth of the dive. As the diver ascends, however, the mix in the tanks becomes suboptimal, and they need fresh tanks containing a mix richer in oxygen. The extra oxygen in the replacement cylinders means the deep diver can sustain life and continue decompressing if they have to bail off their unit.

The job of support divers is to ferry these replacement cylinders to a predetermined meeting point in the deep, so the deep diver has the correct mix to breathe in an emergency. In pairs, they hang in the dark, waiting until their diver appears from below. Then, carefully, they swap the cylinders they are carrying for the ones their diver has clipped away.

Once they have swapped the cylinders, support divers shepherd their diver towards the surface and a meeting with a second team, or a third. Then off they go, hauling tanks topside while the replacement team takes over and repeats the process. In the shallows, support divers might fetch their diver a warm drink or something to eat. For most of the time, they just hang there, a guardian with a bailout bottle burden, watching the diver for signs of anxiety or trouble.

Their presence allows an explorer to make it to the depths and search for a cave or claim a record. In essence, they are hauling someone else's dream. They put them down to the depths and, when their diver is finished, they bring them back up. They might never see the uncharted reaches of what is

75

being explored, certainly won't have a name in the record books if their diver becomes the deepest. But that is the job, and they know the deep diver can't do theirs without them. That's why you catch them speaking in terms of 'our' and 'we': we dived; we're searching for; our diver reached one hundred metres; we found the cave; we all got out safely. The diver is their diver, and they are vital to his or her success.

Sergei Gorpinyuk assumed his role as the organiser of the support team after he talked with the expedition organisers. They had worked together previously on the exploration of Orda cave, in the Ural Mountains. Gorpinyuk believed he could learn much from working with this 'famous British diver' and agreed to give up his time that January. He was a sturdy brown bear of a man; the sausages, meats and cheeses he brought to the get-togethers with members of his scuba diving club had gradually found their way to his middle. He carried with him the black and white outlook of an IT engineer. Which was what he'd been previously until he decided to permanently swap his computer for scuba gear. He lived in Moscow and had come to the sport in 2000 after spending the previous decade crawling around in dry caves. When water blocked the way, Gorpinyuk knew the only way he could move forward was to learn how to dive.

At Blue Lake, he was asked to arrange the support divers into three teams: deep, intermediate and shallow. That required careful thought. 'To be a support diver is hard work because they are looking after the life of the deep diver,' says Gorpinyuk. 'They have to understand everything about their own equipment; they have to understand everything about the diver's equipment, understand all the gases being used, understand the dive plan. They have to check everything for their deep diver, and they take part of the work away from them so the diver can concentrate on the dive.'

Gorpinyuk chose the most experienced divers for the deep support and then arranged cover for the shallower parts of the dive according to training. The deep support team would be the first ones down to meet Robson at a depth of between 90 and 120 metres. Gorpinyuk named himself to the team along with Andrey Bykov. Bykov was one of the best divers he knew, one of the best technical divers in Russia as far as he was concerned. He was the chief of the Black Sea Wreck Club, and he had been nominated in 2010 for an archaeological award after recovering amphorae from an eleventh-century shipwreck.

The intermediate support team, which would meet Robson at about sixty metres, included Roman Dunaev and Andrei Rodionov. Engineer, mechanic, rally driver, diver, researcher, photographer, Rodionov was the all-action epitome of Russian masculinity. Thirty-eight years old, he worked for Moscow-based Neptune Expedition, a non-profit organisation which specialised in all things marine: archaeological research, seabed surveys, artefact recovery and ship maintenance. As president of Neptune's in-house club, he marshalled research tours for well-heeled Russian divers curious to see the country's underwater cultural heritage. He also organised off-road motor rallies across the wilds of Russia or the dusty interior of Central Asia, and once took first place in the Ladoga Rally.

Everyone else was assigned to the shallow support team which would look after Robson during the final phase of decompression, including his time in the habitat. Among the group was Alla Popova. Of all of the team members, Popova probably had the most experience as an expedition support diver. A former saleswoman for a medical supplies firm, the thirty-two-year-old had assisted an international cave exploration project in Mexico. The project aimed to create a three-dimensional map of The Pit, a freshwater sinkhole at the end of a three-mile dirt track surrounded by a jungle of piich and amatl trees, ankle-twisting rock and marching ants. By any measure, the cave system was impressive. A series of tight passageways linked giant chambers large enough to swallow a Boeing 747. Popova worked as shallow support. Underwater, she accompanied the lead explorers as they set off, and she met them on their return. She helped them into the habitat, and as they decompressed, she hauled bailout cylinders and underwater scooters, food, water and weights for them.

When she wasn't doing that, Popova sat and waited, just in case the surface manager needed her to run an errand underwater. Tough as it was, Popova enjoyed the experience, and, when told of the Blue Lake project by Vashchenko, she agreed to help. 'There were a lot of experienced divers,' Popova says. 'I wanted to see how they organised expeditions and how they worked together.'

Safety, everyone knew, hinged on timing and the team conducted a series of practice drills to fine-tune the operation. The dives followed a similar pattern. After the group had finished preparing their equipment, they congregated in the preparation room and, over hot tea, ran through the plan. Specific details were written on a large whiteboard in black marker. At the top of the board was the time Robson left the surface and began his dive. Noted on the subsequent rows were the times and depths the support teams were to meet him. The times were exact, says Gorpinyuk, because he knew the importance of being there on time. To be sure, he noted in parentheses the time each team needed to be in the water ready to descend. Written at the foot of the board were reminders for preparing the habitat.

Underwater, all the support divers would be required to handle Robson's emergency bailout cylinders, and the test dives offered an opportunity to iron out any issues when it came to swapping tanks. Decompression cylinders are rigged with a handle made of nylon webbing sheathed in rubber. Fastened to the cord at the neck and base of the cylinder are bolt snaps that cost about £5 apiece. The snaps are clipped to metal D-rings threaded on the diver's harness. Divers use 316 marine-grade, stainless steel, swivel-eyed bolt snaps that they lever open with their thumbs. They are a holdover from cave diving where they were favoured because they couldn't be opened accidentally and snag a diver on the line. Divers steer clear of carabiners for that very reason; they refer to them as suicide clips.

Since each batch of cylinders was filled with a different breathing mix, they had to be labelled correctly. For the expedition, the decals were white and featured a statement printed in red: 'this cylinder contains something other than air'. In the empty space below, written with a black marker, were two numbers separated by a slash, 5/82, for example, or 32/11. The first indicated the percentage of oxygen in the breathing mix, the second, helium. A cylinder marked 5/82 contains 5 per cent oxygen. Five per cent oxygen would not sustain Robson's life at the surface, but deep underwater it was more than adequate. A helium content of 82 per cent ensured he had a clear head down there.

The cylinders were grouped according to their maximum operating depth, the limit of safety for them to be breathed from, and then handed to the support divers who would carry them to Robson. A typical arrangement was to clip the cylinders to their harness at the collarbone and hip. Some used a leash to group the cylinders and clipped the leash to their harness. The support divers might have to carry as many as four bailout cylinders for Robson alongside three or four for themselves.

When the support team met Robson at the predetermined depth, Robson lay horizontal in the water, arms outstretched in front of him, and adopted what he called the tailor's dummy approach: lie still, pretend you're a mannequin and let the support divers undress and re-dress you. One support diver hovered just below Robson and reached up to swap the battery pack for his heated vest. Then, they began to remove the bailout tanks. The diver then manoeuvred the cylinder to their left side, thumbed open the gates to each clip and snapped them onto the harness rings of their own equipment. It can be a challenge to see past the hose of the breathing loop, so the divers needed to know instinctively where their harness rings were. The cylinders were heavy enough to sink to the bottom if dropped, and no one wanted to chase one into the deep, so the diver didn't release the clips until they were happy it was secure. They repeated the exercise until they had removed all the cylinders from Robson. Only then did the second diver approach. They repeated the process in reverse, unclipping cylinders from their harness and clipping them to Robson's.

Being confident about handling equipment underwater was critical to a smooth changeover and ten minutes was, according to Gorpinyuk, enough time to complete everything. Once the job of exchanging equipment was completed, the support divers and Robson signalled each other with an affirmative okay. They checked their depth and dive time and, together, continued their slow, silent ascent to the surface. At a predetermined time and depth, another support team arrived, and, like a tag wrestling team, they took over responsibility for Robson. The handover allowed the first team to continue its ascent.

By the time they had swapped out Robson's cylinders, everyone in the water was running a decompression schedule. As they shallowed, dissolved gases flowed from the body's tissues and into the capillaries, the smallest structures of the circulatory system, along the venous circulation towards the capillary beds of the alveoli of the lung to be breathed harmlessly away. All the same, their bodies were probably starting to fizz a little as hundreds of thousands of microbubbles appeared. The bubbles were so small, sub-clinical in the language, that they were not in themselves going to be responsible for a bend, but they were there, a sign that everybody was under pressure.

On the surface, there were daily reminders the expedition was as much about the research as the diving. The scientists involved worked with plastic bottles, tape measures and flow meters to map and measure the lake. Ulyana Zhakova could be found standing thigh-deep in the lake's outflow river taking precise flow measurements, her daughter watching from the side, Professor Maksimovich noting down the readings. At other times she paddled a dinghy into the middle of the lake with her Italian colleague, Professor Giovanni Baldino, from the University of Turin, to set and retrieve a crude sample collector, affectionately named Monster Trap. Made from a plastic drinks bottle which had been cut and taped, the trap was sunk into the depths to gather heterotrophic micro-organisms, simple bacteria that belonged to the dawn of time.

Meanwhile, Bogdana Vashchenko's abilities as a saleswoman had become apparent and her persuasive spiel about history, hidden treasure and danger had attracted crews from news channels including MIR 24, News Kabardino-Balkaria (a regional news programme broadcast on Russia 1) and NTV. Before Robson went in for a dive, or after he surfaced, he often found himself in front of the cameras. The interest in the project had surprised him, but he was always willing to accommodate.

The news crews invariably wanted to go outside to the patio, since the view over the lake offered a stunning backdrop. Robson tuned his hearing into the Russian as, inevitably, each journalist asked about the dangers of deep-water diving. When those questions came, Robson didn't wait for the translation, and he sidestepped the drama with guarded sound bites: we don't take unnecessary risks, he said; or, we have trained to eliminate the dangers; or, the whole diving suit is heated, even the socks and gloves, so we don't get frozen.

Another person who sought him out at the end of each dive was Roman Prokhorov. He was the workman who built the habitat, and he always asked Robson what he had found underwater. One time, Robson removed rock samples from his pocket and placed them on the bench.

Prokhorov asked if he could take a look.

Of course, Robson replied, and with that, Prokhorov scooped up the samples and disappeared through a doorway at the end of the corridor. Robson followed after him. Beyond the door, he entered a workshop, and Robson could see the Russian communing with a microscope.

Prokhorov looked up as Robson entered. Good, good, he said.

If one person had to be honoured for pushing Blue Lake, it was probably Roman Prokhorov. Whether he was the first diver to explore the lake is not known and the particulars of his first dive there are somewhat blurred. It was in June 1982, apparently, that he arrived in the mountains as an ambitious nineteen-year-old geology student from Moscow, keen to stake his academic claim. Back then, at least according to an entry on the dive centre's now-defunct website, there was a building close to the site where the dive centre stood. There may even have been a gaggle of onlookers as this young man on a shoestring budget splashed into the lake's chilly waters. Prokhorov wore a homemade wet suit and had fashioned a diving cylinder from an old carbon dioxide tank. He had made a rudimentary depth gauge, the needle of which flickered towards seventy metres as he descended. Floating in the void, he could only look in frustration as the wall dropped out of sight beyond the feeble light of his torch.

Rising to the surface, Prokhorov was left with far more questions than answers. The secrets of the lake lay out of sight, but its lack of physical coherence held a multitude of possibilities.

In his mind, Prokhorov built a research centre on the banks where he could devote himself to study.

The dream had to wait more than twenty years. Diving got in the way. While standing in line at Moscow airport in the late 1980s, Prokhorov got talking to the man next to him and discovered they shared a love of caves. That man was Igor Galaida, and the two became good friends. Together, they charted Orda cave, found more than twenty shipwrecks in Russian waters and led archaeological expeditions to recover artefacts from them. Their 2003 discovery, the tsarist flagship *Oleg*, which had sunk in the Baltic in 1869, would be visited a decade later by Russian president Vladimir Putin in a mini-submersible.

In September 2000, while working as a dive instructor in the Black Sea resort town of Gelendzhik, Prokhorov decided to return to Blue Lake and he took Galaida with him. They spent three days exploring and returned again and again over the next four years. In 2004, Prokhorov and Galaida asked the republic's then-president, Valery Kokov, for permission to build a dive centre and research facility at the lake. The proposal became a reality the following summer. Galaida was named the centre's director, and Prokhorov became technical director.

You know, those two men are heroes of Russia, someone had told Robson, a few days into the expedition. Yes, they are the country's deepest scuba divers. They set the record here at Blue Lake six years ago, 180 metres.

Robson was impressed. Yet as he observed Prokhorov at the microscope, Robson thought he seemed more interested in rocks than records.

Robson left Prokhorov in his workshop and returned to his

equipment. As darkness enveloped the corridors of the dive centre, he worked late into the night cleaning his equipment and filling cylinders in preparation for the next day. The cold air was heavy with a particular tang which oozed from damp neoprene and vulcanised rubber diving suits and pooled as water on the tiled floor beneath rebreathers. The compressor groaned and the voices of other expedition members pitched that bit louder with stories of a day underwater. Together they had smoothed the rough edges from the equipment exchanges, and now they were primed to start looking for a cave. That, after all, was the reason they had all converged at this mountain lake in the borderlands of Russia, miles from anywhere.

UNDISCOVERED CONTINENTS BENEATH OUR FEET

Every field of human endeavor from Tiddly Winks to space exploration has its champions and its marks for human endurance and achievement. Without them there would be little or no human progress for we would have nothing to measure our efforts by or encourage us to try harder.

Sheck Exley, *Caverns Measureless to Man*

Most cave divers have faced *The Question* at some point or another, perhaps during a dinner party, at a bar or in a queue at an airport boarding gate: 'Cave diver, eh. So, tell me, what do you find there; other than some rock?'

What they are really asking is: why? Why bother? What's the point? Inevitably, the diver doesn't have a retort to rival George Mallory's 'Because it's there', or even Jacques Cousteau's 'If I knew that, I wouldn't go'. But cave divers understand why they put every ounce of their body and soul on the line. The why is in the magic hidden in the 7 a.m. mist clinging to the water when the diver enters the cave, and it's in the warmth of the evening sun when they re-emerge. The why is in the excitement of entering an alien world off-limits to all but the most committed, of following a natural time machine to a point where man did not exist. It's in the miracle of Mother Nature's design found in rock sculptures and flowstone; and the sensation of life at its prime in a dark, amniotic comfort, where there's just them, the hum of their breathing and the sweet flow of blood, down in a place where their will and skill combine to show them exactly who they are. And who but a cave diver can understand that?

Robson had his answer to *The Question*. 'Imagine what it's like to walk on the moon,' he'd say. 'It's a pretty barren, desolate place but you are enjoying the act of being in an environment where few people have been and using all the technology it took to get you there. Now imagine you're not on the moon but inside the moon with the most amazing geological structures, carved into the most otherworldly shapes by the water. Now put in your mind a picture of a barren desert from *Lawrence of Arabia*; I know what you're thinking of straight away, but instead of seeing dunes seven metres long and two metres high, imagine them scaled down to the size of sand on the seabed. Now imagine rock carvings like that surrounding you, up, down and sideways, and you are weightless in water so gin-clear it hurts your eyes, and all you want to do is see what's around the next corner. Then you come to a deep drop-shaft where the water looks like it's not there, only it's coming up with such a force that there is a boil in the water. And you drop in because you want to know, you want to see what is down there. . .'

If people were interested, Robson could spend hours talking about the delights of cave diving. 'There's a place, King's Bypass, in Jackson Blue cave, Florida,' he would say, a pressure cooker of excitement now struggling to keep the lid on. 'The

87

roof's very low, the passage very tight and there's so much silt, and you have to be so careful because your very presence stirs it up. Sneeze and that would be it; you won't be able to see anything. Or the exit to Little River, when it's in flow,' he would continue, jumping from detail to detail. 'As you emerge from the tunnel, you look up, and you see this beautiful blue pool of the surface above. The next thing you see is the trees and the sky. The current whips you up in a second if you're not careful. . . And what about Saint-Sauveur, in France? You come to a passage, and you think it's a dead end. It's not. Have you seen *Indiana Jones*? In the third movie, *The Last Crusade*, Indiana Jones must take a leap of faith to find the bridge crossing a canyon. He can't see it because it's disguised, but he knows it is there. The cave is the same. You have to swim right into the rock, that's your leap of faith. If you're at the right point, you find the passage opens up beneath you, dropping down into another chamber.'

If that didn't work, he could highlight divers who had discovered something so significant they had rewritten history. For that, he might turn to Mexico's Yucatan peninsula, a region that has been a premier diving destination since the 1980s when it was charted by members of the Florida caving scene. The pioneers lobbed rolls of toilet paper from aircraft windows to mark sinkholes deep in the jungle, they used horses, mules and local guides to transport their gear and spent days hacking trails by hand. Underwater, they made spectacular finds: fossils protruding from the walls, columns of minerals stretching from floor and ceiling, and freshwater crustaceans unknown to science. Then, in a void that would be named Hoyo Negro – Black

Hole – divers found the perfectly preserved skeleton of a young girl that turned out to be 13,000 years old. Anthropologists would later conclude that the skeleton was the oldest ever found in the Americas. The girl, they would suggest, had fallen into the pit when it was just a well for drinking water. Following the Ice Age, water levels rose and preserved her remains alongside those of other long-extinct mammals, including a sabre tooth tiger, ground sloths and a primitive elephant-like creature called a gomphothere. Nicknamed Naia after a mythological Greek water nymph, she challenged the perceived wisdom of who the first Americans were.

So, when someone asked Robson what he was in it for, he had an answer: I'll tell you what I'm in it for, I'm in it for the history, my friend!

'There are four types of people who want to dive caves,' says Canadian dive pioneer Paul Heinerth, a man with fifty years of cave diving behind him and the instructor who taught Robson to cave dive. 'For some, they've been open-water ocean diving long enough and are seeking another challenge. Others are interested in handling new equipment and the opportunity of seeing where it can take them. Next, you have those who are already technical divers who see cave diving as the top of the pyramid, the pinnacle of achievement. And then there's a small percentage who just want to go where no one has gone before.'

Martin Robson wanted to go where no one had gone before. The first time he experienced an underwater cave in 1997, he had to squirm through the rock-strewn, letterbox entry of Trou Madame, in the Lot Valley of south-west France. It was backbreaking work, crouched under the low ceiling, dragging his gear behind him, inch-by-inch, scrape-by-scrape, but cold sweat and adrenalin drove him towards a place in the world where he would finally feel at home.

The child of a nomadic Royal Navy family, Martin grew up on the Indian Ocean paradise of Mauritius where his father was stationed at a Cold War listening outpost. There he found happiness hiking into the jungle and climbing in the mountains. Occasionally a friend or two from school would join him, but he didn't need them. Martin wasn't withdrawn or unsociable: he was just happy in his own company, alone but never lonely.

If he drifted by at school, he was a high achiever in the outdoors where he attacked everything head-on. He'd seek slabs of rock, scrabbling for a foothold or a handgrip, and begin climbing, driven by a stubborn ability to soak up the surroundings. He pushed himself harder and further. During one sortie, Robson, no more than ten or eleven at the time, found himself stuck on a sheer rock face, with nothing between him and the ground below. There, he learned he could rely on no one but himself. It was a valuable lesson he would carry throughout life.

His second lesson came sometime later while snorkelling in the turquoise waters of a lagoon. He wasn't the only one there. He remembered a couple of other children splashing in the surf and a group of adults partying nearby. Everyone stopped when they heard a guttural scream come from the sea. Martin saw the water turn red as a man thrashed at the dark triangle of a shark fin. The sight of the man's body being hauled up the beach, painting a blood-red streak in the sand, stayed with Martin for years. Nature's a cruel mistress, he acknowledged, be careful of what's lying out of sight beneath the surface.

When Martin was in his early teens, the family returned to Portsmouth, in southern England. He left school at sixteen, climbed when he could and fell into a series of dead-end jobs. One night, after coming home tired from pulling pints in a bar, he turned on the television and caught the final seconds of a recruitment advertisement for the Royal Marines. The images of young men in the wilderness spoke to his heart and mind, and questioned his very being: have you got what it takes? The following day Robson went down to the recruitment office and, believing that he did, in fact, have what it took, signed up to 3 Commando Brigade. The odds of surviving basic training were against him. On Day One, the drill sergeant barked at the fifty-six recruits, the short ones, the fat ones, the ones with long hair, and the ones who barely looked old enough to have left school, and he told them: most of you will not make it. So unremarkable did Robson appear, he was identified as a likely drop-out. The officer was correct in one respect. Most of Robson's cohort didn't make it. Yet he emerged top of his class.

Robson thrived as a bootneck where preparation, wits and improvisation – to adapt and overcome – were preferred to brawn and bludgeoning firepower. He learned to study the enemy, anticipate their actions and plan his reaction. He boxed, played rugby, trained in martial arts and rowed, sports which, looking back, required a particular tolerance for pain and discomfort. He pushed himself on the rock until a disastrous slip at a place called Stanage Edge sent him plunging fifty feet to the ground below. He smashed his left ankle on a small outcrop on his way down, and the thing blew up instantly. Robson's climbing buddy helped him limp to the car. When they reached it, his friend confessed that he couldn't drive, so Robson squeezed behind the wheel, lifted his leg in behind him and headed to Royal Hallamshire Hospital, in nearby Sheffield, wincing every time he pressed the clutch. He remembers screaming when doctors removed his boot.

Robson wanted to specialise in mountain warfare but was instead selected for the diver training school. He didn't remember seeing much on his first dive, not in the dank, dark pond into which he had been thrust. Submerged just a few metres, he crawled forward and let his hands do the work of his eyes. Cold, muddy, and I absolutely loved it, Robson would tell those students who asked about his first dive. In April 1982, aged just twenty-one, Robson went to war as part of an amphibious task force sent to liberate the Falkland Islands in the South Atlantic. He yomped fifty-six miles across the frozen, boggy plains carrying his eighty-pound pack before engaging in fierce combat with Argentine troops. If Robson ever killed a man, it was not something he ever felt minded to discuss. When asked about the conflict, the memory he was comfortable with sharing was of lying in a foxhole reciting Monty Python sketches with a comrade only to be reprimanded by an officer: you two are not taking the war seriously enough.

He left the military four years later and became a firefighter because an officer told him that's what ex-Marines did. Robson saw little difference between the uniformed services. Both required self-discipline and physical fitness, and he rose through the ranks. He went to night school to learn Russian and he returned to scuba diving, certified as an instructor and taught at weekends whenever firefighting duties allowed.

If Robson was searching for something, the underground passages of Trou Madame proved an unlikely answer. As he drifted above the guideline, propelled by frog-like flutter kicks, his torch threw light at the fractured yellow of the Jurassic-era limestone walls and cast shadows in the velvet blanket of silt draped over the floor. Robson saw the cave as a black hole to an unambiguous world where nature, unshackled, challenged his very being. With each breath, each kick, each twist in a passageway, he propelled himself further into the unknown.

Trou Madame heralded a seismic shift in Robson's life, and he threw himself into cave waters like a man dying of thirst. He yearned to explore and saw the caves as his last opportunity. Humans might not have seen the depths of the oceans with their own eyes, but they could describe the topography and marine ecosystems. In essence, Robson already knew what he'd find. It was the same with wreck diving. He could examine a ship's plan and draw in his mind what lay on the seabed. But with caving, he didn't know whether he would have to go up, down, left or right. No technology could tell him that – he just had to be there.

He decided to push his limits underground, and, in the autumn of 1997, he headed to Florida. Under the tutelage of Paul Heinerth, he completed big dives in several famous caves, including Peacock Springs, one of the longest systems in the continental United States, and the remote Eagle's Nest sinkhole. Now, for better or worse, his life was set: he was a cave diver. He looked up to the likes of Tom Mount, Sheck Exley and

Jochen Hasenmayer. They were the folk heroes who made life seem that much bigger, those who answered to no one, and whose stories inspired him to reach for opportunities he only dared to dream of.

'Martin was a natural,' Heinerth says. 'He was a very good diver, and the learning curve was relatively short. He said he wanted to teach cave diving and I normally tell people to go away and get a hundred dives under their belt first, but I felt he was pretty much ready to go. He's the only one I've ever done that for. He had a keen sense of how it should be done safely and properly. That requires a lot more experience than the average person.'

Within the intensely idealistic community of cave diving, Robson found a camaraderie he'd not felt since military service. He appreciated his place within its ranks was not determined by overbearing machismo or tribal politics, but by his underwater prowess. The sport's participants were characterised by the total command they held over their bodies and minds. Anything less than perfection served only as the first step towards a mishap. And mishap had a habit of shaking hands with death. It was precisely the physical and mental challenge Robson had been seeking.

If Robson was a natural, it helped that he understood the balance sheet of cave diving. When extreme environments present extreme consequences, it requires an obsessive approach to overcome them. If any of the divers paid attention to Robson at the inland dive sites he frequented near his home, they would have seen some particular exercise habits. They would have seen him hovering in the shallows, simulating the various ways a rebreather could malfunction. He would practise bailing off the unit onto the open-circuit cylinder at his side. He did it every time, dive after dive, the same routine, driven by the maxim: if you're so worried you can't remember the proper procedures, you're as good as dead. No matter how proficient he thought he was, Robson accepted the cave was the final judge.

When asked, he would speak eloquently about cave diving, with almost spiritual reverence, unusual for an atheist. If his visions fired the excitement among his students, Robson tempered it with reality. Sitting in front of Joan from Sweden, or Heinrich from Germany, he would take out a blank piece of paper and draw the axes of a graph. The y-axis is about risk, he said, writing 'max' at the top. Across the x-axis, he wrote the factors which could reduce that threat. *Training* was the first, followed by maintaining continuous *Guideline*, then *Air/gas management*, observing *Depth limitations* and, finally, *Lights*. Each factor has a series of subsets, but these are the headlines, he explained, the things you need to consider before a dive.

He plotted the points on the graph and finally drew a line showing a sharp decline in risk before it tailed off and ran just above and almost parallel to the x-axis.

See, said Robson, pointing to the capitalised letter of each of the critical factors. Thank. God. All. Divers. Live.

The diving industry loves its mnemonics, and Robson stressed the message: you cannot eliminate the risk, but get these right and it's possible to enjoy the caves safely without fear.

Don't forget, though, he'd remind them, it's a round trip. The summit of a mountain is only halfway. You're responsible for ensuring you get home safely.

*

Buried within the pages of the *Memoirs of Frédéric Mistral* is an intriguing passage, the significance of which is most likely passed over by readers dissecting the life of the French poet. In a chapter entitled 'How I Passed My Baccalaureate Exam', the writer recounts a dinner party conversation about the knowledge necessary to succeed; the battles, the kings, names of all the nations, of all the regions, all the mountains and the rivers. The conversation was interrupted by a gravel-voiced gardener from Château-Renard with a question on an exasperating enigma of subterranean hydraulics, known as the Fontaine-de-Vaucluse, a spring that erupted from the base of the giant limestone cliff for five weeks each year. The gardener asked Mistral if he knew the whereabouts of the source of the spring because he had it on good authority that a shepherd had dropped his crook in the water and had found it again seven leagues away in a spring at Saint-Rémy.

Seven leagues? That was more than twenty miles of caves. Some water, indeed! That a cave diver wanted to know whether the tale was true or not says a lot about cave divers. They take the smallest of clues, the titbits picked up from conversations with locals, they examine how water flows through a confined space, perhaps how silt clings to one side of the rock and not the other; and they use the information to drive them on to new frontiers in search of an answer to a simple question: where does this go?

In 1946, French diving pioneers Jacques Cousteau and Frédéric Dumas travelled to the heart of wine-making country in Avignon to solve the mystery of Mistral's Fontaine-de-Vaucluse. The two men were not the world's first cave divers, not by a long way. Seventy years earlier, a man called Nello Ottonelli made the first documented cave dive at Vaucluse wearing the surface-fed, tinned copper helmet. Staring through the helmet's condensation-soaked viewing port, Ottonelli ventured no further than the dimly lit entrance.

The Frenchmen arrived with their revolutionary new self-contained underwater breathing apparatus – SCUBA – that Cousteau had developed in wartime France from a demand regulator used to feed cooking gas to car engines. A crowd of villagers, including a priest, gathered on the rocky auditorium surrounding the spring's entrance in the late August sun to watch the men splash into the head pool and fin for the throat of the cave. Cousteau's wife, Simone, was said to have stood on the shore with her arms folded before retreating to a café in town to wait anxiously for news of her husband's return. Wearing rubber diving suits over woollen undergarments, Cousteau and Dumas roped themselves together and descended into a world of perpetual darkness, the safety line paying out behind them. With little underfoot, Cousteau plunged down a sharp fifteen-storey incline at tigerish speed. He was focused on the beam of his torch when rocks began to tumble past him, and one hit him on the shoulder. Turning, he saw Dumas trying to dig his heels into the cave floor to break their fall and knew his buddy had a problem.

Cousteau hit a plateau, the elbow in the drowned tunnel, forty-five metres down, a place that would become known as the Great Hall of Night. His eyes still hadn't adjusted to the darkness when his mind was flooded by nausea and confusion. Gasping for breath, Cousteau could sense Dumas was also in trouble. Gripping his friend with one hand, Cousteau tried to

97

swim back to the surface. He clawed at the rock walls for purchase, the dead weight of Dumas holding him back. Overwhelmed, Cousteau wrapped his now feeble fingers around the
safety line that led to the surface and jerked it six times. Six
tugs meant pull us up. Above, the support team began hauling
furiously, hand over hand.

After breaking the surface, the two men were pulled to the
shore as they gasped for fresh air. Tests later found their cylinders contaminated with carbon monoxide. Apparently, their
new compressor sucked in its own exhaust gases. Cousteau
described it as his worst experience in 5,000 dives.

As a result of Cousteau's dive, Vaucluse assumed mythic proportions for European cave explorers. In some ways, it became
their Everest. Only the pinnacle remained out of sight. When
an underwater robot named Telenaut dropped into the depths
in 1967, it reached one hundred metres yet still did not find the
bottom. Speleologists began circulating the idea that Vaucluse
was the funnel for a labyrinth of underground rivers, the subterranean equivalent of the Triveni Sangam confluence in India,
transporting rain and meltwater from 1,000 square miles of
French countryside.

While Everest was summited in 1953, the deep of Vaucluse
was still unconquered three decades later. A prohibition order
issued by the local government enforced a ban on all diving.
Some said the decree was to preserve the quality of water
which fed local villages, others that it was to protect the archaeological heritage of the cave. The more mischievous suggested it
was simply designed to keep out foreigners. In fairness, divers
were not short of caves to occupy their minds. There were so

many passageways in France, about 20,000, that if one tossed a stone into the bush there was a good chance it would land with a *plop!* in a head pool leading to a largely unexplored cave with a name like Landanouse, La Doux de Coly or Source de la Loue. But Vaucluse was the one.

In the 1980s, Jochen Hasenmayer, a monastic German explorer with a thick Swabian accent and a big cave obsession, turned his attention to Vaucluse. As a teenager, he had been gripped by the exploits of cavers at Falkensteiner Höhle, in southern Germany, and decided to follow their footsteps. The frigid water was torture to the young boy's body so, to protect himself, he made a crude dry suit from rubber bed sheets. At the start of each dive, he glued himself into the suit using a bicycle puncture repair kit, and at the end he had to cut himself free. Like those who went before him, Hasenmayer did not find the cave's end, but his experience at Falkensteiner sparked a love affair with caving.

In the late summer of 1981, Hasenmayer learned that rival caver Claude Touloumdjian had secured permission to explore Vaucluse. In October that year, the Frenchman planned to break the record for the deepest cave dive and see if he could bottom-out the shaft. A week before Touloumdjian arrived, Hasenmayer crept into Vaucluse under cover of darkness and, using his homemade rebreather, spent five-and-a-half hours laying line down to a then-world record cave depth of 143 metres. Even then, he was still nowhere closer to the end.

Following the dive, Hasenmayer slipped away; the only evidence to his presence was the guideline left waiting for the Frenchman. When news of the encroachment emerged, journalists whipped the incident into a duel, the French versus

Germans, trenches dug, battle-lines drawn between divers, the cave a No Man's Land. A few days later, Touloumdjian added ten metres to the record. By then it hardly seemed to matter.

One balmy September evening, two years later, Hasenmayer returned to Vaucluse. The only public record of that night is a handful of black and white photographs of the German at the surface. In one, he resembles an alien from a 1950s sci-fi movie. Tubes and hoses snake around his shoulders; insect-like eye-pieces of his mask bulge from a rubber face protector; spare metal regulators hang around his neck; three lights project from his helmet; a spherical compass sits on his left wrist. Curved around his back are four cumbersome, twenty-litre tanks. Out of shot was a sled containing five more cylinders which Hasenmayer towed behind him. The tanks contained an exotic blend of helium, oxygen, nitrogen and a fourth gas which, to this day, he has never identified. He even blended food for the journey which he carried in a baby bottle affixed to his helmet. The photographs were taken by Hasenmayer's wife, Barbara, the only witness to the events that night. Perched at the water's edge, she watched as the dark waters enveloped her husband and then she sat there, alone, waiting for him to return. Underwater, beyond the steep slope where Cousteau and Dumas had found trouble, the cave continued its vertical elevator fall into the darkness. Hasenmayer pushed on for forty-five minutes until he decided to stop. Pausing for one adrenalin-packed second, Hasenmayer looked at the band of rock circling him and the blackness beneath. He was beyond the tip of believable. Then he turned for the surface. The mythical source of the spring remained out of sight.

Nine hours later, Hasenmayer returned from a corner of the world no human had ever visited before. He'd also set a depth record so extraordinary as to have been unthinkable, the world's first 200-metre, surface-to-surface scuba dive. When asked, years later, what motivated him to push deeper into the unknown earth, Hasenmayer replied: undiscovered continents lie almost directly below us.

The story electrified Robson's cave obsession. By accident of age, though, he found caving at a time when all the easy places, the ones with sunlit head pools reflecting the blue sky above, or the secluded coves surrounded by lush forest, had already been visited, claimed and mapped. Many of the difficult ones had fallen, too. To find something new he needed to go beyond what others believed was possible and push the line of an old cave others thought had been walled-out. He chose Durzon, in France.

Source du Durzon is hidden in the Grands Causses, in the south of the Massif Central, in southern France, in a 400-metre-thick limestone and dolomite landscape shaped by water. Expeditions by French, German and British divers had mapped the cave for 1,125 metres until coming to an abrupt stop at what divers referred to as a choke. In caving terms, a choke is a seemingly impassable blockage which puts the brakes on progress. By 2002, the cave was given up as done, but Robson was convinced the way on could be found. At night, after work, he studied hand-drawn outlines, photographs and poorly translated accounts of those earlier expeditions. He sought opinions from other experienced divers.

If the way on is there, one caver had said, I think it'll be beyond most people. It will be a small opening, and the current will be pumping. You'll have to fight your way through. It'll be right up your street, Martin.

By the time Martin and Vikki arrived in early November 2002, the entrance to Durzon was already in the grip of nature's headlong rush towards winter. The trees hung with skeletal hostility, clawing at the deadened grey pool which gasped and gurgled through the stranglehold of the valley. A few days earlier, the area had been occupied by French cavers, all blue dry suits, long fins and homemade valve protectors. Apparently, they'd heard he was on his way and crashed the site, not wanting the cave's record to fall to *le Rosbif*. When they stumbled out later that day having failed to find the way on, equipment was thrown to the ground, and the air was blue with frustration. Well, that was the story. Whether it happened exactly that way did not matter to Robson, he liked the image.

Martin and Vikki approached exploration in the same way mountaineers prepared for a push to the summit. The first day, they spent time staging caches of bailout cylinders and other back-up equipment along the first section of the cave. These would be crucial to Martin's survival if his rebreather malfunctioned and forced him onto conventional open-circuit scuba.

Then, shortly after noon the following day, Vikki watched from the surface as Martin set off on his epic adventure.

He wriggled through the jumble of boulders at the cave's chimney-like entrance. Shards of bright light streamed in behind him only to yield to the vast darkness beyond. Powering up a sixty-kilo scooter he nicknamed Fat Boy, Robson set off.

Tight at first, the meandering, dark grey passageway gradually opened wider as Robson followed the mainline, a white, plastic-coated strand of steel installed by earlier divers as a guide. When he reached the waypoint, 300 metres in, Robson was still only twenty metres deep. Over the next 300 metres, the cave plunged three times that depth, reaching fifty-eight metres at a spot known as the Dune de Sable. Thirty minutes later, Robson glided past the last cache of bailout cylinders, which sat 750 metres inside the cave on a limestone ledge next to the back-up scooter he called Black Pig. His emergency reserves were at the extremes of survival. If anything went wrong with his rebreather from that point on, the only gas he'd have to breathe was in the bailout cylinders he carried with him.

Robson pushed on. He was an inconsequential bubble of light and life moving horizontally through the cave. The bright white halo from his high-powered lamp reached out into the void ahead. Temporarily subdued, the darkness stepped aside as he passed, and, once he had gone, it closed behind him. Walls, up to ten metres apart, disappeared beyond his torch beam into the blackness of a thousand midnights. The ceiling, high above his head, remained unlit, empty of even the tiniest of details as if the reality of its barrier did not exist in Robson's mind. He glided past limestone platforms, jagged walls and vaulted ceilings. He saw ripples in the rock which resembled desert dunes. At some point, Robson found the decaying remains of a cave reel, covered in the orange-hued concretions of iron oxide, half-buried in the silt. This was a spool used years ago by renowned French diver Olivier Isler who first passed through this place.

Then, a little way ahead, the guideline disappeared into a wall. Robson turned off his scooter and approached the wall. Among the breakdown of a rock which had collapsed from the ceiling, he could see a narrow tunnel snaking between the boulders. The way on was a rat trap all sides round, not much wider than a man's shoulders with scheming little outcrops waiting to snag his equipment. Nothing was inviting about the view, but other divers had slithered through; the line told him so.

Robson scanned the way forward, preparing his approach in the same way a climber rehearses their route. Then he set off. Clenching his muscles as if to make himself pencil-thin, Robson squirmed between the boulders. He could feel the gentle tug of the rock on his rebreather case and hear the aluminium bailout cylinders scraping along the claustrophobic limestone collar. He breathed slowly, and moved slower, careful not to spring the hammer. It's rattly in the boulders, he thought. Rattly plays horrendous tricks on the mind.

Back in the 1980s at a place called Creature Sink, in Florida, Robson's friend Lamar Hires was diving with Woody Jasper, rubbing and grinding against a tight passage trying to make it go further. Jasper was pulling at rocks and Hires was there to keep the rubble from filling in behind him. When they reached a dead end, the men had nowhere to turn, so they had to reverse their way out, blind, before eventually making the surface. In the early hours of the morning, Hires' wife woke to find him backing off the bed, taking the blankets and everything with him. Startled, Hires woke and shouted: I got out.

Then there was American diver Parker Turner, who in 1991 became the first recorded casualty of a cave collapse underwater when debris from an overhanging roof of the entry cavern avalanched down the slope and plugged the narrow entrance. Robson dared not contemplate such a catastrophe. Instead, he slithered through the rib-cracking twists and turns until first his head, and then his body, popped out the other side, his dry suit covered in limestone dust.

Looking ahead, Robson saw the passageway drop sharply, a thin braid of nylon leading on. He triggered the throttle of his scooter and took off, to see what was down there. Following the line into the languid current, Robson felt the pressure in his ears as the cave dropped below ninety metres. More than a kilometre inside the earth, he pushed on until the line ended. Just like that. The thin braid was wrapped around a small needle of rock. This was it, the end. The furthest anyone had been.

Robson unclipped a cave reel from his harness and looped the white braid around the mainline. Finning forward, the nylon thread unspooling from his reel, he swept his torch from side to side, reading the cave, seeking the next passageway. Directly ahead, the roof met the floor in a jumble of rock. Robson couldn't see beyond this impasse. If the way on is there, it will be a small opening and the current will be pumping, he recalled. Robson looked again, studying the limestone, the way one side looked smooth and clean, the opposite rough and shaded with silt. To Robson, the side covered in silt was facing the flow of water. That was the direction he moved, divining a way forward from the half-exposed clues.

Robson missed it at first but caught it on his second sweep. It was the black opening, about the size of an oven door, hidden at the top of a mound of gravel. Moving towards it, he felt the punch of cold water hose-piping through the gap. He thrust his hands deep into the gravel, anchors against the torrent which tugged at his mask and scoured his exposed cheeks. He jammed his feet against the roof, took a breath and then launched himself forward a few inches in a frantic scramble towards the gap. The water jostled the hose of his rebreather, and he bit hard into the mouthpiece. He dragged a hand from the gravel and punched another hold. His reel spooled out another few centimetres of guideline. Silt billowed up to cloud his face before being swept away with the flood funnelling through the hole. He moved his other hand, jabbing the scooter's propeller shroud into the gravel. Shingle skidded over his hands and cloaked the beam of his torch. His feet scraped along the cave roof looking for purchase. He scooped at the stone until he made the entrance big enough to squeeze through. Inching forward through the enlarged gap he slammed another handhold into the floor. And another. And another. He was breathing hard.

And then the resistance capitulated. Robson toppled through the other side and crashed into the floor. It was ungainly, but he was through.

Away from the opening, the water was calm, and Robson hovered there, wide-eyed and motionless. He was staring at virgin cave. There was a wall, no more than two metres high, on his left. To his right, there was nothing, just a void. Whatever was there lay beyond the reach of his torch. Staring into the blackness, Robson estimated the distance to be at least thirty metres. But it could easily have been twice that.

Spooling out some line, Robson looped in around a hook of rock and kicked forward, a few metres above the virgin passageway's floor. The water was crystal-clear; finning through it felt like flying. His eyes zinged everywhere. They were the first to see this. The white nylon line from his reel in his left hand paid out behind him. Robson was exploring.

In the glow of his torch, the cave surrendered its brutal beauty: oversized boulders from the land of the lost, mineral seams crushed paper-thin, knobbled columns of crumbly limestone projecting a few inches from the floor. He had found the cave's gold, encrusted in a layer of fine orange silt which glimmered in his torch. To Robson, it was unlike anything he had seen in the dark grey sections of the cave; unlike anything he'd seen in any cave before. It was his Ilha Formosa, Beautiful Island. Unseen since the dawn of time, the sights had no pre-existence, they had not appeared in a coffee-table book or video presentation. They were as pure and timeless as the first view of the Grand Canyon which seized the eyes of the conquistador García López de Cárdenas in 1540. And Robson made sure to shine his light on as much as he could.

Astronaut Frank Borman once described venturing into the unknown as the essence of the human spirit, while George Mallory labelled it an indomitable desire. Scientists had even tried to quantify it and give it a name. In the 1990s, they found a gene mutation called DRD4-7R and labelled it the Adventure Gene. Robson just felt the adrenalin fizz from his ears, and his mind twitch like a live wire. He had crossed a frontier, physically and psychologically, and felt the cave with every fibre of his being. Something about this cave had drawn every last effort from him, and he was now experiencing the deepest sense of who he was. Everyday life now seemed so far away.

Gripped as he was, Robson forgot to heed his turn-time, the moment he was to halt his explorations and turn for the exit and a meeting with Vikki. Instead, he pushed further. He was almost 110 metres deep, and now he was running late.

At the surface, Vikki climbed into her rebreather and, at 3 p.m., slipped into the water to meet Martin. She was his 'cave slave', and they were to rendezvous 300 metres into the cave so she could support him during his decompression stops and ferry his cylinders back to the surface. The lonely wait had been horrendous, and Vikki was happy finally to be in the water. As she followed the mainline into the cave, Vikki tried not to think about the meeting ahead. If she did, a grave disquiet took over her mind. What happens if he is not there? She couldn't allow a place for those thoughts; she would not be able to swim on if she did. So, Vikki focused on her finning technique and the distance markers on the line that led her ever closer to Martin.

Vikki arrived at the meeting point as scheduled.

Martin was nowhere to be seen.

Staring into the black tunnel ahead, Vikki prayed for a flicker of light to emerge. She waited for five minutes. A wave of anxiety rolled over her body, chilling her faster than the surrounding water ever could. Dreadful thoughts swept through her mind, thoughts of Martin trapped in dark recesses of the cave, either dead or dying. She wanted to press forward, to go to him, but Martin had drilled cold rationality into Vikki: if I'm not back, don't risk your life looking for me.

She waited for ten minutes. For eleven. For twelve. Each agonising moment piling on top of the one before, and the one before that. The clock ticked over another minute, but she did not dare to move forward.

Fifteen minutes. Other divers might not have been so disciplined. Consumed by thoughts of a friend in peril they may have pressed on with reckless oblivion to the dangers stacking up against them. He would be there, in their mind at least, thrashing to free himself from some catch point. The image would be so indelible they would forget to look at how deep they were, how much gas they had left. At some point the brain's safety mechanism, the fuse which keeps people from doing stupid things, would trip, the diver would stare at their gauges, and one of two things would happen. Either they would acknowledge their vulnerability and turn in hope, or they would recognise, with grim realisation, that they didn't have enough gas to make it out. This was their event horizon, their point of no return.

Hovering in the cave, Vikki was at her physical and emotional extremes. Her head pounded. She was not waiting for anybody or any buddy; she was waiting for Martin. He was twenty minutes behind schedule. How long should she wait before giving him up for dead? She agonised about abandoning him to the cave, of swimming out alone, knowing he would not be coming home. She imagined herself sitting in a field in France, surrounded by their possessions. She thought of the telephone call for help; of dealing with French officials and their particular formalities; discussing whether others should go and retrieve his body.

Vikki smothered the thoughts and breathed deeply. Then she noticed something, an ethereal wisp in the darkness. Light.

Getting brighter. Martin? When he came into view relief swept her along the line towards him. She grasped his hands and pushed her mask against his. Tears flooded down her face. Her body shook with relief, and he was oblivious to it. He held up his exploration reel, now empty of line.

'Vikki had come in to see how I was getting on. I gave her an underwater hug. I think she guessed I had got through as I was grinning like a Cheshire cat,' he later wrote in a magazine article about the endeavour.

Composing herself, Vikki stayed with Martin as he completed his decompression stops. She ferried out the bailout cylinders and returned when he had just twenty minutes to go so that she could accompany him to the surface.

Eight hours, and two exhausted torches, later, Martin surfaced. He peeled off his mask, pulled the breathing loop from his mouth, and his smile said it all: he was the first person to break through into Durzon's next level.

At the camp, Vikki made him a cup of tea while he pulled his equipment from the water. As he sat down, she opened up.

I can't go through that again, Vikki said.

Go through what?

When you weren't there, I thought you were dead. I can't sit here on my own, waiting for you like that, assuming you're not coming back. The risk is one we both accept, but if the worst happens, I want someone there to support me.

For his part, Martin was mortified by what Vikki had been through, and he resolved never to miss another underwater deadline.

The pair returned to Durzon two months later, in January

2003, with Vikki's father Ed and fellow diver Trevor Clark. Snow lay thick on the ground and water washed from the cave entrance. Progress was slow, visibility in some sections less than a metre. Robson managed to push the line another fifty metres into the cave before he called the dive.

It didn't matter, though; his dive was such an achievement that in the next decade the number of people who repeated his journey could be counted on the fingers of one hand. Another team explored the cave two years later and claimed to have finally reached the end of the cave. When he heard the story, Robson turned to Vikki and said: there's still more to find down there.

A GRUELLING ACT OF SUBMERSION

If you want to compete, play football. If you need to demonstrate physical prowess, go bear hunting with a knife. If you
have to see other people lose, take up tennis. In the underwater
world there is no room for machismo; it might kill you; or
worse, it might kill someone else. Diving is an activity in which
people need to work together. Lives depend upon it. It is not
just something you do; it is something you join.

Gary Gentile, author of *The Technical Diving Handbook*,

aquaCORPS magazine

The line at which diving became too deep for the Royal Navy in
the early 1900s was drawn at thirty-four fathoms (62 m, 204 ft).
That was the maximum depth stated in John Scott Haldane's
staged diving tables. Haldane had promised the risks of decompression sickness would disappear if his procedures were
applied and compressed air illness had become a thing of the
past. Salvage divers knew they could be sent down into the
deep and brought safely back without getting hurt as long as
they stayed within the lines. They were veterans of decompressing on air, moving shallower in ten-foot increments and
ever-lengthening pauses. For two decades everyone seemed
happy with that. Then, the Royal Navy lost two submarines

and the Admiralty was compelled to look again at the limits of deep-sea diving.

When the *M1*, pride of the British submarine fleet, was lost with her crew of sixty-nine, 239 feet (73 m) deep in the English Channel, in November 1925, navy divers had neither the experience nor the equipment to find her and attempt a salvage. Instead, commanders were forced to send for the Germans and their tin-man, bubble-armed, Neufeldt and Kuhnke armoured diving suit. Then, *H47* sank off the South Wales coast, in July 1929, in 325 feet (99 m). The First Lord of the Admiralty, Albert V. Alexander, had to tell the House of Commons, with regret, that no hope could be entertained of the twenty-one crewmen being alive. Her salvage, in such deep waters, was, he said, most improbable. Suddenly, the need to get divers deeper underwater became important again.

The US Navy had already put divers deeper underwater than any other nation had achieved when, in 1915, divers salvaged the submarine *F4* lost off the coast of Honolulu. Eleven dives were made to depths greater than 270 feet (82 m) using extrapolations of Haldane's tables. Divers surfaced with joint pains but escaped serious injury. The Admiralty considered this a remarkable piece of diving and saw what was possible. Six months after the loss of the *H47*, the Lords established a new Deep Diving Committee. The principle was to recommend, in detail, what was needed to get divers in standard rubber dress deeper underwater; and nothing less than fifty fathoms (92 m, 300 ft) would do.

The problem with Haldane's tables, if there was one, was that the time spent decompressing was far greater than that spent in useful work, and there were those in the navy who questioned whether the game was worth the candle. Among them was Dr Leonard Hill, the director of the Department of Applied Physiology at the National Institute of Medical Research, and an authority on diving work. Hill believed he could reduce the time divers spent decompressing in two ways. His first theory was the human body could tolerate an over-pressurisation on ascent greater than the 2:1 ratio Haldane had proposed. A diver could, in Hill's theory at least, save time by skipping deeper decompression stops. His second idea was to have divers breathe pure oxygen instead of air on the shallow decompression stops. Pure oxygen, he posited, would rapidly flush nitrogen from the diver's body and shorten time underwater even further.

Hill employed a statistician to make the calculations and codify the results into a series of oxygen decompression tables for use by divers. By the time these new tables were shown to the navy men, they had already been tested on animals at the Lewisham factory of marine engineering firm Siebe, Gorman & Co. An animal colony was set up at the firm's Neptune Works, and a variety of creatures were enlisted in the battle to beat the deep. The goats, baboons, pigs, dogs and a donkey began their training inside a steel air-pressure chamber. They were placed under increased pressure to simulate a deep dive and then decompressed. The pigs and dogs were found to be unduly susceptible to compressed air illness, while the baboons, Tarzan and Pongo, were particularly immune. So, the doctors prioritised results from the goat experiments. The unfortunate ones, most of them, in fact, like Ermyntrude, Geraldine and Kate, showed signs of decompression sickness. These signs didn't seem to worry the bean counters too much; the number of injuries suffered by goats was considered statistically acceptable to allow the tables to be tested on humans.

In the summer of 1930, twelve volunteer divers boarded HMS *Tedworth* in Portsmouth and left for Argyllshire with nervous anticipation. The grey hulk, whose single stack coughed out black clouds in such volume sailors nicknamed her 'Smokey Joe', was home to the Royal Navy's diving programme after the First World War. On the main deck, coils of India rubber hose were placed next to banks of gas cylinders. On any given day an officer in a windcheater sat hunched in front of the gas mixing panel, eyeing pressure gauges and working the stopcocks to control the flow of air to a test diver somewhere in the deep below. Nearby was a communications man, headphones wrapped over his head, listening to the diver at the other end of the wire. This was the place of hot tea, peaked caps and Yes Sirs. Further aft, profanities mixed with smouldering cigarette smoke in sea salt air as diving attendants, in canvas overalls and Clark Gable haircuts, loitered at the gunwales. A standby diver, already dressed in his three-light six-bolt suit, was perched on a four-legged stool ready to splash in the event of an emergency involving his buddy. This was diving for Royal Navy men and, right then, they were pushing a new frontier of deep-sea exploration.

Slung over the ship's side was the Davis Submerged Decompression Chamber (DSDC). First proposed by Hill two decades earlier and developed by Siebe, Gorman & Co., the chamber was a pressurised, tin can diving bell in which the diver could shelter during decompression, and no other navy had anything like it. The principle was simple: the chamber was like a halfway house. It was lowered to a predetermined depth, ready to collect the ascending diver, who would clamber inside through a hatch at its base. Inside, a waiting chamber attendant would remove the diver's helmet and hand him an oxygen breathing mask. With the lower door sealed shut, the pressure inside could be controlled by an officer back on the surface. The whole thing could then be winched onto the deck of *Tedworth*, where the remaining decompression could be completed in relative comfort. The DSDC was cramped and clammy, and the two men inside had to take turns sitting, but divers preferred that to hanging under a ship, see-sawing on their safety rope in a heavy swell, retching into their helmets, ears throbbing with the pressure swings.

Once the usual components of sea trials — the work-up dives and equipment testing — were completed, the dives became progressively deeper. Underwater, the men relied more on guts than knowledge; they simply didn't have any real idea of what was going to happen once they pushed beyond 240 feet (73 m). On the bottom they worked out as directed, searching for equipment intentionally thrown overboard, recovering anchors or cutting links from a chain with a hammer and chisel, anything that mimicked the spadework they might do for real.

By 17 July, seventy-seven dives had been carried out at depths up to 344 feet (105 m) without a single case of the bends. That Thursday was the final day of the trials. On the roster were five divers who had not yet carried out long excursions in deep water. The plan was for each to spend twenty-five minutes at depths up to 320 feet (98 m). Chief Petty Officer

David Robertson was first to go down. He was on his sixth dive of the trials, his deepest so far, and he was not sweet on the idea. Six days earlier, he had blacked out at 300 feet (91 m), his mind going for a walkabout until he was hauled off the bottom.

Robertson left the surface at 9:07 a.m. with instructions to attach an air pipe to a buoy sunk nearby. Three minutes later his voice, from the glens of east Scotland, crackled over the radio: 'On the bottom.' Robertson spent twenty-two minutes there and at 9:30 a.m. his rope man gave a sharp tug: time to come up.

Robertson didn't answer. Three hundred and twenty feet below he was out of it: his thinking became muddled, and then he developed amnesia of the most paralysing kind.

The minutes ticked away. The radioman tried to raise the diver; only static came back along the telephone cable. Surface attendants were ordered to take up the safety rope and start pulling. The radioman kept on at the microphone: diver, are you all right? Are you all right? The deck crew continued hauling. A hundred-foot length of rope lay coiled at their feet when Robertson came back to life as if someone had thrown a switch to his brain.

All right now, he said.

Five minutes later he reached the submerged decompression chamber and clambered inside. He didn't look well. The chamber attendant unscrewed the faceplate, and Robertson vomited. Asked if he had finished his task on the bottom, Robertson couldn't answer. He wasn't trying to hide anything; he just didn't have the first clue. The chamber attendant dogged the hatch closed, and the DSDC was hoisted aboard *Tedworth*.

As the two men inside took turns to stand, Robertson felt his legs weaken, but he held his tongue. He just wanted the whole thing over. As soon as the men finished their decompression and the lid opened to fresh air, Robertson was up the ladder and out. He was done. Tired and shaken, he fell onto a coil of air pipe and said: that's the end of my deep diving.

Robertson was helped out of his suit and he stretched out on a bench sipping a cup of hot, sweet coffee. A medical officer took his pulse, and that's when Robertson realised he might not walk away from his last dive. He couldn't move his left leg at all and couldn't lift his right more than six inches. When Robertson's reflexes were tested, his knee didn't jerk when hit, and pinpricks felt like dull touches. The men who had hauled him to the surface now carried him to the recompression chamber. They'd probably heard of cases like this, but they'd never seen one. To them, compressed air illness was a bend, a gnawing in the joints quickly cured by a press in the chamber. It wasn't a deadness in the limbs.

Inside the chamber it was a different reality. Despair mounted as five, ten and twenty minutes passed with little improvement in Robertson's condition. After ninety minutes under pressure, he still couldn't move his legs. That's when doctors decided there was no point continuing the treatment.

Robertson was taken ashore. Later, while languishing in Greenock Infirmary, he suffered a bladder infection that caused inflammation of the kidneys. The infection spread. On 11 August, his heart failed, he was declared dead and his wife, Mary Scott, was now a widow with a fatherless child. Robertson's medical file listed the cause of death as septicaemia, and cystitis, secondary to paraplegia caused by caisson's disease, subsequent to deep-diving trials.

Robertson was one of three men who bent that July day, but he was the only one not to recover. His death was damned sobering for the navy men, and it turned the expectations of the Deep Diving Committee upside down. They had been pre-pared to declare the decompression schedule safe for divers to carry out satisfactory work at depths up to 320 feet. Now, they faced the inconvenient truth that their calculations offered nothing like the guarantee the navy brass were after.

The development of dive tables was built on such tragedies, and, amid an air of frustration, everyone returned to Neptune Works that autumn for new experiments. Dr Hill was convinced his method of decompression was sound; he needed something else to blame the bends on. He questioned whether the oxygen breathed in the decompression chamber was pure enough to wash the nitrogen from the diver's body at the rate prescribed by his table. At one stage, he insisted the problem might have been the result of gases in the alimentary canal as if a diet of greens were the trigger for bubbles in the blood vessels during the first, aggressive phase of the ascent. He even suggested rules to make decompression safe: a diver had to allow time to let his last meal digest before deep diving, and he had to be passed free of flatulence by a doctor.

Sir Robert Davis, director of Siebe, Gorman & Co., privately believed the old ways of Haldane offered more opportunity. At his own cost and initiative, he engaged Captain Guybon Damant, the officer who had been part of Haldane's study twenty-five years earlier, to carry out a parallel line of research. From the outset, Damant had no faith in the new methods of calculating decompression schedules. Experience told him to trust Haldane's approach. When he salvaged £5 million of gold bullion from the wreck of the *Laurentic* between 1917 and 1924, Damant rigidly applied Haldane's decompression tables, and his team suffered no severe injuries during more than 5,000 dives. Experience told him the answer lay in simply extending Haldane's theory of staged decompression by extrapolation.

Rather than rely on mathematics, he favoured the old ways of discovery, trial and error. Damant again chose goats as the standard experimental animal for research purposes, and two additional steel pressure chambers were installed at the factory. The animal testing, on the face of it, seemed particularly cruel. Goats were subjected to aggressive decompression schedules that were likely to result in bends. Inevitably, some of the animals had to be sacrificed − painlessly, apparently − when the symptoms showed late and became too crippling to reverse. Others died when a short circuit started a flash fire inside one of the chambers. Researchers hid behind walls as the building pressure blew out rivets which held the chamber walls together.

At the start, Damant extrapolated Haldane's calculations, hoping they would hold as true for a thirty-minute dive to 300 feet as one to 120 feet. The results were disconcerting. Of the dozen goats that went into the chamber, only seven emerged. Two died, three others were bent. That was enough to reveal Haldane's 2:1 rate no longer held good under higher pressures, a finding which Haldane himself had predicted might be the case. Damant tinkered with the ratio, reducing it to 1.75:1. A single dead goat was enough to reveal the idea unsafe.

When compared with Dr Hill's work, Damant's tests may have resulted in more bends, but they didn't cause anything near the misery of his competitor. Dr Hill killed four goats and paralysed three others, and all further work on his proposals was cancelled. The Admiralty still required reliable results, though, so Damant added an arbitrary 15 per cent supplement to the time of each decompression stop. Forty-eight goats underwent the new schedule. One died, but the fatality was dismissed because she was pregnant. That was good enough for the Committee, and Damant created decompression tables covering 200 different exposures for depths up to 300 feet.

The Royal Navy scheduled the next round of manned deep-diving trials for the summer of 1931. Five divers were retained from the previous year, and the call went out to the ranks for five fresh recruits. The requirements were that they were young, about thirty, thin and wiry with good ears, and no active venereal disease. Those with short necks, or thick ones, were turned down, and nervous men told they need not apply. They may have been nothing more than lab goats in rubber diving suits, but the pool of volunteers was considerable; the pay was that good. In late April, at the Siebe, Gorman & Co. factory, the men went through a preliminary screening. Doctors made them do the forty-millimetre endurance test. They were asked to blow into a tube attached to a column of mercury. The idea was to time how long they could hold the mercury at forty millimetres with the pressure of their breath. About a minute was considered a good result. Then, Shipwright Albert Gaisford, aged twenty-nine, blew everyone away with a time of 143 seconds. Next, the doctors made the men do the 'fifty test' to assess their aerobic fitness. The men were told to bend down and touch their toes fifty times in two minutes. Able Seaman Ernest Elias Tomkins, a former van driver brought up in Sutton, Surrey, barely broke a sweat. The doctors then made the men do 250 toe-touches in ten minutes. They made the men do breath-hold tests and balancing tests.

They took the top five recruits, and the five old hands, shut them inside the large pressure chamber, three or four at a time, and kept pumping air until the inside simulated a depth of 300 feet. The men sweated through their thick woollen jumpers, their faces shone, and their breath beaded into silver droplets on the walls. When they stared at the words written on pieces of paper their vision might have blurred momentarily, but no one wanted to admit anything more. They didn't want to lose their spot on the trials, certainly not the nine shillings a day in deep diver pay, because of a momentary glitch in sight. During the dive, small strips of blotting paper treated with carbol fuchsin, a chemical dye now used as a microscopic stain in tests for mycobacteria, were bound to one hand. The test had been developed in Japan and purported to detect mental excitability in people; if the subject's palm was stained deep red at the end of the test, it meant the men had sweaty palms and were, apparently, mentally excitable and not suitable for deep diving.

At the end came the psychological evaluation. Psychiatrist Millais Culpin interviewed the men, and they had to be careful when answering his questions. No one wanted to suggest they were anything other than evenly balanced, not when the slightest kink in the psychic chain, a phobia or common-or-garden funk, was believed to trigger dangerous reactions underwater. When Culpin picked at the men's earliest memories for anxieties or obsessions, they did their best to come off as cool and composed. They certainly weren't afraid of the dark. When talk turned to an afternoon stroll, they certainly didn't want to show any sign of introspection; not when a fellow was deemed suspect because he said he wouldn't go into a tearoom alone and would rather go hungry for fear everyone was watching him. No, that was enough to get you canned. Instead, they knew to say things like: 'Look, ordinary diving has a fixed history; you know what can happen. Deep diving has no fixed history, so we have to pave the way. The pioneer stage of anything is risky, but there's a job to do down there.' That way, they were seen as an intelligent, non-imaginative kind of individual.

Back in Scotland, the manned sea trials started with an air of uncertainty. Things got worse when Able Seaman Frederick Hilton suffered a bend in the right elbow. The twenty-four-year-old Essex man had only been on a short practice dive to 167 feet (51 m). Leading Seaman Richard Oliver, from Christchurch, Hampshire, was hit twice in a matter of days, first in his right elbow, then his left, just days before his thirtieth birthday. He'd barely got past 164 feet (50 m). Shipwright Gaisford, the man who beat the forty-millimetre test, was barely out of his dive suit when he suffered pain so sharp he had trouble 'repressing exclamation' as it exploded in his left elbow, spread down his forearm, and dropped him to the deck in two minutes flat. The sick book made depressing reading, and they weren't even past the practice dives yet.

Members of the Committee looked again at the dive tables.

There was no time for any further animal tests, so they made some modifications. Firstly, they increased the 'dead time', which was the time allowed for the diver to climb into the DSDC and get undressed before the decompression clock began ticking. Then they added a 25 per cent premium to all the shallow decompression stops.

Shipwright Gaisford was a martyr to the bends, pain his constant companion, particularly on damp days, and the Committee decided the former docker was a bad subject. They wanted perfect results, and this imperfect subject was preventing that. Indeed, with his experiences excluded, the number of bends fell by almost a third. So, the Committee eliminated him from the final round of dives to 293 feet (89 m). That worked. The test results looked healthier in an instant. The trials finished with eight dives, eight fit divers, and zero bends. The Gaisford fudge had worked. Damant tweaked his tables to take full advantage of Hill's oxygen breathing schedule during shallow decompression stops, and the Committee's final report was rubber-stamped by the Admiralty. Diving was now approved up to fifty fathoms (91 m, 300 ft).

A series of confirmation trials was held two years later. Eighty-five deep dives were conducted, and five cases of compressed air illness were reported. Three of these cases were so slight, a supplementary report noted, that without medical examination they would not have been detected. The Deep Diving Committee considered this number to be expected. Simply extending decompression times to eliminate the risk to everyone entirely would result in a great waste of time underwater, it was decided. The result was that when divers hit the water on deep dives, the chance of getting bent was a hazard – a vanishingly small one – that they just had to accept because the Admiralty couldn't do anything more about it.

Just before midday on Tuesday, 10 January 2012, Martin Robson sat in his equipment on the bench closest to the door leading outside, with a ritual of accumulated habits waiting for him. Holding the mouthpiece of the breathing loop between his lips, he pinched his nose with his right hand and, head down, carried out the pre-breathe to test his rebreather. For five minutes, his eyes stayed focused on the unit's handset as he watched the readings flicker as expected.

He held his mask in his left hand because he refused to wear it during the procedure. Doing it this way, he would still be able to catch an involuntary breath of fresh air if the loop was contaminated with harmful gas, and he started to faint.

When he had finished, he closed the loop and removed it from his mouth. He secured his mask to his face and swept his thumb around the skirting to make sure it was tucked under his hood. Next, he ran his hands over his chest and his waist to ensure the clips, buckles and hoses were connected as they should be. Then he checked his torches were working, pointing each one at the palm of his left hand and turning them on and off again.

Finally, he placed the loop back between his lips and opened the mouthpiece. He took a few deep breaths to clear his mind and began to play out the whole dive and what he needed to do.

He conjured up a picture of the two divers checking his equipment for leaks at six metres. He visualised descending the shot line to the target depth, using his left hand to alternately squeeze air into his buoyancy wing with the low-pressure inflator, and depress a button on his counterlung to add gas to the volume in his breathing loop. He saw himself using his right hand to equalise his ears. He pictured himself fixing strobe lights to the line to illuminate the way home. He envisaged opening the throttle of his scooter, cruising along the wall, eyes scanning the beam of his torch as he searched for the cave. And then he conjured up images of the ascent, the pitstops with his support team, his transition into the habitat, and everything he would do until surfacing.

Then he began contemplating the multitude of things that could go wrong: all the parts of the rebreather – and he could name every single one – that might fail. What if the solenoid jammed open and the loop's oxygen level spiked? Mentally, his hands traced his equipment: come off the loop and reach for a bailout regulator; reach behind with the right hand and close the valve to the oxygen cylinder; look at the cylinder contents gauge and watch the needle fall to zero; go back on the loop and flush it with diluent gas; watch the sensor readouts on the handset and feather the valve to add oxygen when needed. And if the solenoid jammed closed? Bail off the loop; check the oxygen cylinder valve is open; check the contents gauge of the oxygen cylinder to ensure it is not empty; go back on the loop; do a diluent flush to freshen up the gas in the loop; check the sensor readouts and add oxygen manually.

And what if it crashed out on him? That had happened to him once seventy-two metres down off the coast of Sydney. Robson was teaching a course when the rebreather handsets went dead. Using a practice known as minimum loop volume, in which he manually added oxygen to the loop to replace that which had been metabolised just as it felt like he wouldn't be able to get a lungful of gas, he swam horizontally to the shot line. Switching to his bailout cylinder, Robson ascended to six metres and then went back onto his rebreather and ran it intuitively, flushing the loop with oxygen and then using the minimum loop practice to add oxygen when needed. He'd had better days, obviously, but he hadn't considered his life was in danger.

He had rehearsed these drills thousands of times in his head, and thousands of times more underwater. This clinical rehearsal was not just a personality trait. Going underwater was risking life and limb, and this was a survival skill: know your equipment until it becomes part of you, as cave divers had been counselling for fifty-odd years.

With the mental drills completed, Robson slipped into the water and stood on a stone step just beneath the surface. The cold water rose up to his waist and squeezed the air from the legs of his dry suit. A murmur of excitement swept through everyone lakeside.

It was hard for Robson not to feel that he was the centre of attention there. It was a dazzling day; a warm winter sun lit the surface of the lake a brilliant white and drew a crowd to the courtyard overlooking the dive platform. Those at the front leaned on the safety railings to catch a glimpse of Robson as he prepared to set off, and a news cameraman from MIR 24 was ready to capture it all on tape.

Divers crowded the patio, and anticipation hung thick in the air. Roman Dunaev was there, his dry suit folded down at the waist. Eduard Khuazhev was there, too, taking a break from the compressor. Anna Kozlova was there taking photographs and video as she had done over the previous week. A diver was underwater making last-minute checks to the habitat's communication system, and Sergei Gorpinyuk was speaking into the microphone. Andrei Rodionov was standing in the water, waiting to clip the bailout tank to Robson's harness. Medics from the local Ministry of Emergency Situations, the national search and rescue service known as MChS, or internationally as EMERCOM, were on standby with a dinghy in the water and an ambulance in the parking lot. Just in case.

Robson was about to head off on an adventure into the darkness below, and no one said very much. No one wanted to divert him from his thoughts, and no one wanted to jinx the dive; no one wants to be the one responsible for giving their diver the hoodoos. Robson's cave diving friend Lamar Hires was once about to explore a sinkhole near a church cemetery when his buddy, JT, said: Do ya think they ever dropped a body in here instead o' buryin' em? After that, Hires saw human bones among the tree roots scratching at his body. 'I'd kept all that emotion out of my head until his comment right before I went down. Then I'd snag a valve on a root, and I'd be thinking "Somethin' grabbed me".'

When everything had been done, Robson let the water take his weight, and he floated away from the step. He put his face in the water and finned gently towards a black plastic buoy attached to a guideline that led into the depths. The crowd standing on the banks of Blue Lake watched the lone pilgrim launch himself, not so much with a bang but with a *shhh!* and a gurgle as he released air from his buoyancy wing and sank beneath the surface. He didn't disappear from view straight away. From their vantage point on the patio, the onlookers could see Robson through the clear water, four, five, six metres down, until the lake threw a veil over him and the deep took hold.

Once Robson had disappeared from view, the divers turned their attention to a whiteboard propped against a cylinder at the entrance to the dive centre. The board contained a series of numbers that had been added when Robson briefed the team that morning. In marker pen were the times for every significant event that was to occur underwater.

The blueprint of the dive stated Robson was scheduled to begin his descent at 12:55.

Written below were the words: '+45 mins @ 90m – 13:40.'

Below was another entry: '+75 mins @ 40m – 14:10.'

And so on. Each entry on the board indicated a particular time and depth support divers were expected to meet him to exchange cylinders.

The clock was ticking, and one by one, the divers moved inside, eased into their diving gear, and began their rituals.

Ten minutes into the dive, and with the weight of Blue Lake pressing against him from all sides, Robson squeezed gas into his buoyancy wing and arrested his descent. The faintest blue tendrils of sunlight had long since given up their struggle with the depths, and he found himself in the dark of a moon-forsaken night, 150 metres down. It was silent save for the sound he made pulling and pushing gas around his rebreather: *Shhh! Ummm! Shhh! Ummm!* The shot line continued downwards, swallowed by the deep beyond the reach of his torch. Robson had lost sight of the wall on his free-fall and he hung there in the utter blackness.

He directed his beam ahead, hoping to catch a glimpse of rock. He had expected the shaft to continue down into the depths, but it appeared the walls had been eroded by water. The lake had taken on the shape of a bulb. That idea mattered only in as much as Robson now needed to swim off and find the wall before his search could begin.

To venture into the darkness, destination unknown, Robson needed to leave a trail to find his way back. He unclipped a jump reel loaded with nylon line from his harness and looped the string to the shot line. Facing the black, Robson throttled open his electric scooter and headed into the void. There was no time to waste.

Robson was festooned with equipment. The rebreather, the size of a small domestic printer, was strapped to his back with a webbing harness. Slung under his left arm were two aluminium bailout cylinders that ran the length of his body like bombs fixed beneath the fuselage of a jet fighter. Clipped behind him, on a leash, bobbed four more cylinders. His Santi dry suit was black; but then everything was black in technical diving. A small cylinder of argon gas was clipped to his right side to inflate the suit and stave off the effects of the cold water. Beneath his suit, he wore two layers of low-bulk polyester and nylon insulation, and an electrically heated vest and undergloves. When getting dressed he needed the help of a support diver to clip together the various power cables that connected, via a waterproof seal in his dry suit, to an external battery back. To an outsider, it looked like a man-at-arms being dressed for a medieval tournament. A thick neoprene hood covered Robson's head. On his hands, over the pair of heated gloves, he wore blue dry gloves. They were thick PVC, similar to the kind used in decontamination work and industrial fisheries.

He fastened the electronic handset of his Inspiration rebreather, the size of a cigarette packet, to his left arm. The Vision handset displayed readings from the unit's oxygen sensors and its computer also provided advanced decompression calculations. On his right arm were more gauges, two Liquivision Xi computers to monitor depth and time, and provide back-up decompression details, and also a compass. His powerful Cathx Ocean torch was looped to the back of his right hand. Strobes were attached to the side of his rebreather. Pinging with metronomic regularity, they signalled his whereabouts to the support divers as they reached the rendezvous point. In a pocket on his thigh, he carried his back-up torches, spare mask and a waterproof pad so that he could make notes as he went. On his feet were short-bladed Scubapro Jet Fins, a favourite with technical divers. He'd borrowed these from Eduard Khuazhev. Written on the underside, in white, was the big man's nickname, Mountain Diver. Robson rarely took fins with him. When you're transporting dive gear by air, and every extra kilo costs a tenner, you can save fifty quid by leaving your fins behind. All that equipment weighed more than one hundred kilos, and on dry land he could barely move. But floating weightless underwater, he displayed grace in form and action.

The scooter prop spun with a high-pitched *whrrr* and pulled Robson into the blackness. The jump reel spun between his fingers and unspooled a lifeline as he went. Robson felt relaxed. He stared ahead, his eyes reaching out with expectation. In the bright white beam of his lamp, he began to pick out the faintest of outlines looming ahead. He powered on until a giant rock face appeared.

Robson craned his neck, eyes shooting everywhere. He could see the vertical stone wall disappearing into the darkness in all directions, and the *Shhh! Ummm! Shhh! Ummm!* of his breathing filled the blackness. A speck against the impenetrable monolith hulking over him, Robson felt insignificant.

The cliff face was ragged and hewn, large chunks of rock having separated along worn fissure lines and tumbled into the depths. Robson looped his line around a small knot of rock jutting from the wall, checked his gauges and turned to his left to begin his search for a cave. Sweeping his light left and right, his eyes scoured the shadows as the scooter carried him along. As much as he hoped for a yawning chasm, the target could just as easily be a small opening surrounded by jagged rock. Robson knew of many systems where the entrance could be missed by people who didn't know what they were looking for: Saint-Sauveur, in France and its trompe-l'œil, for one, a seeming dead-end passage that continued straight downwards if you knew where to look.

To outsiders the search might have seemed archaic in an age when remotely operated vehicles (ROV) could be piloted from the comfort of a warm room and stay down for hours on end. In Vashchenko's original press release, she sold the involvement of an ROV and three-dimensional scanner. One had been used to examine the lake before. In December 2009, the Russian Centro-spas disaster rescue team tested its 13-million-rouble underwater spacecraft, nicknamed Falcon, to a depth of 255 metres. When Robson learned the ROV wouldn't be available, he told the organiser not to worry. The robot doesn't have skin, he said; it doesn't feel the water like we do.

Hovering next to the wall, Robson couldn't feel the cave. If 70 million cubic litres were pouring into the lake, they weren't coming in there; the surrounding water was perfectly still. So, Robson gathered rock samples and noted where he had found them. He took water samples and recorded the temperature. Then he set off again. He searched for the layers of rock Ulyana Zhakova said would demonstrate tectonic movements in the region. He rechecked his gauges and pressed on until his time was up. Then, Robson slid his finger from the scooter's drive switch and drifted to a halt. It was time to turn and head back.

One hundred and fifty metres above, the first team of support divers were finalising their preparations. Shortly after Robson had left the surface, Sergei Gorpinyuk and Andrei Bykov had rigged themselves into their rebreathers, picked up their fins and walked to the water. Divers were in the water to help the pair clip on their bailout cylinders and secure the tanks they carried for Robson. Gorpinyuk hurried people along. By turn blunt, affable and demanding, he appeared to like the role of boss. More than most, he sweated the small stuff, and that's why, in the years that followed the expedition, he had a support team whenever he dived deeper than eighty metres. For the most part, he wanted everything to go as planned and didn't want to miss a deadline.

Once, on a hot day on the south-east Sinai, in Egypt, Gorpinyuk and a buddy had been making a deep dive inside the submarine sinkhole known as Blue Hole. He was working with a support team. Ascending, Gorpinyuk had arrived at the depth of the planned rendezvous, but his support divers were nowhere to be seen. He had no time to search for them or wonder why they weren't there, so he continued upwards. When he surfaced and removed his mask, Gorpinyuk saw his friends staring back at him, relieved. A debrief revealed the problem. 'We had all been at the same depth, but in different positions,' he says. 'When we arrived at the surface, we could see they had been very scared about us.'

With those kinds of concerns on his mind, Gorpinyuk secured the mouthpiece of his rebreather's breathing loop and signalled to Bykov. The two men released gas from their buoyancy wings and sank out of sight. A new entry was made to the plan on the whiteboard. In black marker the time '13:35' was added.

Alone in the dark, Robson retraced his steps to the shot line. Twenty-four minutes after submerging, he began his ascent. In total, he'd spent just fourteen minutes on the search. Imagine all that effort for fourteen minutes. But one small step, and all. Apollo 11 took eight days to get to the moon and back, and Neil Armstrong had spent two-and-a-half hours walking on the lunar surface.

During his time in the depths, Robson's tissues had soaked up the nitrogen and helium contained in each breath like a dry sponge immersed in water. Climbing back towards the surface, he now had to purge the gases from his body. Ahead of him lay almost 400 minutes of ever-lengthening decompression stops calculated to settle his debt with the deep.

Before the advent of personal dive computers, all 'deco stops' were just that: stops. Divers planned their dive using theoretical dive tables with stops measured in minutes and depths in ten-foot intervals. Once a diver reached their deco stop, they would level off and wait long enough for the pressure of nitrogen inside their tissues to fall sufficiently far to allow a move up to the next stop. If drawn on a graph, depth along the vertical axis, time along the horizontal, the ascent line was stepped. Many short, sharp vertical lines, representing the diver moving up through the water column, were punctuated by ever-longer horizontal ones, as the diver waited for the pressure to swing back into their favour. Real-time dive computers changed that by reducing the time and depth parameters to seconds and centimetres, allowing a diver to creep up through the water column in smaller stages. Plotted on the same graph the same ascent showed an almost smooth, steep curve that only plateaued towards the end of the dive when the lengthy decompression stops began in the shallows.

Following his computer dive plans, Robson was, in essence, flying the curve of decompression towards his first meeting, eleven minutes after leaving the bottom, with his deep support team. Yet even with his computers to smooth out the edges, the ratio of boredom to pleasure in deep diving was pretty much off the charts. Robson found it wearying in the extreme. He tried to stack the odds of enjoyment at the bottom in his favour. But beyond that, he had learned to tolerate decompression. There really was no escaping it.

From his vantage point high in the water column, Gorpinyuk caught sight of Robson's dive light getting brighter, and he relaxed. It meant Robson was okay and on his way up. So far, so good.

When they reached each other, Gorpinyuk signalled 'okay' to Robson, who replied in kind. Then, he and Bykov went to work. They exchanged the bailout tanks as practised. One diver stripped him of bailout cylinders, another snapped the replacements to the metal harness rings. Then they relieved him of his scooter. So far, so good.

Robson didn't need them to do it for him; he chose to let them because it was his way of showing trust. In some respects, Robson didn't need the help of support divers at all. When drawing up his decompression strategy, Robson planned to be able to survive on his own. Always have a pathway to the surface, was his deco maxim. Even if his rebreather went bang at the point when he began his ascent – when he had the most significant decompression penalty – his six bailout cylinders would last until he was in the shallows. Before the dive, Robson had also agreed with Igor Galaida, the director of the dive centre, a way of signalling the surface if he needed more tanks.

The two divers hung next to Robson, and they continued the ascent together. The decompression curve had become staggered, with short pauses every three metres. Robson would have been content to be on his own. He was indebted to the support divers for their assistance, but once they had served their purpose, he wanted them to get out of the danger zone. It was the kind of detached pragmatism that was perfect for planning deep dives, but which others could easily misinterpret as aloof. More than anything, he didn't want to be fussed over. Eager support divers had a habit of drifting too close or repeatedly asking if he was okay. At some point, one was bound to ask what his decompression obligations were. Robson didn't need reminding of what lay ahead. He knew the numbers would not make comfortable reading, and no one else could do the time for him.

At forty metres, Gorpinyuk and Bykov finally left Robson's side. Like a tag team, they handed over his care to the intermediate support team and continued upwards, following a shorter decompression schedule back to the surface. Once they had moved out of the way, Andrei Rodionov and Roman Dunaev set to work.

Dunaev would only admit, months later, to his disappointment about the role he'd been given. 'I felt insulted,' he says. 'I had expected to be used at a deeper phase of his decompression.'

Robson told his friend to stick with it because he would actually have a harder job. The decompression stops would lengthen, Robson said to Dunaev. As a result, he'd be in the water longer; the transition to the habitat was complicated and needed his expertise. Robson told him that he wanted the best diver on the team to be with him during that time – someone he could rely on 100 per cent – and he considered that to be Dunaev.

Of all the people on the project, Dunaev had known Robson the longest. They first met in August 2008 when Robson hosted a diving course in Crimea. A year later, they were diving together again in Egypt, Robson teaching Dunaev mixed gas diving techniques, and the experience set their friendship. In September 2010, Dunaev travelled to the UK so that Robson could train him on his new rebreather, a Sentinel Expedition. The course was intense but, according to Dunaev's online report, he appreciated Robson's 'tough military approach to training and unconditional discipline'.

Dunaev's own journey to Blue Lake had begun three decades earlier during summer seaside holidays spent with his family. As a seven-year-old, he was given a snorkelling mask and fins and encouraged to investigate the shallows. At twenty-five, he completed an entry-level scuba course and was instantly hooked. Within a year he was exploring underwater caves in the Caucasus Mountains with his friends. Dunaev soon began looking to the deep. When he couldn't find an experienced Russian instructor to show him the rudiments of technical decompression diving, he taught himself with an English-language manual and an English–Russian dictionary for the words he did not understand.

Dunaev finally picked up his first cave diving qualification in 2004. That same year he was part of a team that found almost fifty unidentified shipwrecks in the Black Sea. In July 2006, he and Andrei Bykov went to the Baltic to photograph the wrecks of eighteenth-century trading vessels. Finding the wrecks lay at the extreme end of scuba, so he bought a rebreather.

In June 2009, he was part of a joint Russian–Bulgarian effort to identify a submarine found at the bottom of the Black Sea. While no one could be certain, the wreck was believed to be that of the Second World War Soviet submarine *L-24*, which disappeared in December 1942 with all hands. The tragedy touched Dunaev deeply. His first sight of the wreck was her cigar-shaped frame silhouetted against the green twilight of the Black Sea, her sharp nose hanging in the water. 'Complete silence and tranquillity; it is difficult to imagine that there, inside the body, were fifty-seven people, painfully waiting to die.'

When he emerged from the water, Dunaev decided if he wanted to explore – and he did – bottom time was more important to him than the depth, so he drew a line in the deep. From then on, he would limit his dives to 110 metres.

Dunaev was not originally part of the Blue Lake expedition team. He was planning an expedition with a friend who had discovered a cave system in the Dominican Republic when word got around that Robson was heading for Russia. Shelving his own plans, Dunaev contacted the organisers to offer his assistance.

We don't need you, he was told, but Dunaev travelled to Blue Lake anyway, taking with him two rebreathers and all his bailout gas, ready-mixed. Robson assumed Dunaev was part of the team and when everyone saw how warmly they greeted each other, Dunaev's place on the expedition was assured. No one questioned his involvement or tried to dictate to Robson who would support him underwater. And Dunaev took the job as seriously as it was possible for him to take it.

On the surface, everything appeared to be going to plan. Eduard Khuazhev sat squashed in a blue plastic chair at the water's edge, his eyes scanning the lake. He had assumed the role of surface marshal earlier that day and had not strayed too far from the patio since Robson had vanished. Khuazhev looked at his watch and then over to the dive plan set down on the whiteboard. Getting everybody safely out of the water was only a matter of time.

Time had been on his mind all afternoon. He'd been the one to give the support teams a ten-minute warning to get into the water before their allotted descent time. He'd been the one who noted on the whiteboard, in parentheses, the minute they left the surface. No diver had provided him with a complete decompression schedule, so he had no detailed information to determine their position in the water at any given time. He only knew their dives were over when they broke the surface. Staring at the lake, he was trying to make the mental calculations that might give him some clue about where everyone was in the water column. Beyond that, there was not much else he could do but watch and listen and be ready to react.

Being a diver, he had a good handle on most things that could go wrong underwater: the possible equipment failures that could snatch a diver into the hereafter; the gas narcosis that could confuse their minds; the cold water sapping their strength. That knowledge didn't help his mood.

Khuazhev looked at his watch again.

As the mercury plunged, he pulled on a thick thermal fleece, the kind he usually wore beneath his dry suit. He added a coat when it dropped further. Then a beanie hat. When Gorpinyuk and Bykov had surfaced Khuazhev had asked how things were going. They hadn't reported any problems. So long as things stayed on course, he thought, everyone else would be out of the water by 8 p.m. He looked at his watch: still some hours away. The crowd of onlookers had now disappeared and the sun was about to follow them. Khuazhev remained squashed into his chair. Then a headset resting over the arm crackled into life. Khuazhev settled the speakers over his ears and folded down the microphone.

Martin, Martin, he said. The first to get his attention, the second to see what he wanted. On the other end was Robson, speaking from the habitat.

Martin has sent us a text message from the depths, Khuazhev joked as divers gathered around him. Keying the microphone open, he said: we are pleased to hear you are comfortable.

Electronic pulses fired his words from the microphone and along thirty metres of cable to the habitat where Robson was curled up on the small wooden seat, knees tucked into his chest. The habitat was a lonely place to be with a lot of time to pass and not much to do. Robson unclipped his dive computers from his wrist and put them to one side, hiding their faces. The decompression time was the last thing Robson wanted on his mind. The only thing he thought about now was getting warm. After the excitement of the dive, Robson's experience had been a gruelling act of submersion. At each decompression stop he had hung motionless, hunkered down against the raw cold of the water pricking away at him, waiting for the clock to count down: twenty-three minutes at a ceiling of fifteen metres, almost half an hour at twelve metres, forty minutes at nine metres. Before Robson had entered the habitat, a support diver had connected an umbilical power cable to a connector on his dry suit. The cable powered the heated undergarments he wore and provided a layer of warmth. Sitting there, on the wooden bench, he also felt the temperature inside the habitat slowly begin to climb, simply because of his presence. Within an hour, it could be four degrees warmer than the outside water.

Inside the habitat noise echoes off the wall and it sounds as if your head is in a bucket. Alone, Robson was buttonholed by the monologue of his rebreather. *Shhh! Ummm! Shhh! Ummm! Click! Spritz!* Squinting at the bright light that bounced around the white walls of the container and burned his eyes, Robson examined the rebreather's handset and the readouts from the oxygen sensors. All was working well. Then he reached up, flicking the light switch to off. It was almost 5:30 p.m. Not that it made any difference to him.

Killing time was the same for the support divers who hovered outside the habitat. Hanging around in the water just in case Robson emerged with a problem was tedious, so they busied themselves delivering food and drink from the surface. What else was there to do?

The bubbling surface waters of the habitat's moon pool shook Robson's eyes open. Looking down, he could see a hand breaking the surface holding a plastic slate aloft. Robson took the slate as the diver emerged and looked around with childlike wonder.

Scrawled on the slate was a message. Would you like red wine?

Robson laughed to himself at the inside joke. Decompressing in a habitat in Hérault, or some such place, Robson had been handed Bordeaux and a chunk of Roquefort cheese. The small sip of wine had made him feel giddy, but it was a welcome treat, nonetheless.

Ya, he wrote.

With little more than a nod, the diver disappeared with a *sploosh!* A few minutes later, they were back with a clear, plastic bottle. The pale brown liquid was a strange colour for wine, Robson thought, but he convinced himself it was the result of the low light inside the habitat. If only he had taken off his mask and sniffed the liquid. Instead, he just opened the bottle and took a swig. Then he felt a white-hot thump in his throat.

Robson coughed. Cognac.

Thanks for the drink, he croaked into the microphone.

Laughter echoed back down the line.

When it came time to eat, there was no Roquefort cheese. Food in the habitat came in a small waterproof sachet. Ripping the tab, he stared blankly at the white gunk which clung to the opening like curdled milk. This will provide essential minerals and sugars, he had been told, to help replace lost energy. He held the sachet to his tongue and squeezed. The congealed paste slithered a trail of sweet slime down his throat.

Inevitably, the final hour was tedious, and Robson filled his time thinking through all the things he needed to do to exit the habitat. When his dive computer indicated that, theoretically at least, his body had purged enough nitrogen and helium for it to be safe to surface, he finally stirred. Robson disconnected the power cables from his dry suit and dropped his legs into the water. He could see a support diver in the water below, and he passed his fins down to them. The diver placed the fins on Robson's feet, one at a time, and tapped each leg when each spring-heel strap was secured. Robson rechecked his rebreather handset and slipped out of the habitat. It was utterly dark, and Robson could count the safety divers only by the beams of their torches. Together, they all headed for the surface.

Shortly after 8 p.m., 416 minutes after he left the surface, Robson re-emerged. Members of the expedition team had gathered to greet him. Igor Galaida took Robson's right arm, supporting him as he climbed out of the water and walked into the dive centre.

Robson lowered himself onto the bench. Divers crowded around, and Khuazhev handed him a cup of tea. Robson joked about the cognac.

I took a swig, he said, and it was. . . Robson stuck out his tongue and made a gagging sound.

It was lost in translation because Roman told us you wanted cognac, Vashchenko said, and everyone laughed.

As the cold crept along the dive centre's main corridor, the divers left Robson to get undressed. He slipped out of his equipment, hung up his dry suit and pulled his coat around his shoulders. The compressor was silent for the first time in days, its groan replaced by the cocktail party noise of eager conversation coming from another room. Someone cooked some hot soup, and then a bottle of vodka appeared. Khuazhev finally allowed himself time to relax. He poured himself a shot of vodka and then a second, a hundred grams in total. Special decompression liquid he called it.

MARTIN, WE'VE LOST ANDREI

The dive itself is like hunting a tiger in a thicket. Fear keeps me
alert. I am constantly attuned to every feeling in my body,
every function of my equipment and every happening in the
surroundings. Off guard for a minute and the tiger is on my
back. I've learned to handle the fear by what I call controlled
paranoia, a combination of meditation and experience. The
meditation clears and settles my mind, allowing me to stay at a
high state of alertness. My experience has taught me how vulnerable I am.

Sheck Exley, quoted by Ned DeLoach in
'The Deepest Dive: A Study in Controlled Paranoia'

Robson phoned home whenever he could. He had sourced a
Russian SIM card so he could make cheap calls to Vikki from
his mobile phone, but reception around the lake was patchy,
and one of the divers had to drive him to the top of the mountain to get a signal. Vikki had long since stopped expecting him
to call the moment he had finished a dive. She understood
preparations could take longer than originally planned and
excursions could run late. Martin didn't promise to call at set
times because he understood a missed call could add unnecessary stress for those back home. They operated on the theory

that no news is good news. And that worked for them. He didn't have to go chasing a signal immediately after surfacing, and she didn't have to worry if he didn't call straight away.

Vikki was eager to learn of his adventures all the same, and he would talk through his dive. The topic of conversation was not particularly important to Martin; simply hearing Vikki's voice was enough to smooth the rough edges of his day. After they said their goodbyes, Martin was driven back down the mountain and right back to the demands of the expedition.

When there wasn't a deep dive to prepare for, the team trained or posed for photographs. They donned their equipment, dropped into the shallows of the lake and hovered around while Viktor Lyagushkin set up the lights and took his pictures. Or they'd be asked to illuminate the subject with their dive torches so that he could capture the experience in all its Technicolor glory. In the waters of Blue Lake, he had all the props needed to show the complexity of the experience, and he had a lot of toys with which to play. One image captured a diver in the darkness, floodlit from behind, bailout cylinders surrounding his body, a speck against the orange cliff face. It was the sort of image that made this kind of diving look cool. This was expedition diving. Hardcore.

There were other photographs as well. A month earlier, Lyagushkin made a trip to the lake with Russian champion freediver Natalia Avseenko. He dressed her in traditional Balkarian costume and photographed her perched, ghostlike, on a petrified tree a few metres underwater. Eduard Khuazhev also found himself in national dress, posing at the water's edge alongside his wife, while the image was taken from just beneath the surface.

On days when there wasn't some other expedition work to perform, the group passed the time walking in the mountains, sharing dive stories while eating in the café, or just hanging out with each other. Khuazhev liked Robson's company, and the two men had become close despite the apparent language barrier. One day, Khuazhev took him to a local bathhouse. Robson was handed a little towel that barely wrapped around his waist and a felt hat that reminded him of the Bill and Ben the Flower Pot Men. Khuazhev had a hat with small devil's horns on it, and they went into the hot room where they slapped each other with leaves tied together in a bundle. They dipped them in water, to drive the heat into their bodies, Khuazhev said, and a few slaps later Robson felt as if his insides had been set on fire.

Robson also joined Khuazhev for dinner with his family on the outskirts of Nalchik. The house was modest, with a large lounge and a small kitchen. Khuazhev's wife Angela cooked for them, although her husband had once shown his culinary skills when the couple appeared together on a TV cookery show called *Today's Menu*. Sipping wine at the kitchen table, Khuazhev was persistent in everything he said, his gravelly voice on repeat, as he tried to make Robson understand what he was saying. A fan of Manchester United, Khuazhev would have struggled to get Robson to talk about the benefits of Robin van Persie over Wayne Rooney, or whether the defence was creaking, but the diving stories they shared were good, once they found a way to communicate with each other.

Khuazhev's two youngest daughters, sitting opposite Robson, whispered to one another as their father pressed on in growing frustration. When he failed, Khuazhev turned to his eldest, twelve-year-old Lika, and instructed her to help. She was studying English at school, and Robson was surprised at her grasp of vocabulary.

Retiring to the lounge after dinner, Robson sat in the armchair and watched Lika brush the hair of her little sister who winced every time the bristles snagged. Leaning forward, he asked Lika to fetch a better brush. Under the glow of a table lamp, Robson twisted the youngster's locks into a plait. After he had finished, the girls looked at the results and smiled at Robson; it was messy. Angela told him Eduard had never done that, ever, for any of his daughters. Russian fathers don't do that.

At some point, Lika asked her father if Robson would attend her school to talk about the expedition. Robson had agreed to visit her class with his equipment and host a 'show and tell', but no date had been set. When she asked her father again, Lika was told: after the next dive.

In the early days, diving was done exclusively on air, and the Royal Navy accepted that 300 feet (92 m) was the boundary of deep diving. Pushing past that point had presented all manner of unfathomable complications that went beyond decompression sickness. During the deep trials of 1930, divers had surfaced with mysterious tales of their minds wandering until they could remember nothing of the dive.

What threw divers like Petty Officer Richard Coombs off-track was the way the blackouts came on in the deep when he most needed his wits. At forty fathoms (73 m, 240 ft), the twenty-nine-year-old former messenger felt dizzy; at forty-five, he was in a nightmare. Alone in the dark, hands fumbling with the rope and shackle, helpless as if he was being put under with ether, his brain fogged, and the world closed in. One minute he was alert; the next? Coombs came to, hanging heavy on his lifeline as the tenders hauled him upwards, with no idea how he got there. He saw his face in the glass viewing port of his helmet. Only it was outside his helmet, a ghostly apparition, tinged green, staring right back at him. Coombs was not the only one. Engine Room Artificer Ronald Poe, the kind of man who would get lost at the first sign of danger, completed his task at the bottom but knew nothing more until he reached the decompression chamber. In almost every case, the stricken diver continued to answer signals on the breast rope and, in some cases, even spoke to the radio operator, but they had no recollection of the events which took place in the deep.

Unable to explain the disorder, doctors laid the blame firmly at the feet of the divers. Sufferers were obviously highly strung; claustrophobic; they were the kind of people who felt all eyes were on them; or they had fallen into a state of pathological terror that doctors of the time said was similar to that seen in men suffering from shell shock. (This was many years before post-traumatic stress disorder was recognised by the medical profession.)

These attacks, however, had nothing to do with nervous breakdown, or terrors. The fact was, there was simply too much nitrogen in the air they breathed at depths beyond 220 feet (67 m). In the mid-1930s, US Navy doctor Albert R. Behnke proved the mental fog experienced by deep divers was caused by the anaesthetic effect of nitrogen under increased pressure.

Elevated levels of nitrogen dissolved in the blood were thought to impair the conduction of nerve impulses, mimicking the effects of drinking alcohol. Divers could become woozy, euphoric, disoriented, fixated, anxious. Jacques Cousteau would later describe the condition as the rapture of the deep. Today it's known as nitrogen narcosis.

While the British had discovered the physiological threshold of deep diving on air and set the limits accordingly, the Americans would come up with something that would allow men to venture into the unplumbed depths. They found the antidote to the dulling effects of nitrogen in helium.

Named after the Greek word for the sun, the noble gas – odourless, tasteless and invisible – was discovered in 1900 in incredible quantities in the natural gas wells of Texas. Like nitrogen, helium is chemically inert, but it is only one-seventh the density and the least soluble of gases, perfect for diving mixes.

Inventors, chemists and physicians interested in diving and mining had been casting a curious eye on the benefits of helium in the post-war years. They suggested using the gas as a replacement for nitrogen to cut the time it took divers to decompress and reduce the chances of them getting bent. In 1925, the US Navy and the Bureau of Mines conducted trials using a synthetic breathing mix containing four-fifths helium and one-fifth oxygen, now commonly referred to as heliox. The helium took no effort to breathe, divers found, although they said it left them feeling colder than usual, and their voices became a high-pitched, nasal whine. Divers still got bent though, just as badly, if not worse, than on air. As a result, the trials were interrupted, and the idea of using helium fell by the wayside.

Then, a decade later, a young salvage diver from Milwaukee hit the bottom of Lake Michigan with a cry of 'holy smoke' and proved to those who were interested in such things that a cocktail of oxygen and helium could take divers deeper than ever before.

Diving was a college dream for a twenty-seven-year-old MIT graduate named Max Eugene Nohl, and he had designed a helmet with wrap-around windows that looked like the lantern panes of a lighthouse. Using a primitive homemade rebreather and working with a decompression table created by a professor from the Marquette University School of Medicine, in Milwaukee, Nohl wanted to test how deep he could go. On a bitter December day in 1937, he steamed from the town of Port Washington aboard the Coastguard cutter *Antietam*. Twelve miles from shore, Nohl threw himself overboard and sank into the blackness until he hit the bottom. He couldn't see more than six inches in any direction and spent nine minutes trudging in the mud looking for a stone to bring back to the surface as a souvenir. An echo sounder revealed his depth as 420 feet (128 m), more than a hundred feet deeper than anybody had been before. Nohl was slowly lifted and spent an hour at the end of his line, decompressing under the vessel before surfacing. Under the strict navy standards, one newspaper reported, more than eight hours would have been needed to decompress; in fact, the report went on, decompression tables of the navy have never allowed for that depth.

Nohl's achievement breathed new life into the use of helium. The US Navy Experimental Diving Unit (NEDU) launched an extensive testing programme to develop new decompression tables for the artificial gas mix. Unravelling the mysteries of decompressing from a deep helium dive, however, proved complicated and, at times, disappointing. Scientists experimented on the solubility of helium in oil and water and monitored how it was absorbed by the human body. They injected helium into the intestines and calculated how quickly it was breathed away. Then they double-checked the results by recording the amount of helium in urine at various intervals. They computed how much oxygen a diver might burn working under pressure. They determined how much carbon dioxide and water vapour were in the lungs, and how much was carried in the arterial and venous blood. They monitored how quickly divers ascended and noted when they reported itching over their bodies. Then they took the results and used them to compute the theoretical uptake and elimination of helium at increasing pressures. The investigations led to the creation of the thirty-seven decompression tables known as US Navy Helium Partial Pressure Tables, for depths up to 600 feet (183 m). Test divers still got bent, suffering pains in their joints, skin rashes and itching, but they did not suffer grave attacks of paralysis.

Whatever the results, divers reported helium mixes sharpened their senses. At 300 feet (91 m), they were as alert as a diver at thirty feet. To test these anecdotal reports, a typist attached to the unit was placed in a chamber, pressurised to simulated diving depths up to 250 feet (76 m), and told to copy from a book. When the yeoman breathed air, mistakes peppered the page, three times as many as he made on the surface. Whole lines of text were missing even though the typist was unshakeable in his belief he was word perfect. When he breathed a helium mix, he made no mistakes.

Across the Atlantic, the British dismissed the use of helium for diving because it was felt it had no practical interest of a medical kind, and the Admiralty saw no need to dive deeper. Navy submarines had a maximum crush depth of 300 feet (91 m) and divers could reach those depths.

After the Second World War, the position changed and the Royal Navy was encouraged to increase the maximum permitted diving depth. Commanders favoured the technologically advanced Panzer Tauchergerät, the pressurised, German Ironman suit with articulated joints. They had seized an unboxed suit from the Kriegsmarine, the German Navy, at the end of the war. The operators, though, were less impressed. The arms and legs were not as useful as the makers claimed: cranes were needed to move divers underwater and few tasks could be completed with the suit's lobster claws. Those inside saw themselves as nothing more than a man in a can, a can that slowly leaked.

This was not deep diving to Captain William Shelford, head of the Royal Navy's Experimental Diving Unit. The deep-diving record got to him, and he dreamed of sending a signal to the Admiralty: this day, one of my men broke the world diving record. With some lend-lease helium left over from the war effort, he planned to take back the record. First, he went back over the decompression instructions of the US tables and spent months experimenting with helium-oxygen mixtures until he was confident the decompression numbers were right. Finally, in August 1948, his divers headed to Loch Fyne on the west coast of Scotland to conduct tests using helium-oxygen mixtures they called Yankee Gas or Stuka Juice, after a nickname for a coarse Maltese wine.

ₗord sent eighteen divers down to progressively deeper
ₗhs in the full knowledge they were working at the extreme
ₗmits of diving. He made a cartoon depth chart, not unlike the
paper thermometers used to record fund-raising efforts, which
the divers used to mark their achievements. The Olympic
Games were being held in London at the time, and the men
made their own torch which was passed between them whenever a diver went deeper. Each new holder had to lap the deck
in his diving boots. Going deep was a competitive business.
Underwater, some men lay down and pressed themselves into
the seabed to record a few extra feet of depth. The helium
diving record set by two US Navy divers in 1941 was finally
broken on 26 August, when Petty Officer William Soper reached
451 feet (137 m).

The last helium in Britain was almost breathed out, just
enough left for one diver and his standby, but Shelford wanted
a proper stab at a new record. He'd made the decompression
calculations for a sub-500-foot dive and two men, Soper and
Petty Officer Wilfred Bollard, were in the running. The captain
called a meeting of the dive team. The two men were asked to
draw straws – whoever picked the long straw would dive.
Bollard, the shy Leicester man, the junior of the two, won. He
was just about the last man Shelford expected to be his chosen
diver. When Bollard joined the team, he'd overrun his air, and
almost passed out on shallow dives. He'd come around smartly,
yet he'd only completed four helium-oxygen dives and he still
wasn't certified as a deep diver.

On 28 August, HMS *Reclaim* was anchored over the seabed
540 feet (165 m) down, and Bollard jumped into the water.

Shelford worked the gas mixing panel on the deck himself, switching over to a mix containing just 11 per cent oxygen when his diver passed 200 feet (61 m). When Bollard's voice pitched to falsetto, everyone knew the helium mix had reached the helmet. Bollard continued his free-fall until hitting bottom at a record-breaking depth of 535 feet (163 m). On the surface, someone hung a sign on the Panzer suit: Out of Date.

Bollard spent five minutes on the bottom then began his ascent. It took him seven minutes to descend, but almost four hours to reach the surface. Stripped out of his diving suit, Bollard cradled his left elbow.

It was a bend everyone should have known was coming, and soon navy scientists were off scrabbling to find a new way to protect their divers in the extremes of the deep. The US Navy Experimental Diving Unit developed new helium-oxygen tables that got men down 561 feet and safely back again, but the divers spent so little time on the bottom that the dive was considered of little value. When the bottom time was doubled to twenty minutes, divers surfaced with fatigue, muscular aches and pains in the joints. When divers were sent down to 495 feet and asked to work, almost half suffered a bend. A report into the trials concluded that the accepted physics of decompression might not be valid for working dives to depths greater than 430 feet for more than ten minutes.

Then, in the mid-1950s, in an effort to safely extend working times on the bottom, reduce decompression obligations for divers hanging in the water and also slash the risk of them getting bent, navy scientists went right back to Haldane's work and the very idea of how much over-pressurisation different tissues compartments in the human body could tolerate. Examining the data, scientists discovered the hypothetical tissue types did not have a uniform tolerance to over-pressurisation that Haldane had assumed. Instead, they found the so-called safe decompression ratios varied not only from tissue to tissue but also in the same tissue according to the depth of the dive. All of a sudden, the task of recalculating safe practices of the Standard Air Decompression Table and the mixed gas table took on gargantuan proportions. The amount of information that needed to be analysed to map nitrogen pressures inside the body during a dive was eye-watering. Manual calculation of the decompression schedule from an air dive was tedious by any procedure, and instructions ran to more than six pages. The project team turned to the Bureau of Ships UNIVAC computer to crunch the numbers before testing the findings on the NEDU men. More than 600 test dives were conducted in the unit's wet pressure tanks. Underwater, the divers had to lift up a sixty-eight-pound weight thirty inches ten times a minute for ten minutes, rest for five minutes and do it all over again. They spent more than 8,000 hours trying to solve the problem and eighteen divers got bent before they had a workable air decompression table for dives to 300 feet. Another 2,600 hours was spent developing a table to cover prolonged dives to 300 feet as a protection for a trapped diver. The tables were considered a success even though some of the test divers were injured. A minor bend became an occupational hazard. A table that would be safe for all divers, one report concluded, would be unnecessarily long.

While the US Navy was crunching numbers, scientists at the Royal Navy Physiological Laboratory (RNPL) were busy on their own theories. The Royal Navy demanded, for pressing operational matters, new surfacing procedures that prevented the bends without taking an unreasonably long time to complete. All scientists needed to do was find the missing truth of how inert gas passed through the body.

The navy's prime men for the project were Cyril Rashbass and Henry Valance 'Val' Hempleman. The two scientists were different in every respect. Rashbass, the younger of the two by five years, was a bookish Cambridge graduate seeing out his National Service at the RNPL. The son of an orthodox rabbi, Rashbass was quiet and somewhat shy, a difficult man to get to know, but those who turned to him for help got the support of a fine Trinity College mind. He obeyed strict kosher dietary laws, yet smoked heavily, just not on the Sabbath. Hempleman, on the other hand, was the quintessential gentleman scientist. The son of a sea captain, as a child he developed a precocious interest in science and once blew up a garden shed containing his chemistry lab. As an adult, his voice pitched towards ultrasonic when bubbling over some breakthrough by a peer. He was tall, dark-haired, with a knowing smile, and understood that even the most complex problems could have the simplest of solutions. Hemp, as people called him, had a story which he had liked to tell staff struggling with a question. He recalled buying a strip of plastic for a DIY job, and his eye was drawn to lettering printed on one side. Unable to work out how to remove the unsightly mark without damaging the plastic, he asked the shop assistant for advice. You turn it over, sir.

Hempleman was struck by the curious way the first signs of decompression sickness appeared as pains in or around the joints. The evidence suggested one tissue type, maybe a tendon or cartilage, was involved in the bends. Hempleman speculated that preventing over-pressurisation of that tissue would free divers from attack and his slab diffusion model took shape. It was accepted wisdom at the time that a diver could spend twenty-two minutes at a hundred feet and still ascend to the surface without getting bent. So Hempleman fashioned an equation to determine the severity index of diving exposures and the level of nitrogen units a diver could safely absorb. Multiplying the depth in feet by the square root of time in minutes, he defined danger with a single number: 475 units of nitrogen.

From this simple equation, a new set of no-stop times was created for various depths in the water column. These limits tested well on goats and human subjects in a test chamber. Next, mathematicians developed an increasingly complex formula to calculate decompression stops for longer and deeper dives and used the results to create new diving tables. According to the tables, short, shallow dives required much less decompression when compared with tables created using the Haldanian method. Deeper and longer dives required more.

A team of divers, medical officers and civilian scientists were drafted in to test the validity of Hempleman's theory. The responsibility for testing on volunteers sat heavily on his shoulders. He'd been a guinea pig himself, as a young man during the war, standing off the beach up to his armpits in the water while explosives were detonated near him to test the effects of underwater blasts on men. The research helped develop protective equipment used by divers from the Landing Craft Obstruction Clearance Units who were sent in to clear the beaches of underwater obstacles and mines in advance of the D-Day landings. Later, having thrown himself into his post-war career of diving medicine, Hempleman nearly died from mercury vapour poisoning when a thermometer broke during an experiment that he was conducting inside a steel chamber.

The sea trials for his new tables were conducted, in October 1953, off the coast of Falmouth in Cornwall. The enterprise was arduous, uncomfortable and, at times, painful and the early promise of the new tables was not entirely fulfilled. One diver was shot with pain across the shoulders; another needed treatment for a bend in the left bicep that reappeared in his right knee; a third had a bend in his right arm after becoming snagged on a shot line. And on it went. If divers weren't doubled over in pain, they seethed over the itching. The itching was an indicator of decompression sickness; it was not serious from a clinical point of view, but it told everyone they had reached the limits of safety. The itching came on so often, just beneath the skin, like insects crawling over the back of their hand and up their arm, that it sapped any confidence divers had in the new methods.

An analysis of the injuries found that most occurred in the final week of testing. Hempleman posited that men who dive frequently in deep water over a long period gradually accumulate, in certain tissues, a residue of nitrogen which did not entirely disappear even after more than twenty-four hours. No matter, the early promise of Hempleman's tables faded: the proportion of bends was too high to justify them for general use. In one sense, he couldn't quite marry the theoretical maths with the reality of the human body; but that wouldn't stop him trying. (In the years that followed, Hempleman would cement his place in the field of decompression procedures. He developed the 'Blackpool Tables' for compressed air tunnelling work, which would become a worldwide industry standard; his theories formed the basis of the Royal Navy Physiological Laboratory Tables, released in 1972; and he led a research project into deep saturation diving, which established a new world deep-diving record at the RN Physiological Laboratory, when two men spent ten hours at a simulated depth of 457 metres of sea water. A modified version of his original concept for calculating decompression tables was used in the development of the PADI Recreational Dive Planner.)

While Hempleman continued his research, Rashbass began beavering away at his own numbers. His equations grew longer and more complex. More experiments were conducted. The dry dives in the chamber yielded positive results, but the results of sea dives were always less certain than predicted. Divers were plagued by itches, deep under the skin. One developed a rash. Then another was cut down by a spinal bend. The margin of safety in the deeper dives, Rashbass stated, was too narrow for the tables to be adopted in their entirety. In a follow-up report, Report IX, published a few months later, he added that the difficulties in finding a solution threatened to reduce the prestige of British diving techniques in the eyes of more progressive diving nations. The Americans could set the standards for diving around the world, the Admiralty feared, and the Royal Navy Diving Manual – for fifty years the Good Book on the subject – might no longer be universally accepted as the authority on diving.

As all of this was going on, Hempleman was asked to lend his expertise to another deep-diving project. Officially, the reason for the deep trial was to learn about the physiological limitations of the use of helium-based breathing gas and to establish the maximum depth at which a diver could rescue survivors from a sunken submarine. Unofficially, it was an attempt to break Bollard's deep-diving record. Hemp tailored his decompression theories with the information known about helium diving and drew up a plan. The man chosen to push the subaquatic envelope was Senior Commissioned Boatswain George Wookey.

He was not matinee-idol handsome, but the square-jawed grocer's son from fishing country in Portishead was nevertheless a charismatic adventurer. In 1938, aged sixteen, he'd joined the navy as a boy seaman to serve on submarines. Six years later, he volunteered as a diver. Stationed in Malta, he once calmly walked out of a bar, jumped into the harbour, diffused a mine in zero visibility and strolled back to enjoy his evening pint. In time, he would go on to recover whisky from the wreck of the SS *Politician*, made famous by the 1949 film *Whisky Galore!*

The deep trials took place in October 1956, in the Norwegian fjord of Sørfjorden, the closest body of water to the United Kingdom where a man could be swallowed by one hundred fathoms (182 m, 600 ft). Test divers surfaced complaining of muscle aches and fatigue. After a dive to 450 feet (137 m), the attendant in the submerged decompression chamber suffered a bend in the elbow and knee. On another dive, the chief diver was hit in the knee. Much the same was waiting for Wookey. The fjord's surface was whipped to whitecaps when he left, and the descent seemed to last forever. When Wookey reached the bottom, he was at a world record depth of 600 feet (183 m), and he stayed for five minutes, long enough to unscrew several shackles dropped to him. His mind was clear. He was breathing a mix containing 91 per cent helium and just 9 per cent oxygen.

Ascending, Wookey was helped into the submerged decompression chamber by his attendant, 'Geordie' Clucas. He removed his helmet and he sat there as the chamber was surfaced, a record breaker unable to properly celebrate his achievement for six hours.

As his final decompression stop came to an end Wookey reached to hammer open the clips from the hatchway above his head. Pain shot up his arms and across his shoulder blades, and he recognised the agony. He'd had several bends in the past; the last one had landed him in hospital. Wookey's crew mates carried him to the recompression chamber, and he spent five hours undergoing treatment. At the same time, Clucas reported pain crawling up his legs and over his sternum. Doctors took ten hours to put him right.

Wookey was awarded an MBE in the 1957 Queen's Birthday Honours. The newspapers mentioned it briefly. In the photograph, Wookey looked dashing in his framed cap and dress uniform, elbow propped on his diving helmet. His appearance hid the more significant problem; an answer to the decompression problem remained elusive. The best minds had worked on it, and would continue to do so, in search of a method that would give divers an operational advantage – to stay down longer, to go deeper, to reduce decompression times – with reasonable safety. However, a report into the episode concluded that the risk of decompression sickness by any present method of calculation could not be avoided.

*

Martin Robson's next deep search dive finally took place on Friday the 13th. The team had spent the previous days in the water fine-tuning the sequence of swapping cylinders and transitioning Robson into the habitat. He'd also conducted a number of training dives for some of the divers to develop their knowledge of expedition diving. By the 12th, they were ready for the deep again, but the dive was postponed for a day to allow some members of the support team to enjoy an evening off.

Support diver Roman Dunaev had returned home for a few days the previous afternoon. Don't dive until I get back, he had said to the team before leaving, but Robson didn't have the time to wait. In ten days, he would have to return home and pack for the teaching job scheduled to take place in the Philippines, whether he had found the cave or not.

He intended to search the western side of the shaft, north of the outflow river, and a buoyed shot line had been installed to help guide his descent. The plan itself was very nearly a duplicate of the earlier dive, a 160-metre plunge into the lake, a search of the depths and a series of pitstops with his support team on the ascent. With Dunaev absent, there was a gap in the support team, and that presented a problem because Robson had insisted from the outset, had made it a point in his briefing, that no member was ever to dive alone. Alla Popova had ruled herself out of filling in because she was having difficulty staying warm on the long, deep dives. Robson understood Andrei Rodionov was to be joined by photographer Viktor Lyagushkin, and he considered the plan set.

By the time Robson stomped outside with his rebreather on his back, fog had charcoaled the sky and smudged the far side of the lake from view. Momentum was in his favour at that point, and no one said anything to suggest concern over the make-up of the support teams. Robson completed his pre-dive rituals and stepped into the water where Rodionov was waiting to clip bailout cylinders to his harness. Two members from the region's EMERCOM unit paddled an inflatable dinghy at the surface and watched Robson disappear from view. It was 11 a.m.

Robson took twelve minutes to reach his target depth, but tough conditions from the outset hampered his search. He descended into an opaque cloud that could have been sulphur, and visibility, according to Robson's logbook, was down to a metre or so. His light bounced off particles suspended in the water, creating a whiteout that filled the visor of his mask and dazzled his eyes. Robson acknowledged that he could have swum right past the cave entrance and still not seen it in the milky water, but he persisted with the search until it was time to ascend towards his first rendezvous.

Gorpinyuk and Bykov met Robson at ninety metres, as planned. He paused there as they swapped his cylinders, and they continued their ascent together.

At the surface, Andrei Rodionov was getting ready to dive. His understanding of the dive plan differed from Robson's in one crucial element: he and Lyagushkin had agreed to meet up with each other at the rendezvous point with Robson and accompany him from there, but they were not diving as a team. As far as they were concerned, they both had different jobs to do – Rodionov to carry out the duties of a support diver, Lyagushkin to take photographs – and to all intents and purposes they were operating independently from one another and following different dive plans.

Having spent the morning filming the preparations, Rodionov was now standing waist-deep in water making his final pre-dive checks as a news cameraman from the channel NTV filmed him. Rodionov had his rebreather on his back, black mask clinging to his forehead and yellow fins gleaming underwater. Lyagushkin was at his side. Alla Popova, still dressed in combat trousers and yellow waterproof jacket, helped the men with their equipment, leaning over the photographer to help straighten the shoulder straps of his harness before handing Rodionov his two bailout cylinders and the two he was carrying for Robson.

'Black. Big. Deep. The First,' he said from behind his neoprene hood, cut like a Spetsnaz mask to cover all but his eyes, nose and lips, to some off-camera question.

By all accounts, Rodionov planned to descend to the habitat to station an underwater video camera in preparation for recording footage of Robson entering the habitat. Then he intended to swim to the shot line and continue down to sixty metres to meet the deep divers as scheduled at 12:26 p.m. By that time, Lyagushkin would be there. Rodionov had agreed with Popova that, once he had met Robson and exchanged cylinders, he would inflate his delayed surface marker buoy and dispatch it to the orange surface marker. She would then have twenty minutes to finish her preparations and enter the water.

After securing the tanks to his harness, Rodionov heaved his video camera system into the water. To those on the surface, he seemed calm and relaxed. He secured the rebreather mouthpiece between his lips and slowly began to breathe. Then he sank from view, the radiating circle of ripples the only evidence of his presence. Lyagushkin had descended a few minutes earlier.

Among the support team, there appeared to be no real misgivings about the men's decision to enter the water at different times, nor about a technical diver being alone underwater for a dozen minutes or so. 'Everybody understood that Viktor [Lyagushkin] dived with his camera and Andrei was a support diver,' says Popova. 'There had to be two teams; Viktor had to shoot photographs, and we had to support Martin. There was something Andrei planned with Viktor. I decided to dive later to cover all of the other things we needed to do. We were okay to dive as a single person; we had done it many times before and it was not a problem. We thought that nothing could happen.'

Arriving at sixty metres, cold and downbeat, Robson scanned the water. He had expected the intermediate support team to be waiting for him, but no one was there. Hovering in the water, he looked up. There were no light beams, no bodies silhouetted against the light from the surface, no sign of Rodionov with his bailout cylinders. He didn't recall seeing Lyagushkin either.

Robson wasn't unduly worried but, hovering next to him, Gorpinyuk felt something had happened to delay the men, didn't quite know what, but sensed it was serious. He signalled to Robson that he would stay with him. The Brit waved him off, but Gorpinyuk and Bykov refused to leave Robson on his own. They adjusted their decompression schedules, and the three men continued the slow ascent to the surface.

The support divers' failure to show was not disastrous as far as

Robson was concerned. It wasn't even bad. His bailout cylinders contained a trimix of 16/50: 16 per cent oxygen, 50 per cent helium and 35 per cent nitrogen. (Divers don't refer to the amount of nitrogen in the mix when recording the details on their cylinders.) While they were set up for the deep, the gas was breathable all the way to the habitat if Robson's rebreather packed in. His decompression obligation would be lengthy, but he would have something to breathe. And that was good enough.

As the three men reached thirty metres, Gorpinyuk and Bykov finally left Robson. They needed to complete their decompression, and he had signalled that he was fine to continue without them. Hunkered down against the elements, he carried on up, giving little thought to the reasons why his support team had not shown up as planned; no doubt he'd find out soon enough. He was preoccupied with staying warm. 'Bit chilly during deco this time,' he would write in his logbook after the dive, and if Robson used the word 'chilly', it meant the water really was bitterly cold. Occupied by the steady *Shhh! Ummm! Shhh! Ummm! Click! Spritz!* of his rebreather, Robson continued his ascent, blind to the events going on above him.

Deep diver Andrei Bykov was the first to see Rodionov, whose yellow Mares Avanti Quattro fins were unmissable. The support diver had come into the clear shallow waters as his decompression ceiling lifted. After cresting the ridge which separated the lake's deep shaft from the shallower plateau, Bykov had left the shot line and was finning north along the edge of the lake towards the habitat. Gorpinyuk was following some way behind. He was being towed by a scooter having hurt his leg climbing from the water after an earlier dive. Bykov had probably started to relax a bit as he prepared for a long stop in the shallows. Then the flash of yellow below him caught his eye, and there was only one diver in the team who wore yellow.

Bykov must have known instantly there was a problem, even before he'd dropped down to the motionless body, sixteen metres below the surface. Rodionov was lying flat on his back on a small ledge, a barren patch of rounded stone and gravel in a field of reeds that ringed the habitat's mooring. The rebreather mouthpiece hung free from his lips. A small stream of bubbles trickled past the silicone bite tabs. Behind the black face mask Rodionov's glassy eyes stared blankly into the cold space of water.

Some way behind, Gorpinyuk was surprised to see his buddy fin downwards fast. Very, very fast. It was odd, but he still pointed the scooter towards his buddy and followed. By the time he reached the plateau, Gorpinyuk could see Bykov preparing to lift their friend's body from the bottom. He reached for a delayed surface marker buoy clipped to his harness, inflated the tube and sent it up to warn those on the surface there was a problem.

Glancing at his computer, Gorpinyuk knew they both had to clear a considerable decompression penalty before they could ascend. But that didn't stop his friend. Gorpinyuk watched Bykov wrap his arms around the unresponsive diver and missile for the surface.

A few members of the dive team were milling outside the dive centre at 12:45 p.m. when the orange marker buoy splashed to the surface.

Eduard Khuazhev was talking to an EMERCOM official and

the television crew news team were kicking their heels. An inflatable dinghy floated on the surface, two EMERCOM workers relaxing inside. Shallow support diver Alla Popova was standing by herself at the corner of the patio, a dry suit hanging around her waist, waiting to begin her dive. Popova was impatient to get in the water; the sooner she did, the sooner she would be out. She found nothing particularly inspiring about Blue Lake to stay underwater longer than necessary.

Surface marker buoy, over there, someone said.

Help! Help! The words came from the lake and everybody looked.

Smashing through his decompression ceiling, Bykov arrived at the surface with Rodionov. He paused long enough to get someone's attention and then disappeared again to reduce the chances of getting bent.

Diver at the surface!

The television newsman shouldered his camera and pressed record.

Khuazhev, already dressed in his dry suit, thrust his hands into a pair of dry gloves.

The two men in their inflatable dinghy jabbed paddles into the water. Off to their left was a figure resting barely inches above the water, a yellow bailout cylinder still clipped to his harness. Nearing the body, one of the men lunged to grab the stricken diver. Clasping the body to the side of the boat the rescue worker turned to his colleague. Go!

As the boat arrived, Khuazhev leaped into the water. He reached out to his friend and flipped him over, so that he was face up. Peering into the mask, Khuazhev couldn't quite believe who he was staring at; the face didn't look like Rodionov any more. The life had leaked out of his eyes, they appeared cold and leaden, his skin charcoal grey. He looked dead. But you don't make that call; you don't give up, you don't even remember this is a friend, not when your only task is to try to save a life.

Khuazhev pulled the body towards the bank and those on shore grabbed hold of Rodionov's arm, his harness, the rebreather, anything to give them purchase as they heaved him onto the patio. Water sloshed at their feet as the body was dragged across the concrete. Rodionov's head fell to one side. Then the body let out a gasp of air and for a brief moment there was hope he was still alive.

Immediately they began pulling at buckles and pinching clips to strip away his equipment. Galaida crouched down and checked for vitals. There was no sign of either a pulse or breathing. Without pause, he and Popova began to administer cardio-pulmonary resuscitation. Popova blew hard, trying to blow life into Rodionov's lungs; Galaida pumped his chest vigorously. One, two, three, four, five, six, seven, eight, nine, ten. . . Eighteen seconds later he had completed thirty chest compressions.

Breathe. Popova tilted Rodionov's head back to open his airway and puffed air into his mouth. Rodionov's chest rose. She blew a second time. Galaida began pushing on Rodionov's chest again, hard and fast to propel the air around his body.

Another eighteen seconds. Breathe.

The relentless rhythm continued, halting only when they swapped tasks. Rodionov's skin had now gone blue and his eyes remained lifeless, but Popova continued on autopilot. She could not accept what was happening.

In the car park above, an ambulance driver sat gunning his engine. People crowded around Rodionov and each grabbed a limb, carrying him up the stairs and into the back of the vehicle. Paramedics continued working on Rodionov as the doors slammed shut. With a wail of sirens, the ambulance sped off towards the GBUZ Central District Hospital, in the village of Kashkhatau, seven miles away. As the blue lights smeared in the fog and the siren's two-tone echoes faded into the distance, the reality of the previous five minutes began to register in the minds of those involved.

Bogdana Vashchenko was at the habitat attaching a sponsor's banner to the frame when Gorpinyuk and Bykov appeared. Usually, the two divers were a picture of poise: you might not even know they were there if you hadn't seen them. But this time was different. She felt their presence because the bubbles they vented from their equipment surged past her and disrupted what she was doing. They were gesticulating and shouting at each other through the mouthpieces of their rebreathers, but they were too far away for Bogdana to make out what they were saying.

She had seen them five minutes, maybe ten minutes earlier, through the milky water beneath her. She thought Andrei Rodionov was with them because she had seen a set of yellow fins. They were pointing up to the surface as if their wearer was lying on his back. But it couldn't be Rodionov, she decided; he was in the deep with Robson, wasn't he?

The bubbles kept coming past her and made it hard to hang the banner. Eventually she approached Gorpinyuk with a message written in her notebook asking them to stop. Didn't they realise they were disturbing her? He looked at her as if she was crazy and smacked a hand to his head. She didn't understand what he meant and backed away, returning to what she was doing.

A short while later, Viktor Lyagushkin appeared at the habitat. He pulled out his notebook and wrote a message for his partner: How Andrei dead?

Vashchenko stared at the words. The reality shook her body like thunder, and the water holding her up seemed to give way. Her buoyancy slipped and she sank a metre or two. She scrambled to regain her composure and moved back into position.

Taking the notebook, she wrote: Who?

Viktor replied: Rodionov?

He would later tell Vashchenko that he had been worried when Rodionov did not appear as planned. He had stayed with Robson for as long as his gas allowed and had surfaced anxious and angry. That's when he discovered what had happened.

Now Vashchenko knew, and she couldn't quite believe it. Rodionov was breathing and laughing just an hour before and then. . . he was gone. Darkness swept into her mind.

Alla Popova walked into the dive centre shortly after 1 p.m. and stood next to her equipment, dumbstruck. She was in no fit state to dive. The events were almost too much for her to comprehend. She didn't want to let go of the thought of the last time she had seen Rodionov at the lakeside, his broad-beamed smile gleaming. He was a good friend, an experienced diver. They'd been on wreck-diving expeditions together; had others lined up. He couldn't be dead, could he? She couldn't believe what had happened. Then, who else could?

Similar thoughts were occupying Eduard Khuazhev. The pair had been friends since Rodionov had visited Blue Lake some years earlier. If Khuazhev had a problem, Rodionov was the first to help. If a piece of equipment needed repairing, he would fetch tools from his truck; if cylinders needed filling, he would stay behind; if people were still in the water after dark, he would rig up his arc lights to illuminate the dive platform. If only he had not been diving alone. Khuazhev struggled to shake the memory of his friend lying motionless in the water, one that would haunt him for many years.

Only now did people begin to consider the ramifications of the previous few minutes: Rodionov was on his way to hospital; Bykov had burst through his decompression ceiling and was now underwater trying to keep the bends at bay; and Robson was somewhere between thirty metres and the habitat, diving alone.

Bogdana Vashchenko was still zipped into her dry suit when Galaida approached.

I want you to go and check on Martin, he told her.

Vashchenko shouldered her double cylinders and pulled on her neoprene hood. It had playful little horns protruding from the head. Sitting on the step at the water's edge, she ran through a plan written in a waterproof notebook. Then she disappeared underwater.

Robson heard Vashchenko approaching long before he could see her. The exhaled bubbles of her open-circuit regulators sounded like the thunder of an approaching summer storm rolling ever closer, until it was right above his head.

Arriving at his side, Vashchenko signalled: okay?

Taking her waterproof notebook, Robson scribbled away with his pencil: Problems? Alla? Andrei?

She took the pad and wrote back: We don't know exactly. How are you?

Robson wasn't sure what she was holding back, but whatever it was there was nothing he could do about it right now.

Clutching her mask and fins, rebreather on her back, Popova walked towards the water. She was heading to the habitat to wait for Martin. No sooner had she descended, than Popova wanted the dive to end. As she reached the habitat, she could see Rodionov's camera hanging from a clip. Popova stayed long enough for Robson to arrive, long enough to take his bailout cylinders and remove his fins, long enough to see him climb inside for his final hours of decompression. When Khuazhev joined her underwater, she decided it was time to turn for the surface.

Bewildering thoughts fogged Popova's mind as she climbed out of the water and walked into the dive centre. An unnatural quiet enveloped the building; even the compressor which always hummed was silent. As far as she was concerned, the expedition was over. Popova decided right there she would take no further part and, though it wasn't her call, she wanted a halt called to further diving. The price had just become too high for the prize of discovery.

*

Shortly after six that evening, Martin Robson surfaced and looked up to see Galaida standing at the water's edge. Night had fallen, and sleet glistened in Rodionov's arc lights set up on the patio. Robson's cold hands fumbled as he unclipped a small bailout cylinder. Galaida took it from him and then helped him out of the water. Taking Robson's right arm, the Russian walked him into the centre and along the corridor to his seat on the bench.

Robson looked around and became aware that the usual post-dive buzz – the chatter of stories, the clinking of glasses filled with vodka and the hum of the compressor pumping cylinders – was absent. The red and blue coats of EMERCOM professionals had been a perpetual presence at the water's edge during dive days, but there seemed more of them than usual. Mixed within their ranks were many new faces, officials in uniform and serious-looking men wearing black leather jackets.

Robson climbed out of his rebreather and was sitting back when Vashchenko approached. They looked at each other for a moment. Then she spoke.

Martin, we've lost Andrei.

FOR ANDREI 209 M

You probably wouldn't do this kind of diving if you didn't have a little bit of ego because you probably wouldn't have the confidence to do it. I think there are a lot of times when we let our crocodile mouths outweigh our asses, as the red necks say. Even knowing that we may have overstepped our boundaries, we feel compelled to live up to the challenge we put ourselves into. That gets a lot of people in trouble.

Tom Mount, *aquaCORPS* magazine

Water trickled from Robson's gear, pooling on the floor beneath the bench, and he felt the life ebb from the expedition. Sitting there, under the cold blue of the fluorescent lighting, he could only shake his head in dismay as the enormity of Bogdana's words sank in. Emotionally anaesthetised by combat, he felt neither a great wave of sorrow nor pity, he was just annoyed. How had this happened?

Standing up, Robson walked over to Rodionov's Megalodon rebreather that was propped up on the bench. With a pathologist's precision, he began to analyse the unit in search of something, anything, that looked out of place. It did not take long for him to trace the most likely cause of the tragedy; probably no longer than it took Rodionov to realise his dive was going wrong.

Looking at the top of the unit's head, he could see that the oxygen feed hose, marked with a ring of green tape, was hanging loose. The push-fit connector linked the tube from the rebreather's on-board oxygen tank to the supply intake feeding the loop. Uncoupled as it was, there was no way for fresh oxygen to be automatically added to the breathing loop, no matter how forcefully the unit's electronic brain demanded. With each breath Rodionov had taken, with each lungful, he had withdrawn some of the oxygen from the loop and deposited carbon dioxide. In short, Rodionov was breathing himself to death and didn't even know it.

Picking up the computer wired to the unit, Robson keyed into the memory function and examined the data collected throughout the dive. In the numbers that filled the screen, he saw Rodionov die.

Andrei Rodionov slipped away 104 seconds after leaving the surface and eighty-four centimetres from safety.

In the moments before, he had filled his lungs with a breath of cold mountain air. Then he secured the mouthpiece of his rebreather, deflated his buoyancy wing and left the surface with a sigh of bubbles. It was 11:56 a.m. Finning towards the habitat, he inhaled slow and deep. The gas was warm and moist, and his rebreather hummed with each breath. Occupied in the early moments of the dive, Rodionov may not have looked at his handset. If he had done so, he would have seen the oxygen in the loop dropping like a pebble through water.

A minute into the dive, Rodionov had descended to 10.5 metres. About now, his body may have started to show the early signs of oxygen shortage, known as hypoxia. Chemoreceptors in the blood vessels detected the diminishing amounts of oxygen and encouraged a change in cardiac output: his heart began to beat faster. Rodionov put the brakes on his descent. He paused for a few seconds. He may have received a 'low oxygen warning' on his rebreather. The illuminated heads-up display would have blinked, a bright red smack in his field of vision. Rodionov needed oxygen.

One minute into the dive, he began to ascend. Twenty seconds later, he had reached eight metres, and his computer showed he paused for ten seconds. His chest heaved, and it probably felt like he couldn't catch a breath. Then he kicked for the surface. Fourteen seconds later, a minute and forty-four seconds into the dive, Rodionov had climbed seven metres. He had kicked past the habitat, past the petrified trees, past the meadow of stoneworts, and he was within touching distance of the surface. But his exertions were using up the limited amount of oxygen in the loop. His ascent stalled. He was less than a metre from fresh air. So close he could almost taste it. That's where Rodionov, the man who lived for diving, who was a friend to all on the expedition, who Robson thought was a super guy and good diver, blacked out.

Gravity took over. Unconscious, Rodionov began to drift downwards. The breathing loop falling loose from his lips, he sank from the surface, falling through the ice blue waters of the lake towards a spot beneath the habitat. The fall took forty seconds and he settled on a ledge of cold, bare stone. Sixteen metres down. Where the water plants grew verdant. Where the habitat cast its shadow in the mid-morning sun. For forty-three minutes he lay there in a vacant spot in a field of green, where stoneworts swayed in the current, and no one was around to notice.

Two days later, Robson sat at a table at the back of the hotel restaurant nursing a cup of tea as the ramifications of Andrei's death continued to ripple outwards. The expedition had come to a halt, divers were packing up to return home and an official investigation had been launched by the Investigative Committee of the Russian Federation (ICRF).

The previous day, the officer in charge had summoned Robson to attend the police station in Kashkhatau to answer his questions. At noon, the young detective ushered Robson, Vashchenko and Khuazhev into an office which sat on the edge of the open-plan precinct. Clean-shaven with short, dark hair and wearing an open-necked shirt, a black leather jacket hanging from his chair, the officer said he was finalising his preliminary report.

Robson had little idea why he was there. He was not party to Rodionov's decision to dive alone and had not been present during his final moments. When his statement was read back to him, Robson soon understood: he was the rebreather expert who could point the finger of blame at operator error so everyone could move on.

I'm not signing this, Robson said. As far as he was concerned, the examination of Andrei's equipment had been for his own benefit, to help him make sense of the events. He didn't consider his findings conclusive. To be sure, Rodionov's rebreather needed to be forensically examined, the data held in the computers officially interrogated.

Khuazhev and Vashchenko translated Robson's response, and they kept going until the officer agreed to rewrite the statement. In the end, the argument over the account was academic. Three days later, the ICRF released a statement that said, basically, according to preliminary data, Rodionov drowned as a result of improper use of his rebreather.

After leaving the police station, the trio joined other members of the expedition team at a funeral home to pay their last respects. They all filed into a room where the bodies of five other recently deceased people had been laid out for separate viewing. Andrei was at the far end. The group stood together, whispered conversation and, one by one, walked up to the open coffin, crossed themselves and said a prayer or whatever they felt was appropriate. Watching from the edge of the room, Robson stood in solidarity with those shouldering the burden of losing a friend. When the viewing ended, they all filed out and said their goodbyes. Sergei Gorpinyuk and Andrei Bykov later left to accompany Andrei's body back to Moscow, and to attend his funeral at the city's Khovanskii crematorium. Alla Popova packed up with them. She had been the one to call Rodionov's wife after the tragedy and had decided to head home to Moscow. Before she left, Robson had seen Popova walking along the corridor in the dive centre, and he had hugged her. I'm so sorry for you, he said. She hugged him and walked away without looking back.

Photographs were now all that marked Rodionov's involvement in the expedition. That's him standing at the water's edge with the communication headset rested over his ears, talking to Robson in the habitat. That's him standing thigh-deep in the lake, fully equipped and ready to go diving. That's him looking over his shoulder to the camera with his piercing blue eyes, giving an okay sign.

With everyone else gone or sequestered in their rooms, Robson was on his own in the hotel restaurant, staring out of the window as grey cloud erased the mountains. Wooden tables with white tablecloths lined the walls of the long room. A waitress appeared briefly with a plate of eggs and then again to clear the table when he had finished. Beyond that, the only sound came from a television set which flickered away at the far end of the room. Robson was thousands of miles from home and not due to leave for another week, so he decided to do the only thing he could: go diving.

Leaving the hotel, Robson trudged down a flight of concrete steps and took a path through the pine grove, towards the dive centre. The building was quiet. The three staff members were there, working away at something. Robson called them together, and in his best Russian he discussed his plan with them. Khuazhev was concerned he would be diving without a safety net, so Robson offered a solution to ease their anxieties. I'll keep my dives shallow, he said. If I have a problem, I will send a marker buoy to the surface. One of you can row out in the boat, clip bailout cylinders to the line and drop them down to me. They agreed.

When Robson entered the water, he found visibility much improved. Letting his underwater scooter carry him deeper, he powered on down alongside the wall. His light poked feebly into the darkness. And then the rock just disappeared. Robson hovered before a considerable overhang. He peered beneath it but could not see how far it stretched. He started to inch forward. The darkness beckoned. Within a few seconds, he was deep under the overhang, but he had still not reached the wall. The roof looked bright against the blackness below. Pulling the notebook from his pocket, Robson jotted down some details to help him find the location again and then turned for the surface.

The following day, Robson woke to find winter had dumped itself on the mountains. The edge of the lake looked like a picture-postcard scene, snow clinging to the branches of the bare trees, the still water coloured silver. Someone up there doesn't like us, Robson thought. He still went diving, but visibility had again deteriorated as he descended, and his scooter repeatedly shivered in his hands as if it was not appropriately balanced. Robson found the overhang and followed it down as it curved past one hundred metres. Again, he came up frustrated. He made another attempt the following day, on 17 January, but the visibility in that part of the lake had worsened still.

That afternoon, as he tidied away his dive equipment, Robson was approached by Bogdana Vashchenko. Her appearance surprised him. Following the death of Rodionov, Vashchenko and Lyagushkin had barely ventured out. They hadn't known him that well, but that didn't mean they had been untouched by the pain of having someone die so close to them in the same water.

They had spent some time going through the images of the expedition. Looking at photographs of Andrei, Vashchenko recalled one of the few times her grandfather had opened up about his experiences during the Second World War. He told her that he knew when a comrade was going to die because, a few days before, he sensed a shadow, a sign of death on that person. Vashchenko recognised her grandfather's words in the images of Andrei. The portraits upset her because in them he already seemed marked by death's shadow.

Vashchenko and Lyagushkin had sensed the spirit of the expedition slip away the day of the tragedy. Until then, they felt they had a team who were inspired to complete the enormous task ahead of them. Now, everyone was depressed. The pair weren't ready to go home, though, and they had come up with an idea.

Martin, we have lost a friend in Andrei, Vashchenko said. We do not want the project to end in such a way. We want to have some success, so it means something to him.

Robson listened as Vashchenko explained that both Andrei Bykov and Sergei Gorpinyuk were willing to return from Moscow to support the dive. Another experienced diver, Vladimir Grigoriev, had agreed to join them. A few days earlier, Roman Dunaev had returned from his brief visit home.

We will have the divers, she said. Will you continue with us?

Robson said yes instantly. Yes, because they had asked him, and it was what thcy wanted; yes, because he wanted the opportunity to explore the lake further; yes, because he felt a sense of duty to continue out of respect for the way they wanted to pay tribute to their friend.

Robson spent the day of the 18th planning the dive and setting up his equipment. He thought hard about where to go and opted against going in search of the cave. If I don't find it again, it will be a wasted effort for what is an important dive, he explained. That's when the decision was taken to make a symbolic dive into the deep.

183

Speaking with Igor Galaida, he learned of a buoy that hung on the far side of the lake. The plastic float held a weighted shot line that plummeted down to about 200 metres where it was believed the weights rested on the crown of the lake's base which sloped another sixty metres deeper. That was enough for Robson. He decided it was time to go and see what was at the bottom.

When the sport of scuba diving hit the mainstream in the 1980s, research into decompression sickness shifted focus. The military was content with the numerous air diving tables that had been developed through years of trial and error tests and the accumulation of experienced judgement. In common with the commercial world, they had shifted their attention to extreme saturation diving techniques for dives to the deep seabed. The recreational diving industry, meanwhile, did not need to go fishing for ways to protect divers in the deep; it wanted to ensure those diving in the shallows for fun or sport did so safely. Until then, sports divers had relied on the US Navy or Royal Navy decompression tables to execute their dives. And who was going to argue with their numbers? When, in the 1970s, US Navy researchers analysed a set of dives made over an eight-year period, they found the rate of decompression sickness to be 1.25 per cent. The incidence of injury was so low, in fact, that their safety statistics for 1981 showed only thirty-five divers suffered a bend out of 92,484 dives. As far as sport divers were concerned, these tables had been validated with thousands of dives over decades of work: they had stood the test of time, they were straightforward to use, they were readily available and they were reliable. Unfortunately, they weren't designed with the sport diver in mind. The tables had been designed for military divers, fit young men with a surface air supply typically working at a single depth, whose ascent could be carefully controlled. Sport divers simply didn't dive that way. They spent their dive at various depths, often for shorter periods, made repetitive dives over multiple days, and often ascended far faster than recommended.

Those with a mind for physiology found the square wave profiles of the navy tables did not fit the topography they were diving, such as that found in south Florida. That was the playground of a diver and dentist named Raymond Rogers. He'd become fed up with the length of time the navy tables kept him out of the water between dives. When he asked diving instructors why this was the case, they tended to reply: these are the navy tables. Rogers didn't share their reverence for the sanctity of the charts. He picked apart the research to reveal the assumptions that lay at the heart of the tables, and then he began to crunch his numbers on a pocket calculator with the aim of creating a no-stop dive table that could be used for making multiple dives a day. He built a level of conservatism into his calculations, for the sake of safety and to allow for the physiological differences between recreational divers. His research caught the eye of US diver training agency PADI. After a two-phase testing process which pushed to the limits of the table, and beyond, with only one case of decompression sickness, Rogers produced the Recreational Dive Planner. The table allowed sports divers to map the way their body absorbed nitrogen on a dive and off-gassed during surface intervals so they could enjoy more time underwater on subsequent dives. Since its introduction it has been used successfully by millions of divers worldwide. Similar tables were developed by the British Sub Aqua Club in the United Kingdom, by NAUI (National Association of Underwater Instructors) in Florida, and in Canada, which have arguably made the sport more accessible and much safer for recreational participants.

If uncomplicated planning tables opened up the sport, the introduction of the digital dive computer revolutionised it. Now, divers could carry with them a device that monitored their dive and calculated no-decompression limits and decompression obligations on the fly. In sharp contrast to tables, computers allowed divers to move anywhere in the water column and get real-time information about their exposure to inert gas. The user trusted as accurate the information that flickered across the screen and used it to stay down longer than traditional tables allowed.

Just like the dive tables that preceded them, all dive computers, no matter which brand name is stamped on the front, are underpinned by a decompression model – a theory – about how the body works underwater. Diving models seek to address issues of gas uptake and elimination, the presence of bubbles, their growth and collapse, and the changes in pressure during an excursion underwater. These assumptions can be expressed as mathematical formulae and go by names that resemble alphabet spaghetti: ZH-L16C+GF, VPM-B/E, RGBM.

Names aside, the models of inert gas transport and bubble formation all have the same aim, that of trying to prevent decompression sickness. If the biophysical and biochemical processes that led to the bends were known, so the idea went, it would be possible to compute a gold standard model. The problem is, these processes are not known, and modellers only have pieces of the decompression sickness puzzle to work with. They all face the same unknowns, dilemmas they call them, that they must find a way around. Chief among the unknowns is exactly how quickly the body exchanges gas between tissues, but there are others: how bubbles form and grow, the trigger point for the onset of symptoms, the site of the attack, and the nature of the critical insult (in medical language) causing bends.

The Bühlmann decompression algorithm was developed by Swiss physician Dr Albert A. Bühlmann during the 1960s and 1970s. Backed by the French and American navies and with support from Shell Oil Company, Bühlmann built on the work of Haldane, to find a practicable system of decompression with the largest possible assurance of safety. He modelled the human body on sixteen tissue compartments that absorbed and released inert gas at different rates. Bühlmann believed there was a maximum pressure of nitrogen each tissue could tolerate before symptoms of decompression occurred. That maximum changed with depth, so he derived two constants – 'Factor a' and 'Factor b' – that could be used to calculate safe decompression stops. To confirm his theories, he conducted a series of experiments, including dry chamber dives with human test subjects, and, where necessary, adjustments were made to his calculations. Published in 1983, the model was regarded as the most complete public reference on decompression calculations, with formulae that could easily be adapted to breathing mixed gases or diving at altitude. The open release allowed divers to study the work that went into the decompression calculations and also make modifications, of which there were plenty, to improve the safety of the model. Eventually, the mathematical equations were plugged into software and the model became popular as a computerised dive planning tool.

While some modellers, like Bühlmann, built on the work of Haldane, others approached the decompression puzzle from a different perspective and created what became known as bubble models. Bubble models are a rule-based approach to calculating decompression based on the idea that small seeds, known as bubble nuclei, are found in the human body. Simply put, these nuclei are stable microbubbles of gas that are prevented from collapsing by an elastic surface skin, like that seen in washing detergent. They are about a third the size of a red blood cell. Researchers in Hawaii came up with this theory after discovering the presence of small bubbles in dishes of agarose gelatin that had been sent on a simulated dive.

When a diver ascends, so the bubble theory goes, gas dissolved in the tissues migrates into these micronuclei, and the bubbles grow. The model assumes the human body can tolerate a specific volume of gas in bubbles, known as free-phase gas. Anything above that value could cause injury. Keeping a diver safe, then, was all about keeping this free-phase gas below a critical volume, thus preventing it from popping into a fully formed bubble. Plugging the information into the model's equations would yield values for such things as critical gradients and allowable tensions in each tissue compartment, which could, in turn, be used to compute decompression schedules from various exposures.

Drawing upon the concept of bubble dynamics, Bruce R. Wienke, a program manager in the Nuclear Weapons Technology Simulation and Computing Office at the Los Alamos National Laboratory, in Santa Fe, developed the Reduced Gradient Bubble Model (RGBM). The model was highly complex, with a series of assumptions built in, and addressed a wide spectrum of information to calculate real-time decompression obligations. Over the years, Wienke extended the model to cover repetitive diving, diving at altitude and breathing a mixture of gases. The RGBM found favour with a large number of dive computer manufacturers who installed modified versions of it onto their devices. Alongside the conservatism built into the model, the devices also offered an option for divers to make the results it churned out more conservative or more aggressive, a choice that could be important for both physical safety and psychological comfort.

A similar conservatism construct, called gradient factors, was developed to give divers a dynamic way to manage risk, and was actively applied to the Bühlmann decompression algorithm. The Bühlmann model became the go-to algorithm for technical divers, who used the model to successfully complete thousands of mixed-gas dives to the kind of depths that were once the preserve of military and commercial divers.

The problem is that the desire of technical divers to push the extremes, and the quality of life-support equipment they use to do so, can far exceed the known capabilities of decompression models employed to get them safely back from the deep. Technical divers venturing into the unknown might be relying on decompression numbers that have never been validated in human trials. The decompression model might go to those depths, but their body might not behave in the way modellers assume. In short, they may be experimenting on themselves.

Hunched under the weight of equipment, Martin Robson tromped to the edge of the lake, Igor Galaida at his side. The pair had discussed the dive, and Robson had listened to his concerns. Now Galaida guided him into the water, the role Andrei Rodionov had completed less than a week earlier. After handing Robson his bailout tanks and helping with his fins, Galaida looked Robson in the face and flashed the 'okay' sign. Robson nodded acceptance as he prepared to do an extraordinary thing. On a grey winter's afternoon in southern Russia, Martin Robson prepared to dive deeper into the mysterious lake than anyone had gone before. It was an audacious plan, to descend more than 200 metres into the unknown in order to complete the expedition's symbolic goal for Andrei.

But Robson knew the risks. Sitting at the water's edge, he went through his ritual of accumulated habits. He contemplated all the things that could go wrong and then rehearsed how he would respond, to prevent a foreseeable threat becoming a foregone conclusion. For safety. Then he visualised the dive: he imagined the two divers checking his equipment for bubbles at six metres; descending the shot line, past the point where the bright blue water gave way to blackness, and it felt like he was spacewalking; fixing a strobe light to the end of the line to illuminate the way home. There was scant information about what he would find in the dark, but Robson knew precisely what he would do when he got there: he would go off exploring.

When he was ready, Robson floated into deep water. Air spilled from his buoyancy wing as he sank out of sight.

It was 12:25 p.m. The clock was running.

Khuazhev watched the tell-tale circle of bubbles ripple across the lake and wished someone had halted the dive. He was here to help, knew what he had to do, but he was still dead set against the whole endeavour. One friend had died, and his loss should have been enough. What was this dive going to accomplish? Nothing. Yet it was still going ahead. So, he was there. Supporting the divers in the water, looking after Robson as planned, were the only things he could do now.

As Robson vanished, support divers Gorpinyuk and Bykov began their pre-dive rituals. They were to start their dive exactly twenty-four minutes after Robson has descended. They would be called up in twelve, a warning to be ready.

Robson let the shot line run through his right hand as he slipped from the grey surface waters. His left hand alternated between equalising his ears and injecting air into his wing to offset gravity's downward pull. His wrist-mounted computers counted the increasing depth and calculated his decompression obligation, his extraordinary endeavour rendered into an orderly existence by the numbers displayed on the instrument's face. From behind his mask, Robson saw the light grey waters give way to twilight and then fade to black until the white nylon line was the only break from the darkness. The line dazzled so brightly in the beam of light it almost burned his eyes, and the feel of the nylon running through his gloved hand was a good indication of how fast he was sinking. Sixteen minutes into his fall, Robson reached the end of the line.

Hanging from the shot line were two lumps of lead, gently swaying in the dark space. Robson halted his descent and hovered next to them. His dive computers said he was at 190 metres. Robson peered hard, eager for his first glimpse of a strange land that was meant to be covered, or so it was said, with bejewelled weapons of Tamerlane and Nazi field artillery. There was nothing.

This can't be it, he thought.

All around him was blackness. He hovered there for a moment and considered his situation. If he ascended now, he would have enjoyed a pointless bounce dive to nowhere and back again. What would that prove? No, Robson wasn't going to bounce, sixteen minutes down and hundreds up. He was going to do precisely what the sport's folk hero Jochen Hasenmayer had done on his own, submerged more than 200 metres down in Fontaine-de-Vaucluse.

12:43 p.m.

Robson clipped a strobe to the line and switched it on. He vented air from his wing. He began to sink. To explore. To see what was there. For Andrei. So, he pushed on to the beat of his rebreather. *Shhh! Umm. Shhh! Umm. Click! Spritz!*

Shining his high-intensity light downwards, Robson strained his eyes for a glimpse of rock or silt. He didn't want to exert himself down there. Under pressure, there was a high-consequence menu of reckonings that could cascade from being too physical: oxygen toxicity; gas narcosis; carbon-dioxide induced coma; helium tremors; a very rare phenomenon known as effort-independent respiratory failure, in which an overworked diver suffers a partial airway collapse and suffocates on their own carbon dioxide. Robson knew them; you don't get this far without understanding those dangers, without being able to control your emotions and put everything to one side in full acceptance of the risk and reward, price and prize.

Descending through the darkness, Robson peered at his computers. As he passed 200 metres, a mystery shadow developed like a latent image on photographic paper submerged in chemicals. The bottom? A shelf? Robson kicked towards a desert of plaster-grey silt which sloped away from his light.

Robson reached the silt bed and went off swimming. Alone in the icebox grip of the lake, he was remarkably relaxed, breathing slowly and deeply. *Shhh! Umm. Shhh! Umm. Click! Spritz!*; thirteen or fourteen breaths a minute as he revelled in the fact that he was the first human ever to see this spot. The bed sloped away from him, and Robson followed, a bubble of light and life gliding over a lunar surface in a sea of tranquillity.

With measured strokes from his fins, Robson drifted deeper. Downwards for Andrei. Decorated with white light, the bottom looked like a sandy beach, only with no footprints on it. The cold, dense water around him was still, and the bleak sweep of microscopic matter settled silk-like in permanence. Everything seemed still.

Periodically, he turned to look at the path he had come along, back referencing, he called it. He did it so nothing would look strange on his return because he had seen it already.

Robson checked the Vision handset linked to his rebreather.

The recorded dive time, depth, decompression calculations and readouts from the oxygen sensors were as he expected. Then he looked at the two computers on his right wrist. He noticed one had malfunctioned. The immense pressure down there had overwhelmed the computer's pressure sensor. The digits on the depth reading had frozen at 214 metres. The other computer showed his depth as 209 metres. Two-zero-nine, that would be the number he'd write down in his logbook, Robson told himself. Two-zero-nine. The equivalent of forty-seven London double-decker buses stacked one on top of another, or the height of two Big Ben clock towers, with seventeen metres to spare. Two-zero-nine – the pressure down there was equal to a small car sitting on his chest, but he felt nothing. He was a happy man. At some point, he'd record the depth on a plastic slate: Для Андрей 209 m. For Andrei 209 m.

He kicked on for another minute or so. The bed continued to slope away beyond the light from his torch, and he prepared to turn. He was not ready. He wanted to carry on, but another minute would add thirty minutes to his decompression time, and that was not the plan agreed with the support divers.

Reluctantly, Robson headed back to the shot line. Retracing his journey, he could see the strobe he had placed on the end of the line pulsing in the darkness to guide him back home.

Twenty-five minutes into the dive, he finally left the bottom. All told, he had spent just seven minutes there.

12:50 p.m.

Almost ten hours and more than fifty decompression stops lay between him and the surface, such was the amount of nitrogen and helium washing around his body. As he climbed through the water column, a series of vanishingly small variables and low probability events were beginning to converge inside his body.

THE SURFACE IS NO FRIEND

If it happens, you can be paralysed in your sleep, so that you wake up to find yourself a cripple for life. It can choke you to death, kill you instantly, or twist you into a screaming lump of agony with awful pains in your joints. You might get off with only a headache or a rash. Do not feel reassured if you have only minor symptoms. They can be a prelude to agonies which would be the envy of any medieval torturer.

Peter Throckmorton, *The Lost Ships:*
An Adventure in Undersea Archaeology

Getting bent is a hazard all deep divers must accept, or they don't stay deep divers for long. They plan on spending a lot of time climbing through the water, guided by a £1,200 computer strapped to their wrists, and they generally put their faith in the maths it's using to get them out safely. Yet everyone running a deep decompression schedule knows their computers are churning out numbers based on a mathematical model that offers no concrete guarantees they won't burst like a pop bottle.

The idea of suffering a bend is almost unfathomable to a holiday diver. They know there's not much trouble they can get into exploring the shallows. Diving science can predict, with a high degree of certainty, how to stay free of the bends when returning from thirty or forty metres, and the US Navy has a good idea how to ascend a diver from a hundred-metre dive safely and plenty of experience surfacing divers safely from the shallower water. By the time you reach 200 metres down, you are way beyond the range of any serious study into safe decompression numbers.

That's because computer algorithms which calculate decompression schedules are what one expert calls a limited mathematical representation of the reality of diving. That is, they are limited in what they measure and in the assumptions upon which they were constructed. Not all computerised decompression algorithms are based on comprehensive human testing in the deep. The models that were tested on humans more often than not sought to find the limits by conducting experiments in comparatively shallow water. The findings were used to tweak the mathematical equations and then used to extrapolate decompression obligations throughout the entire depth continuum. The biggest drawback to decompression algorithms is that the physiology of a diver is much trickier than simple maths. Divers can do all the calculations they want to compute the uptake and elimination of inert gas. Yet they know the work still won't provide a cast-iron guarantee when it comes to decompressing from extreme depths because there are myriad variables that equations can't yet measure. The variables include thermal status, exercise intensity, joint forces and a host of individual predispositions that are currently not well understood, let alone quantifiable in their impact on decompression stress. Decompression algorithms are superb at carrying out programmed mathematical computations, and they provide important guidance for users. Still, they are blind to the many issues a thoughtful diver needs to consider. It is up to divers to avoid confusing a computer's decompression information with the truth. Treat dive computers like a politician, is an adage some divers follow: do not believe everything they tell you.

Every deep dive is a natural experiment, one leading specialist in the field of decompression sickness told a diving conference in 2016, dive computers just get you in the ballpark. Deep divers know, then, it's all about risk; and the risk of some of the deep, technical level exposures may be extortionately high. No more unambiguous a warning can be found than in the text that accompanies the computer-generated numbers of a decompression schedule. Most divers don't want to pay attention to the disclaimer because the text spotlights all the perils they are doing their best to forget, particularly when it reads something like this: this dive schedule could indirectly kill you. The author doesn't guarantee it won't get you bent or dead. It might add that the programme is simply a number cruncher, that calculations are at best a guess of the real physiological decompression requirements, and no procedure, dive computer or dive table will prevent the possibility of decompression sickness, but it will remind you that you really are risking your life. That's because diving is fraught with risk, it might state. Decompression adds another layer of risk, and diving deep with mixed gases, including helium, or on a rebreather is about as risky as it gets.

Inevitably, deep divers know they are going to be running decompression profiles which exceed stress levels most people would find acceptable. In the abstract terminology of diving, they are called provocative diving exposures. Of the handful of

divers who died of decompression sickness between 2010 and
2013, and whose deaths were recorded by Divers Alert Network, at least half were running provocative profiles. Then
there are stories of those who escaped with their lives – just –
like the diver left with short-term memory loss, bowel and
bladder incontinence, balance difficulties and chronic leg pain
a year after being hit.

Such stories are enough to make some people think hard
about how deep they will go. The hardened few, though, are
prepared to stomach such risks, because they view decompression sickness as a predictable part of deep diving. They know
the only sure way of avoiding the bends is not to go diving, and
they're not going to do that, not when there's a shipwreck to
find or a cave to explore. They have transcended the stigma and
fear of the illness. They may see a bend as an occupational
hazard – and maybe they've already had a hit or two – in much
the same way as a busted knee is to a skier; a hazard that if
treated promptly and properly may just be a disagreeable incon-
venience rather than a life-threatening trauma. Or maybe they
will remind you nothing in life is free from risk. Look at the
automobile, deep-diving pioneer Jon Lindbergh said at a 1968
symposium on the physiological problems of living and
working underwater. If people were willing to drive at ten
miles an hour on a highway, he said, the number of fatal colli-
sions would be small. But because people drove at seventy
miles an hour there were 50,000 fatalities each year on the
highways. People obviously thought getting from A to B
quickly was worth the risk. A similar outlook, he argued, could
be applied to diving.

Scientists can talk about incident rates for decompression sickness in the fractions of 1 per cent, or they can point to statistics that indicate Americans are eighteen times more likely to be admitted to accident and emergency with a bowling injury than with one earned while scuba diving. Technical divers, then, do not throw themselves blindly into the water and hope for the best. They accept the possibility of decompression sickness, plan for it and prepare themselves to deal with it. They look for every advantage to stay safe, and they respect the fact that the small things matter. A good diver like Martin Robson starts by drinking plenty of water at least twenty-four hours before the dive. That prevents dehydration, one of the causal factors of decompression sickness. They stop doing aerobic exercise about the same time. They take into consideration when they last dived. More than a day can pass before the human body has completely purged excess nitrogen and helium, and what's still swishing around the body at the beginning of the next dive can bubble over if not compensated for. Divers analyse their breathing gas mix and account for every last percentage point of the constituent elements in their tanks. When diving inland, they calculate how far above sea level they are. They check the atmospheric pressure down to the last millibar and load all of this information into their dive computers. They make sure they have a good night's sleep and eat a balanced meal before the dive; being fatigued at the start can lead to a seriously bad day. They try not to get too hot while gearing up and don't exert themselves when hauling their equipment to the water. A pounding heart and huffing lungs only serve to load the body with more inert gases than planned.

Deep divers also take care when switching on their bat-
tery-heated undergarments. Slowly warming the body on the
ascent is good, but they certainly don't want to jack the temperature too high. Rapid heating can cause gas to pour from the
tissues, increasing the chances of bubble formation. Equally,
divers don't want to be chilled during decompression. That
could cause blood vessels to bottleneck and trap gas inside the
skin. This could result in marbled lesions, red, purple and blue,
or painfully swollen areas pitted like orange peel. These are a
warning: a skin bend often heralds neurological symptoms
hidden in the body.

That's a lot to think about. An inventory of the fundamental
contributory factors to decompression sickness runs to around
thirty separate details. On top of that, there are three issues –
age, gender and genetics – which can't be changed but still
have an influence on how deep you go. All that's playing in the
margins, though. Deep divers know their adventures are like
space flight. Everything can be written down, but hidden variables will always crop up. In the end, they have no option but
to rest their safety on a theoretical decompression algorithm
that maths say will get them to the surface. And theory is as
good as it gets because maths can't answer all of the questions
posed by physiology. The human body is so incredibly complex; there are so many variables to consider and too many
assumptions to compute, it's so far proved impossible to model
with any precision.

'There are endless algorithms for calculating decompression
profiles, but none of them are based on any known physiology,
and that's because we don't know how the body works,' says Dr

James Francis, former head of Undersea Medicine at the Royal Navy's Institute of Naval Medicine, and medical director at the UK's Defence Evaluation and Research Agency. 'If you push them beyond the pressure range they've been calibrated to, they break down, and that's because the human body is fantastically complicated nobody has been able to model it. The most elegant demonstration we haven't yet got this right is the fact there are so many decompression algorithms. It's a bit like influenza. If you go to the chemist and trawl along the aisle of flu remedies, you will find thousands of them. Why is that? It's because none of them do any good. The same is true of decompression algorithms; there are many because none of them actually work reproducibly over a limitless range of diving depths and times.'

Martin Robson, gloved hands clasped out in front as if in prayer, hung motionless, suspended in more than a million gallons of water. Legs bent at the knee, abdominal muscles engaged, he was spirit-level straight as programmed. Divers call this neutral trim, the perfect horizontal position for decompressing. Robson had practised this position during hundreds of dives and thousands of hours underwater, and his coordination was just so. Cocooned in his heated dry suit, he supped on the cocktail of helium, oxygen and nitrogen served by his rebreather, *Shhh! Ummm! Shhh! Ummm!* as he rode the decompression curve upwards. There was a mountain of water above him, and Robson had settled in for the slow climb to the surface. In the icebox grip of the deep, he was content.

Robson had left the bottom three short minutes earlier and was hanging around. This seemed the easiest part of his dive.

As he ascended, the small change in relative pressure had stirred a shift in Robson's body. He felt nothing as helium and nitrogen that had massed in his tissues with each *shhh* in the deep now flowed in reverse. Molecules of inert gas siphoned into the capillaries that branched into his veins. Held in solution, the helium and nitrogen hitched a ride with the blood streaming towards Robson's lungs. Sweeping through the alveoli, the gas escaped from his body each time he *ummmed*.

Robson was heading to the surface.

This was the most dangerous part of his dive.

The buoyed shot line signposted the way from No Man's Land and Robson concentrated on his decompression schedule, making sure he hit the right depths at the right time. When the countdown of the sixty-second stop reached zero, it was time to ascend to his next stop. Robson lifted his shoulders and pivoted a few degrees upwards. He drew his feet together and kicked gently, rising a few metres. Levelling out, Robson fine-tuned his buoyancy and relaxed into the new decompression stop. He had practised this move thousands of times before, and like this, he would seesaw gently upwards, all the way to the surface from 200 metres down.

Two hundred metres; 665 feet. In physical terms, it doesn't sound far at all, just an eighth of a mile. Usain Bolt ran it in little more than nineteen seconds at the London Olympics in 2012. Robson had calculated it would take him almost ten hours to cover the same distance. He had done the depth and now he had to do the time. One was a consequence of the other and Robson didn't see any point arguing with consequences; he couldn't change them.

Sixty seconds later, Robson moved again. Stopped again. Waited again.

This, Robson knew, was the role of a diver during decompression: to be patient, to move only when told to, to be resilient. With no choice but to accept the penalties necessary to settle his debt to the deep, one instalment at a time. Robson looked at the black numerals on the rebreather's green decompression computer clipped to his left wrist. At the bottom left, beneath the minutes and seconds of the elapsed dive time, was a number followed by the letters 'TTS'. TTS stood for Total Time to Surface, an aggregate of his decompression stops. When Robson settled into his seventh deco stop, at 150 metres, the figure stood at 5-5-4 – 554 minutes. This was a sharp reminder of what lay ahead, where every minute was just like the one that had gone before: hovering in the darkness. Patient in the darkness. Focused in the darkness.

Twenty minutes into his ascent, everything was going according to plan. Riding the decompression curve to the surface, Robson had ascended to 120 metres. He had made twelve stops to get there. His breathing went *Shhh! Ummm! Shhh! Ummm!* Stable. Relaxed. Inside his body, nitrogen and helium molecules siphoned, streamed and swept their way towards his lungs. Controlled.

Part way into the ascent, Robson scanned the lines of handwritten numbers in his waterproof notebook. He was looking at the entries to ensure his decompression schedule was running to plan. He'd compiled the record the previous day while preparing for the dive.

Before each deep dive, Robson ran the planned depth and

204

bottom time through decompression planning software on his laptop to generate a decompression schedule. Like most deep divers, he then changed variables like ascent and descent speeds and created another plan. Next, he altered the gradient factors and reran the dive. Then, he did it all again, this time using different dive planning software. After all of that, he compared the results of the tests. What he was looking for was an expectation; what he expected to happen at various points on the dive. If the results churned out by the decompression planning software didn't meet that expectation, if they suggested something out of the ordinary, or if they just felt off, he went over them again, line by line if necessary, to understand why he was getting a particular set of numbers.

After all that research, Robson then developed what he believed to be the best plan to match what he wanted to do underwater. Then all the information was handwritten into his waterproof notebook and rechecked to ensure there were no mistakes. Robson committed to memory crucial details of the plan: his bottom time, his first deep stop, the time it would take to arrive at his first stop, time to arrive at first decompression phase stop. Then the notebook was placed into the pocket of his dry suit as he got dressed for the dive and taken with him underwater.

Leaving the bottom, Robson had removed the notebook from his pocket and clipped it to his harness for easy reference. He wasn't going to follow his dive computers slavishly; referring to the notes was a good way to ensure the real-time information coming from his on-board dive computers matched, as close as dammit, the dive plan. The written plans were a good form of insurance, just in case the numbers from his dive computers did not look right. He'd been on dives before when computers had done strange things. Once, Robson's computer had informed him he was seven metres shallower than he actually was. Another time, he was decompressing following a dive to 107 metres when his computer raced away from him. According to readouts on the screen, he was shooting to the surface. In fact, he was stationary in the water on a deco stop. It was at times like that when his wet notes came into their own. It was at times like that that his handwritten dive plan would take over.

Right then, everything was going to plan.

Sergei Gorpinyuk and Andrei Bykov were waiting for him, as scheduled. Under the glow of torchlight, the men swapped the bailout cylinders. The exchange was completed quickly, and Robson got back on track.

Shhh! Ummm! Shhh! Ummm!

The two men settled in around him, but Robson was the kind of person who was happiest on his own. He didn't need to be around others all the time, and, if he was, he didn't need to engage in idle banter. That's because he didn't always enjoy it; sometimes he found it uncomfortable. Diving on his own helped keep the rest of the world at one remove, and he had no problem focusing his energy on the trail of white nylon line which cut a vertical path through the blackness.

He spent two minutes at ninety-six metres. Two more at ninety-three. At ninety metres, Robson stopped again to settle another instalment. After two minutes, he moved again. And stopped again. Another instalment. Stop. Go. Stop. Go. On and on. Up and up.

Decompression suited a man whose personality was contained, controlled, guarded. The very act demanded command of buoyancy, and Robson was an exhibition of exact skill. Stationary, he held himself at the perfect point of balance, zero-degree bubble on the spirit level. When the time came to move, he was able to pull from his imagination and project in real life where he wanted to be. He arrived at each stop with certain placement. Robson enjoyed the physical challenge and would dive particular caves, not because they were beautiful, but because they invited him to think every second about his buoyancy control and movement.

During decompression, Robson could feel the cold nipping at his toes, clawing at his cheeks, a frost on his skin. It was now 1:30 p.m. and his rebreather shushed and hummed with reassuring regularity. His breathing was steady. Nitrogen and helium swept from his body with each exhalation. He checked the pressure gauge of his rebreather's oxygen cylinder, and then he examined the information on the unit's handset. Above the readouts from the oxygen sensors, a bar graph indicated the chemical activity inside the rebreather's carbon dioxide scrubber. The amount of carbon dioxide his rebreather could remove was the real limit of his life support, not the amount of oxygen he carried, because he could always get more of that. He couldn't do anything to replace the scrubber underwater. No, he had to nurse it. According to the manual, the scrubber unit was good for three hours. Robson had studied the test data and concluded he could push the scrubber beyond the limits as long as he didn't exert himself during decompression.

Ninety-five minutes into the dive, Robson arrived at sixty metres to find Roman Dunaev and Roman Prokhorov waiting.

Fingers flicked signals – okay? Yes, I'm okay – then they went to work as planned. Robson hovered next to the shot line, and Dunaev switched the battery powering active in-suit heating for a fresh one. Then they swapped the bailout tanks.

Baton passed, Gorpinyuk and Bykov continued their ascent alone leaving Dunaev and Prokhorov to stay with Robson as he continued his slow climb upwards. The penalties were longer now. Some divers refer to them as decompression hangs because that's what they feel like, hanging. Robson spent six minutes hanging at forty-eight metres. Eight minutes hanging at forty-five metres. Nine minutes hanging at forty-two metres.

Shhh! Ummm! Shhh! Ummm!

For thirteen long minutes, Robson hung at thirty-three metres. Thirteen minutes hanging again in the darkness. Thirteen minutes daydreaming again in the darkness. Thirteen long minutes clock-watching again in the darkness.

The fatigue produced by the last two weeks of hard dives, and long deco hangs, had put dark circles under his eyes, but Robson knew he just had to suck it up for a little bit longer. He was on his way home.

Roman Dunaev kept a close eye on his friend throughout the climb. During one stop, he spotted something that concerned him. 'I noticed that Martin's trim was not very good,' he says. 'That made me start to wonder if everything was okay.'

Robson's hands were still clasped out in front, legs bent at the knee, as usual, but he lay at a slight angle. Robson's legs sat lower in the water. His trim was no longer zero bubble.

*

Thirty-three metres above, in the cold hours of the winter afternoon, Eduard Khuazhev pulled the woollen beanie down tight over his ears. Squeezed into his dry suit, he stared out over the lake. Soon enough, he would be getting ready to enter the water to be on hand when Robson approached the habitat. Only then would he feel comfortable because at least then he'd be there to look after him.

The water's edge was a lonely place to be with a lot of time to pass and nothing to do but think. Five divers were decompressing somewhere in the water column below, and he juggled the different deco schedules in his head. Occasionally he would turn to the dive times committed to the whiteboard to remind himself of the dive plan. He could use the times to infer where the other divers were. Dunaev and Prokhorov should be with Robson; meanwhile, Gorpinyuk and Bykov should be in the shallows nearing the end of their dive.

They knew what they were doing, he told himself. That didn't make him feel any better, though. Andrei Rodionov had known what he was doing and that hadn't prevented him from dying. Khuazhev still could not get the images from his head: the shout for help; the sight of the body at the surface; the grey eyes. Those images would continue to cloud into tears every time he recalled them.

In the dive centre behind him, divers were conducting final checks of their equipment. They would be committed to the water soon enough.

Right then, Khuazhev just wanted the dive to be over.

*

After more than one hundred years of decompression sickness research, joked one authority on the subject during a conference in 2003, we can be fairly sure of one thing – that bubbles have something to do with it. Within the audience of hyperbaric physicians, the comment raised a laugh, but it also highlighted the vast grey areas which still exist about the disorder. Doctors have an idea about what is responsible for decompression sickness, but they don't exactly understand why. Although much is known about the illness, the evolution of the injury is still not fully understood. And while it is commonly thought of as a bubble disease, bubbles are probably only the gateway to a complex array of consequences and effects that spread through a diver's body when bubbles explode. 'We're talking about a very complex disorder,' says retired Royal Navy specialist Dr James Francis. 'Decompression sickness is very difficult to nail down; it is, in a way, similar to syphilis which tends to present itself in an absolute myriad of ways. The disease is a great mimic of all sorts of different conditions.'

There are so many biophysical and pathological components to the disorder, in fact, that no one theory can fit all the known clinical presentations; all might be valid. Short of bending human test cases in a laboratory and then cutting them open to see what is happening to their insides – 'I'm not sure that would pass the ethics committee,' jokes one doctor – it is impossible to map the real-time effects in humans. Scientists, then, are left with animal testing and the interrogation of historical studies to try to understand the body's response to decompression bubbling.

The mechanics of bubble formation are both strikingly

obvious and extremely complicated. All that is required for them to form is a sufficient number of gas molecules to be present in the same location at the same time as there is a rapid decrease in ambient pressure. Bubbles, though, don't just appear from nowhere, de novo in medical terms. The extreme drop in pressure required for that, so physical theory goes, would be greater than could ever be achieved in conventional scuba diving.

All bubbles, then, start as gas nuclei, just a few molecules together, but how exactly they form in the body has baffled scientists over the years. They do not know with any certainty where and how bubbles form, their pathways through the body, nor the exact chain of events that cause decompression sickness.

All that is left, then, are the theories. One of these theories suggests these nuclei are formed by a rubbing together of two solid surfaces, like movement inside tissues or simple muscle motion. This creates pressure differentials inside a microscopic area of the body, in much the same way as cracking a knuckle (the crack is thought to be gas rushing into the vacuum created by the action of pulling). This is known as tribonucleation. Another theory, sometimes referred to as the crevice model, proposes that minute pockets of gas gather in the tiny imperfections in the tissue walls. It's why you see bubbles forming on the side of beer glasses. A third hypothesis suggests that small pockets of gas protected by a shell, called micronuclei, are ever-present inside the body and act as a seed to bubble growth. Then there are studies which suggest bubbles might form when molecules come into contact with a hydrophobic, or non-wettable, surface such as body fat.

Whatever the reality, once the right conditions exist the gas loaded in the body is ready to bubble. Held in solution under pressure, the mix of nitrogen and helium is volcanically unstable in much the same way as nitroglycerine held in a jar, and one bump is enough to trigger detonation. In the case of divers, the trigger is an abrupt decrease in the ambient pressure of the surrounding water.

Bubbles are more likely to form in fatty tissues over aqueous ones, which makes the white matter of the spinal cord, the body's communications infrastructure, a favourite nesting site. It is lipidic and has relatively low blood flow. Within the cord itself, the neck and lumbar region are particular target sites, thanks to quirks in the circulation system. As a result, every spinal cord bend can claim half a dozen different architects. If the diver loses movement and sensation in their limbs and struggles to breathe, bubbles could have overwhelmed the diver's lungs and forced their way into the arteries, a process known as the arterial bubble embolus theory. If a diver suffers pain and immobility an hour after exiting the water, it could be that the venous drainage of the cord has become inundated with bubbles. This is known as the venous infarction theory. With the rapid onset of the paralysis, one suspect is something called the autochthonous bubble hypothesis.

Hyperbaric doctors have a term for autochthonous bubbling in the spinal cord. They describe it as an explosive event. An explosive event describes the moment bubbles erupt spontaneously, in their hundreds along the length of the cord. Swishing around inside each bubble is a cocktail of gases – nitrogen, helium, carbon dioxide, water vapour and a small amount of oxygen. Those bubbles in the spine are not spherical. They are elliptical, shaped by the cellular structure of the cord. Each bubble generates a three-dimensional crater, known as a space-occupying lesion. Around the crater are smooth areas of compression where the free-standing, signal-conducting fibres, known as axons, have been flattened by the blast. Outside the immediate blast area, other axons are stretched by up to a third as they wrap around the bubble's surface. If enough of the fibres suffer physical disruption, the diver will soon know about it; if more than 30 per cent lose their ability to transmit sensory information, the spinal cord will show decreased function. In the dry terminology of medicine, the body is suffering a neurological deficit.

The bubbles don't need to be too large to cause a neurological deficit. Their size is measured in micrometres – a millionth of a metre. All it takes to jam a capillary, the smallest blood vessel in the body, is a bubble with a diameter of seven micrometres. An embolus of that size is so tiny as to be practically invisible to an X-ray or MRI scan. By way of comparison, the average human hair is between seventeen and 191 micrometres in diameter. Studies have found bubbles between twenty and 200 micrometres are enough to take out the control of limbs.

At 4:05 p.m., Robson hung next to the line. The horizon above glowed a twilight blue. The Vision handset on his left wrist and the Liquivision X1 computer on his right wrist both told him he was at twenty-four metres. The other dive computer on his right wrist hadn't worked since he had left the bottom and still displayed his depth as 214 metres. Robson still couldn't quite believe he'd been down there to the moonscape drifting into the depths beyond his light. He'd go back in a heartbeat.

In the background, his rebreather went *Shhh! Ummm! Shhh! Ummm!* Steady.

Inside his body, nitrogen and helium now sloshed from tissues.

At that moment, Robson might have been thinking about caves he had dived, what he fancied for dinner, or more likely he would not have been thinking of anything in particular. He might even have closed his eyes and daydreamed for a moment; buddies sometimes thought he was asleep during long hangs.

He didn't register the sprinkling of pinpricks tickling his thighs, or the cold, clammy feeling which wrapped around his legs like a damp pair of running tights.

Robson prepared to move up again. He'd been underwater for three hours and forty minutes. He had another six hours to go.

And then it hit. Robson's spinal cord was carpeted by a wave of explosions. Considering what happened next, they probably erupted in the section of the spine doctors refer to as L2, which controls hip motion; in L3, which directs knee extension; in L4 and S1, which govern foot movement; in L5, which controls knee flexion; in S2 and S3, which control bladder and bowel activity.

It was as if his body had uncorked.

Immediately Robson's world turned, and his breathing lurched a gear. *Shhh! Ummm! Shh. Umm. Sh-um, sh-um, sh-um.* His legs flopped beneath him. The momentum whipped him around. Caught in a motion he was helpless to control, he moved through almost ninety degrees, snapped vertical in the water like a jack-in-the-box, as if the depths had taken him by the ankles.

The only way to free himself was to kick back.

Robson tried to flex his legs, but he couldn't feel them. They didn't respond in any way.

Sh-um, sh-um, sh-um.

Work! Work! he silently pleaded with his body, but there was no response below the waist. He couldn't move a damn thing.

Sh-um, sh-um, sh-um.

Something had sliced through his body. There was no crack, no rip, no pain tearing at his back; no warning, just an absolute change one would get from flicking off the power switch. At a stroke, his memory went from being able to use his legs to not. They flopped beneath him, lifeless. In the post-mortem that would follow the incident, he described the moment as like being shot in the back.

Sh-um, sh-um, sh-um.

This attack was not something even he had foreseen. For survival he needed to respond. His neck muscles contracted involuntarily, and he blinked. His arms stiffened, and his tattooed shoulders raised. Both featured animals in a war cry, a war eagle on one and a tiger pouncing through clouds with a dagger behind it on the other.

Sh-um, sh-um, sh-um.

In that enormously elongated second, his eyes were in the front of his mask and the white shot line unravelled before them. The line. Robson instinctively clawed for the line with both hands, yanking hold of it with the muscle of a tug-of-war anchor preparing for titanic combat. He had on his dry gloves, locked at the seals, and he squeezed his fingers tightly into his palms to catch a grip.

215

Sh-um, sh-um, sh-um.

If anyone on the surface was looking out over the water at that precise moment, they would have seen the buoy bob violently as it took Robson's dead weight.

Robson hung over the abyss, confused. Blank. He could only stare at his legs as if they no longer belonged to him. His left leg, everything below the hips, stubbornly refused to work. His thigh, his knee, his ankle, his toes, trying to move anything was a dead loss. His right leg was exactly the same, useless beneath him, and he was dangling from the shot line; his life now quite literally hanging by a thread, the very thread he could see running through his gloved hands.

Damn, damn, *damn.*

Right then, he wasn't spooked so much as disappointed by the fact that something had gone wrong, and for a brief moment his wits were split like his body. One half looked at his predicament with unemotional objectivity; the other hoped it was trivial. He didn't want it to be a bend, and he'd have taken anything else: a flooded dry suit, perhaps, or cold legs.

Robson knew the bends, though. Once, in the mid-1990s, he was dragged to the surface while assisting a diver who'd swum to him at fifty metres slashing a hand across the throat. Robson donated his spare regulator and tried to calm the man. Instead, he missiled for the surface, and Robson went as well. The Coastguard helicoptered them out. In the twenty-one minutes it took to reach the recompression chamber, Robson's toes had started to tingle. The doctor diagnosed a possible spinal bend and pressed Robson for eight hours in a recompression chamber, a run made only slightly more bearable by a Chinese takeaway that was delivered to him through an airlock.

Robson had seen a few more close calls over the years as well. There was the cave diver in Florida who walked into a dive store with pains shooting through his shoulder wondering aloud whether he had been hit. Then there was a guy on a boat in Egypt who climbed out of the water pale as a ghost, eyes looking in different directions, unable to find his mouth with a cup of tea. No one else saw him splash back into the water. Robson understood he had suffered a bend and had gone back underwater to try to cure himself, so he dived in to keep the man company while they waited for rescue.

Yes, Robson knew the bends, and this was it. But even he never imagined getting hit underwater. Who in their wildest dreams ever did? Neurological decompression sickness only ever came on at the end of a dive, that was the received wisdom, had been for years. The symptoms might come on quickly; you might still be climbing out of the water, but at least you were at the surface. One in ten got hit that way. Almost 20 per cent collapsed within five minutes of surfacing, the seventy-two point something majority were twisted in pain within an hour; that was what the textbooks and medical papers said. That was what he discussed with students. A spinal bend never came on underwater, never during decompression, and a spinal bend causing paralysis underwater? The medical literature didn't contain any of those.

Yet the unimaginable had been recorded in divers over the years. In a 1989 research paper, Dr Francis, who specialised in spinal cord decompression injuries, found twenty-nine cases where a spinal bend appeared during the dive. There were other statistics if someone wanted to go looking for them. Twenty years earlier, the US Navy's Experimental Diving Unit compiled research into the problem. There were concerns that experimental long-duration, deep dives in hyperbaric chambers had triggered an increase in the incidence of decompression sickness under pressure. Men breathing mixes containing oxygen, helium and nitrogen were at particular risk. In a ten-year period, fifty-four divers suffered injuries during deco; nine were hit by severe symptoms affecting their central nervous system.

Sh-um! sh-um! sh-um! . . . Shh! Umm. Shhh! Ummm!

I've got to get out of this place, Robson thought.

Robson took control of his breathing, but he didn't move except to withdraw into himself. For a full minute, he was still. Behind his mask, he assessed his options, looking to swing the odds back in his favour. The fact was, it felt natural to him to be dispassionate, to rationalise and compute, because, if he wasn't restrained, he would be unnerved: by the slim chance of getting out of there in one piece, by the icy grip of the water seeping into his bones, by his dwindling supply of breathing gas, by the death exploding along his spinal column and taking with it any chance he might have of walking again.

An unnerved man would bolt. He would decide, right there and then, to take his chances on the surface where he would find sunlight and warmth, where comrades were waiting for him, where there was life. As far as Robson was concerned, the surface was no friend.

Shhh! Ummm! Shhh! Ummm! Shhh! Ummm!

Looking up, Robson followed the shot line until it blurred into the supernatural light from the surface above. He knew Khuazhev was there, probably stamping his feet to ward off the cold. Alongside him would be the EMERCOM medics who were on permanent standby. For all the comfort offered by the sanctuary of a warm, dry ambulance and healing dose of oxygen, Robson may as well have been on the dark side of the moon. Blocking his path was his decompression ceiling. If he broke through it, the heads-up display in front of his right eye would blink a furious red, and his computer would flash, alternating the word 'DOWN' with six arrows demanding he immediately change direction.

In Robson's mind, heading for the surface was like popping a bottle of champagne or opening a soda. If the 4,125 millilitres of carbon dioxide in a bottle of cola could shower people with 250 million bubbles, what would a volume of gas orders of magnitude greater do to his body? The bubbles in his spine would balloon to three-and-a-half times their current size. They would crush more of the signal-carrying fibres. The reduction in pressure would trigger a fresh bombardment. So many bubbles could erupt in his body that his blood would boil dry, leaving nothing behind but foam and froth. In all probability, his heart, brain or both would cease not long after the first breaths of fresh air made it to his lungs.

No, Robson wasn't going up; he already knew that. The idea of staying put also made him shudder. Time was no great healer underwater. By the time his decompression obligations had cleared, the sickness could have consumed him, the damage made permanent.

Robson didn't need science to tell him that, but the evidence was available. When the US Navy compiled statistics for injuries among its deep-diving test subjects in the 1970s, it listed the treatment each received. Tucked away in the register was accident file 4009. It related to an unnamed serviceman, a thirty-six-year-old member of the Navy Experimental Diving Unit. After a dive to 450 feet (137 m), the man was struck by neurological decompression sickness. Nothing was done to help him for 315 minutes – five-and-a-quarter hours – less time than Robson had left to go. When the diver was finally recompressed, he was taken down to fifty metres and left there for more than four hours. Not that it mattered. He never recovered the use of his legs.

Shhh! Ummm! Shhh! Ummm! Shhh! Ummm!

The elapsed dive time on Robson's computer clicked over a minute: 2-2-1. In that minute, his whole outlook had changed. Any fear he may have had dissolved. He wasn't living a nightmare. Not yet.

Ask any dive medic and they will tell you that of all the sport's habits, denial is the worst. Scuba divers will come up with all manner of creative and wilful ways to dismiss the notion that they have suffered a bend. The disorder can leave some confused, while others don't want to admit to their predicament because of what they think it says about their abilities. Admitting they are bent is akin to saying they can't hold their liquor. Robson wasn't one for denial. He stared down at his useless legs and he could see it all – I've ruled out A, ruled out B. It's got to be C. He didn't have a choice any more; he had identified the way out even if, to some, what he was thinking seemed like an act of suicidal madness. All Robson knew was that if he were to find salvation from his paralysis, it would be in the black hole beneath him. And that meant experimenting with a procedure that many in the mainstream diving community consider borders not so much on lunacy as invades it wholesale.

Sixty seconds after his legs were swept from under him, Robson prepared to let the deep take him.

The science behind the theory of in-water recompression is so obvious that many of its proponents question why the time hasn't come for the practice to be firmly embraced by the mainstream diving community. In simple terms, divers use the increasing pressure of the surrounding water at depth as a means of reducing the size of offending bubbles to the point of relief. That is precisely what recompression treatment in a hyperbaric chamber does. While both treatments use the same scientific principle, in-water recompression remains a controversial topic.

Yet, at one extreme is a small band of doctors who champion the practice as a legitimate emergency first response when immediate recompression chamber treatment is unavailable: a hyperbaric version of pumping the chest of someone in cardiac arrest before the electronic thump of defibrillation is delivered. There are those operating at the outer limits of diving who have, for years, brushed aside conventional medical advice and consider in-water recompression the best way of treating themselves in an emergency. There are no data that establish the benefits of in-water recompression when compared with conventional treatment. Anecdotally, however, strikingly good outcomes have been achieved with quick action, using short, shallow in-water recompression treatments. One panel of diving medicine experts concluded that in-water recompression using oxygen was an option for an injured diver trapped in a remote location without ready access to a hyperbaric chamber facility and showing significant or progressing symptoms threatening life or limb.

The practice of in-water recompression actually precedes the modern hyperbaric chamber. A hardscrabble Greek sponge diver, when paralysed, found submerging again helped the 'starting' of his limbs. Another man, stricken so deaf he could not even hear the clatter of the chain, recovered his hearing after diving again. The treatment was used by the Greek divers who moved to Florida in the late nineteenth century, and those who dived for black coral in Hawaii. Independently, pearl divers in Australia found that returning to depth helped treat their injuries. Even today, the abalone fishermen of Australia and the indigenous Sea Gypsies of Thailand, the Urak Lawoi, see it as a valuable cure for the bends.

Meanwhile, a study of the fishermen divers in Hawaii found almost 90 per cent recovered from injury following in-water recompression. In the 1980s, when Frank P. Farm Jr, then director of the Hyperbaric Treatment Centre at the University of Hawaii, saw a diver collapse on a boat, paralysed from the nipple line down, he strapped a tank to his back, rolled him over the side and dragged him underwater. When no benefit was seen at about ten metres down, Farm continued to descend. At fifteen metres, the victim gave an okay signal with his hand. He'd drained his first tank, and another was sent down to him.

The diver breathed that dry as well. When the boat slid back into the harbour that evening, the diver stepped off and swore the only difference from any other day was that he felt a little more tired than usual.

Then there was the case of two Hawaiian fishermen who developed severe symptoms of decompression sickness shortly after surfacing from their second dive of the day. The skipper throttled the boat for the harbour, thirty minutes away. One of the divers refused to go, and he rolled over the side of the boat with two scuba tanks to recompress underwater. When the captain returned two hours later to pick him up, the diver was, apparently, cured. His friend didn't make it. He died of severe decompression sickness in the medevac helicopter on the way to the recompression chamber.

Hardcore Hawaiian divers simply had a different mindset to the practice, according to deep-diving pioneer Richard L. Pyle. They were aware of the dangers of in-water recompression, but saw it as a viable option, one which had saved many lives, including their own. If they suffered a bend shortly after surfacing, there would seldom be much deliberation about getting back into the water.

Such experiences have not dislodged the conventional conviction: divers with signs of the bends should never, under any circumstances, be placed back in the water. Diving instruction manuals disapprove of the practice, and the Divers Alert Network does not currently recommend in-water recompression of any type. The idea of placing a person already suffering from a potentially debilitating disorder into a harsh and uncontrollable underwater environment is one stacked with dangers.

'As a doctor, my view is guided by the overriding principle in the Hippocratic Oath,' says Dr Francis. '*Primum non nocere*: First, do no harm. There is a list the length of your arm of hazards associated with in-water recompression. When this requires the patient to be stationary in cold water for many hours, the hazards of hypothermia outweigh any benefit, especially as there is no guarantee in-water recompression would result in a cure.'

Shhh! Ummm! Shhh! Ummm!

When Robson decided the deep offered his only salvation, it should have settled into his stomach like a heavy meal. Only, right then, there wasn't even a numb awareness he might be gambling with his life by going all in on his one hope. He was not thinking of what he needed to do to avoid dying, but what was necessary to cure himself. This was simply something he had to do, and there was no point wasting time agonising about it.

Robson let go of the line.

He seemed to hang motionless for one tense moment, gloved hand clasped in front of him, rag-doll legs dangling beneath him. Then came the pull of gravity. Robson began to sink. The light from the surface dimmed as the deep cast its black veil over him.

BETWEEN THE DEVIL AND THE DEEP

The dividing line between the successful and the not-so-lucky will not be seen on the ideal dive, but instead, on the dive that had a problem. The experienced diver will know how to react when things begin going badly, and will be better prepared to recover presence of mind in time to make the crucial decisions that will save his life. Only by allowing the unthinkable to enter into consideration can the serious cave diver expect to survive the unlikely.

R. D. Milhollin, 'Sheck Eckley's Razor:
The Nature of Limits', *Underwater Speleology*

His life was in free-fall. He could tell by the depth gauge on his working computer which flickered with increasing pace – 25, 26, 28; by the pressure squeezing his ears; by the way his dry suit compressed his body even though everything felt strange from the waist down. Beneath him, there was nothing but the dark discouragement of the deep.

It's going to be a big dive, Robson had told Vikki when they spoke on the telephone the night before.

Do you want to talk through the plan? she'd asked because they usually did when he was planning a big dive. But they hadn't discussed the details of the dive, maybe because he didn't want to worry her.

Now Robson could only watch the shot line zip past his eyes as the grim reality of his situation came crashing in. There was no question he would have preferred to have been anywhere else at that moment, but he wasn't. He was in a situation that he knew needed to be addressed immediately and that's all he was focused on. He had staked everything on heading down, and the descent was all he thought about. That way, he could anticipate what was coming. He needed to head deeper. Deeper increased the pressure around him. Deeper crushed the bubbles in his spine. Deeper gave him a chance of restoring movement to his legs, and if he could move his legs there was a chance he might, in every sense, walk away from this.

Trailing close behind was Roman Dunaev. He was the only one to move. Having seen Robson flip in the water, he'd had a sinking feeling. He'd swum over to Robson and asked if he was okay. He'd understood it when Robson had responded with a gladiatorial thumbs-down. I'm descending, it said. Anyone else might have thought the decision crazy, but the Russian hadn't tried to second-guess his friend; he decided there was nothing he could do at that point but follow him. 'The only thing I knew for sure was that I must stay with Martin till the end,' he says. 'I wouldn't leave him alone for any reason.'

The only thing that concerned Dunaev was the cold water.

The temperature of the water had not registered with Robson. His mind was trying to calculate other issues. Having decided he was trapped between the devil and the deep, he had little idea when the benefits of free-fall would kick in. He didn't worry himself with the question, when will it work? His only thought was to continue plunging through the water until it did.

Since the pathological mechanics of decompression sickness in the central nervous system are still open to debate, no one can say with any degree of certainty what was going on in Robson's spine as he descended. Scientists, though, have a hard-thought theory that depicts one such frightful scene: following the explosive bubbling event, the spinal column is pockmarked with ovoid lesions. Around these cavities, large numbers of axons lie dead, displaced or damaged, and the microcirculation has been disrupted and distorted. As Robson descends and the bubbles begin to compress, blood flows into the hollows and swamps more tissue. These haemorrhages are known as non-staining, space-occupying lesions. In a low-power cross-section of an injured spinal cord, they have the appearance of incoming fireballs, jagged areas of blood surrounding the circular bubble crater.

Evidence to support the theory can be found in a handful of medical journals, some dating back more than a century. In 1908, Graham Blick, the district medical officer for Broome, Western Australia, compiled one of the most extensive cata-logues of autopsies on divers claimed by the bends. For eight years, Blick covered the largest pearl diving industry in the world. In that time, he was called to treat 200 men with the bends. Sixty died of their injuries before he'd even arrived at their bedside. Cutting open the dead, Blick found sections of the spinal cord that looked semi-disintegrated. Probing further, he noticed the presence of haemorrhage. Some were mere points

227

of blood. Others were so large they had practically cut the cord in two.

In 1980, doctors examined the body of a British diver who, four years earlier, had suffered decompression sickness after a rapid ascent from thirty metres. The bend should have crippled him, doctors thought, but he seemed to make a full recovery, even though his legs trembled in cold weather. Following his death, which was unrelated to diving, doctors performed a post-mortem examination and found multiple areas of dead tissue up and down his spine, the damage so bad the doctors thought it remarkable he had recovered in the first place.

In the *Long Island Medical Journal* of April 1907, Harlow Brooks MD outlined the findings of a post-mortem examination of a caisson worker who died thirteen hours after being para-lysed from the navel down from decompression sickness. On opening the spinal canal, Brooks wrote, he found large quanti-ties of blood and serum. The veins of the spinal canal were congested, and haemorrhages were numerous. Even though they were small, Brooks concluded that it was beyond question that their appearance in the spinal cord was sufficient to kill a man.

About thirty-three metres down, Robson clenched his arm tight against the shot line and brought himself to a halt. Dunaev sig-nalled to see if everything was okay. Robson shook his head: he was facing another pressing problem. During the descent, the tank he used to add gas to his dry suit had emptied. Under the pressure of the water, the material squeezed him like shrink wrap on a slab of supermarket beef.

Examining his bailout tanks, Dunaev found one with a hose attachment and hooked the cylinder to the inflator valve on his friend's dry suit. Robson then flooded his suit with gas, bringing his buoyancy under control. As he did this, a curious thing happened. His legs moved. It was curious not so much because his legs were working – the in-water recompression protocol was designed with that end in mind – but because it was as if someone had just turned them back on. And, for a brief moment, it felt good to dream, to hope, that maybe he had been wrong all along, because if he were, it would mean he wasn't bent, and instead of suffering a debilitating injury, maybe his suit had flooded.

Why hadn't I figured it out before?

Icy water pooling in the legs of his suit would explain why his suit had been weighed down and his limbs chilled to the point of numbness.

While the idea was encouraging, Robson knew deep down that it was futile optimism: nice day, fluffy clouds, just a dry suit squeeze. He couldn't escape the fact that his thighs ached, his joints were stiff, and his skin prickled with an unusual sensation he'd not felt before. He knew he was bent.

The increased pressure of deeper water had put a squeeze on the gas bubbles responsible for his paralysis, and that had relieved the pressure on the signal-carrying axons. Those not obliterated had flickered into life and were spitting signals from his brain to his legs. The bubbles were still there, though. Waiting. Lurking. To wash them away, he needed to breathe pure oxygen. The only problem was that breathing pure oxygen was confined to the shallows and the regulator which supplied it was thirty metres above him, at the end of a hose dangling from a hook inside the habitat.

Even though his legs were working again, Robson still hugged the shot line with both arms. Hovering little more than an arm's length away, Dunaev removed the weight of bailout cylinders from Robson's equipment, to help make things easier for him. Still, he wanted some way to fix Robson to the line. Seeing a strobe light on his rebreather, he hit upon an idea to jerry-rig a tether. Attached to the beacon was an ascender, the mechanical equivalent of a friction knot favoured by climbers. Fixed to a rope, the device would run freely in one direction but, once weight was applied, would grip if pulled in the other. Clipped to the shot line, Dunaev reasoned, it could give Robson a foothold.

Pulling a loop of cord from his pocket, Dunaev fashioned a knot around the device. The effort took him a few minutes because his fingers were numbed. When he finished, Dunaev fastened the ascender to the shot line and snapped the other end to a D-ring on Robson's harness. Relinquishing his grip of the line, Robson allowed himself to drift a few feet away from the line until the leash snapped taut. The *Shhh! Ummm!* of his breathing calmed and his morale spiked. Less than five minutes after the deep had taken hold of his legs, Robson had regained a semblance of control.

Looking to Dunaev, he gave a thumbs-up and reached for the ascender. When it came to move upwards, all Robson had to do was slide the device along the line. He could let go during stops because the locking action of the device prevented it from slipping. Robson began to climb towards the surface.

Settled into the rhythm of ascent, Robson pumped his legs. The more he moved them, the more they seemed to want to move. Things were not right, though. They worked, in a fashion, but only under duress.

Despite the new air of optimism, Robson wasn't thinking about his future: too many unknowns for that. He wasn't thinking about much beyond the actions in front of him. The only thing he was confident of, though, was his desire to survive. I'm not going to let myself die here, underwater, he told himself.

He'd seen his share of death over the years. Once, he and a fellow diver were called to raise the body of a deceased diver from Little River cave in Florida. Underwater, Robson tried to ignore the waxy face and glassy eyes of the victim. On land, he couldn't help but notice the grim details of a man's last moments: his mask full of frothy blood, mud under the fingernails. On another occasion, Robson was in an ice hut warming up after a dive in Finland when a fellow diver flung open the door. We need your help, the man said. Robson made it outside just as an unconscious diver was hauled out of the water and onto the ice in front of his tearful wife. Robson ordered two divers to cut away the victim's dry suit and begin cardiopulmonary resuscitation while he prepared the emergency oxygen. He then intubated the casualty to establish an airway. By the time the ambulance arrived, they had managed to get a pulse. The diver lived for a few days in hospital before dying and Robson was troubled by the thought that his actions had given the man's wife false hope. He was determined not to put Vikki through such a trauma, but he couldn't escape the feeling that he had let her down.

So, he continued his climb to the surface. Advancing upwards, centimetre by centimetre, at the end of his leash.

The shot line Robson was attached to went to a surface buoy. To reach the habitat, he needed to swim twenty-odd metres and switch to another vertical line. Given his condition, he didn't want to be untethered from the line. If the bend hit again and he had nothing to grab for support, he'd tumble, end-over-end, towards the cliff edge, clawing at the water to stop himself sinking. In a flurry of hand signals, Robson asked Dunaev to run a horizontal line between the two vertical shots so that he would have an unbroken guideline to follow.

Looking up, Dunaev could see the silhouette of support divers hovering overhead, Valkyrian figures against the flawless surface. Flicking his torch from side to side, Dunaev beckoned them towards him. He unclipped a reel from his harness and fastened the end to the shot line. Then he handed the reel to one of the divers and signalled for them to run the line up to the habitat.

While this was going on, Robson spied another length of cord running off to his left. This one trailed off to a set of old decompression bars installed some years previously for divers to hang onto while finishing their dives. As the support divers swam off towards the habitat, Robson beckoned Dunaev and signalled for him to watch. Unclipping himself from the ascender, Robson stared hard at the bars in the distance. Moving his legs, he propelled himself along the nylon trail. It wasn't perfect, but he covered the distance. Reaching the bars, he used his fins to turn himself in a tight circle like a helicopter and finned back to the start point.

His legs were heavy, but they worked.

He repeated the swim a couple of times, better to understand, with Dunaev's help, how crazy his legs looked. No matter how hard he fought to convince himself everything was fine, Robson knew it wasn't. They still felt wet and cold, and he couldn't shake the unease which accompanied the wave of pinpricks rippling their length. Deep down, he suspected the bubbles would rebound at some point; there was little he could do but wait.

There was no question he would sooner be out of the water if he had the choice. But a choice was the one thing Robson didn't have. In the gamble for his life, he didn't have another card to play. The only one in his hand was 'stay in the water'; 'I want to get out of the water' wasn't in the deck, it just didn't exist.

He'd been here before, frigid in the glacial grasp of water and wishing he could be anywhere else. At the end of a deep penetration dive into Durzon, Robson had sat at twenty-three metres, battered by cold with hours of decompression still to do, when he began to waver. I can't do this, he thought. But decompression wasn't optional, as in: 'Would you like to do some deco?' 'Well, not today.' He didn't have a choice then. He didn't have a choice now.

From his position in shallow water, peering down into the deep, Vladimir Grigoriev watched Robson inch his way towards the habitat and knew something was wrong. He had taken up his position, fifteen metres down, ready to support Robson in the shallows. Strapped to his harness were two heavy sidemount cylinders. The eighteen-litre tanks were cumbersome items, but they were big enough to sustain life at this depth for hours. Hovering there, Grigoriev could see a disorganised mess. Below him, he'd only expected to see another diver with Robson. But there were four or five others crowded around him. Some were carrying his bailout cylinders. Meanwhile, Dunaev was still there, ascending close to Robson, when he should have been long gone. Everything about the picture looked out of place.

Grigoriev, forty-two, had been introduced to diving by his maternal grandfather, Vasily, as a nine-year-old. Vasily was a chief engineer for an oil company in what is now Kazakhstan. One summer, he strapped a scuba tank to his grandson and took him beneath the surface of the Caspian Sea. After that, Grigoriev felt destined for a life in the business. He ran a travel agency for a while, owned a dive centre in Moscow and a dive charter boat somewhere warmer, and he designed Arctic survival suits for the military. He had, apparently, come up with the idea of the Blue Lake expedition, but had been in Sri Lanka, guiding a tour group with his business partner, Dimitri Biskup, when everything started in early January. Then he got the news about Rodionov's death. He'd packed his gear into a car and driven down to Blue Lake to help with the final dive. His job was to help Robson into the habitat. He had volunteered to assist with the dive, even though he was still recovering from a fractured shoulder blade.

Looking down on the rabble of divers, their bubbles thundering to the surface, Grigoriev guessed something was wrong, but he couldn't quite work out what it was. 'It wasn't obvious that Martin had a problem with his legs,' he says. 'His trim wasn't perfect, it was usually perfect, but then it wasn't perfect.

Sometimes, when people have been in the water for a long time, and they are tired, their movements can look strange.'

But everyone else seemed to be working from another dive plan, and that meant something *had* gone wrong. So, he stayed there, keeping a respectful distance, ready to act if needed, and watched Robson make his way to the habitat.

When he got there, a support diver plugged an umbilical power cable into Robson's dry suit. Connected to the mains, the cable buzzed with warmth as it delivered power to his heated undersuit. Then Robson did something that surprised Grigoriev: he came off his rebreather and reached for the regulator attached to the emergency oxygen tank.

Switching from his rebreather to the open-circuit regulator was an environmental awakener to Robson; suddenly the sound of his breathing had been cranked several notches to a roar as exhaled bubbles spilled from his mouth and rolled towards the surface. The high pressure of the delivery also meant the gas was cold and dry, wicking moisture from his mouth and heat from his body. Still, he sucked it up because it was doing him good.

The support divers watched as Robson pulled himself over the metal platform, his actions mirrored in the still moon pool above him until disturbed by the exhaust bubbles from his regulator. Photographer Viktor Lyagushkin appeared at the other side of the platform with his camera and pointed it towards Robson, pinging off a few frames. Robson pulled a white slate from his pocket. On it were the words he'd scrawled after leaving the bottom: Для Андрей 209 m – For Andrei 209 m – and Lyagushkin took another picture.

Continuing, Robson managed to kneel and then stand, his head breaking the surface of the air-filled capsule. Standing upright for the first time in hours, Robson felt the combined weight of his equipment press down through his weakened legs. They held him upright, but they didn't feel right. In the dark waters below him a support diver removed his fins one at a time and handed them up. Then Robson lifted himself onto the seat.

Roman Dunaev waited for a moment and then settled in to finish the final minutes of his decompression obligation. He had been with Robson longer than planned and had shepherded him as far as he could. He was chilled, and he needed to get out of the water. 'I was thinking only about Martin's life, and it helped me not to worry about my problems,' he says. 'I didn't realise how cold I was.'

For Grigoriev, meanwhile, watching all this happening in front of him, there came an awful recognition that Robson was in trouble.

He turned for the surface to get help.

Six metres above, Dimitri Biskup stood alone on the platform outside the dive centre trying to stay warm. From his position, he could see down through the clear water to the silhouettes of divers moving around the habitat. There seemed to be a lot of bubbles on the surface, but Dimitri was relaxed. He'd been due to dive that afternoon but had pulled out feeling sick. When Grigoriev had volunteered to take his place, he'd found something else to do.

As the dive began, Dimitri had taken a spot at the water's edge and he'd been there all afternoon. To help keep things on track, he referred to the whiteboard which sat on top of a row of diving cylinders by the entrance to the dive centre. Written in black marker pen were the initials of each support team along with the depth and the time they were scheduled to meet Robson. A third column was headed 'To Tell', and listed the times each dive team was to receive their countdown to enter the water. There were reminders to turn on the power and oxygen to the habitat and someone had noted the menu: soup, a cutlet, fruit salad, red wine.

With so many moving parts, this was a serious dive, and Dimitri knew it. If everything went as planned, though, he figured Robson and the support teams would be back on the surface soon enough.

All but one of the support teams had been committed when Dimitri spotted a lone diver a few metres down and moving towards the concrete steps. When he saw the sidemount cylinders, he immediately recognised Grigoriev. Seconds later, his friend surfaced at his feet and removed his regulator.

We have a problem, he said. I think Martin is in trouble. We need oxygen.

Dimitri didn't have time to consider the ramifications of what he'd just been told. There was certainly no time to reflect on causes, because no one on the surface had any idea what had happened underwater. So, he did what he was asked and went to fetch a cylinder of pure oxygen.

At the same time, Grigoriev replaced one of his sidemount cylinders. Anticipating he could be underwater for some time, he decided to load up on breathing gas.

The appearance of Grigoriev brought more people outside

and they began to wonder whether there was something they needed to be doing. Handing the cylinder down to his friend, Dimitri asked: shall we call MChS (the national search and rescue service)?

Grigoriev couldn't answer. He didn't yet know what the problem was.

Two lifelines, a power cable and an oxygen hose snaked from the surface, through water and into the habitat where Robson sat. He was weary. He had slipped out of his rebreather and curled into the seat, his legs lifted free of the water. The warmth emitting from his heated undersuit was a welcome relief. Only then did he allow himself a moment of solace. It was hard to believe he had made it this far when just a few hours earlier he had been fighting against the paralysing grip of the decompression sickness.

In the time it took him to climb inside, Robson's whole outlook had changed. He no longer feared losing control of his legs again. Now he dared to think he could make it to the end of the dive in one piece. Perhaps his legs didn't feel sound, but, right there and then, Robson could have been forgiven for thinking: I've made it. Now he thought that a precautionary press in a recompression chamber might be enough.

The electric light inside the habitat bounced off the white plastic walls and burned so bright that Robson had to close his eyes. He couldn't avoid the echo of his breathing as he inhaled oxygen from the open-circuit regulator. When he exhaled, the excess gas bubbled from the moon pool and the plastic sanctuary shook around him. Coming from a compressed gas cylinder on

238

the surface, the oxygen was cold, and he felt the chill in his lungs, but it was doing him good. Robson breathed slow and deep, and let his mind wander.

At some point, Robson removed the oxygen regulator and went back onto his rebreather to give his body a break from breathing high levels of O2.

Having switched, Robson settled back on the seat and closed his eyes. He relaxed and the minutes began to drift by. Then something happened inside his body that jerked him from his daydream. Robson's legs shuddered, and he cursed.

A lightning strike of pain shot up his left leg. His right leg flared almost as bad. The pain was unbearable. He could still use his legs, but every movement was accompanied by an incomprehensible agony, like the worst kind of cramp magnified beyond reason. Things were not playing out according to the neat script inside his head. The pain was a point of clarity, a defining moment in the midst of the attack, and Robson's internal voice commanded him, clearly and sharply: get back underwater now.

Robson removed the full-face oxygen mask from its stowage hook. The set looked similar to the breathing apparatus he had used as a firefighter – an exoskeleton frame encasing a visor and regulator, and a silicone skirt sealed against the face. Holding the mask to his face, Robson took a couple of breaths to ensure it was working and then he pulled the spider strap over his head. Swinging his legs from the bench with gritted teeth, Robson pushed his fins out ahead of him and splashed into the water.

Robson's appearance must have come as a shock to the two support divers hovering outside the habitat. In the white glow of their torches, he came sprawling onto the platform, clawing for a handhold and venting gas from the dump valve on his shoulder.

Holding himself down, Robson looked for the emergency weight belt that was fastened to the platform for such eventualities. The belt was threaded through large lead weights to prevent a diver popping to the surface if they were forced for whatever reason to leave the habitat without their equipment on.

Dazzled by light from the habitat, he couldn't see the faces of the divers who approached, and had no idea who was there to help him. He pointed first to the weight belt, and then to his waist. No one moved. Robson gesticulated again, stabbing his finger at the belt and then his waist again.

Finally, the divers reacted. One reached for Robson's fins and clipped them to his feet. The second diver dragged the belt over Robson's hips but fumbled with the buckle. C'mon, Robson silently pleaded, as the diver struggled to cinch the belt tight. Once it was fastened, Robson dragged himself clear of the platform. With all that weight around his wrist, he plummeted from the habitat, into the twilight waters below. The nine-metre oxygen hose and the power cable unspooled above him. Robson felt the jolt as they twanged taut and he popped upright into the water.

Dangling, like a puppet on a string, from a hose nine metres down, Robson sucked hard on the oxygen, the cold gas flooding him with euphoria. What he was feeling was relief at being in the best possible position to force the bubbles into submission. What he was hearing, as the oxygen hissed into the mask with each breath, was danger. The very thing Robson had hoped to avoid by taking an air break had now become his new reality.

To some in the medical profession, oxygen is a slasher. In much the same way as people might describe themselves as a writer/ fitness trainer/nutritionist, oxygen is a multifaceted molecule that has a myriad of effects on the body, good/bad. On the surface, under normal barometric pressure, oxygen is the chief component in the process that sustains life. The body needs the chemical element to fuel the engine of the cells. We cannot survive without it. There is, however, a downside to breathing oxygen over a sustained period. It is, according to one physiologist, a chemically promiscuous element, because it's always on the lookout for other chemical components with which to mate. The resulting interactions form highly reactive materials known as free radicals, super-oxides and radical anions – body rust – that interfere with the physiological processes of the body.

Divers, perhaps more than most, recognise that oxygen doesn't always wear a white hat. When the concentration of oxygen is increased, say under pressure when underwater, more body rust is produced. The toxic effects of high-pressure oxygen can be likened to acute poisoning, a multi-system, multi-organ prejudice which affects the lungs, the eyes, the bone marrow, the kidneys, the gonads and the liver. The particular strain divers are alive to is known as central nervous system oxygen toxicity. Sufferers can encounter cerebral changes, visual blurring, a tinnitus-like ringing in the ears, nausea, facial twitches and the dizziness of vertigo. The unequivocal endpoint of oxygen toxicity is a convulsion, which can strike without warning. Having a convulsion underwater is the last stop on the line before death; unless you are wearing a diving helmet there is a good chance you will lose your mouthpiece and drown. There are some divers who admit that getting decompression sickness, while not fun, is not something to be feared. But an oxygen hit? Seeing video footage of someone getting a hit is enough to scare the hell out of them.

The human body can tolerate higher than normal pressure of oxygen for a short time before it transforms from Dr Jekyll to Mr Hyde. How much can be tolerated was determined by a British doctor, Kenneth W. Donald, during the Second World War, when the Royal Navy wanted to develop charioteers to pilot torpedoes. At the time, covert divers used rudimentary oxygen rebreathers and were restricted to a maximum depth of thirty-three feet. The navy brass needed to determine if they could go deeper and the search for the limits of safe oxygen use took on an extreme urgency. A cadre of volunteer divers was dunked in a wet pot, a modified submarine escape apparatus which was partially filled with water, sealed and pressurised to simulate different depths. The divers breathed pure oxygen for predetermined periods, and Donald noted the effects on their body. The first test divers were sent down to fifty feet for thirty minutes, and one in four were hauled out unconscious after convulsing. The next diver up often had to step over the last casualty in order to take his turn in the pot. Donald's work demonstrated that the dangers of breathing pure oxygen under pressure were far greater than previously thought and made diving on pure oxygen below twenty-five feet of seawater a hazardous gamble.

Over the following half-century, the restrictions were tweaked and changed on the basis of experience and observations. Eventually, the National Oceanic and Atmospheric Administration (NOAA) in the US laid down limits which remain the standard for recreational scuba divers.

The amount of exposure it takes to produce oxygen poisoning is basically a function of the partial pressure of the gas in a particular breathing mix, its percentage represented as a fraction of atmospheres absolute (ata). Normal breathing air contains 21 per cent oxygen and under normal atmospheric conditions has a partial pressure of 0.21 ata. With an increase in pressure comes an increase in gas density and divers then enter a state of hyperoxia. Ten metres down, where the pressure is two atmospheres, the partial pressure of oxygen in the air is 0.42 ata. A scientific analysis of data on oxygen toxicity found that for all symptoms of central nervous system toxicity, 1.3 ata was the threshold, with convulsions appearing once the partial pressure reached a threshold of 1.7 ata. The Oxygen Exposure limits published by NOAA reined in the acceptable limits to 1.6 ata. That's why, these days, sport divers consider the idea of breathing air beyond a depth of sixty-six metres as too dangerous.

With pure oxygen, then, which has a partial pressure of one atmosphere at the surface, the risk of oxygen toxicity is reached in as little as six metres. To monitor their exposure, divers look to the 'Oxygen Clock' which states the single dose they can take. With exposure to 1.6 ata, the clock ticks more than three times faster than one of 1.4 ata. A diver breathing pure oxygen at six metres reaches their maximum dosage after forty-five minutes.

Like most things in diving, however, the line to mark the absolute limit between safe and unsafe might not be so fixed. That there might be some wiggle room, particularly for expedition-level deep divers whose oxygen use during long decompression runs far exceeds the recognised guidelines, all depends on the circumstances, of course. And with so many interactions going on in the body, it's hard to finesse the data. The retention of carbon dioxide is considered a major risk factor for oxygen toxicity. Working hard, particularly at depth where the simple act of breathing is harder because the gas is denser, is enough to raise the carbon dioxide levels in the blood. This results in a marked increase in blood flow and the delivery of higher than normal limits of oxygen to the brain tissue. That's when the toxicity of oxygen spikes. When it comes to resting in the shallows on a long decompression stop, research shows there is no trend of carbon dioxide retention. Arguably then, so the theory goes, the risk to a decompressing diver of exceeding the oxygen limits is not as significant when they are in the shallows as it would be if they were in the deep. It's not enough to throw out the oxygen limits, but it's enough of a subtlety to help those breathing beyond them.

For the majority of divers, the NOAA oxygen exposure recommendations remain a conservative and well-respected limit. Unfortunately, for others, the idea of measuring exposure to oxygen can give them a false sense of security. Researchers have recorded an extreme variation of tolerance not just among divers, but also for the same individual from one day to the next. Donald found one of his test subjects convulsed after spending twelve minutes on oxygen at fifty feet, but then completed a hundred minutes at the same depth without suffering any symptoms two weeks later. Six days after that, he again convulsed at fifty feet, but after completing more than thirty-two minutes underwater.

Dangling at the end of the hose, Robson shivered in the cold water and sucked on the oxygen as if his life depended on it. By the time he had steadied himself, his exposure to oxygen was already enough to push him into hostile territory.

The dose of central nervous system toxicity is measured in percentage terms, and, according to Robson's plan, his dive was pushing more than four times the recommended safe limit before things took a turn. He had also maxed out on the second measure of poisoning, known by divers as units of pulmonary toxicity dose, or oxygen toxicity units. These measure the effects of oxygen exposure on the body over the medium term. One unit is earned by breathing pure oxygen at one atmosphere for one minute. Conservative limits suggest an average daily exposure of between 300 and 850 units per day depending on the diving one is doing. Under Robson's original dive plan, he was due to rack up more than 1,000 units.

And yet there he was, breathing pure oxygen at nine metres, trying to rationalise his decision as a necessary consequence of his predicament. He needed to be there to subdue the painful effects of decompression sickness. Still, things felt as though they could spin off into the deep at any moment because this was the end of a path of narrowing options which had left Robson with two choices: stay or go. There was nothing in between. If he stayed there, he risked suffering a convulsion; if he ascended, he feared he could lose his legs.

Robson might have been disappointed that the choice he had made, to dive deep at the end of a long fortnight, had put him in a position where he now had to pile risk upon risk to stop things unravelling further. As far as he was concerned, he needed to stay. He'd computed the risks and decided to take his chances breathing oxygen. The furthest Robson would realistically look was the next minute, and, if he survived, to the minute after that. And so on. He hung there, breathed oxygen and examined himself for any sign or symptom of poisoning. Looking at the computer on his wrist, Robson read the digits on the dive time and quickly calculated how long he had been there. One minute. His vision was okay. There was no ringing in his ears, just the wheeze of ice-cold gas coming into his mask as he inhaled, and the rolling thunder of escaping bubbles as he exhaled. Twitching? His facial muscles weren't trembling. Nor did he feel dizzy.

Robson looked at his computer. Two minutes.

Breathing slow and deep, Robson spotted a halo of light from above. The appearance surprised him. Visual disturbances? He blinked. The beam was brighter, closer. In the darkness, he could make out the individual LEDs showering him with light. It was the first real evidence that he was not alone, and he realised one of the support divers had followed him down. Three minutes. He couldn't make out who he was, the darkness shrouded the diver's identity, but someone was with him.

Eduard Khuazhev had been stationed near the habitat, in the darkness of the lake, when he saw Martin Robson drop into the water. Ordinarily, Khuazhev hovered just outside, watching and waiting. At times like that, he might be able to see the fuzzy outline of Robson relaxing inside, silhouetted by the light, like an embryo in a sac. He'd stay there on standby until he was relieved by another support diver. He'd never had to do anything before and hadn't been expecting to have to do anything now.

This time was different: his friend was in free-fall. Khuazhev felt his heart sink as he watched Robson crash through the moon pool without a rebreather on his back and plunge towards the plateau beneath the habitat. Battling fear and confusion, Khauzhev kicked after him.

As he followed the hose, through the dark waters beneath him, Khuazhev saw Robson hanging at the end, and he was worried, chiefly because Robson wasn't wearing any equipment. That meant he was lighter than usual, and Khuazhev thought Robson might pop to the surface, carried by the air trapped in his dry suit, trailing the hoses like a child's balloon. Perhaps he hadn't realised Robson was weighed down by the emergency weight belt, so he finned in from behind and did the strangest of things. He wrapped his arms around his friend in a bear hug. He'd be his anchor.

Robson was conscious, Khuazhev had worked that out. He couldn't see his face but could tell from the bubbles that burst from the mask at regular intervals. The Russian had been through technical diver training and understood, theoretically, what was going on with Robson. But this was the most severe incident he'd ever seen, and he held on tight.

Robson looked at the luminescent glow of his computer handset. Four minutes. All his movements became slow and deliberate. Five minutes. He mentally examined his body for anything that might worry him. Except for his legs, of course; they still throbbed. Six minutes. They weren't useless, though. He could still move them. Seven minutes. He mentally examined his body again. Eight minutes.

Battling the cold which clawed at his body, Robson knew if he suffered an oxygen hit now, nine minutes in, he would convulse. Ten minutes. For someone who hated looking at the time on his computer, Robson had become transfixed, and for the first time he asked himself how long he should give himself down here. Eleven minutes. Each fresh breath now came with an expectation that it might kick-start a chain reaction that would only end one way, with him flopping at the end of the hose like a hooked fish. Twelve minutes. Hopefully, he'd still be wearing the full-face mask when the tremors subsided. Thirteen minutes. Robson started to question how long he could stay put. Another minute. The pain which had shot through his legs had all but vanished, to be replaced by a deep-seated ache.

Just one more minute. What's one more minute? Robson wouldn't know if it hit him anyway. He'd be unconscious in seconds, and after that, he might be dead, a splatter on the windscreen of nature's juggernaut. Others would know, though. Khuazhev would have a front-row seat to his demise, and his friends above would bear witness to it. Someone would have to tell Vikki. Fifteen minutes. He knew what oxygen toxicity could do to him; he'd witnessed a few central nervous system hits in his time. Sixteen minutes. Once the first spasm hit, his mind would check out. Seventeen minutes. He would stare ahead blankly, unresponsive. Eighteen minutes. An arm or a leg might twitch. Nineteen minutes. Then he would drift in and out of consciousness. Twenty minutes. Robson wasn't prepared to wait for that to happen. The lake had taken enough from him. Robson decided it was time to swim slowly up towards the sanctuary of the habitat. At least his legs still worked. For now.

After collecting a spare oxygen cylinder and a hot drink for Robson, Vladimir Grigoriev descended. From his position, five metres down, he could see Robson, silhouetted by the light, curled up inside the habitat. The Russian had been at the surface when Robson had bailed out on the oxygen face mask, and by the time he made it back underwater the immediate drama had passed and Robson had returned. Everything now seemed quiet and still.

He swam up to the habitat and clipped the spare oxygen cylinder to one side. Then he knelt on the platform beneath the moon pool entrance and popped his head inside.

His appearance seemed to surprise Robson.

Grigoriev passed him the waterproof bottle containing tea, and the two men looked at each other for a moment. Robson removed a notebook from his pocket, scribbled a message in pencil and handed it over. Grigoriev understood the message: Decompression not going well.

He scribbled a reply and handed the slate back to Robson. Beneath Robson's message, he had written: We know. The ambulance is ready.

Then, just like that, Grigoriev disappeared.

Grigoriev then took up a spot just outside the habitat, hovering. He hung there as other divers breathed through their cylinders and cycled in and out of the water, until he couldn't remember anyone else being alongside him. The cold water pricked at his body, but he didn't feel it. He was wearing a double-thickness insulation suit beneath his dry suit.

Robson's message had confirmed what he had been thinking since he saw the first signs of something wrong in the disordered group of divers ascending some while back. He knew things were not looking good, but all he could do was watch the habitat and wait to see what happened next. Breathe and wait. Just stay cool and be ready, that was how he approached the task, and when it's time to react, make everything as swift as possible.

The habitat glowed white and cast an eerie light in the water.

Inside, Martin Robson was in a mess. The plunge on oxygen had taken the pain from his legs, but they still didn't feel right. He'd been diving for so long, little now surprised him, yet nothing had prepared him for this. He was exhausted. The whole episode had pushed him to his physical limits, and he had no idea when it would stop. The temptation to say he'd had enough was huge. Only Robson wasn't going to wrap his hand in. Wrap his hand in was marine-speak for quit, and Robson was no quitter, no matter how much he wanted to be out of there. He simply accepted that his survival depended on being realistic about his position: assess the situation and take proactive decisions to improve it, promptly.

A hyperbaric doctor might tell him to take his chances and go for the surface, with a reasonable expectation he could make it there in one piece. If a helicopter was on standby to whisk him to the nearest hyperbaric facility, and everything was lined up in his favour, Robson could find himself getting treatment within an hour.

Looking at the time to surface readouts on his computers, Robson knew the values were as good as useless. 'As much use as a duck's udder' is how one hyperbaric doctor described the decompression information. No decompression algorithm has been developed to take a bend into account. There was no mathematical model that could come close to predicting how big a reservoir of inert gas was still washing around Robson's system. 'If the computer algorithm didn't know he had a bend – and how would it? – he couldn't believe what was on the screen,' says Dr James Francis. 'Any advice it gave about how much of a decompression obligation was left was, at that point, just arrant nonsense.

'I wouldn't be at all surprised if what happened while he was breathing oxygen was that many, if not most, of the bubbles would have shrunk. But there would still have been bubbling in his circulation when he moved to the surface. The bubbles that had not disappeared would start to grow again, and he would get a new onset of symptoms. There could have been a lot of bubbles in his lungs and showers of arterial bubble emboli.'

A night in a recompression chamber was inescapable now, Robson thought. With that uppermost in his mind, he began to prepare a checklist of things that he needed to do, the steps he would take to give himself a fighting chance. He still had enough gas in his rebreather to descend again. He would put that on, unhook the power cable heating his suit, and drop into the water. He would inch his way to the surface, taking as long as his body could cope with the cold. He would give the bubbles another squeeze, one last push to buy himself some time – and time was the only asset he could bank right then – at the surface to get treatment. Having analysed his options, Robson moved, promptly.

Grigoriev, still hovering in the spot he had taken outside the habitat, saw Robson drop into the water, which he expected to come at some point. He knew Robson was in a bad way, and exiting the habitat meant he was not comfortable. But when Robson plunged to the plateau sixteen metres below, it surprised him. Why was he heading down? Grigoriev didn't try to answer the question. His only response was: he's out. Okay, I need to follow him.

Grigoriev stuck to him like a shadow.

The beam from Robson's torch sliced through the darkness and he followed the habitat mooring line down to the bottom. He paused there for a while and assessed his body. He took several deep breaths and tried to work his legs. He could move them, but they felt odd and the sensation, like the cold, wouldn't leave him. Once he was ready, he started upwards, clinging to the contours of the bank as it rose steeply to the surface. Unplugged from the mains, and with no power feed into the suit, his undergarments soon lost their heat. The bitter grip of the lake began to take hold of Robson's body and squeezed any other thought from his mind. Just a few more minutes, he told himself. Robson's survival was now a matter of holding out for as long as possible; to give himself a fighting chance, he told himself. A few more minutes.

On the surface, the support divers couldn't believe how

Robson managed to withstand the cold. It seemed, Bogdana later wrote in a magazine article about the incident, that Robson had anti-freeze coursing through his body.

Underwater, the cold still clawed under Robson's skin and reached deep into his body. He was running on empty but he still stayed put. Just a few more minutes.

Robson had done all he could to fight the disorder and now kicked towards the glow radiating from above. He surfaced into a pool of bright lights and television cameras. He closed the mouthpiece of his breathing loop and let it flop around his neck. Then he just floated there, not moving.

All eyes were on him.

At the water's edge, Dimitri Biskup leaned down to him. How are you feeling?

I'm okay, Robson replied.

Do you need anything?

Just a moment to relax and something to drink.

Dimitri filled a metal cup with hot tea or water and handed it to Robson, who still hadn't moved.

If anyone expected him to rush from the water, they were mistaken; Robson wasn't in a rush to do anything. He took a drink from the cup, passed it back, moved to the steps and prepared to climb from the water. Just before he did, he looked at the newsman with the camera on his shoulder and said: I don't want you to film this.

A week earlier, Robson had watched the nightly news broadcast of Andrei Rodionov's death. A three-second close-up of his body floating at the surface featured in the report. That sat uncomfortably with Robson, and he didn't want any footage of him shuffling from the water to appear on television.

Would you mind turning off your cameras?

The newsman nodded and lowered the camera.

Robson removed his fins, and then shuffled out of the water. Each footstep was deliberate, but he didn't need help; he stepped from the lake in the same way as he had done after every dive. Water spilled from his equipment and sloshed on the floor. As Robson continued into the dive centre, someone held him by the hand and guided him to his spot on the bench.

Robson sat there for a minute or two without saying anything, and everyone looked at him, worried and uncertain. They all knew what had to be done to help him, and they couldn't quite believe he was taking so long. Then, Robson shrugged off his equipment and changed from his diving suit. Members of the support team were sat in the kitchen waiting to move. He joined them and sat quietly at the table, eating from a bowl of soup. All the time, he appeared lost in thought. 'It was like he was assessing what was wrong with him,' Biskup says. 'He was the best barometer for that. We all understood that something was wrong, we were all ready to do something, but no one knew what to do because it wasn't possible to see what was happening to Martin.'

Then someone asked Robson how he was, and he replied: I don't feel so comfortable.

Someone left the room and went to summon the ambulance.

A few minutes later, Khuazhev came into the room: Martin, I think it is time.

Nodding, Robson heaved himself to his feet and everyone watched as he shuffled to the door. Viktor Lyagushkin was there with his camera. Before Robson had a chance to say would you mind putting that down, he took a photograph. There was Robson dressed in an oversized red jumper and black gilet. A red woolly hat was pulled down over his ears, and his hands were shoved into thick gloves. Looking directly at the camera, Robson wore an expression that was somewhere between a smile and a scowl.

To those watching, he appeared calm on the outside, but inwardly a million things were happening to him, and none of them were good.

A RACE AGAINST TIME

We do not really know where bubbles form nor lodge, their migration patterns, their birth and dissolution mechanisms, nor the exact chain of physico-chemical insults resulting in decompression sickness. Many possibilities exist, differing in the nature of the insult, the location, and the manifestation of symptoms.

Bruce R. Wienke and Timothy R. O'Leary,

Los Alamos National Laboratory

So, this is how it goes.

Puddles of water splashed beneath his faltering feet as Robson crossed the courtyard and two men wrapped their arms around his waist to stop him from collapsing. He tried to move his legs, but they wouldn't respond as expected; they felt like they were dissolving into the concrete. He knew he just had to get away from this place, make it out of there right now.

In a few short steps, Robson had gone from standing on his own two feet to having his legs pulled from under him. First, he needed the help of one man to hold him up. A few steps later, he needed another to help. On one side, Khuazhev held him tightly around the waist. Igor Galaida was on his other side.

Reaching the ambulance, the two Russians lifted Robson

inside. They scooped his legs up and squeezed him onto a bench seat, and then climbed in beside him. Viktor Lyagushkin and Bogdana Vashchenko jumped in after them. The door slammed shut, and the vehicle sped from the lake in a streak of white and blue light.

The ambulance moved quickly along the mountain road towards Nalchik, forty minutes away. Robson's friends looked down at him, expressions solemn, heads bowed. Sprawled across the seat, he could only stare at the ceiling, the sirens wailing above his head. He felt helpless for the first time. The bubbling inside his body had pitched up a notch to the level of fury, and there was nothing he could do to reverse the creeping numbness. He could not flex his toes or feel his thighs, but almost simultaneously he understood they were in excruciating pain.

Robson had expected his paralysed legs to flop beneath him. Instead, they were locked in a rigor mortis-like spasm, known as spastic hypertonia. Electrical pulses from his central nervous system were misfiring, and a confused loop of activity had taken hold, creating a wave of painful shock-like contractions, starting at his ankles. It felt as if his muscles were being petrified from the inside out; the worst kind of muscle cramp he had ever known multiplied by a hundred.

For the first time, he noticed discomfort in his abdomen. Girdle pain, doctors call it. While no one in the medical profession could satisfactorily explain the underlying pathology, girdle pain was believed to indicate bleeding in the spinal cord.

Robson breathed slow and deep. No time for panic.

But what about oxygen? Why aren't I on oxygen?

257

He heard someone make a phone call, and a few minutes later the vehicle stopped. The back doors were flung open and flashing lights filled the cabin. Robson saw Roman Dunaev standing outside holding a scuba tank.

Dunaev had been chasing after the ambulance in his truck, the cylinder of oxygen sliding around on the passenger seat. He'd seen it in the dive centre as he was about to leave with the ambulance. He'd picked it up and tossed it into the truck, couldn't explain why he thought to do so. Now he was glad he had.

Robson pressed the mask to his face and breathed as the vehicle set off again. The journey took some time, but soon he arrived at the place where he believed they would be able to reverse the thing that had stopped him from being able to move his legs.

The ambulance crew wheeled his stretcher into the Republican Clinical Hospital and a private medical bay scrubbed so clean that Robson could taste the disinfectant.

He was going to make it, he was sure.

Only nothing seemed to be happening.

Left alone in the bay, Robson stared at the walls and the ceiling and wondered what was taking them so long. Occasionally, a doctor appeared from behind the curtain at his bedside, looked at him, curious, mumbled something and then left. They were followed by one of his friends who arrived with an update. We're trying to sort things out, they told him, we're trying to get you to a recompression chamber. When he asked how long it would be before he was moved, they replied: soon. Only soon didn't seem to be in a hurry.

Time ticked on.

At some point, Lyagushkin walked into the medical bay with his camera, held it up to his eye and started to take photographs. I have to document this, Robson heard him say.

You don't take pictures of people in distress, Robson replied. Don't you take my picture. Lyagushkin decided to leave the room.

Someone brought Robson a telephone, and he called home. He woke Vikki.

I'm in hospital, he said. I've got a bend.

It took Vikki a few moments to understand what he was saying and when she did, he tried to reassure her.

Don't worry, I'm okay, Robson continued. He told her what had happened but tiptoed around the severity of his injury.

She heard him say his right leg was numb, but his voice sounded all right, and she didn't want to believe it could be that serious.

Vikki asked: What about treatment?

There's a local chamber here, Robson replied. I'm just waiting for the doctors to move me. I don't think I'll be coming home at the weekend. Can you call the airline and rearrange the flight? I'll call you when I can, he added before hanging up.

And time continued to tick.

Eventually, a hospital porter arrived, and Robson was on the move again. He was wheeled along the corridors on a gurney, fluorescent lights streaking past above his head. Towards the recompression chamber, he believed. Robson had imagined a cylinder-shaped recompression facility the size of a small room, complete with beds, a shower, toilet, video monitoring, computer displays, an airlock to receive food and medication, and a control panel of knobs and buttons; a unit capable of holding pressures high enough to squish the bubbles in his spine. Essentially, a unit where he could live in relative comfort for a few days.

What Robson got was more like a pressurised coffin.

Is this it? Robson asked as he craned his neck from his pillow to look at the pod.

In the centre of a small white-tiled room sat the one-person hyperbaric oxygen therapy unit. An attendant stood beside it, hands in the pockets of his pristine lab coat. The cramped unit was about the size of a single bed with a lid that opened like a chest freezer. The patient lay down and the lid closed on top of them. A thick acrylic viewing dome above their head offered the only window to the outside world. The control panel was a stand-alone unit, the size of an industrial boiler, with rotary switches and tiny red reflector lamps straight out of the 1970s. The thin, sheet metal casing vibrated nervously with the idling compressor.

Roman Dunaev was at Robson's side; he was out of the water, but he wasn't going to quit looking after his teacher.

It's the best we've got, he said.

The hyperbaric oxygen therapy unit Robson stared at was the kid brother of a recompression chamber. It worked, in principle, in precisely the same way. The significant difference was that it was designed to treat medical conditions such as diabetes, burns, infections, chronic cerebral palsy and ulcers, not decompression sickness. When fully pressurised, the environment inside was the equivalent of diving to twelve metres.

Yet Robson and the legs he couldn't feel were squeezed into

the cramped casket anyway. The lid closed in on him with the thud and he stared up through the dome to the featureless ceiling above. Periodically, a head would appear and stare down at him, and he heard the chatter of disembodied voices. Somewhere behind him, a valve opened, and oxygen hissed inside. Robson felt the pressure push against his eardrums and sweat beaded on his forehead as the temperature inside spiked.

And he began breathing for his life.

Only a small amount of pressure was not going to force the bubbles into submission. Robson knew it. Most likely, the doctors and the chamber technicians knew it also. The unit would have been okay if he'd had diabetes, burns or an open wound. But he had neurological decompression sickness which had deadened his legs and would soon begin to numb his abdomen, and all he'd got was a three-metre-long pod; a Coffin of No-Hope.

The thought that he was going to die never crossed Robson's mind, but others were thinking that for him. Looking at the hyperbaric unit, everyone there must have shared the same thought: this was nowhere near good enough.

In the late 1960s, deep-sea diver Jon Lindbergh, son of 'Lone Eagle' aviator Charles Lindbergh, took part in a research project for a device which allowed doctors to see into the bodies of divers. The technique had been stumbled upon by an MD at Seattle's Virginia Mason Medical Center called Merrill P. Spencer. At the time, Dr Spencer was investigating the use of Doppler ultrasound flowmeters in the diagnosis of vascular diseases. Essentially an aural imaging device, Doppler zapped the body with high-frequency sound, between five and ten megahertz, and measured the radar-like reflections to examine the flow of blood through the venous system. The presence of bubbles, Dr Spencer noticed, sent his machine haywire. With an ear for music, the professor had played the trumpet until damaging his windpipe, and he was able to pick out globules of air from the chirrups they made. Dr Spencer wondered if Doppler could be used to diagnose decompression sickness in divers.

The discovery caught the attention of Lindburgh, who was looking for a way to improve the effectiveness of decompression tables. The boss of a commercial diving outfit, he saw the depths of the sea as the last unconquered frontier on earth. Only in his thirties, Lindbergh had already lived a lifetime accented by adventure. As a student on a wreck-finding expedition, he graced the October 1952 cover of *Life* magazine; suntanned, smiling, a dash of a young Clint Eastwood, eyes with the same no-limits twinkle that saw his father take on the skies over the Atlantic. He made the first cave dive in California; served as a frogman with the US Navy Demolitions Team; searched for a nuclear bomb lost when a B-52 aircraft crashed off the coast of Spain; worked as a troubleshooter on oil rigs; and spent forty-nine hours living in an underwater habitat off the coast of the Bahamas. As a deep diver, Lindbergh knew the vagaries of decompression – some days you get bent, others you don't, even when doing the same thing at the same depth, he said – and he'd been hit by a bend, temporarily paralysed in one arm and down one side of his face, while diving for anchors off the coast of San Diego. It bothered him quite a bit, he told a journalist some years later. Fortunately, it just went away.

Lindbergh heard about the research and soon enough signed up to work with Dr Spencer and Seattle dive instructor Spencer Campbell. While conducting experiments, the two divers could often be found perched on a cot in a recompression chamber, hunched over Dr Spencer's silver ultrasound box. One of the men had a probe clasped to his arm or neck, the other clutched headphones to his ears and listened out for the chirp of bubbles hidden within the white noise of blood, which pulsed *whurr-whipp, whurr-whipp, whurr-whipp* around the body.

During a test in 1968, Lindbergh noted the first recognised human decompression bubbles; a series of vague sounds coming from Campbell's veins following a simulated dive to almost 200 feet (61 m). The following year a chamber technician, who was conducting a pressure test on equipment, complained of muscle pains and redness of the skin. An ultrasound examination of his brachial vein, downstream from his upper right arm, chirped with bubbles.

The Doppler ultrasound gave voice to the theory of 'silent bubbles' that had first been proposed in 1951 and would later become central to a number of modern studies of decompression sickness. The hypothesis proposed that bubbles were produced on all dives. The bubbles were referred to as silent because they were too small to interfere with the body's functions and didn't cause the bends, so divers didn't have any inkling they were there.

To some, bubbles twitter like birds, to others they snap, crackle and pop like a particular breakfast cereal. The five-point Spencer Scale was created to grade the size and number of bubbles in the veins. On the Spencer Scale, grade zero is no bubbles; one is an occasional chirp; two is a short birdsong; three is a flock of seagulls. Above that is something you don't want to hear. Grade IV describes the condition as: 'The maximum detectable bubble signal, sounding continuously throughout the systole and diastole of every cardiac period, and overriding the amplitude of the normal cardiac signals.' In other words, the volume of bubbles is so large it drowns out the sound of your pulsing blood.

In the late 1990s, Dr Rob van Hulst, former director of Diving and Submarine Medicine with the Royal Netherlands Navy, volunteered for a study measuring bubble formation in chamber dives to 275 feet (84 m). 'A probe was put on my chest, and I was asked to do two or three knee bends,' Dr van Hulst says. 'I could hear this "chip, chip, chip" sound, very loud.' He was half a grade from being diagnosed with decompression sickness.

Very few mixed gas divers get decompression sickness without first suffering Grade IV bubbling; but the absence of bubbles does not mean there is no risk of the bends. That's still a possibility, but it's measured in fractions of a single per cent. The potential for injury doesn't rise linearly with bubble grading. Between grades II and III it leaps almost six-fold. By the time the white noise of Grade IV bubbling has been reached, the chances of suffering decompression sickness rise to anywhere between one in ten and eight in ten, depending on whose research you favour. In terms of pure numbers, Grade IV bubbling on the Spencer Scale can represent anything up to 10,000 bubbles per minute dumped into the bloodstream. That number doesn't include the bubbles still trapped in the tissues, such as the spinal cord; there's no scientific way of calculating their number.

If the equipment had been available in Nalchik to take a Doppler ultrasound of Robson's vascular system, it is highly likely it would not have been birdsong; it would have sounded like the foxes were in the henhouse.

Let's try to come to grips with what was happening inside Robson's body as he lay there. While the evolution of decompression sickness on a microscopic level is not truly understood even today, scientific studies suggest a complex array of responses is triggered by the presence of a significant bubble-load.

Assuming an attack, the immune system most likely responds with a chaotic blitzkrieg of countermeasures, known as the complement and coagulation cascade. The action is similar to those the body would deploy to tackle any foreign invader, be it a splinter or a lodged bullet, albeit on a larger scale. In the short term, however, these biochemical defence mechanisms may be as much a hindrance as a help.

Lipoproteins in the blood are drawn towards the bubbles but are rendered biologically inactive on arrival in a process known as denaturation. The shells of denatured lipoproteins surrounding the bubbles are now deemed a foreign body, and white blood cells begin to descend upon them. Meanwhile, histamines are dispatched to dilate the blood vessels and boost the flow. At the same time, the walls of the vessels become sticky to glue the foreign body in place. This process, however, causes the endothelium cells in the vessels' walls to break down, allowing the white blood cells to leak away.

Platelets are then sent to the damaged area to begin emergency repairs, and they opt to reduce the flow of blood. The body is contradicting itself. Red blood cells now begin to turn to sludge, exacerbating the disruption caused by the coagulated bubbles. The flow of blood in his body begins to fall incrementally. Haemorrhages break out and cause swelling inside the spinal cord.

Across the body cells are now being starved of oxygen. Unchecked, they will soon begin to break down.

As he lay in the chamber, Robson's body was starting to crash.

A snake's hiss of escaping gas blew into Robson's ears and forced his eyes open. Something on the chamber had cracked, and the mattress under him shuddered. An alarm beeped furiously. Robson stared up through the viewing dome. He could hear the indistinct sounds of activity outside but couldn't see anything.

What's going on? Robson asked, but no one answered.

Outside, the technicians were preoccupied. The chamber's safety valve had blown, and they were trying to plug the leak.

The breach shouldn't have come as a surprise to them. Before sealing Robson inside, they had blocked the valve. They had blown the chamber down to twenty metres, well beyond its operating pressure. They had sent the needle of the pressure gauge into the red, and they had done it with the best of intentions. They thought more pressure might bring a sliver of relief to Robson's body. It was a gamble, and someone somewhere had decided it was worth a try. But the venture had failed. Now they stood by, helpless as oxygen – and life – bled into the outside world.

Robson had been inside the pod for six minutes.

The chamber pressure plummeted as the gas hissed away. In simple terms, Robson was being yanked back towards the ambient pressure of the surface. The bubbles inside his body were popping back to their destructive worst.

The alarm continued to beep and the needle of the chamber's pressure gauge swept an arc towards zero.

Robson heard the muted sound of tapping echo in his ears and felt the pod vibrate. A face appeared at the window, eyes unexpectedly wide, and then, just as quickly, vanished. Robson strained to see out of the viewing dome. He heard tapping again. What was going on? He felt confused and helpless as the events affecting his life were out of his control. The alarm beeped some more, and the muffled sounds of movement continued. A face appeared at the window again. Then the sound of escaping gas made a final high-pitched whine and fell silent.

The technicians had managed to seal the valve. They had stabilised the chamber, and everyone breathed a sigh of relief. A face appeared at the window again, eyes normal, and Robson relaxed, but right then his chances had dropped a notch. He didn't know it then, but no one in the room had any idea of what to do for the best.

On Thursday, 19 January, Dr Gennady Mikhailovich Sokolov had a day at home in Moscow and a busy schedule. He'd been working all day on a research programme, and a plan for his seventy-eighth birthday. He'd decided to go to bed early, knowing he would spend Saturday shopping for treats for friends and colleagues who were due to attend his party on Sunday. He was sound asleep when the telephone rang.

On answering, he was surprised to hear the voice of Irina Kochergina, editor of the dive magazine *Neptune XXI Century*. The pair knew each other professionally, and the magazine had published his articles on safe diving practices over the years.

I've received a telephone call from a young man about a serious problem with a diver in Nalchik, Kochergina told him. She didn't have the full details of what was going on down south, but she asked Dr Sokolov if he would consider speaking with the caller.

Reaching Dr Sokolov was a masterstroke, according to divers on the expedition. 'Every technical diver in Russia knows Dr Sokolov, he is Number One,' says Alla Popova, one of the expedition's support divers. 'He is very experienced, with an open mind and a readiness to help. He is the only one able to help.'

Dr Sokolov crept out of the bedroom so as not to wake his wife, Albina Petrovna, and headed to his study, his mind already working on the problem. A former Colonel in the Medical Corps, he was little more than five-foot-six in his dress shoes and suit, but he stood much taller in the eyes of his colleagues. He had the face of everyone's favourite grandpa, and for a man used to working under pressure he was unusually benevolent. In the racket of a recompression chamber treatment, he would think nothing of handing over his ear defenders if he felt someone needed protecting from the hiss of venting air. As a specialist in hyperbaric medicine and a pioneer in the field, he stood at the centre of everything the Russians did surrounding research into the treatment of decompression sickness; four volumes of medical research he had co-authored and a bookcase full of scientific reports were a testament to that.

A living specialist, as he called himself, Sokolov had lived a life at war with the bends, a war fought in the shadows of the deep, one with many casualties, but no monuments. He had treated young men whose silent bravery could not hide the pain behind their eyes. He had suffered decompression sickness himself, and he had helped to develop experimental treatments for the most severe of cases.

He worked for the Institute of Biomedical Problems of the Russian Academy of Sciences, on the outskirts of Moscow. The Institute researched, among other things, how to send people into deep space and how to get people back from deep underwater. So respected was he, Dr Sokolov could wave people through the building's security screening with a simple 'these are my friends'. Well beyond retirement age, his best years were not necessarily behind him. His eyes still twinkled, and a mischievous smile crossed his face whenever he was asked to recall one of his adventures.

His compassionate demeanour suited a man who as a young boy had watched his mother, Evgenia, care for injured soldiers during the Second World War. Until then, his childhood in Omsk, Siberia, had been blissful. He went to school perched on the crossbar of his father's bicycle and the pair hunted game together. With the outbreak of war, Sokolov's father, who had served with the Red Army before graduating from the Medical Institute, was ordered into the navy medical service in the Pacific. His mother made the rank of captain at the city hospital. He would see her pick up her medical bag and head out to some emergency after hearing a knock at the door during the night. He often saw her go without sleep.

When she was at work, the eight-year-old Sokolov would go to the hospital after school. Awful sights would remain with him forever. Young men missing arms, hobbling around on crutches or burned and wrapped in bandages. His mother told him that, sometimes, during surgery, the anaesthesia wore off and the wounded soldiers screamed and cursed at her. Young Sokolov walked the wards speaking to the injured, singing for them and reciting poetry, reminding them of sons in some far-off home.

Once, he almost blew himself up with a chemistry set, and he nearly drowned when his feet got stuck in the mud of a river that he crossed on his way to school. A fellow student saw his arms waving above the surface and plucked him to safety. He embraced the incident and, after reading a book called *Underwater Wizard*, he knew he wanted to be a diver. Then, he was fascinated with becoming a professional chauffeur. Then a pilot. The one career he understood, however, was being a doctor. By the time he was a teenager, Sokolov had decided to continue the family tradition and become a navy doctor. While at the Naval Medical Academy, he was introduced to diving medicine.

To understand what it took to be a deep-sea diver, he asked to be posted to the Baltic Sea and joined the diving corps. For a learned doctor, it was an odd career move, unheard of until he became the first physician in the country to qualify as a deep-sea diver. Yet he was pragmatic about his decision; he believed it would help him to look at casualties as comrades rather than patients. 'I believe if a specialist in diving medicine is a professional diver himself, he will approach an injured professional diver differently because they are colleagues,' he says.

'When I talk to an injured diver, I can't help thinking that it could have happened to me or maybe something similar did happen to me.'

More than that, he loved the extremes. Diving was not just a simple walk in the depths, it was the excitement of pushing the limits in a dangerous world, having the intelligence to do it safely and return in one piece. It was often grim work, living in tight quarters on a ship, enduring the cold and darkness on long dives and even longer decompression, putting your life in the hands of mechanical equipment and breathing the tinned air it produced. That's not to say he didn't love it. He embraced its heart-pounding challenges, lived for the opportunity to push deeper.

After his time in the Baltic, he spent two years training divers of the Algerian Navy – Sokolov spoke French and German – before returning to Russia to take part in classified research into saturation diving. Saturation diving gets its name from the idea that if you spent long enough at a certain depth, your body would become saturated with inert gas. At that point, you could live and work there as long as you want at that depth without adding to your decompression obligations. Saturation diving would become popular in the oil industry, but back then, the limits were an unknown. The new captain could easily have ordered his juniors into the pressure chamber. Instead, Sokolov took part in the test dives himself, clocking up several intense weeks living under increased pressures, including a 200-metre saturation dive, until senior officers ordered him to stop experimenting on himself. By then, his style had rubbed off on the unit. Some divers readily submitted to spending more than a month living at 300 metres so Sokolov could determine such things as the safety parameters of working at depth, the best way of protecting the climate inside the chamber and how to avoid health issues, such as inner ear infection. By the time he was assigned to the Institute, in 1985, as a senior researcher in the Barophysiology, Barotherapy and Dive Medicine Department, Sokolov was a legend among Russian divers.

Right then, waiting for the telephone to ring, research was furthest from his mind; he was impatient to discover what had gone so drastically wrong in Nalchik to require his late-night intervention. He didn't have to wait long for the call and the phone barely had time to ring. The voice at the other end burst out of the blocks: I'm sorry to call so late . . . friend . . . English . . . decompression sickness . . . no recompression chamber . . . big problems.

In Nalchik, Roman Dunaev was pacing the corridor outside the hyperbaric therapy treatment room. Dr Sokolov waited for Dunaev to pause, and then started asking questions. Who was the diver? What had happened to him? How deep? How is he being treated?

Dunaev peered through a window in the door and at the white coffin where Robson languished. They've put him in a hyperbaric oxygen therapy unit, he said.

That was all wrong. Dr Sokolov knew instantly that the Englishman would never fully recover by breathing hyperbaric oxygen alone. The small pressure chamber was not entirely use-less, but it was next to it. All it was doing was slowing down Robson's inevitable decline. For a brief moment he thought about ordering a halt to the oxygen therapy, but he held his tongue; he didn't approve of the treatment, it was risky and in breach of safety rules, but he understood the decision had been made in the best interests of the patient.

How long has he been in the chamber?

Dunaev explained the blown valve and then said the chamber pressure had stabilised half an hour ago. How do I proceed?

Sokolov thought for a moment and then reeled off a list of numbers: times and pressures for Robson's treatment.

The total time under this maximum pressure is to be one and a half hours, then reduce pressure uniformly over thirty minutes to bring the patient back to ambient pressure.

It was a stopgap, and Sokolov knew it. Without access to a multi-pressure recompression chamber, the situation looked grim for Robson.

Still, the opportunity to help a diver in distress was something Sokolov could not pass up; it was what he'd spent his life doing. 'Why wouldn't I agree to treat him?' he says as if the very question was ridiculous. There's no sentiment, no high ideals, no talk of duty, there's not even mention of the Hippocratic Oath; in all his years as a medical practitioner he'd never been asked to take it. Sometimes, he can appear so matter of fact about his decision as to be underwhelming: 'There's someone who is ill and suffering and someone who can help. One must; if one doesn't, one's not a doctor.'

Following his call with Dunaev, Dr Sokolov made contact with his counterparts in Nalchik and informed them he would lead Robson's emergency care and take on all responsibility for its result. He would, he added, also organise an evacuation plan.

Evacuation plans take time to organise; time was something Sokolov didn't have and he knew it. The critical measure now was how long it took to get his patient to an appropriate medical facility, the time to treatment (TTT). In essence, TTT is a measure of the length of time between the onset of symptoms and the start of recompression therapy.

For years, conventional wisdom has been that patients who receive prompt care are more likely to recover than those who, for whatever reason, suffer a delay. In 1982, physician Kenneth W. Kizer conducted a retrospective review of fifty cases of decompression sickness in divers from Hawaii to examine the effect of delays to recompression treatment. He found that 84 per cent of severely affected divers treated within twenty-four hours completely recovered from their injuries. Beyond that, their chances were little better than fifty-fifty; a flip of a coin. A 1990 study by Dr Rob van Hulst, of the Royal Netherlands Navy, put the recovery rate closer to 40 per cent. Robert Ball, of the Naval Medical Research Institute, in Bethesda, Maryland, slashed the odds even further, concluding that the chances of a full recovery were one in three; no better than playing rock, paper, scissors. Significantly, his report set a threshold of time for successful therapy: treatment greater than twelve hours after onset of injury would not result in substantial improvement for most injured divers.

At home, the curtains drawn to shut out the winter darkness, Dr Sokolov believed his own treatment methods afforded him a little more time, but not much. Then another telephone call from Nalchik; Robson had completed the first round of hyperbaric oxygen therapy.

His condition has stabilised, the voice from Nalchik told him. The doctors had diagnosed a spinal cord injury with the development of lower spastic paraparesis and impaired pelvic organs. What shall we do?

The old man had already done the maths and was concerned. Robson had been breathing elevated levels of oxygen for hours; during the dive, in the ambulance on the way to the hospital, in the coffin. Dr Sokolov was concerned Robson could be suffering the invisible effects of pulmonary oxygen toxicity, which would only make future treatment unpredictable. Oxygen, the very thing Robson was breathing for his life, was now in danger of killing the cells in his lungs. If they died, he would suffer a reduction in vital capacity, a measure of the total amount of air one can inhale. Worsening lung function was the last thing Robson needed. If he couldn't inhale efficiently, he would not be able to get sufficient oxygen to his organs.

To stabilise his patient, Dr Sokolov decided to take a risk. He gambled on the second session of oxygen therapy: two atmospheres of pressure, for one hour; uniform decompression for thirty minutes.

After hanging up the phone, he interrogated his watch. He knew his patient was running a race against time, but without the use of his legs. He needed to find somewhere to treat him. He had to start making some phone calls. This couldn't wait, but it was the dead of night.

Robson had been out of the hyperbaric pod for just thirty minutes before they helped him and his legs back in. The lid was closed, and he stared up through the viewing dome as the

whole thing was pressurised. This time, he could hear a constant flow of oxygen being pumped into the pod and suspected
the technicians were trying to overcome another leak. The
whole thing played havoc with his ears, but he still sucked in
the oxygen like his life depended on it.

Yet even though his situation was becoming increasingly
nightmarish, there was no fear in his mind. Not yet. There was
just a grim sense of reality that things were going a little awry.
Robson felt his optimism begin to ebb. If the oxygen was doing
his body any good, he could not feel it. He still could not feel
his legs.

This can't be all there is, surely?

Dr Sokolov, however, was trying to buy time for an evacuation. The diagnosis of lower spastic paraparesis had given him
hope. It told him his patient's legs were numb, but not yet
completely dead. That's why he had gambled on an hour-long
session.

After it was all over, Robson was lifted from the pod, placed
on a gurney and wheeled from the room. Lying on his back, he
stared upwards as a hospital porter, unshaven, white lab coat,
pushed the bed through a door and into the cold darkness outside. Robson's cheeks felt the sting of the icy wind and sleet.
Then he saw a large metal gate towering above him, glowing
orange in the light of a nearby lamp, heard the jangle of keys
and the click of a padlock. The hinges squealed, and he was
wheeled inside.

The corridor was dark, many of the light fittings were
missing a bulb and those that worked flickered and fizzed. He
could sense unlit passageways disappearing off to each side.

Above him, Robson could see the building's innards, gloomy recesses and bundles of electrical cables instead of ceiling tiles. Then the gurney crashed through a pair of swinging doors and Robson was on a ward. He heard whispered voices and was pushed into a room where two other patients lay asleep. A nurse arrived and shoved needles and tubes into his arms. Three bags dripped intravenous fluids into his body. They were to counter tissue damage and hypercoagulation; Dr Sokolov had asked for them, but no one had told Robson. All he was thinking was that the tingling flow of fluids was not going to save his legs.

What's happening? he asked in Russian. The nurse did not answer.

Robson wasn't screaming, and his eyes weren't pleading; he was from the grin-and-bear-it school. Staring helplessly at the ceiling above his hospital bed, he questioned whether the doctors had the first idea how to treat him. That only confirmed the suspicions he harboured about the medical profession. Once, in between teaching assignments in Florida and Ukraine, Robson was tormented with agonising back pain. Wincing when he stood or walked anywhere, he visited a doctor who diagnosed a bad back. A second consultant diagnosed muscle spasms and sent him home. That night Robson hobbled into his local hospital with the words of a friend in his ears: forget you're an ex-Marine, show the pain like the rest of us. An hour later, he was admitted. The following day he underwent emergency spinal surgery. A collapsed disc had fused with his spinal cord in a rare condition called cauda equina.

Finally, Roman Dunaev appeared and explained the situation to Robson. We're trying to arrange things for you, he added.

Dunaev tried to reassure his friend, but what else could he say that wouldn't unnerve him: that the nearest recompression chamber they could locate was 500 miles away on the Black Sea coast; that they couldn't airlift him by helicopter because the weather had closed in and shut the airport; that the chamber had problems sourcing helium, which could render the entire effort to transfer him a fruitless errand. That would be admitting to Robson that his chances were slim, not quite on the floor, but not far above. Then Robson would have to call Vikki and tell her their life – her life – was about to change irrevocably.

'I realised then that the chamber wasn't going to work, it was a 200-metre dive Martin had completed, and the numbness was spreading; I had a pretty good understanding of what that meant,' says Vikki Batten. 'That's when, and I don't think we said all that much to each other about it, the shock started to set in about what that might mean for us. That's when I realised he might be dying.'

It was sometime on Friday morning, Vikki had just spoken to Martin and was sitting on the sofa, clutching the telephone. Her smile had vanished, and the ill wind inside the house was as heavy as the weather outside. She had barely slept since the first call from Martin the previous evening. The conversations were few and far between now. He was nursing his phone battery and she had to wait for his call. Annoyance piled on top of anxiety and she struggled to absorb what was happening. At any moment she was part of a couple, and at the same time she was alone and facing the possible loss of her soulmate: 'It made everything more frightening.'

And the news from Nalchik wasn't good.

I've let you down. I'm really sorry, Martin repeated.

You've done nothing of the sort, Vikki said, silent tears streaming down her cheeks.

Despite Martin's constant reassurances he was going to be okay, she could hear the uncertainty in his voice. The silences grew longer, and they didn't have the words to express their worst fears.

'I had no idea whether anything was going to happen or if he was just being left to die slowly. And there was nothing either of us could do about it,' Vikki says. 'I knew as well as Martin what was happening in his body; the clock was ticking, and the ticking was getting faster. He was getting more and more frightened. I don't remember him saying it; he didn't need to. His body was under systematic assault and, no matter how fit or healthy he was, bubbles could end up anywhere. We were in a race against time.'

Robson had been in hospital for almost eight hours, but the bend had struck hours earlier. By conventional wisdom, he should already have waved goodbye to his legs. And walking, and diving, and teaching. And he could die suddenly, swiftly, with an aneurysm, or die slowly with organ failure. Or his heart could stop beating just like that because his blood had turned to foam. Or he could die slowly as the paralysis spread.

Finding a suitable facility to treat Robson, Dr Sokolov knew, was going to be a significant problem. Finding a way to transport him across the country was going to be an even bigger one. The truth of it was Robson would probably have had a better chance if he had been injured while diving off an oil rig in the middle of the North Sea.

The Institute of Biomedical Problems where Dr Sokolov worked was a deep-water diving complex, and he knew it would be ideal. The Institute was located at the end of the road in an anonymous industrial estate way out on the outskirts of Moscow. Visitors to it could easily think they had taken a wrong turn. Behind the ramshackle corrugated iron gatehouse, where a man with camouflaged trousers patrolled the red and white barrier, the place looked like a disused tyre factory. The grey walls were crumbling and streaked with rust. But beyond the overgrown gravel parking lot, through the entrance to a grey office block where a dog slept on the concrete floor, past the old woman in a glass-fronted reception booth, up the stairs and along the featureless corridors and down a metal staircase was something special: the GVK-250 research chamber.

Wrapped in an orange tarpaulin, the GVK-250 appeared to grow from iron girders beneath the floorboards. Pipes and hoses protruded from the three-door chamber as if it was wired to the very building itself. The three-part pressure chamber had all the necessary systems for long-term, deep saturation exposures. Run from an imposing control panel of valves, gauges and dials, the chamber could dive six people down to a depth of 250 metres for up to three months. It had been used to test the effects on the body at a cellular and tissue level of breathing gas mixtures under high pressures.

The highly experienced staff who maintained and operated the chamber were on standby. They had worked with the chamber for so long they knew its quirks. If, say, the communications box on the control panel shorted, they could rustle up some spares and have it up and running in no time. Between them, they had been involved in some significant experiments over their years of research. In 1984, they'd sent two men to a simulated depth of 450 metres for three days using a helium-oxygen gas mixture; two years later they'd tested a neon-oxygen gas mixture at 410 metres; in 2009, they had put four men inside to verify the safety of breathing a mix of oxygen, nitrogen and argon.

However, more than 1,000 miles lay between GVK-250 and Robson, with a dwindling number of options to get him there. Driving would take too long, and they couldn't fly him on a commercial aircraft because the reduction in pressure in a cabin would worsen his condition. Besides, Nalchik was in the grip of a winter storm. Temperatures had plunged below zero, blizzards were blowing hard, the runway had iced, and the airport had been closed. Then there were the trains. Dr Sokolov examined a timetable on the internet. There was a daily service between Nalchik and Moscow, but the next departure was not until the following evening. The journey took a day and a half. Dr Sokolov calculated that it would be three days before Robson would receive treatment, and that was too long.

If Moscow was too far, he needed somewhere closer. He knew of a pressure chamber on board the *Captain Beklemishev* salvage tug, based out of the Novorossiysk naval shipyard, on the Black Sea coast of Krasnodar Krai. The ship was 500-odd miles closer to Robson, but it was cramped with barely enough room enough for two divers and could only be pressurised to the equivalent of sixty metres. Dr Sokolov didn't think that was deep enough to carry out his treatment.

The telephone rang again. It was Dunaev. I think we've found a possible solution, he said.

Dunaev had managed to get a call to a man called Oleg Niko-layevich Skalatskiy. Skalatskiy ran a hyperbaric complex at the southern branch of the Institute of Oceanology, at the Black Sea resort town of Gelendzhik.

He's willing to take Martin, Dunaev said, but only on condi-tion you travel to Gelendzhik and take charge of the treatment.

Of course, I'll take charge, replied Dr Sokolov. He asked how they planned to get Martin from Nalchik to the chamber. We're still working on that, Dunaev told him.

After finishing the call, Dr Sokolov checked the airline sched-ules. The first available flight to Gelendzhik from Moscow's Vnukovo airport departed shortly after eleven that morning. It would arrive in the coastal city at about 2 p.m., almost twenty-four hours after the onset of Robson's injury.

The feedback from doctors in Nalchik sounded positive. The second round of hyperbaric therapy appeared to have produced some improvement in Robson's condition, and they felt a third treatment would deliver further improvements. Dr Sokolov dis-agreed. The whole thing was just too risky. He was already thinking two or three steps ahead to the therapy he needed to deliver and was worried more hyperbaric treatment could trigger pulmonary oxygen toxicity.

To be absolutely certain, Dr Sokolov woke an old friend, Pro-fessor Alexei Anatolyevich Myasnikov, the service chief at the Military Medical Academy's Department of Physiology, and asked for a second opinion. The men discussed the incident, and Professor Myasnikov concurred with his colleague's approach: no more hyperbaric oxygen.

For now, the glorious mess that was Robson's body was alive, but not necessarily kicking, on a hospital bed in a ward in Nalchik. The question that most perturbed Dr Sokolov, though, was whether it would stay that way long enough for him to be evacuated.

All this time, the bottleneck caused by bubble accumulation and hypercoagulation was slowing the circulation around Robson's body. That, so the scientific theory goes, causes a host of other problems. The oxygen needed to maintain cell viability is in short supply, and the cells cry out for aid. Nutrients such as glucose and fatty acids have stopped flowing across the cell membranes. The affected areas of the body begin anaerobic metabolism to produce energy. As the cells start feeding off themselves, oedema becomes a real risk. Toxic chemicals released by the damaged cells, axons and blood vessels go to work on their neighbours. A flood of glutamate over-excites nearby neurons, triggering a series of destructive events inside the cells, a process known as electrotoxicity.

Microscopic dead spots start to appear in the spine. The desperate fight by cells to stave off death is producing lactic acid and nitric oxide. The two compounds turn the venous blood acidic.

In a last-ditch effort to arrest this acidosis, the body orders the release of oxygen from the haemoglobin. This action brings temporary relief for its cells, but there is not much to go around.

At this point, Robson's body was on a downward spiral. With each response it chose, a cascade of consequences would follow.

The sun, or something dimly similar, strained through the winter sky over Moscow and Dr Sokolov buttoned up his brown outdoor coat over his charcoal suit jacket and red and black striped tie. He wrapped a scarf around his neck and pulled on his winter gloves. A peaked hat covered his head. Albina Petrovna watched her husband get ready. His leaving for the airport was entirely unexpected – they were meant to be preparing for his birthday – but as the wife of a naval officer she had grown accustomed to her husband being called away for weeks or months at a time. We'll celebrate my birthday when I return, he said.

Though he anticipated being away for some time, Dr Sokolov carried only a small bag of provisions. Inside was a change of clothes and some toiletries. Of greater importance was the book, Декомпрессионная болезнь (*Decompression Sickness*), that he had written with his mentor Dr Vladimir Vasilyevich Smolin. The volume was 600 pages thick with a chunk devoted to the detailed procedures for treating severe decompression injuries. Alongside the book, Sokolov had with him a computer flash drive containing a detailed description of a long-stay treatment, developed and perfected some years earlier by the two men.

Stepping into the Moscow winter, Dr Sokolov's mind was filled with fresh possibility and even more uncertainty. That morning, while packing, he had received a call from Yevgeny Glukhov, the chief diving specialist at the Ministry of Emergency Situations (MChS), a man he had known professionally for years. Since the early morning, Glukhov's staff had been piecing together the elements of an operation to go into Nalchik and rescue Robson. He was due to brief the Minister within an hour in the hope of getting final approval for his plan.

The doctor asked if the plan was still to transport Robson to Gelendzhik.

Glukhov told him they were considering a complex in Sochi on the Black Sea coast. As soon as we have a decision, I will call you, he promised.

Dr Sokolov had heard about the facility; it was relatively new and run by somebody he knew. Sochi was closer to Nalchik, as the crow flies, than Gelendzhik, but the journey time by road was an hour longer because the road crossed the Caucasus Mountains. The bigger concern for the doctor was that he wasn't sure if the kind of treatment Robson needed could be conducted there. He was, however, prepared to go with Glukhov's suggestion.

Glukhov suggested he head to the airport as planned and wait for instructions.

Dr Sokolov walked to the nearby metro station and joined the crush of early-morning commuters heading to work. It was almost 7 a.m., and he had one thing on his mind: 'Martin's condition was very serious and, even being provided with the most efficient treatment, it wasn't guaranteed he would fully recover and not remain disabled.'

The Ministry for Emergency Situations occupies a beige, six-storey building in the heart of Moscow's theatre district, down the street from the Bolshoi Ballet. The restructured neoclassical building allows a view of the five-star Hotel Metropole on the opposite side of the avenue. Expensive cars delivering wealthy visitors roll past the tinted windows of the ground floor and gaggles of tourists mass at the wide intersections gazing off towards Theatre Square. There are no large signs on the building, and the only clues about the tenants are four small flags flying above the front door and a giant satellite dish on the roof.

Known internationally as EMERCOM, the Ministry was led by Sergei Shoigu, a popular, hands-on leader who would often be seen supporting his people on the ground in the aftermath of natural disasters and terrorist attacks.

Waiting outside Shoigu's office just before eight o'clock that Friday morning was Yevgeny Glukhov. His mind was abuzz with the details of a complicated rescue plan for an Englishman with the bends. The details were mixed with fears the patient he wanted to help might not make it through the next twenty-four hours alive. Glukhov was stocky, in his mid-fifties, with the quiet composure that comes with experience. He probably had access to more diver rescue resources than any other civilian rescue service commander anywhere in the world, with a mix of national and regional facilities at his disposal. That morning, he had the elite of Russia's rescue units on standby, and he knew they could overcome almost anything. Yet there were some things for which even he needed to seek approval. Right then, he was anxious; he was about to step into a meeting with his boss, and he was still waiting for a written report containing the latest updates to be handed to him.

Earlier that morning he'd spoken with a deputy named Constantine Rastegaeva who was based at a toytown-coloured, waterside complex in Tuapse, on the Black Sea. Rastegaeva headed a detachment of divers from the Centrospas search and rescue team that was ready to help with Robson's rescue. In official terms, Centrospas is a nationwide airmobile resource providing a 'quick response to emergency situations of natural and man-made disasters; work to save the lives and health of people, the salvation of the material and cultural values, reducing the size of damage to the natural environment'. To the layperson, they are professional disaster rescue specialists. If a crisis develops anywhere in Russia, Centrospas are on three-minute notice to respond. They can have rescue vehicles on the road within an hour and be airborne in three. And they can find themselves anywhere in the world. That's why, for example, following the 2010 earthquake in Haiti, civilians were as likely to find a Centrospas rescue worker searching the rubble as a member of the US Coast Guard.

If Rastegaeva's Centrospas detachment could do the heavy lifting and move Robson anywhere, the next question was how to transport him safely. The answer lay two-and-a-half hours' drive south-east along the coast road from Tuapse, in the city of Sochi. Occupying a three-storey building in the federal South Sports complex on the harbourfront was the Southern Regional Search and Rescue Team, YURPSO for short. The specialist dive team had only moved into the building four years earlier, yet they were as tied to the sea as the fishermen who had plied their trade off the coast for generations. The team of mostly hardened ex-military types specialised in rescue on, in or around water, whether it be pulling crewmen from stricken tankers, searching for children lost under the iced surface of rivers or disabling wartime munitions on the seabed.

One of the many resources the team possessed was a hyperbaric life-raft stored in a secure compound at their Sochi headquarters. The self-contained DART is a transportable recompression chamber designed to rescue injured divers working in offshore oil and gas drilling or remote military operations. Built by Dutch firm IHC Hytech, it looks not unlike the Apollo command module which carried the first American astronauts into space. The business end is the cone-shaped chamber, where the patient rests. Mated onto the base of the cone is the ATEL (Attachable Transportable Entrance Lock) stub cylinder, an airlock that allows attendants to move between the pressurised chamber and the outside world. Astonishingly small, it is not something you climb into as much as put on. But it makes it possible to transfer a patient to a medical facility anywhere in the world in a pressurised bubble up to six atmospheres, equivalent to fifty metres of seawater.

Glukhov knew if they could get the DART to Nalchik, Robson could be locked inside and transported anywhere in the country in the belly of an aircraft. It needed to be one hell of an aircraft; the unit and its accompanying airlock weighed half a ton and sat on the back of a low-load trailer. One of Centrospas's biggest assets is its huge IL-76 cargo plane. Its wings span more than fifty metres and the giant tail fin towers fifteen metres above the ground. An enormous lump of a thing, the aircraft looks like it has no business being in the air, but the four Aviadvigatel turbofans slung beneath its wings can propel it to any destination in the world with room for a fifty-tonne payload of men and machinery. Politics aside, there is nowhere on earth they cannot reach, and no casualty they can't get to hospital. But where to take Robson?

Everyone had been focused on treating Robson at the facility in Gelendzhik. However, there was another recompression chamber, much closer to Robson, in Sochi. Behind a large, shuttered entrance, the YURPSO building also housed a large multi-pressure recompression chamber. The chamber was new and offered comfortable surroundings for Robson and the medical staff, the technicians were well trained, and they could quickly secure enough helium for the duration of the treatment.

Glukhov knew from the outset that timing was going to be crucial, and an awful lot had already been lost. To make the plan work he needed the DART to be delivered to Adler airport south of Sochi where it could rendezvous with the IL-76 cargo plane from Moscow. The whole thing could then make the short flight over the Caucasus. The aircraft was too large to land in Nalchik because the runway was too short. The nearest alternative was Mineralnye Vody, two hours north. Robson would need to be transported there by ambulance. Then they had to find a way of meeting up with Dr Sokolov, who was already on his way to Vnukovo airport, south-west of Moscow.

The major downside with all of this expertise and equipment is that it didn't just roll out of the door on a whim. That's why the Minister was needed to issue the order for the aircraft to leave the runway.

The written report still hadn't arrived by the time Glukhov was called into the Minister's office, so he had to do everything by memory. As he spoke, Glukhov knew all the plans could change in an instant if, for instance, cloud cover fogged the airports or closed the gaps in flight schedules down south.

There's no other exit, Glukhov told his boss.

That was enough. There was a chance to save a life, so Shoigu approved the plan. The meeting lasted only minutes.

Glukhov left the room to make the necessary calls. The engine of rescue was being revved.

The electronic departure screens blinked as flights bound for destinations across Russia took off from Vnukovo airport. Standing beneath them, lost amidst the hustle of travellers dragging bags and pushing trolleys, Dr Sokolov still had no idea where he was going, and he was beginning to worry it all might be futile anyway.

He'd been living on his nerves since the early hours, treating over the telephone a man he'd neither met nor examined. He still had no idea where in the country he was going, and the calls from Nalchik had grown more desperate: Robson's in pain, what should we do? The painkillers don't work, what else should we prescribe? The improvements from the hyperbaric treatment are being lost, what about a third session? No, he had said, drugs only.

Prescribing drugs to Robson was not really the best answer. Dr Sokolov knew the rules; he was the one who had helped write them. Drugs could serve to mask the symptoms of the decompression sickness as it ravaged Robson's body, but using them to stabilise his patient was the only option he had left at that point.

In denying his patient hyperbaric oxygen right then, Dr Sokolov was already thinking longer term; not being sidelined by what others thought necessary to aid Robson over the next few minutes and hours, but what would better prepare his patient for the intense treatment that was to come. He weighed what would happen if he denied the oxygen, and what would happen if he prescribed it. He convinced himself what should be done for the best for his patient, provided Robson survived long enough to reach Sochi and the chamber.

Dr Sokolov had been playing a delicate balancing act with this stranger's health for hours and creeping into his mind, for the first time, was the idea that he might just have confined Robson to a wheelchair. Could the refusal to conduct a third session be seen as a refusal to assist his patient? Was he to be responsible for Robson's worsening condition?

'I started to think about the consequences,' he says. 'Imprisonment? Or just probation if my age was taken into account?'

His telephone rang. It was Glukhov.

The treatment will take place in Sochi, Glukhov said. You have the full authority to conduct the treatment.

Sokolov purchased a ticket for the scheduled 11:40 a.m. flight to Adler, went through the security checkpoint and waited.

His phone rang again, and it was bad news: Martin had been moved to intensive care.

Waiting to board the aircraft, Dr Sokolov couldn't shake the feeling that the treatment he planned to administer might not save Robson's legs; and now he started to worry it might not save his life either.

A HOPE NOT LOST

We know surprisingly few facts about the natural progression of any of the decompression injuries, perhaps because there are many different starting points and thereafter so many possible pathways for the development of the pathology. From several studies we know that the prediction of outcome for an individual case is far from precise, and occasionally it will then appear to have been wildly wrong.

David Elliott, Divers Alert Network workshop

He stared at the six comatose bodies tethered by tubes and wires to life-support equipment which pumped oxygen into their lungs, breathed for them, washed their blood, and monitored them with *bleeps* and *blips*, and he wondered what the hell he was doing there. Around mid-morning on Friday, Robson and his damaged legs had been admitted to the intensive care ward. He didn't know why and, apparently, no one thought it necessary to tell him. He was anxious because this was the place where doctors sent the powerless, the ones who needed the *bleeps* and *blips* to keep a fingertip-hold on life.

He had tubes shoved into his arm, and they dripped clear liquid which dulled the pain and blunted the discomfort around his abdomen, but each breath was still hard. He shivered under the blanket, and his legs remained dead. He'd been in the hospital for more than fifteen hours and had heard sketchy details of a plan to move him, yet still he was there, waiting for treatment.

He watched as a nurse, smart in her crisp ocean-blue tunic, approached a patient, removed something from the endo-tracheal tube in his neck and stuck an aspirator into his throat. There was a slurp of bodily fluids as she moved the suction hose around. When she finished, a cleaner beavered in behind her to disinfect the machine.

Robson winced. He needed to get out, needed recompression therapy now. There's something wrong with me, he wanted to cry to the nurses. What am I still doing here? Why aren't I being treated?

A nurse walked past his bed. Oxygen. I need oxygen, he said.

She mumbled a few words and shoved a thermometer into his armpit. After a few seconds, the nurse removed the instrument and took note of the reading. She wiped the device on her apron and approached another patient to repeat the same pro-cess. All these beeping machines, Robson thought, and just one thermometer.

The clock ticked and the machines bleeped, and the nurses huddled into a corner whispering to one another. His mouth was cottony, his lips were dry, he hadn't eaten for hours, and he lay there holding onto memories of a time when he wasn't in hospital with legs that didn't work.

The ward sister patrolled the room and looked at each patient. She went to Robson's bed. Water, he croaked.

She walked away and returned a moment later with a large plastic bottle. The woman picked a paper cup from his bedside unit, took a syringe and extracted a measured amount from the bottle. Robson watched as she squirted the sliver into the cup and passed it to him.

Thank you very much, he said. He looked inside. The water barely covered the bottom of the cup and scarcely lined his tongue.

Robson held the cup aloft and looked to the bottle.

The sister nodded and repeated the process. As she handed the cup to Robson, a machine beeped behind her, and she turned to see where the noise had come from. He eyed the water bottle and then the distracted nurse.

The crunch of plastic was probably her first clue that her patient was up to no good. By the time she turned, Robson had almost drained the bottle. A smile crept across his face. Another nurse stifled a snigger.

Oxygen, he said again, pointing to a gas cylinder and then to his mouth.

He couldn't understand why he was being denied oxygen. The fact was the nurses couldn't tell him either. They were simply following orders issued down the telephone that told them how to care for this patient and his legs. They just had to keep him comfortable, provide no more oxygen and sips of water only, and he was meant to lie there and wait.

Hanging over Robson like a bad omen was the ghost of another diving disaster, one involving his sporting hero Jochen Hasenmayer. In the spring of 1989, the German was leading an expedition at Wolfgang Lake, in Salzburg, Austria, for a documentary.

Ascending from eighty-five metres, Hasenmayer made a deco stop. He thought he was at forty metres. That's what his depth gauge told him, and the German relaxed into the routine stop; he still had three more hours of deco to go. But the pressure gauge was faulty. Instead of resting at forty metres, Hasenmayer was fifteen metres shallower.

The attack lasted all of ten seconds. Hasenmayer didn't see it coming, and it sent him spinning. At first, he saw a bright light. It was closely followed by darkness. And then light. Then darkness. The surface above and the depths below. Over and over and over, like a cartwheeling car. Hasenmayer was in danger of tumbling into the abyss. So, he did the only thing left open to him. He inflated his buoyancy jacket and rocketed to the surface. By the time he arrived, he was paralysed from just below the chin and couldn't do anything to help himself. Two safety divers waiting on the north shore hauled him up the bank, stripped off his equipment and lifted him into a mobile hyperbaric unit, on standby for such emergencies. Then they blew the chamber down to fifty metres.

Within two minutes, 90 per cent of the paralysis had disappeared. Still, Hasenmayer stayed inside for another five hours as he waited for the nitrogen to be purged from his body. The support divers arranged his evacuation to a recompression facility, in Graz, where his lingering injuries could be treated.

But in hospital the debilitating paralysis returned and took his legs again. Still hoping for a full recovery, Hasenmayer arranged an airlift to an institute in Cologne, Germany. For eleven days, doctors toiled to reverse the paralysis. When they eventually ran out of options, Hasenmayer just shrugged.

Everything was already too late, he told journalist Hubert Kaltenbach, in the months after accepting his life was now confined to a wheelchair.

The aircraft touched down at Sochi airport at two in the afternoon, and Dr Sokolov woke up in his seat. Sweeping over him again was the same feeling he'd had before take-off: have I done enough to save my patient and his legs?

He'd been worried about Robson's condition, and the consequences of his decisions were not lost on him; they had niggled away in the back of his mind for some time. Even he had felt it necessary to seek a second opinion before boarding the flight. Exhausted, he'd fallen asleep for the first time since Dunaev had called him the previous evening. And now here he was, awake and anxious in his seat as the jet taxied along the apron, worried for Robson's life and unable to escape the fear he'd made mistakes in his advice about treatment.

As soon as the plane arrived at the terminal, Dr Sokolov telephoned the doctors in Nalchik and held his breath.

Robson remained serious but stable, he was told. No change.

A certain relief swept over the doctor. His patient was in intensive care, but, so far, all the medical team had needed to do was administer intravenous fluids of saline and glucose.

Making his way through the airport, the doctor was greeted by a representative of the YURPSO emergency rescue team, and he was briefed about the rescue operation that was now in full swing.

Around midday, the mobile chamber had been towed out of storage and lifted onto a trailer, and the driver set out along the

M27 Highway, bound for Sochi. Medical staff from YURPSO were travelling with the truck. Meanwhile, on the outskirts of Moscow at about 1:45 p.m., the EMERCOM IL-76 transporter aircraft had taken off from Zhukovsky airfield with orders to rendezvous with the DART in Sochi. From there, the whole party would fly to Mineralnye Vody, the closest airport to Nalchik still accepting flights.

At the same time, technicians in Sochi were finalising preparations with the recompression chamber. An operational check had been carried out on the facility and all of its operating systems, medical documentation had been filled in, the first aid equipment examined, bedding and food gathered. The oxygen and helium needed to run the chamber was analysed and the paperwork completed. Someone sat down to begin the complicated calculations to ensure there was an ample supply of gas available to safely complete the treatment and provide a reserve for any unforeseen emergencies. Quantifying the oxygen requirements for Robson and one attendant inside the chamber for an extended time required dozens of separate equations that accounted for every minute of the treatment. Added together, the total gave an indication of the volume of gas they had to have at hand. Spare cylinders had to be pulled out of storage. The men apparently had to dip into their own pockets to pay for extra helium when it was realised they might not have enough. Duties had been assigned to each member of the team. Then they had called their families and said they might not be home for days.

Once he was brought up to speed, Dr Sokolov was asked if he wanted to head over to the hyperbaric chamber in Sochi or fly with the DART to Mineralnye Vody. He opted to accompany the DART because he wanted to meet his patient as soon as possible. As the official leader of the treatment team, he wanted to be there to conduct a medical examination, to give instructions on the transfer and accompany Robson during the flight.

As the resources converged on Sochi, there was little for Dr Sokolov to do but find a place to sit and wait, knowing it could be another four hours before he would rendezvous with Robson. More than twenty-four hours had passed since the English diver was first injured and Dr Sokolov couldn't help but wonder if they would get to him in time.

Seven hundred miles away, heading east through the brittle, winter farmland of Crimea, towards the border with Russia, was Robson's closest friend, Mike Shyrokov. He was sitting in the passenger seat of his Nissan pick-up waiting for a phone call to tell him where to go. Mike was really Mikhail. He had a face full of stubble and peppered the soberest conversations with humour and bad language. At the wheel was Oleg Savchenko, pilot, dive buddy, and chief mechanic of Shyrokov's speedboat racing team. They had been on the road since early morning after Shyrokov got a telephone call from Nalchik telling him about Robson's incident.

Shyrokov had burst into Robson's life eight years earlier on the Mediterranean island of Cyprus. Robson was on the second day of teaching a rebreather course in Larnaca when the Ukrainian accosted him. Tell me, what is all this about? Shyrokov had urged, pointing to the rebreather. No sooner had Robson begun to explain than Shyrokov asked to join the course. Robson told him he was already part way through the programme and did not have a training manual in Russian, but to Shyrokov they were minor obstacles. By the end of the week, he had qualified as a rebreather diver. The pair became firm friends, diving around the world, sharing 'rooms, boats and booze'.

The previous evening, Shyrokov had been relaxing in his local banya with friends. The bathhouse was a rare opportunity to escape the pressures of work and was perhaps the only place he was forced to leave his mobile phone at the door. Shut off from the world, time lost to the hazy heat of the wooden steam room and its mint or chamomile scents, Shyrokov and his friends talked politics, sport or the challenges of moving teams of workmen around the world. The conversations had continued as the group moved to the changing rooms. Shyrokov fell silent when he opened his locker and glanced at his phone. 'There was something like thirty-six missed calls from Andrei Bykov,' he says.

He dialled Bykov's number, but his call went unanswered. He tried again. And again. Flicking through his contacts, Shyrokov found a telephone number for Dunaev and called him.

Roman, what's going on? he asked.

It's Martin, Roman replied, before filling him in the situation. We're trying to arrange evacuation to a recompression chamber, but we don't know where yet.

Eventually, Shyrokov got to speak to Robson. I think it's best I come to help with translations, he told his friend. There will be small cultural differences, lots of them. Hopefully, I can work to make them smoother. And, don't forget, I know how to make a proper cup of tea.

Shyrokov went home, packed a bag and checked the airline schedules. With no direct flights to Nalchik, it would take him two days to get there. That's when he called his buddy Savchenko. They pointed the car towards Russia and set off, the destination to be confirmed.

Somewhere on the road through Crimea, Shyrokov's phone rang. Dunaev explained the plan to move Robson. He told him about the involvement of Dr Sokolov and the plan to fly Robson over the mountains to the Black Sea for treatment.

Head to Sochi, Dunaev said. We'll see you there.

At some point during those early hours in hospital, the bubbles massed inside Martin Robson began to shrink naturally as the gas pressure inside his body sought equilibrium with the surrounding atmosphere. On the face of it, this sounds positive, but things might not be as simple as that, according to the science.

Even as the bubbles depart, the lesions in the spine's white matter continue to grow and damage more of the signal-carrying axons, adding to the number already flattened in the maelstrom. It is likely that the level of the waste chemical known as creatinine, which may have spiked eight times greater than normal in the early part of the ambush, remains abnormally high. This may indicate a potential problem in the kidneys. If there is a problem, and that leads to a fall in the hormone erythropoietin, there will be a severe reduction in red blood cell count. This threatens to compromise the efficiency of the body's oxygen transport system.

Elsewhere, however, the medication starts to kick in. The husks of platelets and fibrin proteins surrounding the bubbles are slowly being dissolved by the drugs administered to prevent hypercoagulation and encourage blood flow. This process reduces the chance of stroke or heart attack. Meanwhile, sensory neurons called nociceptors stop transmitting and the feelings of pain begin to dissipate.

The human body is a remarkable machine; its built-in redundancy can compensate for a limited amount of tissue damage and restore function. Lying in hospital, the real issue for Robson was whether his body could find a way to circumvent the destruction. Or was the tissue damage in the spinal cord too much to recover from?

Martin Robson remembers once saving a young girl from a burning building. He'd found her amid baby toys and choking smoke on the floor of her bedroom in a three-storey townhouse in Tunbridge Wells, in Kent. With a firefighter's breathing mask shielding his face, Robson must have looked unearthly to the toddler.

I've got her, he shouted to a colleague who was searching another room. Scooping up the girl, Robson turned for the door and ran for both of their lives, throwing himself at the stairs as the flames chased his boots.

Acrid smoke was already billowing from the front door when he pitched into the fresh air of red fire appliances, blue flashing lights, blaring sirens and spraying water.

My baby, screamed the mother.

Robson's arms were empty. He reached for the zip of his tunic. He looked down, and the eyes of his commander followed. Cradled inside, the toddler looked up at them.

Robson carefully lifted the girl from his jacket and handed her to a waiting paramedic. In that instant, Robson had saved two lives, that of the young girl and her mother. For a few brief moments their lives had been fused by experience, then just as quickly they were parted. Robson never saw the child again, he didn't even learn of her name, it just wasn't his style. Now he was like that little girl; waiting for a stranger to come to his aid.

It was so quiet; he could hear the clock ticking on the wall. The machines still blipped and bleeped, and the nurses still huddled in the corner. From the corner of his eye, Robson saw Igor Galaida at the door. A nurse buzzed him in and handed him white paper boots, a cap and cape.

We are moving you, Robson remembers him saying. For the first time in hours, he allowed himself a moment of relief. He was getting out of there.

The giant IL-76 transporter howled into Adler airport, and Dr Sokolov watched it turn a semi-circle at the end of the runway and lower its loading ramp, engines still alive. In the turbo-fan-charged winter evening, the YURPSO team drove the lorry carrying the DART chamber straight into the cavernous belly of the aircraft and lashed everything down. The doctor was surprised everything fitted, with room to spare.

He took his seat, and the aircraft screamed into the air again. Jammed into the passenger cabin alongside him, among the YURPSO rescue squad, were two acquaintances. He had known them both for some years because of their shared passion for diving medicine. The team's hyperbaric specialist was a man called Igor Constantinovich Gusarov. He had been the one who had put in the effort to get the Sochi chamber complex into operation. The team's medical specialist was Ilya Ivanovich Gaponov, whom Dr Sokolov had actually taught the basics of hyperbaric medicine at his Institute in Moscow.

It was early evening on Friday. Soon, they would be with their patient. Their job was to get him to Sochi in one piece. Dr Sokolov's part in all this was to examine the patient and give an honest assessment: could they save the man? Looking out of the window, he watched the Caucasus Mountains drift beneath them in the orange glow of dusk, but he couldn't enjoy the view, not with so much riding on him.

Part way through the flight, a message was passed to the doctor. There's a problem, Dr Sokolov was told. The medical team at Nalchik have asked for the whole entourage to go to the hospital to collect Robson.

No. Dr Sokolov was firm in his reply. No, because travelling to Nalchik would waste time, because it would risk deterioration in the patient's condition, because it would adversely affect the treatment.

No, they must send him by ambulance to meet us, Dr Sokolov said.

They won't do it unless you take responsibility, he was told. The doctor wasn't going to let bureaucracy get in the way now. Tell them I authorise them to transport him by road, he replied. It cannot be any other way.

The machines in ITU were still beeping and blipping when Robson was unplugged from the tubes. He tried to move his legs, but he couldn't. Somehow, though, he wasn't worried. He

303

was heading for recompression therapy, and he was confident that would put him right. He was lifted onto a gurney, and he was wheeled outside to the waiting ambulance. The cold rush of the air crept under his blanket, and the stretcher's legs collapsed with a bang as his broken body was pushed into the vehicle. An attendant nodded to him and, with a blur of blue lights and sirens, the convoy set off. Robson fought the fatigue as the ambulance rushed to someplace he didn't know. We're with you, his Russian friends said as they accompanied him for reassurance.

Then the vehicle came to a halt and soon he could hear aircraft engines approaching. The engines whined in the winter air, and the doors to the ambulance opened. Robson looked up and saw the faces of two men. Doctors, Robson presumed. The pair climbed inside, and they shut the door. The younger of the two asked him to move his toes. This, Robson understood, was the medical exam the doctors needed to carry out to see if they could restore the life to lower body. Sergei Gorpinyuk interpreted for the group. Robson didn't say much; he just did what he was told when asked to move his toes.

He couldn't wiggle his toes.

Or swivel his ankles.

Or bend his knees.

And the cold numbness had migrated north through his body. It was only when the doctor touched his stomach that Robson felt his hand. Robson didn't complain and tried to stay optimistic, he had made it this far without giving up, but his face said something different. He didn't pay much attention to the old man sitting off to one side, the one taking notes while the younger man carried out the examination.

From the lack of movement, Dr Sokolov knew his patient had suffered a significant spinal injury, but it was what he couldn't see that worried him most. He had no idea how permanent the damage was, but he still had hope. That's why he diagnosed a deep lower paraparesis. The three words were as notable for what they didn't say as much as what they did. The doctor hadn't written lower paraplegia, for example. That would have signalled that all hope had been lost; that everything, the phone calls, his journey from Moscow, this mercy flight, had been in vain. It would have said: there's nothing we can do; his legs are gone. But deep lower paraparesis said: there's a hope that not everything has been lost; there's a chance to prevent this patient from being disabled; there's a chance to fight for his legs using the therapeutic recompression deep method of treatment. The words said: it's time to move.

Giant men in heavy winter coats appeared, and they pulled Robson from the ambulance into the dark and across the snow-covered airfield. Rain fell into his face, and the wind scraped at his skin, and the turbofans whined impatiently. Robson lay there frustrated, unable to help as the men struggled up the steep ramp lined with anti-skid netting and into the belly of the aircraft. They swapped him to a smaller stretcher they were able to lift onto the trailer, and they slid him through the sixty-six-centimetre-wide hatchway and into the DART.

Sardined inside the hyperbaric chamber, Robson watched the younger man who had examined him inside the ambulance, Ilya

Gaponov, climb through the hatch and take a seat. A cigarette dangled from his lips. Robson stared back at him. The man looked at the filter tip and said: I know, and I am a doctor.

The steel door of the DART clunked shut, and gas hissed in to pressurise the chamber. Not much, barely enough to force Robson into equalising his ears. And he breathed deeply for all his worth. He wanted to live and to walk again, and he knew this journey was the next step towards his salvation. The four turbofans growled, and the cabin shook. The trailer shook, and the DART shook as the giant husk of metal that had no place in the skies thundered down the asphalt and into the air. From inside the chamber, Robson felt the aircraft bank as it turned south-west and belted for the heavens.

What Robson didn't notice was the crumpled face of the doctor who peered through a porthole during the flight. Although the maximum working pressure of the chamber was the equivalent of fifty metres, the doctor had made a rather unusual decision to increase the pressure inside the chamber to just one metre. This pressure, he decided, would secure the integrity of the unit as they flew over the mountains and could be depressurised without delay at the other end.

Then the aircraft landed, gas hissed from the chamber and the big men were there again. Four of them, five, maybe six, lifted the stretcher from the DART, down the aircraft's steep loading ramp and into the back of a waiting ambulance. Someone in the back checked Robson's vitals. Then the vehicle raced through the late-evening traffic, lights flashing, sirens hollering, other vehicles moving out of the way.

Arriving at the harbourside complex, the ambulance driver

backed the vehicle beneath a large roller-shutter and into a room dominated by a giant cylinder-shaped recompression chamber. A man with a Mohican haircut approached Robson – the ambulance driver. A proud smile creased his face. Bystro, bystro, he said. Quickly, quickly.

It was gone 9 p.m. on Friday and Robson lay on the gurney in the middle of the room, waiting. A coat was draped over his legs, a blue blanket across his body. A hand, white with cold, poked from beneath the covers. People moved around him, busy with jobs that needed doing. The numbness of fatigue holding him to the gurney, Robson did not say anything and left the men to do whatever it was they were doing. He had made it this far without giving up, made it to the place where he had every confidence they would restore his legs and reverse the damage that had swept through his body.

Standing around the room were small groups of burly, weathered men dressed in padded, fur-trimmed jackets and boots, huddled together like cops congregating over a body at a crime scene. The younger ones wore grey and white camouflage combat trousers, the older ones woolly hats. One lit a cigarette as they talked and waited for the order to move their patient through the circular hatchway of the chamber. A thickset, bearded man in a blue T-shirt which looked like medical scrubs joined them then walked away. Sergei Gorpinyuk, who had travelled to Sochi with Robson, was there in the corner of the room and stood, listening. The doctors who had examined Robson in the ambulance were also there. They were off to one side in conversation with other men he had not met. A video cameraman from EMERCOM pointed the lens at Robson, who pulled the blanket over his face.

Then, a voice he recognised spoke to him, and Robson removed the blanket from his face. Gorpinyuk said it was time to move. Robson lay there helpless as eight men eased the stretcher into the chamber; weak and vulnerable as the bearded man in blue scrubs manhandled him onto the ready-made bed. Gorpinyuk crouched beside him.

Martin, the doctor wants to speak with you now.

Robson looked up. The older man invisible in the background, the one everyone had missed coming into the room, was sitting before him, a picture of tidiness in his shirt and tie and suit jacket. The doctor examined him again, and Robson said he couldn't move his legs, couldn't feel them, that there was pain in his abdomen.

The treatment, Dr Sokolov said, will consist of prolonged stay under pressure.

As Gorpinyuk translated the message, Robson looked up to the doctor. He asked none of the questions one would have thought necessary: who are you? Where are you from? What is your experience?

All he asked was a technical question about the chamber operation: will we be on BIBS? BIBS means built-in breathing system, where the patient breathes oxygen from a face mask. That was it. Just one technical question.

No, was the reply. You'll be breathing chamber gas.

With that, everyone left but Robson and the bearded man in scrubs.

As the chamber was prepared for blowdown, Robson had time to telephone Vikki. There was no answer, so he left a message and the phone was taken from him.

The door clanged shut, valves opened, and the machine came to life with a dragon-hiss.

On the other side of the door, Dr Sokolov stared at the monitor, nervous. He could see Robson slumped on a bed inside the chamber, equalising his ears to the increasing pressure. Then he turned his eyes to the pressure gauge and watched the needle climb steadily, passing the equivalent of fifty metres of water, then sixty, and on towards its final destination, the equivalent of one hundred metres. Dr Sokolov looked back to Robson again, and as the fizz of gas filled his ears the intricate details of the treatment plan flooded his mind. He exchanged a few words with the technician operating the chamber controls and finally took a seat at the tiny fold-down table next to the instrument console. Then he began to write in his medical journal:

20.01.2012 at 22h 30. The patient had complaints of violation of the sensitivity of the lower limbs, pain in the abdomen and lower limbs, the inability of independent movement. There was a violation of the pelvic organs. Diagnosis: severe decompression sickness.

20.01.2012 at 23h 10. Affected air compression was started, and then helium gas atmosphere adjusted to oxygen.

The most important figure, the one uppermost in his mind, was the time to treatment period: almost twenty-nine hours. Twenty-three hours longer than the conventional wisdom dictated for completely reversing nerve tissue damage.

*

Vikki Batten's phone beeped with a voicemail at seven o'clock. Home alone in Somerset, enveloped with a desperate sadness, Vikki had last spoken with Martin a few hours ago when he called to say he was being transferred to a recompression chamber. She'd been waiting to hear from him with an update, but when Martin's call came it hadn't connected. Instead, it had gone straight through to her messaging service.

Vikki dialled the service, and Martin's voice leaped from the speaker. He sounded more positive and confident than at any point over the previous day.

I'm going to be in the chamber for a week to ten days, so I won't be able to speak with you again until the treatment is all finished. Love you. Speak to you when I get out.

Sitting on the sofa, the holiday photograph of happier times on the side, his slippers on the floor by the door, Vikki played the message back repeatedly: twenty-odd seconds of his voice; twenty-odd seconds of welcome news; twenty-odd seconds of hope.

And then she started sobbing. 'It might have been the last time I could have spoken with him,' she says. 'And I missed it.'

THE LONG SOAK

The discomfort of decompression sickness, the confinement in a small metal cylinder, the noise of frequent air changes to prevent carbon dioxide accumulation (and also prevent restful sleep), the loss of taste of food, the lack of comfort in toilet arrangements or bedding, and the resistance to breathing from increased density of air . . . makes the whole process very exhausting and may cause consequent complications for the patient. This might be justified if one could promise success, the prospect of spending up to forty hours more after the initial six to ten hours can be demoralising for patient and attendants.

Donald E. Mackay, former Surgeon General, Royal Navy, Proceedings of the Second Symposium on Underwater Physiology

The first men to suffer decompression sickness in the 1840s rubbed brandy into their aching joints in the hope of alleviating the pain. Such treatment might seem odd, even for those days, but since no one really knew what kind of illness they were dealing with, no one really knew how to cure it. Some physicians dismissed the ailment as rheumatism and prescribed a poultice with laudanum, a mild rubefacient, or a mercury chloride mix, known as calomel, with milk. Some suggested hot baths and warm drinks like chamomile infusion; others injected men with morphine. Sometimes men sought their own medicine at the nearest saloon. When two caisson workers on London's Tower Bridge were seized with joint pains, one danced about and was quickly relieved; the other knelt and prayed. When his religious request went unanswered, he too was said to have turned to dance.

For the first fifty years of hard-hat diving, when men were blown back to the surface in four or five seconds, the only treatment for a paralysed diver was hope and prayer for spontaneous recovery. In the 1880s, there was a Greek sponge diver who, on his seventh dive of the day, spent a single minute ascending from forty metres. By the time the man surfaced, he couldn't move his right arm or right leg. Even so, he went to bed and woke the next morning to find the paralysis had gone. Just like that, he was back on his feet. Nine years later, the same man lost the use of both legs after a dive, and slumped, unconscious, to the deck of the boat. Three hours later, he could stand with the help of sticks. The following morning, he was back at work, apparently well.

Nature's efforts, that's how such occurrences of fortune were explained. In Australia, between 1900 and 1908, Dr Graham Blick treated pearl divers who had been paralysed two or three times, and sometimes more, and he was often astonished at the way some hopeless paraplegics recovered. One can only wait on Nature's efforts, he wrote. And Nature's efforts could sometimes be kinder than expected.

Nature's efforts weren't kind to everyone, though, and doctors at diving grounds around the world watched paralysed men die from septicaemia, bedsores, cystitis or some other unknown complication. Early photographs reveal monochrome horrors of the most appalling kind. One, taken in 1907, shows lab-coated doctors surrounding the cadaverous body of a Greek sponge diver who, thirty-four days earlier, had shot to the surface from seventy metres. Stretched out on a hospital bed and covered in ulcers, the young man's body had withered so much his spine stood proud of his back. He died of sepsis and encephalopathy two days after the photograph was taken, and nobody could think of what could have been done to save him.

Physicians in the mining industry had first suggested treating the bends by recompressing their patients in the 1840s, but it was British civil engineer Ernest Moir who turned the idea into a reality. In 1899, he was appointed to represent a British firm working on the Hudson River Tunnel, between Manhattan and New Jersey. When he arrived in New York, he found tunnellers, or sandhogs as they called themselves, were dying at a rate of one or two a month. He saw a man's veins opened up on the mortuary slab and the blood was so thick and black it had to be squeezed out. With a view to improving the state of things, he introduced the medical airlock. Moir placed his boiler-like air compartment near the top of the shaft at the New York North River Tunnel site so men who fell ill could quickly be re-immersed. Those who went in were often in a bad way. Some were unconscious; others unable to use their limbs. To treat them, Moir raised the pressure inside the chamber to two-thirds that of the working pressure inside the tunnel, and then slowly decompressed the men for thirty minutes. After the airlock was introduced, the works lost just two men in the following fifteen months.

The use of compressed air as a medicine didn't catch on nearly as quickly among divers, though, and the first US Navy diving handbook, published in 1905, didn't even mention the risks of the bends, let alone how to treat the disorder. The idea of asking a disabled diver to re-enter the very environment he blamed for his affliction was counterintuitive and would remain so for many years. When Gunner George Stillson investigated the US Navy's deep-diving programme in 1915, he noted an anxiety about recompression treatment among divers. Some men hid their pain from doctors to avoid a spell in the chamber. Even Stillson was guilty of the practice. Once, while suffering the effects of a bend, he objected to the treatment advised by the navy surgeon. Instead, Stillson went home. Three hours later, he was doubled up in pain and gripped by nausea, willing the doctor to hurry to his bedside.

Another nine years passed before the US Navy introduced the first standardised treatment protocol. Officially, it was called a Recompression Therapy Procedure, although divers knew it as an air treatment table. Published in the 1924 edition of the *Diving Manual*, the procedure called for an injured diver to be rapidly recompressed to forty-five pounds per square inch, the equivalent of three atmospheres of pressure. If the casualty's condition did not improve, doctors increased the pressure to sixty pounds. The patient was left under pressure until symptoms disappeared. Decompression back to the surface took almost five hours.

The procedure was lengthy and often failed to prevent disability or death, so it was inevitable researchers would look for something more efficient. In 1937, a lieutenant in the US Navy

Medical Corps named Albert R. Behnke proposed the use of oxygen to treat compressed air illness. To test his theory, Behnke exposed dogs to an explosive decompression event designed to produce the worst symptoms of the bends. He then recompressed some of the dogs on air and some on pure oxygen. As he predicted, dogs breathing oxygen had a better outcome. Oxygen inhalation combined with recompression, Behnke later wrote, were essential in the treatment for compressed air illness.

His wisdom didn't win over the US Navy Bureau of Medicine and Surgery, however. The Bureau ruled that breathing oxygen in a confined space was not sailor-proof, which meant the risk of a patient convulsing, or of a fire breaking out inside the chamber, was far too great to justify introducing the new protocol.

Behnke continued his research anyway, and, in 1939, reported on the successful use of oxygen to treat forty-eight out of fifty men who suffered decompression sickness while on experimental and salvage diving operations. For severe cases, he suggested recompressing the casualty to a depth of 165 feet (50 m) and then have them breathe hyperbaric oxygen once they reached sixty feet (18 m). If the treatment failed, he recompressed the patient to the point of relief and left them there for twenty-four hours. In May 1944, the Bureau of Medicine and Surgery published a simplified method of Behnke's treatment protocol to provide fleet personnel with a new option to treat injured divers. The schedule became known as the long oxygen table. To divers, long treatments were known as an overnight soak.

The development didn't last long, though. A year later, following reports from across the fleet that the table failed to provide a complete cure in half of the cases, the navy was compelled to take a fresh look at its treatment for the bends. Commander Otto Van Der Aue's approach to testing the efficacy of a treatment table was a novel one and he drew up a report that said, in effect: if a test diver could survive a working dive followed by a course of recompression therapy without suffering a bend, then the treatment table was safe to use. If a test diver suffered decompression sickness, the treatment table would be modified until no bends occurred. For Project X-443, Van Der Aue pulled thirty-three men from the ranks of first and second-class divers and carried out tests on them in a pressurised diving tank. The men, dressed in hard-hat diving gear, were made to lift a length of pipe weighing sixty pounds from a bench to the floor and back again, ten times a minute for fifty-five minutes. The divers then decompressed according to navy guidelines. On the surface, the divers rested for an hour. Then they were recompressed according to the schedule of the treatment table under test. Some played cards, some read, others went to sleep while doctors kept them under observation. Van Der Aue watched to see if the men developed symptoms of the bends.

The results of his study led to the introduction in the US Navy of four therapeutic plans, numbered Tables 1 to 4. On face value, the tables appeared to be a significant step forward. What the experiments really focused on, however, was whether or not the proposed treatment tables would cause the bends in healthy divers; it didn't look at their therapeutic efficacy. And the conclusions were based on slim experimental evidence. The whole project involved just eighty-four test dives; some tables were ruled safe after tests on only six subjects. These tables, however, stood as the US Navy standard for almost twenty years. Navies adopted them around the world, commercial salvage companies embraced them, and everyone seemed happy.

So, it was with a mainly academic curiosity that staff at the US Navy Experimental Diving Unit, at the Washington Navy Yard, began to question the effectiveness of treatment tables. Over the years, the unit had collected hundreds of case reports of decompression sickness in both military and civilian divers. Investigations found 13 per cent of patients either suffered a relapse or saw no improvement after standard treatment. The failure rate on some tables ran as high as 25 per cent among the most serious cases of decompression. In a report dated November 1965, two navy doctors in Washington, Commander Maxwell W. Goodman and Captain Robert D. Workman, described US Navy tables as reliable for treating pain-only bends, but generally speaking, they were insufficient for the management of severe injury.

Finally, in the mid-1960s, the US Navy treatment tables were subjected to a further review. In the interim, diving had changed; it was no longer the preserve only of the military and commercial salvagers. Hobbyists, equipped with scuba tanks, were heading underwater and they were bumping into the accepted limits of diving. They were diving multiple times a day, spending short periods on the surface between excursions, and were completing what the navy described as 'non-standard' decompressions. Non-standard meant anything other than strict adherence to the military school of diving. These sport divers also took longer to receive treatment if they got a bend; some abalone fishermen would treat themselves with aspirin, alcohol and hot baths before seeking help. And it was these practices that were, in part, exposing the shortcomings of the treatment tables.

Encouraged by the work of Behnke thirty years earlier, Goodman and Workman proposed a low-pressure, minimal-recompression, oxygen exposure therapeutic approach to treatment. Under their plan, injured divers would be recompressed to sixty feet and breathe oxygen for three sessions of twenty-five minutes, with an air break between each session. The patient would then be decompressed to thirty feet and have two sixty-minute periods of oxygen breathing interspersed with a fifteen-minute air break. The total time of the treatment was 285 minutes. That was nine times shorter than the previous tables, yet the schedule seemed to cure even the most traumatic of injuries.

The two doctors reported the case of a thirty-three-year-old diver who had completed six dives in one day and couldn't move his left leg. Pain gripped his shoulder, he couldn't feel anything in his lower abdomen, and he had no control over his bladder. Following the use of hyperbaric oxygen, 'recovery was prompt and complete'. Another diver, aged thirty-four, brought in with nausea, vertigo and general weakness, recovered after four minutes under pressure. The two men were so confident in their research they said the treatment would provide complete and firm relief for most divers stricken with severe decompression sickness and should be effective in ninety-eight out of a hundred trials.

Within eight years, the US Navy had introduced the minimal recompression oxygen table to the fleet as Table 6, and the protocol was on its way to becoming the universal standard of care – the treatment of choice, one report labelled it – for treating decompression sickness. The British Royal Navy introduced its version of Table 6, known by the number 62, and the French commercial diving company Comex published something similar. Pretty soon, the type of injury suffered by military and commercial divers appeared completely reversible when treated on-site. Sport divers who were often injured while pushing against the limits of safety with provocative dive profiles, and who took longer to seek treatment, were not always as lucky. Even so, success rates pushed 97 per cent if therapy was delivered promptly. Divers who turned up for treatment with severe injuries hours after the event had a greater than 80 per cent chance of satisfactory response. Soon, recompression with oxygen became the cornerstone of treatment for decompression sickness.

Their relative success then provided little impetus for the development of alternative therapies. But they do exist for use when a diver is brought into a recompression chamber suffering life-threatening injuries so severe that something else is needed. In the field of hyperbaric medicine, they are known as deep tables, and some involve the use of helium-oxygen breathing mixes, known as heliox. Theoretically, deep tables work because compression to greater pressures results in the rapid reduction in the volume of bubbles trapped in the body. Heliox, meanwhile, when used as part of the treatment, is understood to drive nitrogen from the body faster than pure oxygen.

Probably the most common deep table is the Comex 30, developed by Compagnie Maritime d'Expertises, a French company that specialises in deep diving. Patients treated using the protocol are compressed to the equivalent of thirty metres of seawater and breathe a fifty-fifty mix of heliox. Doctors at the Eastern Hospital in Gothenburg, Sweden, have successfully used Comex 30 to treat a handful of injured divers who had failed to show any improvement under a Table 6 treatment. They had one guy who came in nauseous, dizzy and unable to stand on his left leg. Half an hour into treatment, he was back on his feet.

Other doctors reported similar successes with different deep treatments. In the early 1980s, a set of deep air tables emerged in Hawaii to treat injuries faced by a unique subset of commercial divers: black-coral divers who were known to make very deep dives, multiple times a day, day after day, in search of the rare gemstone. Not unexpectedly, some got decompression sickness, and they took up to a day, on average, to get treatment. Doctors noticed many failed to recover using the navy's oxygen tables. When the divers were compressed to the point where their symptoms disappeared, or to the chamber limits, they were able to walk away, apparently healed. This occurred often enough that doctors developed the Hawaiian deep air tables, which involved an initial spike to depths as great as eighty-five metres of seawater before a staged decompression and transitioning to oxygen at eighteen metres. The treatment lasted about six-and-a-half hours. An analysis of 780 cases, between 1983 and 2003, found 93 per cent of divers made a full recovery. One diver died; twenty-four others were left with life-changing limitations. The rest escaped with mild to moderate limitations.

Doctors behind the Hawaiian tables were, according to the report, confident in their use. The idea of deep tables, and those using heliox mixes, did not, however, find consensus among hyperbaric doctors. The case for using deep treatments was simply not established by data, they stated, the clinical evidence of their success was mostly anecdotal, and ethically validating them could be difficult.

Doctors expressed other concerns with deep tables. Maintaining a patient and their attendant under a hyperbaric environment for longer than six to twelve hours introduces the complexities of atmosphere control, fatigue and nutritional and waste management, one report noted. In other words, you need to provide a patient with food, a toilet, washing facilities and also have a way of monitoring the atmosphere inside the chamber to prevent the build-up of carbon dioxide. Then you need a way of managing the risk of oxygen toxicity to both patient and attendant inside the chamber, as well as keeping your staff well rested. Medics who have carried out such treatments have reported suffering from a profound fatigue they likened to jet lag. Such challenges perhaps go part way to explaining why deep tables never found much support when doctors were finding plenty of success with the low pressure, short oxygen tables.

The short oxygen tables were favoured because they had the great advantage of history on their side to show they worked. And they worked well enough to get even the most seriously injured casualties back on their feet. Today, Table 6, or one of its equivalents, is the most commonly used recompression schedule in the world. One estimate suggests 80 per cent of cases are treated using one of the protocols. Most of the time, doctors rarely need to step outside the parameters of the treatment schedule to see a complete resolution or significant improvement in their patient's condition in a single cycle of recompression. But they have options. Occasionally, when faced with a patient with residual symptoms, doctors might feel it advantageous to lock them in the chamber again for a follow-up treatment. If things aren't going well, they might adapt the Table 6 schedule and increase the amount of time their patient is breathing oxygen. Such options, according to doctors, have proved remarkably effective in treating divers suffering from severe decompression sickness. On one occasion a patient arrived at a chamber barely conscious and quadriplegic following a rapid ascent. Faced with one of the sickest patients he had ever seen, the doctor took him down to eighteen metres on a Table 6 protocol. He extended the time his patient was under pressure by almost a hundred minutes but did nothing more elaborate than that. Transferred to an intensive care unit, the diver appeared to have regained all motor movement and reported nothing but minor leg pain. He was back in the water less than a year later.

In Russia, physiologists had been searching for a cure for decompression sickness almost as long as their American and British counterparts. The idea of therapeutic recompression was first recommended in 1902, but it wasn't until 1928 that the treatment found favour in the medical profession. Injured divers were placed in a chamber and recompressed until their symptoms disappeared. They were left at depth for at least fifteen minutes and no more than half an hour, and then slowly decompressed. Back then, doctors treating the most severe of cases noted that when approaching atmospheric pressure, patients often reported that the pains had reappeared, and they had to recompress divers again. In the absence of a pressure chamber, say when a diver was injured at sea while operating from a salvage ship, doctors recommended placing a patient into a purpose-built recompression suit. The suit was made of sealed rubber and braided on the outside with a galvanised chain. A pump was used to blow the suit up to a pressure equivalent to fifteen metres of seawater and doctors could monitor their patient through a porthole in the suit.

The idea of using oxygen to speed up the washout of nitrogen was first proposed in Russia in 1940. Twelve years later the Soviet Navy introduced the 'Instruction for the prevention, first aid and treatment of decompression (caisson) disease', which featured six different treatment regimens, one of which allowed for a deep spike to seventy metres for fifteen minutes. All prescribed the patient oxygen from fifteen metres. The main drawback of these regimens, it was reported, was that very often the maximum therapeutic pressure did not provide successful treatment for the most seriously injured victims, and in 1960 five new treatment regimens were introduced. The regimens recommended pressing injured divers to pressures equivalent to between fifty and one hundred metres and doctors chose the therapeutic depth after assessing the nature of the symptoms and how deep the diver had been when they were injured. The greatest pressure was used to treat severe decompression disorders and, for the first time, the tables introduced helium into the mix of chamber gases.

While the US Navy turned to the development of low pressure, short oxygen tables in the 1960s, their opposites in the East continued to fine-tune deep treatment regimens under the leadership of Vladimir Smolin, arguably the father of diving safety and medicine in the Soviet Union. Smolin continued to adjust the treatment methods throughout the next five decades, and together with Dr Gennady Sokolov, also developed a technique of in-water recompression using oxygen. They tested their theory on thirteen divers who had surfaced with severe pain in bones, joints and muscles and paralysis, taking them down to a maximum depth of ten metres for a maximum of thirty minutes. The divers welcomed the treatment, reporting the disappearance of pain within ten minutes of oxygen breathing. Most were back to work the next day.

Perhaps the biggest problem faced by divers in a country the size of Russia, the doctors noticed, was the scarcity of recompression chambers. That meant it could take hours or days for a diver to reach treatment, and when they finally arrived at a chamber, they were in a bad way. So Sokolov, Smolin and colleague Boris Pavlov put their minds to developing a new treatment regimen to deal with severe cases of decompression sickness in which the patient had been delayed reaching an appropriate medical care facility.

When the chamber door slammed shut on Martin Robson shortly before midnight on Friday, 20 January 2012, the treatment plan ahead was something more elaborate than a Table 6 or a Comex 30. Like the doctors in Hawaii, the Russians were confident in the use of their deep treatment method. As gas hissed into the chamber, Robson was inside for the long soak.

On a makeshift bed at the harbourside complex in Sochi, Robson lay asleep as the chamber thrummed to itself. The hum of the compressor echoed around the compartment's metal walls, and when it murmured in his ears, he stirred from an exhausted sleep. His face was drawn and anxious, and his eyes were tired. Beads of sweat clung to his forehead. Artificial light filtered in through the porthole above his head and dazzled his eyes. He had no idea what the time was, didn't even know whether it was day or night, but he was alive.

Robson instinctively looked down at his legs. He had survived for thirty-three hours after a terrible assault that some thought could have finished him off, but his lower body was still in the worst shape. Nerves compressed. Spinal cord damaged. Both legs numbed. Muscles tied in knots. Pain pulsating down his back and his muscles periodically spasming uncontrollably. He couldn't sense anything from his thighs to his toes; couldn't feel the bedsheet that shrouded his lower body, even though frayed senses told him his legs – which were locked rigid by muscle spasms – were wobbling, like jelly.

Throughout the whole sorry ordeal after his legs went, during the time underwater, lying in the monopod and listening to the beeps of life in intensive care, he'd been confident that everything was going to be all right. He had hoped his body might have sprung back to life after a short period of recompression; like a headache; pop some pills and, puff, it's gone. Only this was nothing like dealing with a headache. Deep down, he understood, given the nature of his injuries, that nothing was going to happen instantaneously. Things were going to take time. He wasn't so much disappointed, that wouldn't help him; no, the treatment was going as the treatment was going. But for the first time, he was forced to acknowledge that it could take longer than expected for a reconciliation with half of his body that still appeared utterly lost.

He lifted his head and looked around at the surroundings. The chamber was sterile and quiet. The padded, vinyl-covered couch that served as his bed ran almost the length of the compartment. A small wooden table was fixed to the bed's base by his head. Another couch ran along the wall opposite. That belonged to the medic who was locked inside with him. The two men shared the small cell that was about four metres long and two metres in diameter. Chains hung from two cables running the length of the room, and the light glistened on rivulets of condensation that trickled down the curved white walls. A 'no smoking' sign hung above the door. At the far end was another circular doorway leading to a second compartment. Inside was a toilet and shower. Beyond that was another entrance to the outside world. In the event of an emergency, the smaller compartment could be sealed off and act as an airlock to transfer medical staff in and out of the chamber. In the far corner was a closed-circuit camera and an intercom that relayed everything happening inside to a viewing monitor outside. A black box recorded everything. Food, drink, medical supplies and everything else came through a small supply lock the size of a dinner plate, located in the wall above Robson's bed.

Robson looked across at the stranger seated opposite him. The man had been the one buzzing around in scrubs when he first arrived at the facility. His name was Denis Morozov. He was there to help provide medical care inside the chamber. Morozov, Robson soon learned, didn't speak a word of English.

The Russian said something, and after a short pause another voice crackled over the intercom, in English this time. Robson could finally understand what was being said. The translator's voice belonged to Sergei Gorpinyuk, the support diver who had travelled with him from Nalchik.

Would you like something to eat? Gorpinyuk asked.

Robson wasn't hungry.

Sometime later, more Russian spilt out from the intercom and Morozov listened intently. Then, a second or two later, Gorpinyuk interpreted the words of Dr Sokolov and explained how the medic would examine him.

Robson lay back as Morozov took his temperature, measured his pulse and counted his respiration. The medic then took his own temperature with the same thermometer and relayed the details to the outside. More instructions came back the other way. Then, the details came into the chamber in English.

Robson looked down as Morozov began to inspect his body. He saw him manhandle his legs, but he couldn't feel anything. Next, Morozov moved to his abdomen, and, as he prodded and pressed, Robson grimaced and screwed up his eyes. Next, the medic moved his hands onto Robson's back and pressed again. Robson's face twisted, but he said nothing. Assertive was how some might have characterised Morozov's approach. Robson felt no compassion in the medic's hands. His companion seemed to have all the bedside manner of a roadside paramedic used to handling patients in the back of an ambulance sweeping through traffic. That had apparently been Morozov's previous job.

After he finished with the physical examination, Morozov reached for a metal tray. On it were a handful of orange pills

Robson had to swallow, and a syringe containing medication he would receive three times a day. He couldn't decipher what the drug was or why it was necessary.

It's to help with your treatment, was all he was told.

He didn't press any more than that. No one was going to give him drugs if they weren't going to be of benefit; there had to be trust, Robson thought, that his doctors were doing the right thing for him. (When, on his return to Russia six years later, Robson asked Dr Sokolov what drugs he was given, he still didn't get a complete answer.)

Morozov leaned forward with the syringe and said something. Robson struggled to make out the words; his ears still hadn't tuned in to the helium-oxygen atmosphere which played havoc with their voices. Words came out as high-pitched squeaks, which would have been funny if Robson hadn't been in such a bad way. He felt Morozov push the needle into his arm, felt the pressure as the syringe's plunger forced the drugs into his body. He then swallowed the five orange pills and glanced up at the porthole at the artificial light of the outside world beyond. At some point, a balloon appeared and Robson was asked to blow into it. This was a test designed to assess how his lungs were responding to the elevated levels of oxygen.

When asked how he was feeling, Robson was lost for words; he didn't have the vocabulary in Russian to accurately describe his symptoms to the medical staff. He needed help.

Around 3 p.m. that day, help arrived in the shape of Mikhail Shyrokov who took over the translating duties from Sergei Gorpinyuk. (Following the arrival of Mikhail, Gorpinyuk returned to Blue Lake to collect his equipment.) When Robson woke, he was relieved to hear his friend's voice emerge from the intercom and fill the chamber.

It's a good job I'm here, Shyrokov told him.

No, he couldn't miss a party like this, couldn't miss out on the steel drums, lots of pipes, helium and all the nuts provided by EMERCOM, he would later joke.

Shyrokov was a big guy from Odessa, in Ukraine, who ran his own shipping repair business which did work for some of the world's biggest cruise liner companies. He was actually Russian, not Ukrainian. He just happened to be studying marine management at the Odessa State Marine Academy when Ukraine declared independence from the Soviet Union in 1991. Given the option of returning home or become a Ukrainian citizen, he had opted for the latter, because he thought living on the Black Sea would be good business. Good business, but tough business. For a boss in such a cut-throat industry he was unusually laid-back; he could disarm anyone with a self-deprecating joke. He had two sons, Denys (who had been educated at Fettes College, in Edinburgh; 'so, he's bloody Scottish now'), and Timothy (at least he's still on this side), and a wife, Anna, who kept the books for his business.

He'd been on the road for almost twenty-four hours to reach Sochi. It was fearless rally-style in my Nissan pick-up, Shyrokov would later recall. There were icy roads, lots of mountains, and this and that. 'This and that' peppered his speech whenever he struggled to find the correct word in English.

He went on: all officials on the border, when we told them what was happening and asked for the fast lane, they did everything out of respect to EMERCOM. It was very touching.

And I'm glad I came. Seeing a tough man like you in a steel

drum with all these Russians around; even I would kill the guard and escape.

Looking at Robson, flat on his back and weary, disturbed Shyrokov. His friend looked bone-tired and full of pain, and that was not the way he thought of his friend. The impression he always carried with him was that Robson was a superman.

Now I'm here I can work to make things smoother for you. As I told you, Martin, Russians are the same as all human beings; they are not strange, just a little different. You know, small cultural differences to become familiar with. Is there anything I can get for you?

Robson asked for a toothbrush, toothpaste, shaving kit and some clean underwear.

And would it be possible to find something to read, please?

Martin, Shyrokov replied, we are in the south of Russia, finding a book in English might be a challenge.

Later that evening, Shyrokov returned with a small number of provisions. He placed them inside the airlock, ready for Martin, and closed the door. A technician opened a valve and began to flood the lock with gas. It took about ten minutes for the pressure inside the lock to equalise with that of the chamber. Only then would the inner lock door open. Among the toiletries and paper, Robson found Shyrokov's Rolex Submariner watch. To help keep the time, his friend had said.

Wrapped around the watch strap was a silver chain Shyrokov wore religiously around his neck. At the end of the chain was a small cross, the cross used during his baptism. Mikhail had been given the cross by his godmother when he was nineteen. He never travelled anywhere without it. Giving it to Robson was Shyrokov's way of telling his friend: I'm not going anywhere.

Robson was not religious but felt the support of his friend well up in his stomach as he clutched Mikhail's cross.

In official terms, the answer to Robson's fate rested not in the hands of God, but in Russia's Режимы 6-а и 6-б лечебной рекомпрессии – Modes 6-A and 6-B of Therapeutic Recompression. The treatment regimens are, in the words of Dr Sokolov, unique, meaning they are unlike anything else in the world used to treat injured divers. Under Modes 6-A and 6-B, patients must accept they will be pressed deeper and stay longer inside the chamber than any other treatment if they are to have any hope of ever walking again.

Under the heading Этапы лечебного режима – Stages of Medical Treatment – are seven columns and forty-nine rows of numbers. Meaningless to the layperson, the numbers offer a roadmap to physical repair for the diver afflicted with decompression sickness of the most destructive kind. Taking an injured diver through the table's numbers is to give them the best chance of recovery. Each junction of the journey is carefully outlined: the pressure, in metres of seawater, inside the chamber; the length of time the chamber remains at that depth; the percentages of oxygen, carbon dioxide and helium in the atmosphere; the temperature. The numbers in row seven, for example, read: 90; 5; 60; 7.0–7.5; 0.05; 27–28; 40–80. That means the chamber is resting at ninety metres and will stay that way for anything between five minutes and an hour. The oxygen in the breathing mix is set between 7 and 7.5 per cent, carbon dioxide is at five-hundredths of a per cent, the temperature inside is about twenty-seven degrees Celsius, and the helium percentage is between 40 and 80 per cent. Although not included on the table, nitrogen makes up the rest of the atmospheric contents.

The table had been developed by Dr Sokolov and his mentor, Dr Smolin, more than a decade earlier, with casualties like Martin Robson very much in mind. At the time, the conventional wisdom in Russia was that a diver needed to be treated within twenty-four hours if there was to be any hope of reversing spinal cord injuries. After forty-eight hours, the results of treatment were said to be negligible. The odds then of fully recovering from a diving incident in a country the size of Russia, with a limited number of recompression chambers, wasn't good. So, in 1998, the two men began to test a theory that deep recompression treatment in pressures up to the equivalent of one hundred metres, and an extended stay in a helium-oxygen-nitrogen environment, might give patients a better chance of recovering.

In time, they would use their long-stay method in the GVK-250 deep-diving chamber at their Institute in Moscow to treat more than 160 people, including divers who had taken up to twenty-five hours to reach help. Among them was a man who was left quadriplegic in a diving incident. Ten days had passed before he arrived at the chamber. Other doctors may have decided there was no hope. Dr Sokolov managed to save his arms. Another diver who had taken more than a week to get treatment was able to get back on his feet with the help of walking sticks. Then there was a high-altitude pilot injured after the emergency depressurisation of his aircraft. Two days after the incident, he arrived at the chamber, unconscious and immobile. He began to walk with a cane after medical recompression. And there was a female marine biologist who arrived at the Institute suffering symptoms of decompression sickness from a diving incident six months earlier. She'd already been treated and told that she was as good as she'd ever be. Dr Sokolov offered to put her through his regimen anyway. He didn't promise anything, but he had hope. During the treatment, the woman suffered sharp pains in her abdomen, and he feared a court case, but she emerged without problems. When asked to explain the pains, she told him that she had previously suffered gynaecological problems which had, apparently, left her unable to have children. Three months later, Dr Sokolov received a telephone call from the woman. She was pregnant.

When asked whether this regimen could deliver a better outcome for Robson than the standard treatment offered in the West, Dr Sokolov is quick to say there is no competition between the schedules. But he also says that in using his method he was able to cure patients who had not been successfully treated elsewhere. 'With other methods, our experience shows, it was impossible to get such good results.' It's a statement that, typically Russian, seems to have it both ways.

The treatment was designed to work in two phases. The shorter part was the deepest. The chamber was first pressurised to thirty metres using air and, after a brief check on the patient, was then pumped to one hundred metres with helium. The pressure of one hundred metres was designed to crush the bubbles in Robson's body and restore the flow of oxygen to damaged tissues. For successful treatment, the Russian medics believed, exposure under the greatest pressure should be such as to ensure the complete elimination, without exception, of all gas bubbles in the organs and tissues of the victim. While conventional wisdom would have it that all the bubbles were gone, resolved of their own accord within twenty-four hours or so, at least one study found bubbles could remain in the tissues of divers for up to nineteen days in the absence of treatment. Depending on the doctor's assessment, the patient would spend a minimum of two hours and no more than four hours under the maximum pressure.

After that, the pressure inside the chamber would be slowly reduced over forty-five hours until it reached a pressure of forty metres. That's when the atmosphere would be enriched with oxygen and the second phase of the treatment would begin. This step aimed to restore the damaged tissues by feeding the body with moderately elevated amounts of oxygen. In theory, this would help restore the circulation to damaged capillaries and kick-start the nerve fibres damaged by ischaemia (restricted blood supply), which resulted from the blockage caused by bubbles. According to the treatment regimen, Robson could be held there for at least five hours, depending on the doctor's examination. In the presence of severe or difficult-to-cure symptoms, he could stay at that depth for up to two days.

During that stop, the medical team had to be alive to the possibility that Robson could experience fresh hurt or intensification of pain and numbness that was not noted at the beginning of treatment. This, Dr Sokolov believed, was quite normal and was

334

associated with the processes of restoring microcirculation and regenerating nerve tissue. At the end of the exposure at forty metres, the chamber would be gradually decompressed over a period lasting four days.

All of that knowledge and experience was wrapped into the 331 cells of information contained in the table which filled a single sheet of paper and offered a bubble of hope, a bubble of possibility that this would rehabilitate the patient and get them walking again. Hanging from a clipboard on the recompression chamber's control panel, the table was at the centre of everything happening in Sochi.

Seated at a small desk making notes in his medical journal, Dr Sokolov listened to Mikhail Shyrokov talk with Robson and dissolved into laughter. Life in the complex had been such a blast since Shyrokov had arrived from Ukraine. He seemed, to the doctor at least, to have put a comforting arm around Robson's shoulder and lifted his morale. But he had a way with him, peppering his speech with slang and curses – the language of bandits, joked Sokolov – that made it impossible not to chuckle when he was in full flow. The doctor was only pleased that his laughter did not reach Martin through the thick metal walls of the chamber.

Things had settled down after the first twenty-four hours, and the medical team had shut themselves off from the outside world. Early in the treatment procedure, when Robson was still under maximum pressure, a journalist from a television company managed to get through to Dr Sokolov on the phone to offer him birthday wishes. He also wished to ask a few questions. The doctor didn't feel he could decline such a polite request so asked the reporter what interested him. The first question was whether it was true that medical assistance had not been appropriately rendered in Nalchik. That, to Sokolov, sounded like a witch-hunt had started. So, he praised everybody, those at Blue Lake, in Nalchik, Adler, Mineralnye Vody, in Sochi, who had done all that had been possible – and almost impossible – to treat Robson. 'Had it not been for their selfless work,' he says, 'Martin could have died and would have definitely remained disabled.'

After that, the medical team decided to limit their communication with the press. Sokolov did not want to be drawn into making hasty predictions at a time when the outcome of the treatment remained uncertain. Perhaps the team's self-imposed silence could be a mistake, he thought, because in a vacuum of information, rumours could spread. But radio silence was also what his patient wanted, and Sokolov respected that.

There was a round-the-clock watch on the chamber and soon they had established a rhythm. At regular intervals, every ninety minutes in the early phase of the treatment, the chamber was vented and moved two metres closer to the surface. A technician was never far away from the control panel, located next to Sokolov's desk, and hourly checks of the gauges were made to ensure everything remained on track. Clinical white, the panel was an imposing wall of dials and knobs and levers. Cranked one way, the valves opened vents and allowed gas to escape. Turned the other, they opened inlet pipes and flooded the chamber with gas. Coloured lines criss-crossed the panel, indicating which valve controlled which dial. When it came time to vent gas from the chamber, the technician informed the two men inside that he was about to start. Then he manipulated the valves to control the discharge of gas from the chamber. He kept a close eye on the pressure gauge to ensure a uniform bleed. When the pressure had reached the correct level, he closed the valve and spoke to the men again. Notes were made, and the clock timer was reset.

While all of this was going on, Dr Sokolov stood there in shirtsleeves and tie, just far enough away so as not to be seen to interfere, and he watched Robson on the monitor. He was looking for anything that might indicate an adverse reaction to the pressure drop.

The doctors tried to stagger their time at the complex, but Sokolov liked to be there whenever the pressure was reduced. He'd become accustomed to working long hours in the navy with little time off; to the doctor, his medicine was work. That meant he didn't stray from the complex, nor would he for another eight days. None of the doctors did unless they were ordered to go home.

To anyone but the medical team, the quarters were austere. The complex itself was clinical. The tiled walls gleamed bright, and the desks were devoid of anything that resembled personal property. When the telephone rang, the sound echoed off the walls. The medical team had nothing but a locker to call their own, and when it came time to catch some sleep, they took turns in two small cots round the back. The bed was in an adjoining room that also served as a kitchen, but even out there they couldn't completely shut out the background noise of the chamber's compressor, which groaned on throughout the day and night.

337

That didn't matter to Dr Sokolov. He didn't complain because this was his world, and he was with his brothers in arms. Tough men in a tough world, they were just like regular guys to him.

The doctor's abilities as a leader impressed Shyrokov. He watched Sokolov shuffling around the facility in his slippers; speaking softly when issuing orders to the technicians – 'No cursing at all, damn it!' joked Mikhail Shyrokov – and stepping back to give the men space to do their jobs without being overlooked; after all, they were all experts in that room.

In the early days, he always seemed to have plenty to do. He could often be seen seated at the desk on which he stacked his reference books, ledgers and clocks. There, he made copious notes about the procedure and laid forth plans for the next stage of treatment. He worked like a watchmaker: one eye focused on a singular detail, like the best percentage mix of oxygen and helium for Robson's recovery at any given moment, the other looking at how each piece of information fitted together in the delicate movement to get Robson back on his feet. Day and night, he would examine the details, hold them up to the light, ask questions of them – how much had the atmosphere inside the chamber been infected with carbon dioxide, for example? – consider the importance of what he was seeing and weave them into his treatment plan.

Mikhail Shyrokov helped the doctor gain access to the final piece of the puzzle: how Robson felt the treatment was going. Alone on the evening shift together that Saturday, Shyrokov and the doctor spoke about what they could do to help each other. Over a cup of tea, Dr Sokolov explained the nature of

Robson's paralysis and said the process of recovery would be difficult, physically painful and psychologically challenging.

The doctor spoke softly, but Shyrokov could sense his concern. So, he took a moment to explain his friend's background, the military service and diving experience, and then what he saw as the key characteristics that would be called upon over the next few days: a scrupulous attention to detail, a self-discipline and a fitness level that belied his years.

How fluent are you in English diving terms? Sokolov asked.

With my poor English and Martin's poor Russian, and our friendship, we might just get by, Shyrokov joked.

It will be a big help if Martin can observe every change in his condition, every tingle, every pain, any new sensations and notify us immediately, the doctor explained.

Shyrokov understood the meaning of this request. He needed to know, when Robson reported a new pain, whether it was like a cat's scratch on the skin or a knife twisting in his back. His conversations with Robson would be critical because they would give the doctor fresh information to build into his plan. Push things to the edge, Shyrokov thought. The doctor seemed genuinely excited. 'Wonderful moments,' Mike says.

Anyone watching Shyrokov and Robson in conversation would have laughed at the absurdity of it. Helium made Robson sound like Donald Duck and it took Shyrokov two days to properly tune his ear. The electronic speakers which relayed his voice to the outside world added a further distortion. To help, Robson looked directly into the closed-circuit camera and mouthed his replies to questions, slowly. Shyrokov watched the black and white images on the monitor and mentally stitched together the audio with Robson's lip movements. Sometimes it appeared as if he was watching a badly dubbed movie, but that was the only way he could fully understand what his friend was saying.

When Robson fell asleep, there was little for Shyrokov to do. Occasionally, he would step outside for a few minutes to clear his mind, to smoke a cigarette or head to a nearby store to grab something to eat. While at the quayside, catching a breath of cold winter air, he noticed a large, tan German Shepherd scampering around. One time, Shyrokov took some food and the stray came to him. He fed the dog titbits and ruffled his fur. The dog was gentle and obedient, and Shyrokov felt sorry for it. So, he took food with him whenever he went out during the long hours looking after his friend.

Bed for the night was one of two cots the team shared on round-the-clock shifts. One of the EMERCOM officials had offered to arrange a room for Shyrokov in the Marina Yacht Hotel a short walk away, but he decided to stay near his friend. After he noticed Dr Sokolov worked the late shift most nights, Shyrokov stayed up late with him and they talked until midnight. Discovering it was Dr Sokolov's seventy-eighth birthday, Shyrokov dug out a bottle of vodka and two plastic cups, and offered a toast to his new friend.

When talk turned to Robson's condition, Dr Sokolov remained sanguine about the prospect of success. 'There is always hope for the patient.'

Vikki and Martin had discussed what they would do if one of them died while diving. It was a short conversation and focused on practicalities. How will one of us survive financially? What insurance do we have? Where is the paperwork? Vikki had also thought about ways she might take 'time out' to start to cope with the loss if she was the one left behind. The one thing they had never discussed was what they would do if one of them was left disabled by decompression sickness. Sitting on the sofa on Sunday evening, friends having been and gone, Vikki had time to ask herself how she might cope if, once all the healing that could be done had been done, Martin returned home in a wheelchair.

Practically, financially, it would be harder to cope with than if he were to die, she thought. Their home would need modifications, but they were in rented accommodation, the bathroom was upstairs; he couldn't come home to this. So, they would have to move. And that raised so many questions. Where would they go? How would they pay for it? Could they get a mortgage on a single salary? And how would Martin cope with being paralysed, unable to dive? How would she cope seeing the man she loved wheeled home along a pathway of broken dreams?

It might not be so bad, a friend had said to her, if the worst were to happen. You know Martin won't be held back, he'll see the wheelchair as a challenge, he'll be trying to break records at the Olympics.

Yes, Vikki told herself, he'd push the limits.

So, she clung to that. There was a story she remembered from Martin's past. It was from back when he was working in London as a firefighter and had joined an amateur American football team. Now, he wasn't really built to be an American footballer, but he was proud and confident and energetic. His contribution outweighed his physical size, she said. He charged into tackles, picked himself up and went again. His coach said he was persistent. Relentless, that was the word Vikki said the coach used; and relentless was the trait she hoped Martin would show, first fighting for his life and then fighting to get back on his feet.

That was all she had. Vikki had heard nothing from Russia since Martin had gone into the chamber and now she was in an agony of suspense. 'I don't really know how I feel,' she wrote in her diary. 'Sometimes numb, sometimes gutted, most of the time just sad, worried, wishing I could be with him and help. I am now just waiting for news on whether there has been any improvement to the paralysis.'

Sometime that evening, Mikhail Shyrokov called.

How is he? she blurted.

I can see him through the window, he said. He is conscious. Everything is going fine. The doctors are dealing with him at the moment, and I don't want to interrupt. The dialect they are speaking in makes it hard to understand, but don't worry; I will get my ear in soon.

I'm thinking about coming out, Vikki started.

From the moment she learned that Martin was in trouble, Vikki knew she wanted to be in Russia. Shyrokov did his best to discourage her. It is not a good idea, he said. You will be in the way and make it worse. Stay at home. I will do whatever it takes; whatever Martin needs I will do.

She was relieved Martin had a friend with him. Shyrokov would become Vikki's lifeline in the coming days as well.

The call ended, and she sat there on the sofa, in a quiet

corner of Somerset, with a prayer on her lips, bargaining with no god in particular: if I'm a better person, will he live and come home in one piece?

You can tell by his neat handwriting the organised manner in which Martin Robson approached his recovery. In well-ordered sections over two pages of notepaper he'd asked for, Robson detailed for the first time the state of his body and its response to treatment. Written in pencil, the words were devoid of sentiment and emotion, hiding his relief even as they described the weakening grip paralysis had on his legs. About his left leg, he wrote:

Small improvement in skin sensation at front of thigh. Muscles very sore sometimes painful. Left calf slight improvement in skin sensation. Left foot improved sensation in skin but still feels very numb. Toes have better movement than earlier but not much sensation.

His right leg was better. There was a definite improvement in skin sensation, he could wiggle his toes, and he could move his leg. They were still punchbag-heavy, as if someone had beaten his thighs over twelve rounds until they set rigid. The pain in the middle of his back had vanished, and he was able to clench his glutes, even though they remained painful. 'Lower back still sore but no recent painful back spasms/cramps,' he added.

Keeping a record was an act of control. It implied he had authority over a situation in which, reality dictated, he was just a passenger. This note, and the ones that followed, were

343

Robson's way of feeling like he was doing something to influence the course of his treatment. Without his input, he thought, the medical team could only measure his progress by viewing him on the closed-circuit monitor. They would have no idea what was going on inside his body, or whether the treatment was working unless he told them.

Once Robson had put down his pen, he lay back. The pain from his injuries had troubled him throughout the night, and he was tired. He tried to sleep, but the periodic venting of pressure from the chamber and the addition of oxygen continually disturbed him.

The note was dispatched through the airlock and handed over to Shyrokov. His day began around six every morning. During each shift change, the outgoing chamber operator updated his colleague on the events of the previous night and shared technical details, such as the levels of oxygen and helium. While this happened, Shyrokov translated Robson's words for the doctors. The information was so important to the treatment plan that he was asked to transcribe everything into a logbook which acted as an official record of all that was going on in the chamber. Beneath each entry he signed his name. After that, he went to make breakfast in the small kitchen so it would be ready for when Robson and Morozov stirred.

Waking up was, in some ways, the hardest thing Robson had to face each day because he would go to sleep thinking things would be better in the morning. Then he'd come around to the reality that things weren't happening as quickly as he hoped. Robson couldn't escape what had happened to him; he was reminded of it every time he looked at his legs.

But he was getting better now, he told himself, even though progress was painfully slow.

Like everything he did in life, Robson dealt with the here and now, what was in front of him. There was no point in trying to tackle the whole thing at once. After being ambushed underwater, he'd focused on what needed to be done to survive. When paralysis marched up his legs in the habitat, he'd focused on what needed to be done to overcome that. When in the intensive care unit, he had concentrated on what he needed to pull through that. One step at a time. Make it through one day at a time and figure out how to survive the next day when it was time. As the second day inside the chamber ticked away, and his legs were still not working correctly, Robson knew he just needed to do more for himself.

He reached up to the chains hanging from the chamber ceiling. Bracing his arms, he began to do pull ups. One, two, three, four. A rhythm he intended to beat during the coming hours and days. Then he shuffled to the end of the bed, shifting his legs by hand as he moved. He sat there and hung his legs over the edge of the mattress. His feet touched the floor – he could see they did – but he couldn't feel any sensation.

Shyrokov's voice entered the chamber: Martin, what are you doing?

Getting myself moving, he replied.

Getting himself moving, right there and then, was the best thing he could do. Getting himself moving was the best thing he could think of to be the man he was; be the man he wanted to be. He could be a victim, or he could be a fighter. He chose to be a fighter.

He began to circle his feet at the ankle, one after the other. His left ankle was stiff, and he had little control over movement. Next, he tried to raise his left foot off the floor. His leg trembled with each move, and he made a pencil mark on the white wall to show the high point of the exercise. Then he switched legs and did it all over again with his right leg. Robson looked at the two pencil marks. The one for his right leg was higher than his left. They were about a foot off the floor. On the road to recovery, he had taken his first step.

'This was an amazing sign,' says Shyrokov, who saw an uplift in Robson's mood as he began to move. The Russian looked over to Sokolov and saw a smile break out across the doctor's face.

The doctor was pleased, but he knew talk about the results of treatment was premature.

There was a rare news conference on the outside, when Dr Sokolov tried to offer context for the progress of treatment. The patient's condition has improved significantly, he had said, and Robson's morale was coming back stronger.

Except inside the chamber, Robson didn't always feel that way. Looking at the thin pencil marks on the wall, he was disappointed they weren't higher, but he couldn't let his mood fall to the nagging doubts hiding in the dark recess of his mind. The truth was, it felt good to be doing something, to get the blood flowing around his body; because if he was doing something he wasn't thinking about the possible consequences of his situation: about being confined to a wheelchair for the rest of his life; about never diving again; about losing the livelihood he had invested his life in; about struggling to pay the bills. He and Vikki wanted to buy a house; they were thinking about starting a family and moving into a new phase of their lives together. Waiting to get better was not for him. He needed to be an active participant in his treatment; to keep up with the doctors as they pushed forward with their plan to heal him.

At regular intervals throughout the day, Robson moved another step closer to the surface as the chamber was bled of gas. The compartment exhaled a wheeze of stale air during each movement, and the pressure inside fell by the equivalent of two metres. By two o'clock that afternoon, the chamber came to rest at fifty metres.

As time ticked on, he lay back on his bed, exhausted, watching everything happen around him. He watched Denis Morozov wipe the condensation off the walls and ferry hot tea that had come through the airlock. Later it would be time for another medical examination, and he watched Morozov assemble the tray of medicines. The medic took Robson's temperature, measured his pulse, counted his respirations, lifted his shirt and pushed and prodded his abdomen, and Robson again winced at his heavy touch. Then the same questions were asked. There was another injection, and then he swallowed the five orange tablets lined up on the table. Robson took them all. He then inflated the balloon with two or three breaths, deflated it and inflated it again.

And, afterwards, he lay back on his bed again. He knew there was no point willing the treatment away, there was already a finite endpoint to the procedure, and Robson just had to wait for it. The clock wouldn't tick any faster (although it stopped ticking for a while when he forgot to rotate the winder on Shyrokov's watch). There was little else to do, so he just lay where he was, and the day passed slowly.

Just another winter's afternoon in Russia.

The confusion about Shyrokov's watch made Robson and Morozov laugh. The two men were with each other day and night, no more than an arm's length apart for much of the time. Robson made every effort to be polite to his companion, manners mattered to him, and his grasp of Russian was enough for them to communicate somewhat. He still found the medic's bedside manner abrupt, but their exchanges were becoming enjoyable. Their limited conversation was aided by a Russian–English dictionary which had been sent into the chamber by Morozov's mother. The first phrase Robson found was 'Покажите мне ваши планы ядерного реактора' – 'Show me the plans to your nuclear reactor' – which made him chuckle. The book passed between the two men frequently as they searched for words to teach each other. They started with items of diving equipment that were familiar to both of them – wetsuit: gidrokostyum; dry suit: sukhoy kostyum; decompression sickness: dekompressionnaya bolezn'; nitrogen: azot. Soon they would be conjugating verbs and working on the different tenses. To the outside world, the pair sounded like birds chirruping.

Sometimes, when he didn't feel like talking any more, Robson tried to read. The only English-language books Shyrokov had been able to find were *Martin Eden* by Jack London, and *Sister Carrie* by Theodore Dreiser. Robson thought it was peculiar that anyone would have these titles – two American novels from the early 1900s – on their bookshelf in this corner of Russia. (In fact, the two men were among a select few US writers to earn Soviet approval because their works offered a critical perspective on capitalist America.) Robson wasn't much of a reader; it just didn't interest him the same way it did Vikki. Starting with *Martin Eden*, he soon found London's central story of a writer's emotional turmoil – a life lived in a melancholy key – hard going.

Even though he was tired, he barely slept at night. Now and then, pain pulsated from his hips and down his legs, and his legs jumped in violent spasms. These kept him awake, and his notes became shorter, sharper:

02:05 Sharp shooting pains from left hip downside of leg.

03:40 Left foot now totally numb. Moving left foot very difficult + little control over this movement. Whole of leg left very tight/stiff painful muscles.

04:10 Breathing no problem but dry cough.

07:10 SICK – had been feeling sick/nausea most of the night.

The chamber had moved two metres shallower during that five-hour bout of discomfort. When everything had settled, the pressure gauge on the control panel indicated that the internal environment was equivalent to forty metres of seawater. Forty metres was the depth, according to the science behind the therapeutic table, at which the second phase of treatment began with the aim of restoring the vital activity of damaged tissues. Dr Sokolov ordered an increase in the oxygen level inside the chamber to 10 per cent. At this depth, that was like breathing 50 per cent at the surface. The elevated partial pressure of oxygen would, so the theory went, mobilise the detoxification capabilities of cells, restore blood flow to the capillaries, regenerate body tissues damaged by the bubbles and normalise the protein metabolism and enzymatic function of the liver.

Inside the chamber, Robson sat up in bed looking at his legs. He made them move in the small ways they could and a bright, clarifying awareness came over him as he began to appreciate the full nature of his injury: the damage done by the bubbles was far more significant than he first realised. He accepted the treatment had not yet been able to gather up the fragments of his body and put them back together in the way he believed it would; the healing process was days away from being complete. The question he asked of himself was no longer: how much of my body can I get back with treatment? The big question now was: will I get it all back?

Right then, he would have loved Vikki to have been there with him for moral support. To tell him everything was going to be okay. Seeing her would make his day. At the same time, he had decided he didn't want her to see him this way. Hurt. Debilitated. Vulnerable. He wished to keep a promise he made to her a long time ago when he headed off on an expedition: don't worry, he said, I always come back. The expression stuck, and whenever he planned a deep dive he would make the pledge. This wasn't some throwaway line; he meant it. He hated letting people down, none more so than Vikki.

I'm coming back, he pledged to her, silently. He wanted her to see him return home in precisely the way he had left it, on two feet.

What everyone else wanted was for the treatment to be over and for him to be better, so they did what they could to buoy his spirits each day.

There was his best friend, Mikhail Shyrokov, who would share an observation, or a joke, 'or just talk bullshit' over the microphone to keep spirits up. You should see it out here, he said. There's equipment I've never seen before. It all looks like space station stuff.

There was Roman Dunaev, who had made the trip from Blue Lake. He typed Russian to English translations on his tablet and held the device up to a porthole so Robson could get practice. They laughed and teased each other about Robson's helium-squeaked pronunciations. You sound funny, Dunaev said.

There were the wives of the YURPSO team members running the chamber who insisted on sending home-cooked meals – buckwheat porridge for breakfast, stews, pies and casserole for dinner – in plastic tubs through the airlock.

He was grateful for the support, particularly from those who did not know him and who had never met him before events had brought them all together. At some point, though, he felt they all stared at him. The idea of people stealing pitying looks at him made him uncomfortable. He was a private person, and he didn't like being on show. It bothered him because he didn't want people to see how badly he had been hurt or how helpless he was when he tried to stand unaided. He saw himself as strong, unbreakable, and that was the image he wanted to uphold.

They all watched him anyway. They watched him through the portholes and on the closed-circuit monitor. They watched him do round after round of pull ups. They watched him trying to shake off the numbness when he sat at the end of his bed and lifted his legs. They watched him as he charted his progress with more pencil lines, each higher than the last. They watched him inflate the balloon with a couple of breaths. They watched as the medic poked and prodded, took Robson's temperature and administered another injection. They watched to see how he was responding to the treatment. They watched because they were concerned; concerned about the state of his lungs, concerned about his kidneys, concerned about how much water he passed. They watched through tired eyes because they had been working around the clock for hours on little sleep, and they wanted to see him get better.

And there was Dr Sokolov, who looked at Robson on the black and white monitor. He was alive to the possibility that Robson's condition could take a temporary turn for the worse as his body repaired itself. In the back of his mind, he also knew that if Robson didn't show further improvement in the coming hours he might never get any better. Right then, watching Robson exercise was the happiest he had felt since receiving the telephone call from Roman Dunaev three days earlier. Everything is looking good, he thought.

What they didn't see, however, that Sunday evening was the slow movement of the needle on the chamber's depth gauge. The internal pressure should have been fixed at the equivalent of forty metres of seawater, only it wasn't. The needle had been creeping anticlockwise for some time. The pressure was dropping. The chamber was leaking.

THE IRON DOCTOR

I had considerable fear about the development and ultimate extent of my paralysis, largely because I understood the possible effect of logistical delays in obtaining treatment. This fear substantially vanished once I was in a hyperbaric unit, but I made a conscious effort to postpone confronting the magnitude of my injury. Once it became obvious that I would not have a rapid recovery I experienced some shock at the idea of an extensive and permanent paralysis.

Neil R. Swanberg PhD, 'The View from the Stretcher'

Everything had been going well, right up until the leak.

A chamber operator was conducting a routine check of the apparatus at about eight that evening when he looked at the pressure gauge and knew the two men inside the chamber were in trouble. The black needle hovered at thirty-four metres. It should have been pointing to forty metres. The chamber had lost more than a tenth of its pressure. Robson and Morozov were slowly being pulled to the surface.

We have a problem, the operator shouted, and the whole room gulped.

The operator knew that the correct emergency procedure for a loss of gas was to open the inlet valves to the oxygen and

353

helium tanks and flood the chamber with compressed gas. This would raise the internal pressure of the compartment and replace the amount seeping out from somewhere.

Dr Sokolov approached the control panel and spoke a few words to the operator. Calculations were made to ensure the correct amount of oxygen and helium were added to the chamber. Then the doctor stood back so as not to crowd the operator as he opened the inlet valves. Everyone in the room pinned their eyes on the pressure gauge. The needle began to nose upwards.

As this was happening, the operator keyed the microphone and alerted Morozov to the situation. The message was redundant. The hiss of gas and the increase in pressure prodding his eardrums would have told Morozov precisely what was happening. He equalised.

Dr Sokolov looked at the black and white image on the closed-circuit television screen. For a brief moment, he saw Robson lying asleep in bed. Then everything changed.

Inside the chamber, gas hissed in Robson's ears and his eyes snapped open. He felt a jolt of pain strike both hips and shoot down his thighs. He knew something was wrong.

Stop. Stop. Stop, he shouted.

The whistle of in-rushing gas turned to a squeal and then fell silent. The chamber came to a halt.

Robson looked at Denis on his feet, standing in front of the camera, talking to the medical team. There was a confusing amount of Russian being spoken, but he couldn't understand what was going on. He waited for someone to explain the sudden increase in chamber pressure; he waited for the translation to come.

Mike? Mike?

Mike is not here, Robson was told.

Mike Shyrokov had left the building for a moment.

Confused, Robson reached for the pad and pen and started making notes. 'Skin + "sub-cutaneous" sensation on front of both thighs worsened,' stated his first entry, timed at 20:10. 'Slight mobility decrease in L leg. Noticeable loss of feeling in L foot. L ankle very stiff.'

Under the orange glow of the desk lamp, Dr Sokolov began to make notes in his ledger. He looked at the instrument panel and noted that the needle of the depth gauge now pointed to forty-two metres. He reset the timer and began to consult his research. Over the following hours, Dr Sokolov filled the page with lines of neat handwriting; each row of ink documenting his observations, his decisions and his reasoning behind them. He had no guidelines to rely on in such a situation; there hadn't been enough incidents like this to give birth to agreed-upon responses. So, everything he did at that point was on a hunch. This was a setback and Dr Sokolov knew he had to rewrite the treatment plan, knew he had to decide whether to raise the chamber pressure again, and knew he had to decide how long to leave it.

The more changes he had to make to the table, the further he would step away from the method that had worked for so many other divers, the method that had received government approval. He knew the further he stepped away from the treatment regimen, the bigger the risk he would be taking with his

355

patient's health. The more trouble he could find himself in if things went awry.

He watched Robson on the monitor and he was struck by several things: Robson sitting up in bed; Robson moving his legs; Robson's face no longer filled with discomfort.

He decided against making any additional changes to the chamber pressure. He made a fresh entry in his ledger.

A search, meanwhile, was under way for the source of the leak, and everyone hoped the chamber had not blown a seam somewhere. (The problem was eventually traced to the medical lock transfer system.)

About an hour after the incident began, Robson scribbled another note:

Direct pain in left and right hip almost gone but radiated pain in lower outer aspect of both thighs still present. Improvement in skin sensation and left foot but left ankle still very stiff.

That was positive news to Doctor Sokolov.

Then, an hour and fifty minutes after being woken, Robson wrote the most comprehensive update on his condition:

No pain in hips (right or left).

Right leg still some pain (much less) in lower outer aspect of thigh.

Right leg everywhere else nearly back to how it was before pressure change including front of thigh.

Left leg pain almost gone from lower outer aspect of thigh but loss of deeper muscle feeling in same area.

Left ankle still very stiff. Still worse than the medical checks this morning.

Left front of thigh some improvement in skin and deeper muscle sensation. Not yet fully returned to how it was prior to pressure change but is improving.

When Mike Shyrokov returned to the complex he went straight over to the microphone. Inside the chamber, his voice crackled over the intercom.

Martin, I'm sorry I was not here, he said. Dr Sokolov wants to know how you are.

Robson gave a rundown of his symptoms, and then he vented.

They can't change the pressure inside the chamber, he said, without first telling me what they plan to do.

Robson was walking an emotional tightrope. He appreciated the doctors' efforts, but it was his body and he would have to live with the long-term consequences of whatever was being done to him by people he did not know.

The doctors are not here to hurt you, Martin.

I know the doctors are doing their best for me, but I can't have that happen again. I need to know when they are going to do things, Robson replied. I don't care if I'm asleep, they must wake me so I can be ready for when they start changing the environment in here.

The speaker fell quiet as Shyrokov translated the conversation for Dr Sokolov. Robson began to worry that essential decisions about his treatment were being transacted in the silence. When the Russians spoke, their conversations seemed, to Robson at least, long and drawn out. When messages were relayed, they seemed shorter in translation than he anticipated. He felt crucial details were being left outside. This frustrated him because he didn't want to be shielded from anything.

You need to tell Dr Sokolov that I'm not here to be experimented on, Robson said when Shyrokov returned to the microphone. Tell them they are not to do anything without my knowledge and consent.

Shyrokov promised to relay the message.

Robson's reaction concerned Dr Sokolov. 'It took us a long time afterwards,' he says, recounting that winter's night, 'to convince him it was an absurd accident and that all our aspirations were directed only at his quickest and most complete recovery.'

Most doctors who have worked in the field of diving medicine for long enough will recognise the failure of expectation that comes with dealing with decompression sickness. Sometimes, textbook treatments fall flat, and patients do not achieve, in medical terms, a good outcome; sometimes their recovery plateaus and they are never the same person again; sometimes they arrive at the chamber too late to survive. There is no eleventh commandment that states Thou shalt get better with recompression, jokes one doctor. 'Recompression therapy is a lengthy, time-consuming and expensive operation,' says former Royal Navy specialist Dr James Francis. 'People do improve, but the ones who have really got it wrong don't usually make a full recovery. It's draining, you do everything possible in the circumstances, and even that might be insufficient. Sometimes you lose people, or they remain wheelchair-bound for the rest of their lives; it's absolutely heartbreaking.'

Over the years, Dr Sokolov had taken his fair share of risks that would shake very strong nerves. He'd spent sixty years studying the disorder and ways to overcome it, and was, in his own words, occasionally prepared to break the rules for the good of his patients. Once, he was on a trip to Algeria when he heard of a military diver who was dying in the first aid post at the naval base. The diver had been training with Italian special forces when he was injured. Local doctors believed he was fatigued and, apparently, that's what they put in the diver's medical report. Dr Sokolov knew the man wasn't tired and he tried to convince the head of the medical department that treatment was needed. He eventually persuaded the medic to take the man to the nearby French hospital for an X-ray. That's when Dr Sokolov 'stole the patient', as he puts it. During the journey, he ordered the ambulance driver to head to the port instead. Docked there was a diving support ship the Russians had handed over to the Algerian Navy. On board was a recompression chamber. Dr Sokolov pressed the patient down to ninety metres and waited. A day and a half later, the man walked out of the chamber. The locals weren't happy, and the doctor feared he would be kicked out of the country. Instead, he received an award from the Central Committee of the Soviet Union Communist Party.

The biggest risk occurred on that summer's day in 1964 during a naval exercise out in the Baltic Sea. Diving from the Soviet salvage vessel *Spasatel'noye Sudno 87*, Sokolov had been down to the seabed 374 feet (114 m) below as part of a simulated submarine rescue mission. That was the dive where he surfaced without an issue, ate some food and went to bed, only to wake up a few hours later with horrible convulsions which shook him to and fro. That was the dive where he should have been pressurised to the equivalent of 300 feet (91 m) for a long soak, and where he heard the chamber door clang shut not knowing if he would walk away from his ordeal. That was the dive where he treated himself with an experimental protocol he had been quietly working on. That was risky. The gamble paid off, though. Five hours later, he walked out of the chamber, a little surprised that the treatment had worked so well.

After everything that had happened inside the chamber following the leak, Dr Sokolov had two choices – decide either it was time to fold and let nature take its course with Robson, or that he was on a winning streak and should go all in. He decided to go all in. He'd been bending the rules a little since he was first asked to treat Robson. He'd agreed to hyperbaric oxygen treatment at Nalchik, not once, but twice, when he knew it was forbidden; he'd agreed to the use of painkillers; he'd been optimistic in his diagnosis when he first saw Robson at the airfield. The success he'd enjoyed playing in the margins over the years may have made him lucky, and Sokolov appreciated that. Equally, years of study and experience had given him the wisdom to determine the best ends and the best means of treatment. 'There is always a possibility to do something if you think about it,' he says. 'Whenever you are faced with a situation, there is always an exit to get you out, even if you can't see the exit. You just have to find it. You never give up as long as there is something new to try.' And he wasn't thinking of giving up on his patient. So, he tweaked the treatment regimen. Just one more risk.

He held the chamber at forty-two metres, a little deeper than originally planned, and set the clock running. There had been a positive change in Robson's condition following the recompression and Sokolov wanted time to see how Robson reacted to the increased pressure. Under the treatment schedule, the minimum stay at this treatment zone was five hours. Sokolov decided to leave him there for another twelve hours.

Of grave concern for Dr Sokolov was the slow build-up of carbon dioxide inside the chamber. He was confident Robson and Morozov could stay inside for up to ten days before dangerous levels were reached. If all went to plan, that would be enough time to get the men out, even after lengthening the stay at depth. A hunch was not good enough, though, and, back in Moscow, experts were asked to model the build-up of gas and its effects on the body under pressure.

Perhaps the greatest concern for the medical team was the potential for pulmonary oxygen toxicity. Extended exposure to higher than normal concentrations of oxygen can cause damage to cell membranes, and lead to pulmonary oedema and the collapse of the alveoli in the lungs. Pulmonary effects can present within twenty-four hours of breathing pure oxygen. Robson wasn't breathing pure oxygen, but, under pressure, he had been inhaling doses equivalent to about 75 per cent for three days. Dr Sokolov needed to balance the dangers of lung damage against the possibility of incomplete recovery. In short, he didn't want to hurt his patient while trying to cure him.

Inside the chamber, Robson did what he was asked and inflated the balloon in two or three breaths, let the gas squeak out and inflated it again. His dry cough had gone, and he felt neither burning nor tickling when he inhaled. As long as he felt like this, he wasn't unduly worried about the problems of oxygen toxicity.

Robson sat at the end of his bed, legs hanging over the side, and stared ahead, his eyes focused, resolute. After the near catastrophe of the gas escape, he woke up ready to get out of bed and back on his feet. He'd been lifting his legs since his second day in the chamber, pencil marks on the white chamber wall highlighting his achievements. The spaces between the lines were tiny, but the improvements they represented were vast. Now it was time he asked another favour of his body.

His legs still didn't quite feel like his own. His left leg was numb and the muscles stiff. His thigh felt like it was swelling up, although it didn't look swollen. His right leg had gained some flexibility, but only if he lifted and pulled at the joints with his hands. His right foot could flex at the ankle without hurting, but he couldn't fully control its movement, as if the signals from his brain were misfiring. Pain, meanwhile, pulsated down his thighs.

It had been five days since Robson had been paralysed by the bends, three days since he'd been locked away in the chamber, and he didn't want to be disappointed any more. He had accepted what had happened underwater; there was no point dwelling on something he could no longer change, even if he was reminded of it every time he looked down past his waist. Just because he accepted things as they were didn't mean that was it for him, that he had no control over his situation. Acceptance wasn't admitting defeat; it was empowering.

If Robson's mind had wandered, he might have thought of a conversation he had had with a physiotherapist two years earlier following spinal surgery. Doctors had told him it would be five weeks before he would be up and about, but Robson wanted to return to the gym sooner and get back to the person he knew he could be. A few days after the operation, he spoke to the physio, and the advice he received struck a nerve.

You have two choices, the physio had told him. You can lie on your back and rest and do what the doctors say, and your recovery will be easier. But, in the end, you will not be as physically in shape as you were beforehand. Nor will you ever be. Or you do what you are doing. Your actual recovery is going to be more painful, but, at the end of it, you will be as good as you can be, bearing in mind you have just had spinal surgery. That was a turning point.

Robson didn't want to lie on his back and waste away then, and he didn't want to now. He needed to get moving soon, otherwise he might never get moving. There was nothing more the doctors could do for him beyond running the chamber treatment and hope for a positive outcome. If he was ever to walk again unaided, he knew that was up to him.

Robson shuffled forward on the bed, a cloth in one hand. He'd watched Morozov wipe the condensation from the chamber walls a day earlier and promised to help him next time. Placing his feet on the floor, Robson pushed himself up. His face was thin and forlorn; he had lost so much weight already that his friends thought he looked less and less like the Martin they knew. The chamber wasn't big enough for him to stand up straight, and he was forced to lean forward. His lower back ached from stooping.

Sweating in the twenty-eight-degree heat, Robson stood there on inflexible legs which trembled with pain and strangeness. He could sense pressure through his thighs, but he couldn't feel anything in the sole of his left foot. It was still numb. It must have seemed oddly strange to know he was standing, yet at the same time not feel the ground beneath his feet, but he was too focused to notice. He shuffled one foot forward, barely above the floor because he still had little control of his ankle, and he planted it down. He swung his other foot forward. Searching for support, Robson found the wall separating the main chamber with the medical lock behind him, and he leaned against it. Then he lifted the cloth and began wiping away the droplets of condensation. At least he felt he was contributing.

Small steps, two or three at first, but Robson had made them. Only they didn't resonate much with emotion or meaning; he wouldn't remember taking them when later asked to recall the moment he realised he would not be permanently disabled. He had approached the moment with a strong belief that they would work, an expectation that the reality of his situation would match the conviction he carried in his mind that everything would be okay.

Outside the chamber, Dr Sokolov watched Robson's efforts on the closed-circuit television monitor. As his patient shuffled around the chamber, the old man allowed himself a moment's relief. After a near catastrophe, and for the first time since the ordeal began, he felt positive. He still had a wheelchair on standby in the adjacent room. Just in case.

*

The headaches began five days into the treatment. Pain throbbed behind his eyeballs, a fist hammering inside his head, and it had grown worse throughout the past few hours. His forehead pounded. His temples ached. The torment would not let up. He became nauseous and developed a fever. His skin was cold and clammy and his temperature see-sawed wildly. The muscles in his legs felt swollen and painful. His left leg felt cold. His face lost its colour and its life. He swallowed some ibuprofen on top of the other tablets he had to take every day, and sank into the mattress. Uncontrollable shivers took hold of his body, and no matter how much he closed his eyes, he couldn't escape the suffering.

He was dressed in the same jumper and trousers that now hung loose from his body as the weight fell from his frame. The injuries sapped him of his strength. At 120 over 80, there was nothing wrong with his blood pressure, but he felt weak, and he had no energy to exercise, so the pencil marks of achievement on the white chamber wall went unchallenged. He didn't want to read, and holding any conversation was just too much for him. It felt like he couldn't do anything except lie in bed, staring at the walls where condensation massed and dripped on the floor next to the bucket he reached for when he wanted to retch.

The chamber was vented that morning. The plan was to leave it resting at thirty-eight metres for six hours before moving to another decompression stop later that afternoon. In the pause, Robson continued to note down the changes in his condition, and the entries were terser and more frequent. The humour found in the previous page – 'Day 400 I have started eating the cockroaches. Tomorrow I will attack the guards and escape' – had vanished. Each entry signalled a fresh setback he needed to overcome if he wanted to walk away from the incident.

'Slow build-up of pain in left hip joint,' he wrote.

'Front of left thigh feels like it is swelling up,' he wrote.

'Pain in muscles top of inside left thigh,' he wrote.

Robson couldn't understand why his recovery seemed to have skidded into reverse; why he was still living with the same shattered body that had come into the chamber days before. How could he have gone from a man who spent three days pushing himself to get better, three days of daily reports, to a man so weary he had no appetite and no energy to help himself? Everyone around him seemed to be at a loss to understand this transformation. He could hear the concern in the voices which carried into the chamber the same questions for him to answer again and again. He could hear the concern in the instructions for Morozov.

Then over came the medic to administer another injection.

Over he came with more tablets for Robson to swallow.

Over he came to conduct yet another medical examination, to prod the same part of his body, hard, and hurt him.

This one time, the medic tried to explain why he was pushing hard on his kidneys. Robson thought he understood what Morozov meant and braced himself. The medic pushed deep, and it felt to Robson as if his hand had poked through the other side. He cried out and screwed his eyes.

Enough. He pointed a finger at Morozov, and the medic sat back.

That was it for Robson. He'd had it with being manhandled. He retreated into the bed and pulled the covers over him, his abdomen hurting and his head still throbbing. Silence filled the empty chamber.

The urologist outside may have been worried about how much water he was passing and whether that meant his kidneys were failing; the physiologist may have been worried about the effect of oxygen on his lungs; Dr Sokolov may have been worried that the treatment was not going as well as they thought it would. Whatever they felt, Robson was no longer in the mood for it. He just wanted to be left alone.

Looking at the video monitor, Shyrokov saw his friend's reaction. He was concerned and started to write a note. Once finished, the paper was sent through the airlock and passed to Robson. During a moment of calm, he unfolded the page and read the words.

'Things on this side of the pond are a little bit different,' Shyrokov opened. 'Since you started learning Russian, you know that we Russians are different. This difference is small and can look embarrassing and quite challenging.

'I want to put things straight. Nobody knows what happened to you in the water. Nobody. Whatever the fault was, nobody cares. Only everybody cares is that you return, not only alive but being healthy, soon, and able to return to your duties. The unit you are in is an emergency committee unit which follows strict procedures; imagine Russian army hospital.'

After finishing the letter, Robson put it to one side and lay down, his head and body thumping. He tossed and turned throughout the night and shivered uncontrollably for two straight hours.

'Numbness in left thigh worse,' he wrote. 'Headache much worse. A lot of discomfort from numbness and coldness in left leg preventing sleep.'

'Still no sleep.'

'Feel weak and light-headed as if I will faint (cool, wet skin, no facial colour, increase in pulse then momentary loss of consciousness),' he wrote on a sheet of notepaper. 'I did not faint, but I felt as if I was going to,' he added.

'Sick again.'

Ninety minutes later, he noted: 'Some of "very cold feeling" now gone and not shivering as much. Headache and overall weakness. Still feel nausea. Not hungry.'

Time slipped by in big gaps of deadness. The minutes when he might snatch a little sleep and forget his predicament; the hours when he tossed and turned, and pain poked open his eyes to remind him of his situation. Again, he asked for something to deal with the headache, and again he was just given ibuprofen. Maybe they don't believe me, he thought, perhaps they don't think I'm telling the truth. It hadn't occurred to him that maybe they were confused and didn't quite understand what he was trying to say.

Later it was time for Robson's medication again, and, afterwards, his companion would be asked to give him another examination and poke and prod him. When the moment came, the two men acknowledged one another. Neither spoke of the flare-up the time before, neither was going to apologise for what had happened. Robson certainly wasn't prepared to apologise for something he had done in the heat of the moment; he had said what he wanted to say and had no desire to return to a quarrel with a man with whom he had developed a rapport over the previous days. He had no idea how Morozov was feeling and didn't ask to find out.

More and more he thought of the letter from Mike:

After talking to these guys and living with them for these days, I found they are spending their own money for drugs and other bits. The atmosphere is really fantastic. Now I am part of this family. The doctors are still sleeping here. Dr Sokolov has spent every minute of your treatment five metres away from your chamber. Denis's daughter turned up without seeing her father, and Dr Gaponov was refusing to leave these premises even when ordered to go home. All of this is for the very simple thing, to return you back.

The days of captivity had begun to run together. Thursday, for Robson, was lost to fits of sleep and moments of discomfort. So was Friday morning. There were no new updates, nothing in the way of meaningful details to recall, and nothing to share with the doctors. Time was marked only by another pressure change. And another. And another. And one more. Following the problems earlier in the treatment, the two men were alerted each time before the chamber was decompressed. Gas hissed away for a few minutes; they moved two metres closer to the surface, then things went quiet again.

The room was starting to smell distinctly like him, and Robson shuffled into the adjoining outer lock compartment to take a shower, more confident on his feet than he had been. He sat down and let the lukewarm water fall on his body and it felt good to wash away the sweat, even though the shower provided another cruel reminder that his body was broken. Cold water felt hot to the touch, and hot water felt icy cold. As a result, the water droplets came down on his legs in a thousand icy needles pricking his skin.

He was tired and frustrated. He slept fitfully. Every time he did manage to sleep he would wake expecting things to be better, only there was just more soreness and disappointment.

During one of the days, Morozov had a visitor. The intercom crackled and he looked towards one of the portholes. Robson followed his eyes. Standing on the other side was a young girl. Her face filling the window. Tears rolled down her cheeks. Morozov broke out into a smile. The girl in the window was his young daughter.

Happy Birthday, he said. She wiped her tears and smiled back at him.

She had celebrated her tenth birthday while her father was inside the chamber, and he had missed it because he had volunteered to help Robson instead. The sacrifice by a family he did not know touched Robson deeply.

Meanwhile, Shyrokov had returned home to Ukraine for forty-eight hours, to take a shower and change his underwear, he joked, and he left Robson a note. 'Please keep good progress (stay in chamber and don't escape), your guard seems like a good chap,' he wrote. 'I am proud with your strength (but I am not surprised) . . . Everybody wants to hug you when you walk away . . . Eat, drink, exercise. Russian should be fluent. And please, please, please don't thank, since it is . . . fuck, I forgot proper English word.'

By lunchtime on Friday there was a shift in Robson's mood. Unable to live with the day-to-day pain in his head, he snapped. Three days of resentment poured out onto half a page of paper:

Please, could you ask the doctors to help me? I have told them every day for the last three days that I have a very bad headache. The headache is primarily from dehydration, but I cannot drink or eat because of the headache. I have asked them many times about this. I do not understand why they are leaving me in so much pain.

The letter seemed to work, and a short while later stronger painkillers appeared in the airlock. The doctors hadn't withheld medicine because they didn't believe Robson, he was told; they hadn't understood him when he complained about just how much pain he was suffering. It's your British stiff upper lip, he heard.

He swallowed the new tablets along with the other medication he had to take and let them go to work. Drifting in the gentle current of painkillers, Robson was aware that, finally, the headache was starting to recede. As it did, his nausea died away. He managed to eat and drink a little, and the chamber was moved closer to the surface.

The percentage of oxygen in the chamber atmosphere was increased by Dr Sokolov, in line with the treatment guidelines. Robson noted that strength had returned to his right leg, although, confusingly, the top of his foot had gone numb. His left ankle had gone stiff again, and the pain in his hip had returned. His legs were sore and rigid, but none of that was going to keep him off his feet.

He hauled himself from his bed onto his feet, leaned against the wall and began exercising again. With the wall as support, Robson began to lower himself a few inches into a squat. Then he straightened up. His chest expanded, he grimaced, and breathed heavily, but he plugged away. Standing with his left leg in the air, he balanced on his right leg, closed his eyes and started to count. Robson managed fifteen seconds before his standing leg trembled and his body began to sway. He swapped legs. Robson found it harder to balance on his left leg; the sole was still numb, he couldn't feel the floor beneath his foot, and his calf muscle remained tight. Eyes open, staring straight ahead, Robson ticked off ten seconds before he lost his footing. Once he took his vision away his situation changed. Closing his eyes, his left leg wobbled, and he couldn't hold himself stable. As long as he was moving, though, things were good.

Mid-afternoon the following day, Saturday, when the chamber was standing at six metres, Robson and Morozov were joined by another man who had been transferred into the chamber, temporarily, via the secondary compartment. Robson recognised Ilya Gaponov as the doctor who had examined him as he lay in the ambulance on the airport runway, and who had climbed into the hyperbaric life-raft with a cigarette dangling from his lips. Since then, he had acted as Dr Sokolov's 'invaluable assistant', barely moving from the facility as he worked alongside his mentor to deliver the treatment schedule. Now, he had been sent into the chamber to carry out a full medical examination.

Robson was fed up with people examining him, but Mike's letter was still uppermost in his mind: all of this is for the very simple thing, to get you back on your feet.

In limited English, the doctor explained to Robson what he needed to do, and why. Robson appreciated the effort, and he softened. He wouldn't have understood much beyond the words for stomach and pain if Gaponov had spoken only in Russian. First, the doctor checked his pulse, took his temperature and blood pressure and asked him to exhale while he listened to his lungs through a stethoscope. Gaponov then asked him to stand up, hold his arms out in front of him and close his eyes. This is known as the Romberg Test and is used to assess the body's sense of balance and positioning.

Next was the inspection of Robson's kidneys. I am not trying to hurt you, Robson heard, but we need to know if it hurts. Robson understood that to mean they were still worried about the proper functioning of his renal organs. Then the doctor told his reluctant patient to lift his shirt, lie face down on his stomach and take a deep breath. Robson inhaled, and he felt the doctor push hard into his abdomen to palpate the organs. He screwed his eyes shut as Dr Gaponov moved his hands to the other side of his body and pressed down again. Robson winced again as he remembered hearing: I will be as gentle as I can.

Then it was done. Robson relaxed. He hoped there would be no more examinations. He'd had enough.

Later, when all this was over, when Robson had emerged from the chamber and Dr Sokolov had made it back to Moscow, both men would ask what, when everything during the dive was going right, had triggered the decompression sickness that left Martin fighting for survival. If he was a recreational diver, he could have explained away the decompression sickness on a rapid rise to the surface, because, simply put, that was more often than not the cause. But a rapid ascent couldn't account for Robson's hit. He'd been slowly climbing through the water, hitting his deco stops as planned when he was ambushed. Neither Robson nor Dr Sokolov could say with any level of certainty what was responsible for the bout of decompression sickness. They did know with some degree of certainty that the bend probably wasn't the result of a single, catastrophic episode underwater. Instead, they suspected the cause of the attack was rather a series of smaller events that, by themselves, might not have been enough to hurt Robson, but taken together were enough to pull the rug from beneath his feet.

The first issue Dr Sokolov considered was Robson's history of diving in Russia that month. He had been in the water almost every day for two weeks, sometimes twice a day, with only a handful of days off. Many of his dives had been between eighty and one hundred and sixty metres, and he had been deeper than one hundred metres at least five times before that fateful dive. Dr Sokolov predicted Robson's body had been in a state of residual saturation for most of the time. Generally speaking, the more diving someone does in a limited period, the higher the presence of residual gases in their blood and tissues. The conventional wisdom is that the vast majority of helium and nitrogen is off-gassed within a few hours, and almost all of it leaves a diver's body within about twenty-four hours. However, following a series of exceptional exposures, the washout time for inert gas could be much longer. In short, a diver's body may still be under the influence of an earlier dive. When Robson started his final dive at Blue Lake, his body may have been in a more saturated state than he believed. By going deep again the pressure of inert gas in his body could have been greater than predicted by the decompression algorithms running on his dive computers, greater than his tissues could withstand as he ascended.

Then there was the dive itself. Even with all the planning Robson had done, even with all the different decompression algorithms he had consulted on his laptop before getting in the water, even with the layers of conservatism he'd added to his decompression schedule, he was still embarking on an exceptional exposure. On ascent, Robson had been working with the decompression data on his dive computers, but there was nothing to guarantee the information was valid for the depth he had been. When all the variables of the dive – the depth, the bottom time, the breathing mix, the residual gas load, the ascent rate, the altitude he was diving, the atmospheric pressure – were combined to give Robson decompression data, it's more than likely that the specific exposure may never have been tested, let alone validated, with human test data. Robson understood that, though, and he was still prepared to take the risk. That's what deep divers do. If they didn't, they wouldn't be explorers.

There were more peripheral issues that both men thought about. Robson had been diving in the mountains, more than 800 metres above sea level, and, even though the lower atmospheric pressure had been accounted for by the divers, Dr Sokolov wondered whether repetitive, long, deep dives at altitude might have had some unknown effect. Robson himself reflected on the long hours he had spent in the cold water over the previous two weeks, and he wondered if that could have had a cooling effect on his core body temperature. Then there was his diet in Russia which was rich in fat and dairy. And he was tired. The long days of diving, the late evenings preparing equipment, the late nights at Khuazhev's house could have all taken a toll on him and his body.

Robson couldn't help but wonder whether some or all of these elements had played a part, however small, in the events that struck him down. He also knew that sometimes a diver could follow all the rules of diving and decompression and still suffer decompression sickness. In the old days, divers used to optimistically call such a hit unearned, undeserved or unprovoked, meaning they had followed their decompression plan perfectly, but these days the medical profession labels them unexplained. And that's how things remained for Robson. In the end, he did not spend too much time thinking about what had caused his bend, because he knew it was a mystery he was not going to solve. So, he didn't try to. He just wanted to move beyond the event and get back to diving.

At dawn on Sunday, 29 January 2012, the last of the pressurised gas began to vent from the chamber, and Martin Robson tried to finish his book. As the compartment inched the final two metres to the surface, he was sitting up in bed, eighty pages of *Sister Carrie* still to go. He'd been carried into the chamber on a stretcher, legs paralysed, and locked away eight days, seven hours and twenty minutes ago. Now it was time to see if he was ready to walk away from his ordeal. On the other side of the door, a wheelchair was waiting, close enough for Robson to reach if he needed help to get to the hospital and then to the airport for his flight home.

It was 6:40 a.m., and everyone involved in the treatment had gathered in the small room to watch him leave. Robson's doctors, the rescue team and his friends were patiently standing by. They had turned out, dressed in their dark blue jackets and cargo trousers, hoping for something to celebrate. As the hiss of escaping gas waned in their ears, the metal door relaxed on its seal and the compartment breathed a huge gasp of air.

The door was swung open on its hinges and Robson looked through the hatchway to see faces staring back into the chamber, waiting to see if the efforts of science and nature had worked. He smiled at them. He had earlier been briefed by Mikhail Shyrokov, now back in Sochi, on the best way to show his appreciation: how do you feel about coming out and hugging everyone? I know you are English, and you don't do hugs, but in Russian culture that will mean a lot to them.

Public displays of affection made Robson uncomfortable. He would stand up and make a speech on an evening to come, which would, apparently, go down well with everyone; that was more him. Right now, he wanted to do the right thing by them, and Mikhail said a hug was the right thing, so that was what he would do.

As they stared, he closed the book without marking the page and stood all the way up. His legs were still sore, and his mobility hadn't fully returned, but he finally felt the ground beneath parts of his feet. He stood for a moment. His legs held, Robson was confident they would, and he shuffled towards the exit. He carefully lifted a leg through the hatchway, bent forward, and shifted his weight to his front foot. Holding onto the lip of the hatch, he pulled his second leg through and stood up.

Robson looked around the room at the faces that welcomed him. He knew he needed to hug them, but what he really wanted to do first was take a shower; otherwise, he thought he'd have to position himself downwind of them. He hoped they understood his request. As soon as he was cleaned up, he walked back into the room and approached each person in turn. He wrapped his arms around them, and they reciprocated. Thank you very much, he said in Russian, I'm so grateful for what you have done for me. They smiled at him. He smiled as they held his hand, and he laughed when they told a joke.

Thank you for what you have done for me, he said to the next man.

Robson couldn't quite believe the warmth he received as he thanked each man. By the end of the weekend, all trace of him would be gone from this place, leaving only a story they could recount to their friends. When he looked back in the weeks that followed, he would wonder about these men, about how much they had given, of their time, of their money, their comfort, to save him, a stranger from another country, and he would wonder: why me?

Thank you very much.

Simple. Understated. Something Robson might say when served a beer at a bar. The expression, there and then, was all he had, but he loaded it with heartfelt gratitude. If the men didn't get the import of his words, he hoped they understood the message in his hug. And they did.

As Robson moved from man to man, offering his thanks and hugging them, Dr Sokolov watched from the edge of the crowd waiting patiently for his moment with Martin. It was a day of enormous relief. And triumph. 'This was for me one of the most joyful days in my life,' he would later state in his report of the incident.

When Robson had finished thanking everybody else, he was guided to Dr Sokolov. Two men from different backgrounds, cultures and countries, who had spent arguably the most important days of their lives separated by a quarter inch of steel, were now stood together, side by side.

Thank you, Robson said. Then the two men embraced for a short moment, and their eyes welled up with tears.

A news crew from EMERCOM was there to capture the moment. The footage showed Robson standing next to the chamber, trying to stay at the edge of the frame. Roman Dunaev was nearby, dressed in a black leather jacket, and Denis Morozov was still in his scrubs, emptying his locker. Robson's face was long and thin; even his cheekbones seemed to cast a shadow. His hands were pushed into the pockets of his grey trousers, and a blue polo shirt hung loosely around the neck. His ill-fitting clothes said he was recovering from an illness. He had lost about thirty pounds, so he thought, while inside the chamber. He appeared uneasy, and he smiled uncomfortably whenever the camera was pointed directly at him. Robson visibly relaxed when Dr Sokolov approached. He reached out with his right hand, and the old man wrapped his own hands around it. The doctor said something quietly in Russian, and a smile broke out across Robson's face. He whispered something back.

Sokolov wrapped his arm around Robson's waist. Robson reciprocated, but, because he was at least six inches taller, his arm went around the doctor's shoulders. There they stood, two men, supporting each other, two men granted a new lease of life following their successful battle against the deep.

An interpreter was called over to help them converse.

It's been very interesting, Dr Sokolov said.

Interesting? Robson laughed and held the doctor tightly.

We have all done our best, he continued, so that you could walk out, so that you can keep diving, maybe not extreme records; so you can keep diving and teaching your students.

Dr Sokolov produced a copy of the book he had written with his mentor Vladimir Smolin, and he discussed some of the developments it contained.

After the crowd had filtered away and the camera crew had gone, Dr Sokolov took Robson to one side and asked how he was feeling. My left leg is still numb in places, Robson volunteered, and the skin sensation is mixed. The doctor decided to conduct a Romberg Test. He kept things simple and first asked Robson to walk across the room. He watched his patient stride from one side to the other. The doctor then asked him to walk back with his eyes closed, and Robson did that too.

Martin Robson has improved significantly, he can walk confidently, the doctor would later say to a journalist, adding that the results of the treatment had exceeded all his expectations.

It really was the most difficult and the most successful treatment Dr Sokolov had dealt with in more than fifty years of service.

Robson was told he needed to go to hospital for further

examinations, but, first, he had a call to make. Clutching Shy-rokov's mobile phone, he walked outside and breathed fresh air into his lungs. Daylight seeped through the grey clouds of a winter's day as he moved across the car park, past the boats in dry dock, towards the quayside. The gentle swell of the sea lapped at the pilings, and the wind made the lines of the small sailboats sing.

Forty-eight hours hence, Robson will be standing near this very spot during his last few hours in Sochi, before heading to the railway station, before cramming crates of diving gear into a sleeping carriage and finding a place to sit between them all. His new Russian friends will be standing there, gathered out-side the grey building, under the grey sky. They will all be saying their final thanks, final goodbyes. They will be standing there looking at Robson, and no one will see the stray that Shyrokov had befriended. The German Shepherd will see Robson, though, and take off towards him. The dog will crash into the group and send Robson toppling to the ground. Robson will try to push the dog away, but his left leg will be in perfect range, and temptation will be too great. The dog will snap its jaws and Robson will feel the sharp bite on his upper left leg. His left leg in pain and his confident walk gone, Robson will hobble to the ambulance. While being patched up, he will look at the mark nature has left on him and the blood, and wonder, of all the people here, why me?

Vikki will cry when she hears that story. She will cry now.

Robson opened the phone and dialled home.

I'm out, and I'm on my feet, he told her. I'm coming home.

She knew he was due out, Mike Shyrokov had informed her, but she didn't quite know how Martin would feel about his recovery. It didn't matter; she just wanted it all to be over. Tears rolled down her face as she listened to his voice on the end of the line. He sounded exhausted but relieved to be out. Mentally, she flew across the world and threw her arms around him.

The call was short. There was an ambulance waiting for him. The doctors are chasing me; they are anxious to run more tests, he told her. He promised to call back as soon as he could.

Elsewhere in Russia, people were learning of Robson's recovery. In Moscow, Yevgeny Glukhov, the man who had pulled together the rescue mission, received a telephone call from Dr Sokolov. The wheelchair is not going to be needed, after all, the doctor said. For the first time in ten days, Glukhov allowed himself a moment to relax.

When the news made its way to Nalchik, Eduard Khuazhev reached for his best cognac; the same age as Martin, he would later joke, and he let his celebration last through two-thirds of the bottle.

The ambulance took a few minutes to reach City Hospital Number Four. On arrival, Robson insisted on walking. He hadn't needed a wheelchair when exiting the chamber and didn't need one to get to his appointment. Mike Shyrokov was with him for support, as were several friends who had travelled to Sochi, and members of the medical team. Denis Morozov wasn't there. He had gone home to see his family. They would invite Robson to visit their apartment one lunchtime and would cook him a Russian dinner, nothing too extravagant, but an act of kindness that would touch him.

As the entourage moved around from department to department, Dr Sokolov walked behind the group, a little way back, and studied Robson's bearing. He was looking to see if his stride had any stiffness that might indicate residual complications. While the movement wasn't perfect, slow and deliberate rather than fleet-footed, the Englishman appeared to move with some confidence. When the group arrived at a flight of stairs, Robson's assurance in his footing faltered. What he once did without a second thought now required conscious effort; he had to think his left leg into action. Dr Sokolov watched his patient take the first few steps upwards, and he could see that he was having difficulty. He took hold of Robson's left arm to steady him. He then reached around Robson's waist to provide further support. Everyone watched as, step by step, the two men climbed the stairs together, the man of seventy-eight at the side of his patient who had not long got back on his feet.

Upon admission to the hospital, Robson was examined by a therapist, a neurologist and a urologist. The doctors were the same faces he had seen in the moments before he was placed under pressure in the chamber. They poked and prodded his abdomen and carried out an ultrasound scan on his kidneys. They spoke in Russian in words he didn't understand. Interpreters told Robson they diagnosed that he was suffering only minor residual effects of decompression sickness. A neurological examination had not revealed any pathological changes in his health; his left leg would get better, he was told. Even so, the medical team wanted to keep him in for longer, to do more tests. Robson understood the medics had his wellbeing at heart, but he was tired. They wanted to finish caring for him; he just wanted to go home. Science had done its best for him; now, he wanted to let nature take its course and finish the healing. Robson said no to further treatment and asked to be discharged.

No one seemed to want to be accountable for granting official permission to leave. The delay frustrated Robson, but he had accepted the level of bureaucracy that inevitably came when interacting with the state: small cultural differences. It would appear again at the railway station when he went to purchase a ticket to Moscow. The self-service machine asked for Robson to enter his middle name, but it wouldn't accept his English one. His friends tried to bypass the question. The computer wouldn't let them. Everyone was becoming frustrated when someone spoke up: give him Dr Sokolov's name. They did, and the ticket was issued. Robson looked at the name printed on it: Martin Gennadyovich Robson. The doctor was his unofficial godfather.

Would you accept me as such? Robson remembered the doctor asking.

It would be my honour, he replied.

As they left the hospital, discharge papers yet to be issued, the group strolled along the corridor towards the staircase. Everyone paused as Robson took the first step. Going down didn't seem to be a problem for him. However, Robson saw Dr Sokolov take a cautious step, so he instinctively moved alongside. Robson took the doctor's arm, reached around his waist and said: here, let me help you.

AFTERWORD

The spirit of a month before, when an international team of divers and scientists had gathered at Blue Lake in search of the Holy Grail of cave diving, had evaporated after the loss of Andrei Rodionov and the injury to Martin Robson. The expedition was centred on a search for a virgin cave system; it had been impossible not to get excited by the prospects of what lay in wait just beneath the surface of the mysterious lake. After Martin was injured, the expedition quietly folded without finding answers to any of the questions posed. In the end, that didn't matter; the divers were just grateful Martin walked away with his life.

Less than a week after climbing out of the chamber, legs stiff but moving, Martin headed home. Late at night on Friday, 3 February, he walked through Heathrow airport towards a reunion with Vikki. 'He looked so vulnerable and wobbly on his legs,' she says of the moment Martin walked into the arrivals hall. If he had hoped to return to her the same man who had left four weeks earlier, Vikki was just relieved to have him home. She wanted to stay to look after him, but the following day she had to leave for the Philippines to honour a work commitment Martin had lined up. They were apart for another six weeks.

Home alone, Martin had no intention of just waiting to get better. Just like his time in the chamber, he knew he had to work himself fit again. So, he hit the gym, built up his fitness, and swiftly returned to his fighting weight. Before departing Russia, Martin was issued with a fit-to-dive certificate by Dr Sokolov, who was philosophical about his patient's return to diving: you'll know when the time is right to get back into the water, Martin remembered him saying. He didn't rush things.

Having to adjust, however temporarily, to a life that did not include diving was tough, but next to what had happened to him in Russia, a few months on dry land really didn't amount to much in the end. By mid-April Martin was diving in Malta.

Vikki asked Martin not to dive deep that year, nothing more than one hundred metres. Martin promised he wouldn't, and he honoured that promise. However, he couldn't resist the pull of the caves, and it wasn't long before he was running cave diving courses in France, Florida and Mexico, and deep wreck-diving expeditions to the Outer Hebrides and Italy.

For a while, Blue Lake continued to exert a hold over Martin's life. In the summer of 2012, he received an email from a friend in Russia asking for help. A diver had failed to surface from a deep dive in the lake and staff there asked if he could suggest where the search team should go looking. Armed with knowledge of the diver's start point, Martin offered his thoughts about where he was most likely to be found. Later that week, the body of Israeli diver Dimitri Sapozhnikov was recovered from 210 metres down by members of the Tuapse branch of Centrospas, the same team that had helped transfer Martin safely to Sochi. Then, in October 2014, he received word that his support diver Andrei Bykov had died while exploring the sunken Russian destroyer *Tenacious*.

The more Martin thought about his exploration of Blue Lake, the more he began to question whether there was even a cave system channelling water. With time to analyse his discoveries, he speculated that the water was not flowing in from one single source. Rather it was coming through many sources dotted around the walls: like a colander.

New research into the lake added weight to the theory. During the late summer of 2016, a team from the Underwater Research Center of the Russian Geographical Society established a field camp at the lake. They brought with them geologists and physiologists, divers and a mini-submersible called *Explorer 3*. For seven weeks, the scientists and divers collected data and carried out a series of experiments. Guided by Professor Nikolai Maksimovich, the man who directed Robson's search, they studied things like the flow and chemical composition of the lake water. Physiologists, meanwhile, studied the divers. Using sonar, the team mapped the lake and created a three-dimensional planogram. The findings suggested an upwelling of water was coming into the lake from deep down, passing through multiple cracks and breaks in the rock wall. The submersible found the bottom of the lake at a depth of 279 metres. The lake might go deeper still, researchers said, possibly through a fissure and along a horizontal siphon. Unfortunately, the way on was blocked by rocks that had fallen from the walls and formed a boulder choke.

During the summer of 2018, Martin returned to Russia and was reunited with Dr Gennady Sokolov for the first time in more than six years. In his eighties and still working, the doctor invited Martin to visit him at the Institute of Biomedical Problems of the Russian Academy of Sciences. Martin took a taxi to an address scribbled on a piece of paper. Dropped off at the end of the road in an anonymous industrial estate away on the outskirts of Moscow, Martin thought he might be in the wrong place. A man in camouflaged combat trousers eyed him with curiosity from his corrugated iron security shed. Trucks trundled from neighbouring yards, kicking dust into the hot summer air.

Beyond the security barrier, a man with a white beard looked over. Martin Robson? he shouted. The man, Martin soon discovered, was Pavel Spirkov, a legend in Russian diving circles. Waving open the security barrier, Spirkov ushered Martin behind the curtain to a place of Russian genius. Martin hadn't even made it to the building when Dr Sokolov emerged from the entrance. The two men approached each other, feet quickening as they neared, and instinctively embraced. Martin held the doctor tightly, and the Russian rubbed his back in return. Neither one seemed to want to break hold. When they did, the doctor whispered something to Martin, and a smile broke out across the face of his former patient.

Quite a group of Russian scientists had gathered, and they shepherded Martin into the building. It seemed as big a deal to them to have Martin visit as it was for him to be visiting. The men were keen to share with him the research they had conducted in the building that led to advances in diving and space flight. Then they showed him something special: the GVK-250 research chamber. This was the chamber Dr Sokolov had considered using to treat Martin before it was decided to transport him to Sochi. Martin stepped through the circular hatchway to look around at what could have been his salvation. The doctor followed. Inside, they shared a private moment away from the others: a heartfelt minute between two men shaped by the intense experience they had shared in Sochi. The old man said something, and Martin's laughter echoed around the chamber.

Two days later, Martin found himself in a van heading into the mountains of Kabardino-Balkaria. He had been this way before at a different time in his life filled with different expectations. He'd stepped off the sleeper train from Moscow an hour earlier, right into the bear hug of Eduard Khuazhev who was waiting for his arrival. Martin looked out of the window as the vehicle trundled along the mountain road. A mile or two out of town, where the limestone outcrops jutted towards the sky, the smell of rotten eggs drifted through an open window. 'The lake,' the interpreter said. 'You can smell it.'

The smell had vanished by the time Martin reached the banks of Blue Lake and looked out across the water. Standing at the patio where his legs had started to give way en route to the ambulance, Martin finally closed the circle on that most dramatic of events. Journalists from the local television news programmes were there to interview him, to capture the scattered glories of his celebrity with the people in this distant corner of Russia. He had fought to survive, and now he was back to tell his story.

Much had changed at the lake in the intervening years. Pop music blared from an outdoor restaurant where a cook grilled salmon for 250 roubles. A summer industry had grown around the lake. Market stalls, staffed by women in headscarves, lined the southern banks. They sold jewellery, stuffed toys and elegant fabric flowers to a steady stream of tourists who arrived in cars. The tourists had come to the lake for reasons that were not too hard to fathom. They were there to lap up the picture-postcard views of cobalt waters which reflected the blue sky above in its mirrored surface. Some stayed for minutes and a quick photograph. Others ambled along the pathway around the lake or sat on a bench gazing out over the water on a perfect afternoon.

The old dive centre had been closed, and a new wooden building stood on the lake's north-eastern bank. Igor Galaida and Roman Prokhorov had long since departed, both going to work for the Underwater Research Center of the Russian Geographical Society. Eduard Khuazhev, the one constant at the lake, had taken charge of the new centre. At some point, he asked Martin about a dive in the lake, and Martin said yes.

Wearing a dry suit and open-circuit scuba gear, he slipped beneath the surface. The water was cold but clear, and Martin could see, still fixed into place, the habitat which had provided him with a sanctuary when most in trouble. He swam over to it, pulled himself inside and spent a moment thinking back to the expedition. Afterwards, Martin dropped down to the plateau where the body of Andrei Rodionov had been found. A small memorial to the Russian had been laid by fellow divers. After a moment's reflection, Martin finned over the drop-off and around the cliff. He did not intend to go deep, and time did not allow him to stay too long, but Martin did what he always liked to do underwater whether there was a cave to find or not: he went off exploring.

NOTES ON SOURCES

This book is the product of a wealth of sources. Chief among them are the memories of a number of those who were involved in the events recounted in the pages and agreed to share their stories with me, as I reported and wrote this story. As stated previously, this book would not have been possible without the collaboration of Martin Robson. I spent many hours interviewing Martin, in person at his home in the UK, on a cave diving trip to France, during our research trip to Russia, by telephone and at various diving conferences. He answered my questions candidly and gave me full access to his files, notes, photographs and dive logs to support his answers. He happily submitted himself to follow-up phone calls to clarify matters or to revisit conversations as fresh information came to light during my research, which generally helped to improve his recollection. That said, there are certain events during the episode, particularly during his time in the chamber, that he does not remember well. He readily admitted when that was the case and never tried to fill in the blanks with false memories. Some of those instances, like him not remembering exactly when he took his first steps in the chamber, might seem odd to those of us who would think to lose the use of one's legs would leave an indelible mark in the mind. Martin was, for the most part, confident that he would walk again and therefore didn't commit the incident to memory. His partner Vikki Batten helped to corroborate many aspects of their diving trips and served as an aide-memoir to some aspects of Martin's life that he was too modest to highlight. Upon my completion of the manuscript, Martin read the pages to ensure what I had written accurately captured the events as they occurred, and to highlight any issues I may have misunderstood. Most clarifications were of a technical nature, but in some cases, his suggestions triggered fresh conversations and deepened the text with more information.

Likewise, the input of Dr Gennady Sokolov was crucial to the reporting for this book. I had the pleasure of spending time in his company at either end of my research trip to Russia. I got to watch him in action as he ran a chamber dry dive to one hundred metres for a group of technical divers and I interviewed him at length. He also provided pages of written answers to my questions and sent me numerous articles and reports he had written about his experiences as a diver and doctor. His file recounting his childhood was particularly wonderful. I am grateful to him for sharing with me his official report of the incident, which was written a few months after the event. This helped to corroborate the recollections of those involved, to point me in the direction of fresh inquiries and to provide specific data that I might not have otherwise found.

Alongside these two men, many people who were involved in the expedition and subsequent rescue of Robson agreed to share their recollections with me in interview and via follow-up emails, to help me build an authoritative account of what happened during that period in Russia. I acknowledge, though, that it is perhaps impossible to ever get a complete account because people see things from a particular point of view and their recollections of events may change or diminish with time. No one's recollection is going to be perfect and all I hoped for was their best memory. I then sought to corroborate these recollections with independent sources. Most of the incidents were independently described by more than one individual and were supported by contemporaneous sources, including news stories from reporters following the expedition, website entries, photographs and video footage, official reports, and online forums to which some of the divers contributed. In all, I have relied on first-hand accounts and have stayed away from anecdotes told second-hand. Inevitably, there are a handful of instances included in the book where it has proved impossible to corroborate the information provided. Most, but not all, of those matters concern some of the deep dives. As any deep diver knows, these excursions are often solitary experiences in which the memory of the participant is the only record available. Hopefully, those instances, when they appear in the book, are clear to the reader. In all other instances, I have made a judgement call on the information provided and the reason for providing it.

Finally, there are some people whom I have not been able to speak with, as a result of a language barrier, bureaucracy or a wish on the subject's part not to engage. I understand the latter and respect their decision. Out of fairness, I have limited their inclusion in the book, but it has not always been possible. The one person I regret not being able to interview is Denis Morozov, in Sochi. Unfortunately, I have not been able to get official clearance to speak with him and have exhausted current channels.

As a technical and cave diver with almost twenty years of experience, I hope I have been able to bring a level of understanding to the manuscript that I believe benefits it in many ways. I've been lucky to have met, spoken with, been taught by and dived with people far more accomplished than me in underwater exploration. The many divers I have had informal conversations with at dive sites, on dive boats and in the bar afterwards have helped inform me and my thinking, and also helped to make this book better than I envisaged.

As much as this book is the product of the people who have opened themselves up to my questions, it also owes a huge amount to men and women no longer with us; the divers, doctors and researchers to whom we owe so much of our understanding of diving physiology and underwater adventures. Having been schooled on many of these concepts when I first started diving, it has been a fascinating adventure to find out how they originated. I have read countless scientific reports and medical studies and attended many conferences where specialists have educated divers on matters of science. I would like to thank members of the medical profession who have helped me to understand matters of the human body. For those interested, *Bennett and Elliott's Physiology and Medicine of Diving* is an excellent introduction to the subject. If I can impart one piece of advice, be prepared for a long journey as you follow the sources from one document to the next. Certainly, those studies will take you to the non-profit Rubicon Foundation website at rubicon-foundation.org, which has a remarkable electronic research repository filled with thousands of documents, many historic and hard to find, that tell the story of diving physiology and medicine. The repository is certainly worth your time and spare change to keep it free and available.

If I were asked to recommend a handful of books to those interested in the history of decompression sickness and the early years of diving, I would suggest the following, all of which make fascinating reading:

Paul Bert, *La Pression Barométrique: Recherches de Physiologie Expérimentale*, G. Masson, Paris, 1878

E. Hugh Snell, *Compressed Air Illness, or so-called Caisson Disease*, H. K. Lewis, London, 1896

Leonard Hill, *Caisson Sickness and the Physiology of Work in Compressed Air*, Edward Arnold, London, 1912

The Report of a Committee Appointed by the Lords Commissioner of the Admiralty to Consider and Report upon the Conditions of Deep-water Diving, London, 1907

The Report of a Committee Appointed by Lord Commissioners of the Admiralty to Consider Equipment and Material Required for Deep and Ordinary Diving in HM Services (Deep Diving Committee): based on experiments and trials 1930–1931

Over the following pages, I have detailed the range of sources that informed each sentence, paragraph, section and chapter in this manuscript.

Mark Cowan

Prologue

1 'He lay there . . . as decompression sickness': Dr Gennady Mikhailovich Sokolov.

3 'Decompression sickness is . . . make disturbing reading': A. O. Brubakk and T. S. Neuman (eds), *Bennett and Elliott's Physiology and Medicine of Diving 5th Edition* (Saunders, Edinburgh, London, 2003) informed general insights into decompression sickness. Richard D. Vann, Assistant Professor Emeritus in Anaesthesiology at Duke University, described decompression sickness as a man-made disease during a lecture titled 'Pathophysiology of Decompression Illness', posted online by Divers Alert Network. Details of the incident involving the U-2 pilot can be found in S. L. Jersey, R. T. Baril, R. D. McCarty and C. M. Millhouse, 'Severe Neurological Decompression Sickness in a U-2 Pilot', *Aviation, Space, and Environmental Medicine*, Vol. 81, No. 1, 2010, pp. 64–8. An introduction to decompression sickness has been provided on the website of Divers Alert Network by following the link: https://dan.org/health-medicine/health-resource/dive-medical-reference-books/decompression-sickness/

4 'When, in 1912 . . . of the navel': A comprehensive record, rich in first-hand observations from doctors investigating the strange new disease that struck down early divers, was gathered by physiologist Leonard Erskine Hill and presented in *Caisson Sickness and the Physiology of Work in Compressed Air*, Edward Arnold, London, 1912 (hereafter Hill's *Caisson Sickness*).

5 'And on and . . . it gurgled loudly': This case featured in both Hill's work and John Scott Haldane's research into decompression sickness, *The Report of a Committee Appointed by the Lords Commissioner of the Admiralty to Consider and Report upon the Conditions of Deep-water Diving*, London, 1907 (hereafter *The Haldane Report*).

5 'Doctors also noticed . . . with a knife': Dr Graham Blick's account was published in *British Medical Journal*, Vol. 2, Issue 2556, December 1909.

6 'In the 1950s . . . caused irreparable damage': The description is taken from a US Navy training video that can be found at https://www.youtube.com/watch?v= jIGOEiPpoe8

6 'This, Sokolov knew . . . Let's go!': Sokolov. Descriptions and details from photographs both provided to me by Sokolov, and which featured on information boards displayed at the Institute of Biomedical Problems of the Russian Academy of Sciences, in Moscow.

Not Strange, Just a Little Different

9 'Once a man . . . their own selves': The epigraph is taken from Hans Hass, *Men Beneath the Sea: Man's Conquest of the Underwater World*, David and Charles, Newton Abbot, 1975; translated from German.

9 'A gentle wind . . . them, everything changed': Martin Robson, Sergei Gorpinyuk, Eduard Khuazhev, Roman Dunaev, Anna Kozlova, Ulyana Zhakova. Descriptions of people and the lake are from personal recollections, supplemented by photographs and video taken by var-

ious expedition members, and news broadcasts from local television stations.

15   'Blue Lake is . . . is not recommended': Zhakova. The description of the lake and surrounding area comes from personal observation from my trip to Kabardino-Balkaria, supplemented by photographs taken by expedition members, articles and news reports about the expedition, and the book Голубое ожерелье Кавказа (*Blue Necklaces of the Caucasus*) by U. V. Eremov. Regarding the Balkar version of the lake's name, I have seen a variety of different spellings, but I opted to use the version given to me by Eduard Khuazhev and interpreter Vladimir I. Belichenko while I was in Kabardino-Balkaria.

18   'Cave diving was . . . with carbon monoxide': Robson, Christine Loew, Phil Short, and numerous other cave divers I have spoken to while at various cave diving sites in Mexico and France.

21   'After his presentation . . . exploration die hard': Robson, Bogdana Vashchenko, supplemented by an interview Vashchenko and partner Viktor Lyagushkin gave to *DivePlanet* (published online 9 February 2012) shortly after the expedition ended, and available at http://www.diveplanet.ru/diving-media/09/83532/

23   'It's not easy . . . two of them': Robson, Vikki Batten.

27   'Robson landed in . . . to find caves': Robson, Gorpinyuk, Khuazhev, supplemented by photographs taken by expedition members and personal recollections gathered by repeating the journey from Moscow by sleeper train. I took the train all the way to Nalchik, and

from there was driven to the lake along the same mountain road.

31 'The water in . . . feared: decompression sickness':
Robson, Gorpinyuk, Dunaev. Description of the lake also
from photographs and video shot by expedition members
and from personal recollection of my own dive there.

35 'Almost as soon . . . hour or more': C. A. Deane (the
helmet's inventor), *Submarine researches on the wrecks of
His Majesty's late ships Royal George, Boyne, and others by
Mr C. A. Deane, in his improved diving apparatus*, repub-
lished by the Historical Diving Society, UK, 2001.

36 'Impressed by the . . . the lower legs': J. J. W. Roberts,
Assistant Surgeon, *The Medical and Surgical Journal of
HMS Success for 12 June to 28 October 1840*, National
Archives, Kew, reference ADM 101/121/1. This provides
a first-hand account of diving activities during the first
year of the salvage operation, and includes a detailed list
of injuries and sickness among those on board. Pasley
documented Philip Trevail's illness in correspondence
with Rt Hon. Sidney Herbert, dated 7 December 1843,
the originals of which are held at the National Archives,
Kew (Admiralty, and Ministry of Defence, Navy
Department: Correspondence and Papers, in various,
reference ADM 1/5528). Trevail's discharge paper is
available at findmypast.co.uk. James Dugan, *Man
Explores the Sea* (Hamish Hamilton, London, 1956) and,
in particular, T. W. J. Connelly, *The History of the Royal
Sappers and Miners Vol. I* (Longman, Brown, Green,
Longmans, and Roberts, London, 1857) provided

supplementary and colourful details not found in the public records.

39   **'That's how it . . . aid of crutches'**: J. B. Green, *Diving With and Without Armor*, Faxon's Steam PowerPress, Buffalo, 1859.

39   **'The star diver . . . of his life'**: Details are found in Sir Robert Davis, *Deep Diving and Submarine Operations: A Manual for Deep Sea Divers and Compressed Air Workers*, Siebe, Gorman & Co., 1935.

40   **'Dreadful to be . . . doctor had permitted'**: Writing in the French medical press, doctors Michel Catsaras, Alphonse Gal and Leroy de Mericourt provided independent first-hand accounts of the activities of Greek sponge divers. Their accounts were summarised in English in numerous books of the time, including Hill's *Caisson Sickness*. For the original French versions: de Mericourt, *Considerations sur l'hygiène des pecheurs d'eponges*, in *Ann. d'hygiène publique et de médecine légale*, Second series. Vol. XXXI, 1869; Catseras, *Recherches cliniques et expérimentales sur les accidents survenant par l'emploi des scaphandres*, in *Archives de Neurologie*, Vol. XVI, No. 47, 1888; Gal, *Des dangers du travail dans l'air comprimé et des moyens de les prévenir. Thèse de doctorat en médecine*, Montpellier, Faculté de médecine de Montpellier, 1872.

42   **'The same was . . . couldn't pass urine'**: The account of the Japanese pearl diver appeared in *The Lancet*, 6 February 1892, by P. W. Bassett-Smith, a surgeon on board HMS *Penguin*, which was on survey work at the time.

43 **'Being a hard-hat . . . and then uncorked'**: The case was reported in great detail in Hill's *Caisson Sickness*.

44 **'Those early years . . . a mystery illness'**: The development of the caisson is outlined in Jacques Triger, 'Mémoire sur un appareil à air comprimé, pour le percement des puits de mines et autres travaux, sous les eaux et dans les sables submergés', *Comptes rendus hebdomedaires de l'Académie des sciences*, Vol. XIII, 1841. The letter was published in *Comptes rendus de l'Académie des sciences*, Vol. XX, 1854, pp. 445–9.

44 **'At a pit . . . well as deaf'**: Blavier provided a background to the work in his paper 'Rapport sur le procédé suivi, à Douchy, pour traverser des nappes d'eau considérables', *Annales des Mines*, 4e ser, No. 9, 1846. Pol and Watelle added further detail in their work 'Mémoire sur les effets de la compression de l'air appliquée au creusement des puits à houille', *Annales d'hygiène publique et de médecine légale*, 2e ser, No. 1, 1854. The work of Triger, Blavier, Pol and Watelle was summarised in Paul Bert, *La Pression Barométrique: Recherches de Physiologie Expérimentale*, G. Masson, Paris, 1878. There also exists an English version, translated by M. A. Hitchcock and F. A. Hitchcock, *Barometric Pressure: Researches in Experimental Physiology*, College Book Company, Columbus, Ohio, 1943.

44 **'Around the world . . . such a manner'**: An overview of the issues facing caisson workers can be found in E. Hugh Snell, *Compressed Air Illness, or so-called Caisson Disease*, H. K. Lewis, London, 1896. A detailed account

about work on the Brooklyn Bridge can be found in Andrew Smith, *The Effects of High Atmospheric Pressure Including Caisson Disease*. Eagle Book and Job Printing Department, Brooklyn, New York, 1873.

46   'They'd been underwater . . . for him alone': Robson, Gorpinyuk, Popova, Kozlova, Khuazhev.

49   'The divers used . . . kill a diver': Robson. Mark Powell, *Deco for Divers* (Aquapress, Southend-on-Sea, 2008) offers a good introduction to trimix. Supplemented with manuals read for my own training in the use of trimix.

50   'The quickest way . . . pair of eyes': Khuazhev, his wife Angela Kucherenko, Robson. Supplemented by information posted on the dive centre's now-defunct website kbrdiving.ru and news story about the couple, 'Divers of Kabardino-Balkaria are preparing to set a new record for Russia in deep sea diving', sk-news.ru, 15 July 2007. Description of Khuazhev also taken from photographs taken by expedition members.

Pay Only When Leaving

54   'Naturally, like any . . . has been before': The epigraph is a quote from Dr George Benjamin, a pioneering cave diver who helped develop the two outlet non-isolator manifold to link two tanks, which featured in Bret Gilliam, *Deep Diving* (Watersport Press, San Diego, 1992), an advanced guide to physiology, procedures and systems.

54   'The stark reality . . . of serious concern': Robson, Zhakova, supplemented by video and photographs taken by expedition members. Details of Maksimovich's career

are from his profile on the website of Perm State University, http://www.psu.ru/personalnye-stranitsy-prepodavatelej/m/nikolaj-georgievich-maksimovich

58 'At the turn . . . they clocked off': Informed by *Siebe, Gorman & Co.'s Manual for Divers: with instructions for submarine operations*, Unwin Brothers, London, 1904; *The Haldane Report*; Snell, *Compressed Air Illness*; Smith, *The Effects of High Atmospheric Pressure Including Caisson Disease*; and Alphonse Jaminet's account of caisson work, *Physical Effects of Compressed Air, and the causes of pathological symptoms produced on man, by increased atmospheric pressure employed for the sinking of piers, in the construction of the Illinois and St. Louis Bridge over the Mississippi River at St. Louis, Missouri*, R. & T. A. Ennis, Stationers and Printers, St Louis, 1871.

58 'In Great Britain . . . was lost overboard': Informed by *Siebe, Gorman & Co's Manual for Divers* and *The Haldane Report*.

59 'By early 1905 . . . specially trained divers': A. S. Evans, *Beneath the Waves: A History of HM Submarine Losses* (Kimber, London, 1986) offers a comprehensive account of British submarine losses. Arthur Lee's quote was taken from Hansard: Navy Estimates, 1905–6. HC Deb 12 July 1905 vol. 149 cc471–503.

59 'Suddenly, the safety . . . had the answers': Martin Goodman provides an account of the extreme life of Haldane in *Suffer and Survive: Gas Attacks, Miners' Canaries, Spacesuits and the Bends. The Extreme Life of Dr J. S. Haldane*, Simon & Schuster, London, 2008.

60   'That he knew . . . pays when leaving': Pol and Watelle, 'Mémoire sur les effets de la compression de l'air. . .'.

61   'The culprit for . . . in the blood': Bert provided a detailed account of his experiments in *La Pression Barométrique*.

61   'Nitrogen is found . . . finally understood it': *The Haldane Report* and A. E. Boycott, G. C. C. Damant and J. S. Haldane, 'Prevention of compressed air illness', *Journal of Hygiene*, Vol. 8, No. 3, June 1908, offer a comprehensive account of the research by Haldane and the Committee. The analogy between the emergence of bubbles during decompression and those in a bottle of soda was made by Haldane and continues to be cited by many scuba diving instructors. Damant's account can be found in Dugan, *Man Explores the Sea*. The claim that Great Britain possessed a means of carrying out diving operations in a way unmatched by any other country was made by Haldane during a lecture for the Auchterarder Literary Society, in the Perthshire seat of his brother, Richard Haldane MP, and reported in *The Scotsman*, 8 January 1908. Descriptions from photographs included in the report and on file at the National Archives, Kew.

70   'Few modern divers . . . is about control': From personal experience and years spent diving and speaking with accomplished technical divers.

71   'When the final . . . rest while decompressing': Robson.

71   'American cave explorer . . . from their mouths':

Details and photographs of the habitat are found on Bill Stone's website https://stoneaerospace.com/history/ and a report on the 1987 Wakulla Springs expedition at https://www.usdct.org/wakulla87.php. A detailed description of life inside the habitat is given in Lisanne Renner, 'Diving "where no man has gone before": 14-member team will explore Wakulla Springs in the Fall', *The Orlando Sentinel*, 14 September 1987.

72 **'Robson would like . . . the deeper dives'**: Robson. Description from personal recollection from my dive in Blue Lake, supplemented by photographs and video from expedition members of the habitat being constructed. Quote from Robson's blog about the expedition.

74 **'Thought then turned . . . his or her success'**: Robson, Khuazhev, Dunaev, Gorpinyuk, Popova, Batten, and various divers I have spoken with informally at dive sites and conferences around the world. Verna van Schaik, *Fatally Flawed: The Quest to be Deepest* (Liquid Edge Publishing, South Africa, 2008) offers an interesting view of what it was like being a surface marshal in charge of support divers during an ill-fated dive. She offered more in an article posted on the website Liquid Edge, 5 February 2008: http://theliquidedge.blogspot.com/2008/02/thank-heaven-for-support-divers.html

76 **'Sergei Gorpinyuk assumed . . . and Andrei Rodionov'**: Gorpinyuk, Robson. Details of Bykov's archaeological honour were reported in *The Day*, a Kiev-based broadsheet newspaper, 14 October 2010. Robson was also involved in the expedition.

77 'Engineer, mechanic, rally . . . the Ladoga Rally':
Popova, Khuazhev, supplemented by videos of Rodionov
on diving expeditions, and a commemorative video
posted to YouTube: https://www.youtube.com/
watch?v=_hgxPi1QLLo. Description comes from photographs taken by expedition members.

77 'Everyone else was . . . they worked together':
Popova, supplemented by a report into The UTD Pit
Exploration Project, November 2009, Tulum, Mexico,
available online at https://docplayer.net/47881797-The-utd-
pit-exploration-project-november-2009-tulum-mexico.
html. Description of Popova from photograph taken by
expedition member.

78 'Safety, everyone knew . . . preparing the habitat':
Gorpinyuk.

79 'Underwater, all the . . . was under pressure':
Robson, Gorpinyuk, Dunaev, Popova, supplemented by
photographs and video taken by expedition members,
and my own experience of handling bailout cylinders
underwater.

81 'On the surface . . . dawn of time': Zakhova, supplemented by photographs and video taken by her and
other expedition members, Robson.

82 'Meanwhile, Bogdana Vashchenko's . . . don't get
frozen': Robson, supplemented by photographs taken
by expedition members and copies of broadcast news
reports from various TV channels. The quoted Q&A
comes from a report broadcast on News Kabardino-
Balkaria, 10 January 2012.

82   'Another person who . . . good, he said': Robson.

83   'If one person . . . became technical director': The story of Prokhorov's first dive at Blue Lake and the development of the diving and research centre was featured on the dive centre's now-defunct website kbrdiving.ru. I made repeated efforts to contact both Galaida and Prokhorov but neither responded and they moved on from Blue Lake.

84   'You know, those . . . miles from anywhere': Robson.

Undiscovered Continents Beneath Our Feet

86   'Every field of . . . to try harder': The epigraph is from cave diving pioneer Sheck Exley, *Caverns Measureless to Man*, Cave Books, St Louis, 1994.

86   'Most cave divers . . . history, my friend': Robson, Loew, Batten, Lamar Hires, Paul Heinerth, Michael Thomas, and many other cave divers I have spoken to informally at dive sites during my diving research.

89   'There are four . . . has gone before': Heinerth.

89   'Martin Robson wanted . . . to be there': Robson, Batten.

93   'He decided to . . . the average person': Robson, Heinerth.

94   'Within the intensely . . . get home safely': Robson. Description of his teaching comes from watching him teach two students on a cave diving course in France.

96   'Buried within the . . . at Saint-Rémy': Frédéric Mistral, *Memoirs of Frédéric Mistral*, Edward Arnold, London, 1907.

96 'Seven leagues? That . . . does this go?' Informed by my experience exploring caves with other divers.

96 'In 1946, French . . . in 5,000 dives': Jacques-Yves Cousteau and Frédéric Dumas, *The Silent World*, edited by James Dugan, Hamish Hamilton, London, 1953.

98 'As a result . . . directly below us': Martyn Farr, *The Darkness Beckons: The History and Development of Cave Diving* (Diadem, London, 1991) gives a detailed account of Hasenmayer's cave diving exploits. Information supplemented by an interview Hasenmayer gave to Jan Murtomaa and various newspaper interviews.

101 'The story electrified . . . find down there': Robson, Batten. Supported with information from an article in the now-defunct *990* diving magazine, along with a contemporaneous document by Vikki Batten, 'A Supporting Role', and a document prepared by her father Ed Batten, 'Cave Slaves'. Descriptions come from photographs supplied by Robson and Batten. Additional information about the cave and reference to Robson's exploration from the French cave diving website plongeesout.com.

A Gruelling Act of Submersion

112 'If you want . . . something you join': The epigraph comes from author and pioneering technical diver Gary Gentile, author of *The Technical Diving Handbook*, in 'Brass Fever', *aquaCORPS* magazine, date unknown.

112 'The line at . . . deep-sea diving': Informed by *The Haldane Report* and H. V. Hempleman, *The History of*

Evolution of Decompression Procedures, in *Bennett and Elliott's Physiology and Medicine of Diving 3rd Edition*, Bailliere Tindall, London, 1982; *The Report of Committee Appointed by Lord Commissioners of the Admiralty to Consider Equipment and Material Required for Deep and Ordinary Diving in HM Services (Deep Diving Committee): based on experiments and trials 1930–1931*, held at the National Archives, Kew (reference ADM 315/1) (hereafter *The 1930–31 Trials Report*); and *The Medical Report on Deep Sea Diving Trials for 1931*, by Surgeon Lieutenant-Commander A. E. Phillips, HMS *Excellent*, held at the National Archives, Kew (reference ADM 212/202) (hereafter *The Deep Diving Trials Medical Report*).

113 **'When the M1 . . . in 325 feet':** *The 1930–31 Trials Report*.

113 **'The First Lord . . . became important again':** 'No Hope for *H47* Crew', *Hampshire Telegraph*, 12 July 1929.

113 **'The US Navy . . . brass were after':** A comprehensive account of the Royal Navy research can be found in *The 1930–31 Trials Report*. This includes details of the death of David Robertson. His gravestone in Caputh churchyard, Perthshire, Scotland, features a Standard Dress diving helmet and states he died during diving operations.

119 **'The development of . . . more about it':** Complementing the above report is *The Deep-sea Diving Committee: Research Papers 1929–1932*, held at the National Archives, Kew (reference FD1/3176), which details Damant's research and the interviews with divers. Further details can be found in *The Report of Deep Diving Committee on Confirma-*

tory Trials at Siebe, Gorman and Co. works and from HMS Tedworth at Inverary [sic] *in 1933*, ADM 315/2. Details of the tests taken by divers can be found in *The Deep Diving Trials Medical Report*. Supplementary information from William A. R. Thomson, 'The Physiology of Deep-Sea Diving', *British Medical Journal*, 3 August 1935.

125 **'Just before midday . . . diver the hoodoos'**: Robson, Khuazhev, Gorpinyuk, Dunaev, Kozlova. Description of Robson preparing for a dive comes from personal observation during my time with him on a cave diving trip in France. Additional information from photographs and video taken by expedition members, from a report of the expedition broadcast on News Kabardino-Balkaria on 10 January 2012, a feature on the expedition that appeared in the Russian version of *National Geographic* magazine, and published online on 23 March 2012, https://nat-geo.ru/adventure/kuvshin-dzhinna, and a report on the dive on the dive centre's now-defunct website kbrdiving.ru

128 **'Robson's cave diving . . . Somethin' grabbed me'**: Hires.

128 **'When everything had . . . the deep took hold'**: Robson. Additional information and descriptions taken from video footage provided by expedition members.

129 **'Once Robson had . . . began their rituals'**: Khuazhev, Gorpinyuk with additional information from photographs by expedition members.

129 **'Ten minutes into . . . and head back'**: Robson. Description comes from photographs by expedition

members and personal observations of Robson preparing for dives.

133   'One hundred and . . . "13:35" was added': Gorpinyuk.

134   'Alone in the . . . no escaping it': Robson.

136   'From his vantage . . . to take it': Robson, Gorpinyuk, Dunaev.

139   'On the surface . . . you are comfortable': Khuazhev. Description of Khuazhev at the water's edge comes from photographs and video taken by expedition members.

141   'Electronic pulses fired . . . he called it': Robson, Khuazhev, Gorpinyuk, Dunaev. Description of experience inside the habitat comes from personal recollection having spent time inside. Description of post-dive conversation taken from video footage provided by expedition members.

Martin, We've Lost Andrei

145   'The dive itself . . . vulnerable I am': The epigraph is a quote by Sheck Exley, which appeared in Ned DeLoach, 'The Deepest Dive: A Study in Controlled Paranoia', *Ocean Realm* magazine, Summer 1988, an article about Exley's pioneering deep dives at a Mexican spring known as Nacimiento del Rio Mante.

145   'Robson phoned home . . . of the expedition': Robson, Batten and personal recollection having spent time with Robson on a cave diving trip in France.

146   'When there wasn't . . . beneath the surface': Robson, Khuazhev, Popova, Kozlova. The dive centre's

now-defunct website kbrdiving.ru included a useful timeline of daily events during the expedition. Descriptions aided by photographs taken by Viktor Lyagushkin.

147 **'On days when . . . the next dive'**: Robson, Khuazhev, Lika Khuazheva, and personal recollection speaking with Eduard about Manchester United, a team my grandfather, Robert Cowan, briefly signed for in 1935. Khuazhev's appearance on the cooking show *Today's Menu*, broadcast on 11 February 2012, can be found at https://www.youtube.com/watch?v=HbWOtaCW5Ko

148 **'In the early . . . the medical profession'**: Investigations into the narcosis suffered by divers during the trials, including interviews with the men, can be found in *The Deep-sea Diving Committee: Research Papers 1929–1932*, held at the National Archives, London, (reference FD1/3176).

149 **'These attacks, however . . . disoriented, fixated, anxious'**: A. R. Behnke, R. M. Thomson and E. P. Motley, 'The Physiological Effects from Breathing Air at 4 Atmospheres Pressure', *American Journal of Physiology*, June 1935.

150 **'Jacques Cousteau would . . . as nitrogen narcosis'**: Cousteau, *The Silent World*. The Frenchman called the experience 'l'ivresse des grand profonduers' ('the intoxication of the great depths'). The title of the chapter in which it featured, 'Rapture of the Deep', obviously sounded much more poetic and that particular phrase stuck.

150 **'While the British . . . by the wayside'**: Charles Momsen, *The Report on the Use of Helium-Oxygen Mixtures for*

Diving, Navy Experimental Diving Unit, Report 2-42, which appears in the collection of documents from the Navy Experimental Diving Unit (NEDU), held by the Rubicon Foundation.

151 **'Then, a decade . . . for that depth'**: Max Gene Nohl, 'Diving Goes Modern', *Popular Mechanics*, October 1937; 'Max G. Nohl Establishes World Record', *Milwaukee Sentinel*, 2 December 1937; and 'Nohl and His Helpers Jubilant Over Record Dive Into Lake', *Milwaukee Journal*, 2 December 1937. AP Archives has footage, titled 'Divers Record', showing Nohl being dressed into his diving suit, lowered into the water and then being hoisted back on deck after the dive.

151 **'Nohl's achievement breathed . . . made no mistakes'**: Momsen, *The Report on the Use of Helium-Oxygen Mixtures for Diving*; Lt. A. R. Behnke and Lt. T. L. Willmon, '*U.S.S. Squalus*: Medical aspects of the rescue and salvage operations and the use of oxygen in deep-sea diving', *US Navy Medical Bulletin*, January 1939; and G. G. Molumphy, *Report of Diving Training in U.S.S. Chanticleer off Key West, Florida, During Period 19 October to 8 December 1948*, NEDU, Report 1-49, held by the Rubicon Foundation. The dismissal by the British authorities of helium as a diving gas is contained in letters in the file 'Research on Using Helium', held at the National Archives, Kew (reference FD1/3177).

153 **'Across the Atlantic . . . of the deep'**: An official account of the tests can be found in the detailed contemporaneous report, *HMS Reclaim: Report of Deep*

Diving Trials 1946–48, held at the National Archives, Kew (reference ADM 315/46). Dugan captures another side of the experiments in his interview with Shelford, in *Man Explores the Sea*.

155 'The US Navy . . . than ten minutes': Commander G. G. Molumphy, *Evaluation of Newly Computed Helium-Oxygen Decompression Tables at Depths Greater than Provided for in the Published Tables*, NEDU, Report 9-50, held by the Rubicon Foundation.

155 'Then, in the . . . be unnecessarily long': Commander Maino des Granges, *Standard Air Decompression Table*, NEDU, December 1956; J. W. Dwyer, *Calculation of Air Decompression Tables*, NEDU, November 1955; and Robert Workman, *Calculation of Air Saturation Decompression Tables*, NEDU, June 1957; all held by the Rubicon Foundation. Workman would go on to develop a new approach to calculating decompression tables.

156 'While the US . . . through the body': Informed by W. E. Crocker, *Investigation into Decompression Tables*, Report IX, December 1957, held at the National Archives, Kew (reference ADM 298/242).

157 'The navy's prime . . . a steel chamber': Hempleman's obituary in *Diving and Hyperbaric Medicine*, Vol. 37, No. 1, March 2007; Dr John Bevan, 'Tribute to Dr Val Hempleman', published by the Minewarfare & Clearance Diving Officers' Association at http://www.mcdoa.org.uk/Val.htm; Rashbass's obituary in *The Lancet*, August 1982; and 'An appreciation of the late Cyril Rashbass', *Perception*, Vol. 11, 1982.

159 'The sea trials . . . stop him trying': *Investigation into Decompression Tables*, Report III (reference ADM 298/137), and *Trials of New Decompression Tables IV* (reference ADM 298/190), both held at the National Archives, Kew.

160 'In the years . . . Recreational Dive Planner': Hempleman's obituaries.

160 'While Hempleman continued . . . in their entirety': *Investigation into Decompression Tables*, Report VI, 1955 (reference ADM 298/221), and Report VII, 1957, held at the National Archives, Kew (reference ADM 298/502).

160 'In a follow-up . . . authority on diving': *Investigation into Decompression Tables*, Report IX, 1957, part of the collection titled *Revision of Decompression Tables*, held at the National Archives, Kew (reference ADM 298/242).

160 'As all of . . . not be avoided': W. E. Crocker and H. V. Hempleman, 'Decompression problems of diving to 600 ft', held at the National Archives, Kew (reference ADM 298/234). An interview with Wookey also featured in David Strike, 'One Hundred Fathoms Down', at http://www.historicaldivingsociety.com.au/articles/one-hundred-fathoms-down/. Captain Shelford's account of the trials can be found in Dugan, *Man Explores the Sea*. The photograph described was featured in newspapers around the world, including the *Milwaukee Journal*, on 25 October 1956.

163 'Martin Robson's next . . . an evening off': Robson, Popova.

163   'Support diver Roman . . . team before leaving': Dunaev, Robson.

163   'But Robson didn't . . . on the ascent': Robson.

163   'With Dunaev absent . . . long, deep dives': Robson, Vashchenko, Popova.

163   'Robson understood Andrei . . . the plan set': Robson.

163   'By the time . . . their ascent together': Robson, Gorpinyuk, supplemented by video taken by expedition members and TV crews.

164   'At the surface . . . would be there': The exact reason behind Rodionov's decision to dive independently and who was party to it remain unclear. I don't doubt the decision taken by members of the support team was made in good faith at the time even though it was at odds with Robson's rule stating no member of the support team was to dive alone. It appears they were confident in their abilities and didn't see it as a risk. One member even said it hadn't seemed a bad idea for Rodionov to dive solo because he would be on his own for little more than ten minutes before meeting up with other divers; at the time they thought what he intended to do was an easy task for a technical diver on a rebreather. I still have some questions that remain unanswered, but I have tried to piece together the events on the surface that morning as best I can. In doing so I have relied on accounts published on the now-defunct kbrdiving.ru; in the article 'Blue Lake: The Beauty and the Beast', published in *Diver* magazine, October 2012;

in the article about the expedition published by the Russian version of *National Geographic* magazine, in March 2012; and in an interview Vashchenko and Lyagushkin gave to *DivePlanet*, in February 2012. These accounts were supplemented by Popova and Vashchenko. In interview, Khuazhev said he was not aware of the decision. Gorpinyuk was not able to offer any information. Rodionov's on-camera response was taken from a news report broadcast on NTV on 16 January 2012. The report, by NTV correspondent Maxim Berezin, is still available online under the heading 'Попытка измерить глубину Голубого озера в Кабардино-Балкарии закончилась смертью участника экспедиции', at https://www.ntv.ru/novosti/260635/.

165   **'Rodionov had agreed . . . nothing could happen'**: Popova.

166   **'Arriving at sixty . . . on above him'**: Robson, Gorpinyuk. Informed by the report on now-defunct kbrdiving.ru, the *Diver* magazine article and the *DivePlanet* interview. An overview of the incident appeared in the Russian version of *National Geographic* magazine.

167   **'Deep diver Andrei . . . for the surface'**: Gorpinyuk. His account of the incident and description of the scene given during interview echoed entries posted shortly after the event by Andrei Bykov on the tetis.ru diving forum, under the heading 'Погиб Андрей Родионов! 13.01.12'. Sadly, Bykov died in a diving incident before I had a chance to interview him. A short account of the

incident was also published by MChS in Kabardino-Balkaria, timed at 14:47 on 13 January 2012.

168 'A few members . . . his colleague. Go!' Khuazhev, Popova, descriptions taken from NTV news report broadcast on 16 January 2012.

169 'As the boat . . . of those involved': Khuazhev, Popova.

171 'Bogdana Vashchenko was . . . into her mind': Vashchenko. She also provided me with copies of the notebook pages and indications of who wrote what.

172 'Alla Popova walked . . . habitat, diving alone': Popova.

173 'Bogdana Vashchenko was . . . she disappeared underwater': Description comes from footage contained in the NTV broadcast.

173 'Robson heard Vashchenko . . . it right now': Robson, Vashchenko.

174 'Clutching her mask . . . prize of discovery': Popova.

175 'Shortly after six . . . we've lost Andrei': Robson. Description of Robson exiting the water comes from the NTV broadcast. Robson remembers Vashchenko using the phrase 'We've lost Andrei,' because he initially thought she was referring to Andrei Bykov. It was only when he saw Bykov walking along the corridor in the dive centre that he realised she meant Rodionov.

For Andrei 209 m

176 'You probably wouldn't . . . people in trouble': The epigraph from Tom Mount comes from an interview he did with Michael Menduno, 'You've Come a Long Way

Baby: Tom Mount Talks Tech', *aquaCORPS* magazine, No. 10, June 1995, available online at https://www.tdisdi.com/aquacorps/tom-mount/

176 **'Water trickled . . . saw Rodionov die'**: Robson. Description of the unit comes from a photograph taken of Rodionov's equipment after it was recovered from the water and before it was handed over to the authorities. Gorpinyuk described seeing the same in interview. This echoed a number of entries posted by Bykov on the tetis.ru diving forum, and the report on now-defunct kbrdiving.ru.

177 **'Andrei Rodionov slipped . . . around to notice'**: Robson shared with me a copy of the dive profile taken from Rodionov's computer. The pertinent details of the profile supported comments made by members of the expedition in the hours after Rodionov's death and various reports mentioned previously.

179 **'Two days later . . . rewrite the statement'**: Robson, Khuazhev.

180 **'In the end . . . of his rebreather'**: A statement issued by the Investigative Committee of Russia on 16 January 2012 stated: 'According to preliminary data, the cause of death was drowning as a result of improper use of breathing equipment (rebreather). In connection with this fact, the Urvan Interdistrict Investigation Department of the Investigative Department of the Investigative Committee of the Russian Federation for the Kabardino-Balkarian Republic will carry out a preliminary investigation after which an appropriate procedural decision will be made.'

180   'After leaving the . . . without looking back':
      Robson, Popova.

180   'Photographs were now . . . an okay sign': Descrip-
      tions taken from photographs taken by expedition mem-
      bers.

181   'With everyone else . . . had worsened still': Robson,
      Khuazhev, Dunaev.

182   'That afternoon, as . . . at the bottom': Robson.
      Vashchenko, supplemented by her interview with
      DivePlanet.

184   'When the sport . . . the deep seabed': David H.
      Elliott and James Vorosmarti, 'An Outline History of
      Diving Physiology and Medicine', in *Bennett and Elliott's
      Physiology and Medicine of Diving 5th Edition*.

184   'The recreational diving . . . of 92,484 dives': M. L.
      Dembert, J. F. Jekel and L. W. Mooney, 'Health risk fac-
      tors for the development of decompression sickness
      among U.S. Navy divers', *Undersea Biomedical Research*,
      December 1985.

184   'As far as . . . faster than recommended': T. E. Ber-
      ghage and D. Durman, 'US Navy Air Decompression
      Schedule Risk Analysis', Naval Medical Research Insti-
      tute, January 1980, part of the NEDU collection, held by
      the Rubicon Foundation.

185   'Those with a . . . of divers worldwide': Roger's work
      was detailed in R. W. Hamilton, Raymond Rogers,
      Michael R. Powell and Richard D. Vann, *The DSAT Rec-
      reational Dive Planner*, Diving Science & Technology
      Corp, 28 February 1994.

186 'Similar tables were . . . for recreational partici-pants': John Lippmann and Dr Simon Mitchell, *Deeper into Diving 2nd Edition*, JL Publications, Australia, 2005.

186 'If uncomplicated planning . . . language) causing bends': Informed by Robert W. Hamilton and Edward Thalmann, 'Decompression Practice', in *Bennett and Elliott's Physiology and Medicine of Diving 5th Edition*. Dr Neal Pollock illustrated the issues in a succinct way in his presentation 'Thoughtful Management of Decompression Stress', given at the EUROTEK 2014 diving conference, Birmingham, UK, October 2014.

187 'The Bühlmann decompression . . . dive planning tool': Informed by Albert Bühlmann, *Decompression – Decompression Sickness*, Springer-Verlag, Berlin, 1984.

188 'While some modellers . . . from various expo-sures': David Eugene Yount (Department of Physics and Astronomy, University of Hawaii, Honolulu), 'Gelatin, Bubbles, and the Bends', September 1991, part of a collection of papers and reports by the American Academy of Underwater Sciences, held by the Rubicon Foundation.

189 'Drawing upon the . . . and psychological comfort': Bruce R. Wienke and Timothy R. O'Leary, 'Reduced Gradient Bubble Model: Diving Algorithm, Basis, and Comparisons', NAUI Technical Diving Operations, Tampa, Florida, February 2002; Bruce Wienke, *Biophysics and Diving Decompression Phenomenology*, Bentham Science Publishers, Sharjah, UAE, 2016; Bruce R. Wienke, 'Modern Decompression Algorithms: Models, Compari-

sons, and Statistics', Los Alamos National Laboratory, Applied Physics Division.

189 'A similar conservatism . . . and commercial divers': Dr Neal Pollock, 'Flexible Control of Decompression Stress', published by Shearwater on 30 November 2015 at www.shearwater.com/monthly-blog-posts/flexible-control-of-decompression-stress

189 'The problem is . . . experimenting on themselves': Dr James Francis, former head of Undersea Medicine at the Institute of Naval Medicine, and medical director at the Defence Evaluation and Research Agency. Francis wrote a number of influential reports on spinal cord decompression. Additional information from Karl E. Huggins, 'Decompression Computers: Pros and Cons'; S. L. Blogg et al., 'Validation of Dive Computers', Proceedings of the American Academy of Underwater Sciences 31st Scientific Symposium, 2012; and Robert W. Hamilton, 'The Effectiveness of Dive Computers in Repetitive Diving', Undersea and Hyperbaric Medical Society Workshop, 1995. All are part of collections held by the Rubicon Foundation.

190 'Hunched under the . . . inside his body': Robson, Khuazhev. Descriptions come from photographs and video taken by expedition members. The times used in the following pages are a best approximation of the dive time. I've not been able to locate a profile of the actual dive that was recorded by any of Robson's computers, but he did recreate the dive for me using planning software. I also have a photograph of the whiteboard on

which he had written the planned schedule for the dive, which includes a running time. Combining that information and Robson's recreation of the dive, I was able to create an approximate run-time for the dive. I have used this run-time for the times, depths and decompression stops quoted in the text. It is not perfect, but it is the closest I am able to get with the information at hand.

The Surface Is No Friend

196   **'If it happens . . . any medieval torturer'**: The epigraph is from Peter Throckmorton, *The Lost Ships: An Adventure in Undersea Archaeology*, Jonathan Cape, London, 1965.

196   **'Getting bent is . . . in the ballpark'**: Dr Neal Pollock has given many illuminating presentations on diving and decompression, including: 'Thoughtful Management of Decompression Stress', at the EUROTEK 2014 diving conference, Birmingham, UK, October 2014; 'Decompression Induced Bubbles', at the EUROTEK 2016 diving conference, Birmingham, December 2016; and 'Thermal Physiology and Protection', at Rebreather Forum 3.0, Orlando, Florida, May 2012.

198   **'Deep divers know . . . as it gets'**: The warning draws from a variety of disclaimers issued by dive planning software and computer manufacturers.

198   **'Inevitably, deep divers . . . after being hit'**: Each year Divers Alert Network publishes a report that features case studies on fatalities and injuries. At one time the publication was titled *Report on Decompression Illness*

and Diving Fatalities, but it later changed to the more innocuous *Annual Diving Report*. Figures are taken from the 2012–15 edition. The case study comes from the 2002 report.

199 **'Such stories are . . . free from risk'**: Robson and many deep divers I've dived with or spoken with over the years.

199 **'Look at the . . . applied to diving'**: Jon Lindbergh neatly summed up a diver's approach to risk in his presentation 'The Need for Practical Methods of Pre-symptomatic Bubble Detection', later published in *Journal of Occupational Medicine*, May 1969.

200 **'Scientists can talk . . . to the surface'**: Robson and many deep divers I've dived with or spoken with over the years. Additional information from Pollock's various presentations, and Francis. Regarding incident rates of decompression sickness, the exact number remains unknown. Over the years, various reports have tried to quantify the problem, with estimated rates ranging anywhere between 0.01 per cent to 0.35 per cent within recreational, technical, scientific, military and commercial diving. Perhaps the only accurate statement on incident rates is that decompression sickness remains a very rare event.

201 **'And theory is . . . depths and times'**: Francis.

202 **'Martin Robson, gloved . . . going to plan'**: Robson. Times and depths come from my re-creation of the run-time as explained above.

206 **'Sergei Gorpinyuk and . . . back on track'**: Robson, Gorpinyuk.

206 'Shhh! Ummm! Shhh . . . himself during decom-
     pression': Robson.

207 'Ninety-five minutes . . . slow climb upwards':
     Robson, Dunaev, Gorpinyuk.

208 'The penalties were . . . his way home': Robson.

208 'Roman Dunaev kept . . . longer zero bubble':
     Dunaev.

209 'Thirty-three metres . . . to be over': Khuazhev.

210 'After more than . . . about the disorder': The
     opening lines paraphrase a joke by Professor David
     Elliott, an authority on the bends, during a conference
     in 2003.

210 'Doctors have an . . . to decompression bubbling':
     Francis, Dr Rob van Hulst.

210 'The mechanics of . . . conventional scuba diving':
     James Francis and Simon Mitchell, 'Pathophysiology of
     Decompression Sickness', in Bennett and Elliott's Physi-
     ology and Medicine of Diving 5th Edition.

211 'All bubbles, then . . . cause decompression sick-
     ness': Wienke and O'Leary, 'Reduced Gradient Bubble
     Model: Diving Algorithm, Basis, and Comparisons'.

211 'All that is . . . as body fat': Peter Tikuisis and Wayne
     Gerth, 'Decompression Theory', in Bennett and Elliott's
     Physiology and Medicine of Diving 5th Edition; Sander
     Wildeman, Henri Lhuissier, Chao Sun, Detlef Lohse
     and Andrea Prosperetti, 'Tribonucleation of Bubbles',
     Proceedings of the National Academy of Sciences of the
     United States of America, May 2014; Bruce R. Wienke,
     'Nucleation, Gas Separation, Bubble Growth and

Destruction', American Academy of Underwater Sciences, 1987.

212 'Whatever the reality . . . a neurological deficit': Informed by James Francis, 'A Current View of the Pathogenesis of Spinal Cord Decompression Sickness in a Historical Perspective', in *The Physiological Basis of Decompression: Proceedings of the Thirty-eighth Undersea and Hyperbaric Medical Society Workshop*, held at Duke University Medical Center, Durham, North Carolina, Undersea and Hyperbaric Medical Society, Bethesda MD, 1989; Francis and Mitchell, 'Pathophysiology of Decompression Sickness'; and T. J. Francis, J. L. Griffin, L. D. Homer, G. H. Pezeshkpour, A. J. Dutka and E. T. Flynn, 'Bubble-induced dysfunction in acute spinal cord decompression sickness', *Journal of Applied Physiology*, April 1990.

213 'The bubbles don't . . . control of limbs': Robert M. Olson, 'Echo Imaging Techniques Determine the Size of Intravascular Bubbles in Decompression Sickness', Brooks Air Force Base, Texas, July 1994; and H. D. Van Liew, J. Conkin and M. E. Burkard, 'How Big are Decompression Bubbles', Proceedings of the XIX Annual Meeting of the European Underwater Baromedical Society, Trondheim, Norway, 1993.

213 'At 4:05 p.m. . . . any of those': Robson.

217 'Yet the unimaginable. . . central nervous system': T. J. Francis, R. R. Pearson, A. G. Robertson, M. Hodgson, A. J. Dutka and E. T. Flynn, 'Central Nervous System Decompression Sickness: Latency of 1070 Human

Cases', *Undersea Biomedical Research*, November 1989; and J. K. Summitt and T. E. Berghage, 'Review and Analysis of Cases of Decompression Sickness Occurring Under Pressure', NEDU, December 1971, held by the Rubicon Foundation.

218 **'Sh-um, sh-um, sh-um . . . damage made permanent'**: Robson. There are a handful of documented cases of divers suffering explosive decompression sickness, including cases reported by Haldane and, in 1992, the death of Chris Rouse Junior, who was fatally injured while exploring the wreck of the U-869 and died during recompression treatment.

220 **'Robson didn't need . . . of his legs'**: Summitt and Berghage, 'Review and Analysis of Cases of Decompression Sickness Occurring Under Pressure'.

220 **'Shhh! Ummm! Shhh! . . . nightmare. Not yet'**: Robson.

220 **'Ask any dive . . . hold their liquor'**: Francis. The issue of denial is a significant factor for hyperbaric doctors, and it is referenced repeatedly by doctors during presentations and in the literature.

220 **'Robson wasn't one . . . deep take him'**: Robson.

221 **'The science behind . . . life or limb'**: 'In-water Recompression', 48th Workshop of the Undersea and Hyperbaric Medical Society, Seattle, Washington, May 1998; David J. Doolette and Simon Mitchell, 'In-water Recompression', *Diving Hyperbaric Medicine Journal*, June 2018, published online at www.ncbi.nlm.nih.gov/pmc/articles/PMC6156824; Richard L. Pyle and David A. Youngblood, 'In-water Recompression as an Emergency

Field Treatment of Decompression Illness', *Journal of the South Pacific Underwater Medical Society* (hereafter *SPUMS*), Vol. 27, No. 3, September 1997; Dr Carl Edmonds, 'Underwater Oxygen Treatment of Decompression Sickness', *SPUMS*, Vol. 9, No. 1, March 1979; James Francis, 'Treatment in Remote Location Hyperbaric Chambers and In-Water Recompression', in *Management of Mild or Marginal Decompression Illness in Remote Locations, Workshop Proceedings*, 2004; Alf Brubakk, 'On-site recompression treatment is acceptable for DCI', *SPUMS*, Vol. 30, No. 3, September 2000; and 'The practice of . . . after diving again,' from Catsaras, *Recherches cliniques et expérimentales sur les accidents survenant par l'emploi des scaphandres.*

222 **'The practice of . . . treat their injuries'**: Carl Edmonds, 'Pearl Diving: The Australia Story', *SPUMS*, Vol. 26, No. 1, March 1996, includes fascinating accounts of in-water recompression.

222 **'Even today, the . . . for the bends'**: David Gold, Alan Geater, Soomboon Aiyarak, Somchai Wongcharoenyong, Wilawan Juengprasert, Mark Johnson and Paul Skinner, 'The Indigenous Fisherman Divers of Thailand: Diving-Related Mortality and Morbidity', *International Journal of Occupational Safety and Ergonomics*, 2000, published online on 8 January 2015.

222 **'Meanwhile, a study . . . the recompression chamber'**: Frank P. Farm Jr, Edwin M. Hayashi and Edward L. Beckham, 'Diving and Decompression Treatment Practices Among Hawaii's Diving Fishermen', UH Sea Grant College Program, Honolulu, Hawaii, February 1986.

223 'Hardcore Hawaiian . . . into the water': Pyle and Youngblood, 'In-water Recompression as an Emergency Field Treatment of Decompression Illness'. Pyle's well-argued position benefits from personal experience in 1986, which he wrote about in great detail in 'Confessions of a Mortal Diver', which was, at one time, available to read on the website of Bishop Museum, in Hawaii.

223 'Such experiences have . . . stacked with dangers': Divers Alert Network https://www.diversalertnetwork.org/medical/faq/In-Water_Recompression

224 'As a doctor . . . result in a cure': Francis.

224 'Shhh! Ummm! Shhh! . . . veil over him': Robson, Dunaev.

Between the Devil and the Deep

225 'The dividing line . . . survive the unlikely': The epigraph is from R. D. Milhollin, 'Exley's Razor: The Nature of Limits', *Underwater Speleology*, March–April 1995.

225 'His life was . . . away from this': Robson, Batten.

226 'Trailing close behind . . . until it did': Robson, Dunaev.

227 'Since the pathological . . . circular bubble crater': Francis and Mitchell, 'Pathophysiology of Decompression Sickness'; and James Francis, G. H. Pezeshkpour and A. J. Dutka, 'Arterial gas embolism as a pathophysiologic mechanism for spinal cord decompression sickness', *Undersea Biomedical Research*, November 1989. Both reports include a number of fascinating electron micrograph images, which aided descriptions.

227 'Evidence to support . . . cord in two': Blick, *British Medical Journal*, December 1909.

228 'In 1980, doctors . . . the first place': The case was outlined in A. C. Palmer, I. M. Calder, R. I. McCallum and F. L. Mastaglia, 'Spinal Cord Degeneration in the Case of "Recovered" Spinal Decompression Sickness', *British Medical Journal*, Vol. 283, October 1981.

228 'In the Long Island . . . kill a man': Harlow Brooks MD, 'Caisson Disease: The Pathological Anatomy and Pathogenesis', *Long Island Medical Journal*, April 1907.

228 'About thirty-three . . . a choice now': Robson, Dunaev.

233 'From his position . . . emergency oxygen tank': Grigoriev.

235 'Switching from his . . . onto the seat': Robson. Description comes from a photograph taken by Lyagushkin of Robson about to enter the habitat, holding the slate with the message 'For Andrei 209 m'.

236 'Roman Dunaev waited . . . cold I was': Dunaev.

236 'For Grigoriev, meanwhile . . . to get help': Grigoriev.

236 'Six metres above . . . of pure oxygen': Dmitri Biskup. Description of whiteboard from two photographs taken independently by separate expedition members and video footage of Robson making entries on the board during a pre-dive briefing.

237 'At the same . . . the problem was': Grigoriev, Biskup.

238 'Two lifelines, a . . . into the water': Robson.

239 'Robson's appearance must . . . his new reality': Robson, Khuazhev.

241 'To some in . . . to Mr Hyde': James M. Clark and
Stephen R. Thom, 'Oxygen Under Pressure', in *Bennett
and Elliott's Physiology and Medicine of Diving 5th Edition*; and *Oxygen Working Party: Report to Underwater
Physiology Sub-Committee on Decompression Sickness*,
held at the National Archives, Kew (reference
FD1/3451).

242 'How much can . . . a hazardous gamble': Kenneth
W. Donald's work on the limits of pure oxygen use
underwater defined the dangers of oxygen under pressure and proved pivotal during the Second World War,
allowing the crews of midget submarines and covert
divers to operate using closed-circuit rebreathers. His
two-part series, 'Oxygen Poisoning in Man, Parts I and
II', *British Medical Journal*, 17 and 24 May 1947, and
'Oxygen Tolerance of Human Subjects in Wet and Dry
Conditions', Admiralty Experimental Diving Unit, 1944,
in the National Archives, Kew (reference ADM 315/19),
make fascinating reading. His work was collated in Kenneth Donald, *Oxygen and the Diver*, Hanley Swan, SPA
Ltd in conjunction with K. Donald, 1992; C. J. Lamb-
ertson, 'Definition of Oxygen Tolerance in Man', Final
Technical Report to NASA, for Naval Medical Research
and Development Command and Office of Naval
Research, December 1987; and Richard D. Vann, 'Oxygen
Toxicity Risk Assessment', Office of Naval Research,
May 1988. The latter two reports are available online
from the Defense Technical Information Center at https://
discover.dtic.mil

243 'Over the following . . . after forty-five minutes': Dr E. D. Thalmann, 'Oxtox: If You Dive Nitrox You Should Know About Oxtox', published online by Divers Alert Network; NOAA Diving Standards and Safety Manual, NOAA, revised 2011.

244 'Like most things . . . breathing beyond them': Informed by Simon Mitchell's presentation 'Oxygen Toxicity During Long Dives', at the EUROTEK 2014 diving conference, Birmingham, October 2014.

244 'For the majority . . . thirty-two minutes underwater': Donald, *Oxygen and the Water*.

245 'Dangling at the . . . was with him': Robson.

246 'Eduard Khuazhev had . . . held on tight': Khuazhev. Robson didn't recall Khuazhev holding onto him, but he did not dismiss the possibility when the Russian described the situation during interview.

246 'Robson looked at . . . worked. For now': Robson.

249 'After collecting a . . . swift as possible': Grigoriev, Robson.

250 'The habitat glowed . . . improve it, promptly': Robson. Description from photographs taken by expedition members.

250 'A hyperbaric doctor . . . arterial bubble emboli': Francis.

251 'A night in . . . Robson moved, promptly': Robson.

252 'Grigoriev, still hovering . . . like a shadow': Grigoriev.

252 'The beam from . . . few more minutes': Robson, Grigoriev.

253 'Robson had done . . . them were good': Robson, Khuazhev, Biskup. Description from photographs taken by expedition member.

A Race Against Time

256   'We do not . . . manifestation of symptoms': The epigraph is from Wienke and O'Leary, 'Reduced Gradient Bubble Model: Diving Algorithm, Basis, and Comparisons'.

256   'So, this is . . . and blue light': Robson, Khuazhev, Biskup.

257   'The ambulance moved . . . the vehicle stopped': Robson.

258   'The back doors . . . glad he had': Dunaev, Robson.

258   'Robson pressed the . . . leave the room': Robson. Additional details from the statement released by MChS in Kabardino-Balkaria, timed at 16:24 on 20 January 2012.

259   'Someone brought Robson . . . continued to tick': Robson, Batten. Vikki also gave a candid presentation at the EUROTEK 2014 diving conference, Birmingham, October 2014, in which she detailed the incident from her point of view.

259   'Eventually, a hospital . . . near good enough': Robson, Sokolov.

261   'In the late . . . chirped with bubbles': Merrill P. Spencer and David C. Johanson, 'Investigation of New Principles for Human Decompression Schedules Using Doppler Ultrasonic Blood Bubble Detection', Institute of Environmental Medicine and Physiology, Seattle, technical report submitted to the Office for Naval Research, July 1974. Descriptions from photographs included in the above report. Details of Lindbergh's career from Robert Sténuit, *The Deepest Days*, translated by Morris Kemp, Hodder & Stoughton, London, 1966; and *Life* magazine, 27 October

1952 and 25 May 1953. Lindbergh talked about decompression sickness in an interview that appeared in numerous newspapers, including Steve Lowell, 'Jon Lindbergh keeps up family tradition for trailblazing', *Independent Press-Telegram*, Long Beach, California, 6 March 1966.

261 **'The Doppler ultrasound . . . your pulsing blood':** Ron Y. Nishi, Alf O. Brubakk and Olav S. Eftedal, 'Bubble Detection', in *Bennett and Elliott's Physiology and Medicine of Diving 5th Edition*; and Neal W. Pollock, 'Use of Ultrasound in Decompression Research', *Diving and Hyperbaric Medicine*, Vol. 37, No. 2, June 2007.

264 **'In the late . . . with decompression sickness':** Van Hulst.

264 **'Very few mixed . . . in the henhouse':** Nishi et al., 'Bubble Detection'.

265 **'Let's try to . . . starting to crash':** Francis. Additional information from Francis and Mitchell, 'Pathophysiology of Decompression Sickness'; Costantino Balestra and Peter Germonpré, *The Science of Diving*, LAP Lambert Academic Publishing, Saarbrücken, 2014. The latter book's associated DAN/medical conference in Brussels, in December 2014, was extremely helpful in highlighting current thinking on decompression injuries. Additional information from: Costantino Balestra, 'An Introduction to the Clinical Aspects of Decompression Illness', in Michael A. Lang and Alf. O. Brubakk (eds), *The Future Of Diving: 100 Years of Haldane and Beyond*, Smithsonian Institution Scholarly Press, Washington DC, 2009; B. A. Warren, R. B. Philp and M. J. Inwood, 'The Ultrastructural Morphology

of Air Embolism: Platelet Adhesion to the Interface and Endothelial Damage', *British Journal of Experimental Pathology*, April 1973; C. Marabotti, F. Chiesa, A. Scalzini, F. Antonelli, R. Lari, C. Franchini and P. G. Data, 'Cardiac and Humoral Changes Induced by Recreational Scuba Diving', *Undersea Hyperbaric Medicine*, Vol. 26, No. 3, Fall 1999; T. Thorsen, H. Klausen, R. T. Lie and H. Holmsen, 'Bubble-induced aggregation of platelets: effects of gas species, proteins, and decompression', *Undersea and Hyperbaric Medicine*, Vol. 20, No. 2, June 1993; and T. Thorsen, H. Dalen, R. Bjerkvig and H. Holmsen, 'Transmission and scanning electron microscopy of N2 microbubble-activated human platelets in vitro', *Undersea Biomedical Research*, January 1987.

266   'A snake's hiss . . . for the best': Robson. The time Robson spent in the pod was provided by Sokolov. He wrote an official report for the Federal State Budgetary Institution of Science, State Scientific Center of the Russian Federation – Institute of Biomedical Problems of the Russian Academy of Sciences, which provided specific details, names and places connected with the incident, and was titled 'Оказание помощи британскому водолазу' ('Assistance to British Diver'; hereafter the ОПБВ Report).

267   'On Thursday, 19 . . . with the caller': Sokolov.

268   'Reaching Dr Sokolov . . . able to help': Popova.

268   'Dr Sokolov crept . . . he knew it': Sokolov. Additional details about the security screening at the Institute and his demeanour when speaking about diving come from

435

personal recollection having visited him there. He provided me with a wonderful account of his early years,
including photographs of himself as a boy, and his parents, titled 'Мое детство и начало юности ' ('My Childhood and the Beginning of Youth').

274 **'The critical measure . . . most injured divers'**: Van
Hulst and his report 'Analysis of ten year diving casualties
1979–1989', Diving Medical Centre, The Netherlands,
*Proceedings of the XVI Annual Scientific Meeting of the
European Underwater and Baromedical Society*, EUBS 1990,
Amsterdam. Additional information from K. W. Kizer,
'Delayed Treatment of Dysbarism: a retrospective review
of 50 cases', *Journal of the American Medical Association*,
May 1982; Paul Cianci and John B. Slade, Jr, 'Delayed
Treatment of Decompression Sickness with Short, No-Air-
Break Tables: Review of 140 Cases', *Aviation, Space, and
Environmental Medicine*, Vol. 77, No. 10, October 2006; R.
Ball, 'Effect of severity, time to recompression with
oxygen, and re-treatment on outcome in forty-nine cases
of spinal cord decompression sickness', *Undersea and
Hyperbaric Medicine*, Vol. 20, No. 2, June 1993; and 'Time
to Treatment for Decompression Illness', prepared by
North Sea Medical Centre for the Health and Safety
Executive, 2007.

274 **'At home, the . . . dead of night'**: Sokolov.

275 **'Robson had been . . . hour-long session'**: Robson,
Sokolov, the ОПБВ Report.

276 **'After it was . . . to change irrevocably'**: Robson.

278 **'I realised then . . . the paralysis spread'**: Batten,

436

Robson. Vikki shared with me some very personal entries she made in her diary during the event that captured her immediate feelings as the event was unfolding.

279 **'Finding a suitable . . . to be evacuated'**: Sokolov, the ОПБВ Report. Descriptions of the Institute and the GVK-250 chamber come from personal recollection during my visit to meet Dr Sokolov. He and his colleagues took me on a tour of the building. I also saw the chamber in operation when they conducted a simulated dive to one hundred metres for a group of Russian divers. Additional information from two booklets about the work of the Institute: *Institute of Biomedical Problems of the Russian Academy of Sciences* and космические техногии – медицине (*Space Technology – Medicine*).

283 **'All this time . . . consequences would follow'**: Informed by Francis and Mitchell, 'Pathophysiology of Decompression Sickness'; and Balestra and Germonpré, *The Science of Diving*, and the book's associated DAN/medical conference in Brussels, December 2014.

284 **'The sun, or . . . the two men'**: Sokolov, the ОПБВ Report. Description of the book comes from personal recollection after Sokolov presented me with a signed copy.

284 **'Stepping into the . . . not remain disabled'**: Sokolov, Glukhov.

285 **'The Ministry for . . . on the roof'**: From personal recollection after visiting the building during my trip to Moscow.

286 **'Known internationally as . . . the Black Sea'**: Glukhov. Additional information from the ОПБВ Report,

and a series of detailed reports into the incident published in three issues of Вестник МЧС России (*Bulletin of EMERCOM Russia*), which included a narrative of events and a timeline (hereafter MChS Вестник).

287 **'Rastegaeva headed a . . . US Coast Guard'**: Glukhov. Additional information on the history of the unit from EMERCOM at the unit's official website www.centrospas.ru.

287 **'If Rastegaeva's Centrospas . . . their Sochi headquarters'**: Details of YURPSO from the correspondence and the unit's official website at urpso.ru.

288 **'The self-contained . . . metres of seawater'**: From IHC Hytech specifications brochure.

288 **'Glukhov knew if . . . was being revved'**: Glukhov, MChS Вестник.

290 **'The electronic departure . . . his life either'**: Sokolov, Glukhov, the ОПБВ Report, MChS Вестник.

A Hope Not Lost

292 **'We know surprisingly . . . been wildly wrong'**: The epigraph comes from David Elliott, in *Management of Mild or Marginal Decompression Illness in Remote Locations*, Workshop Proceedings, 2004.

292 **'He stared at . . . there and wait'**: Robson, Sokolov. The decision about refusal to administer oxygen was taken by Sokolov and outlined in the ОПБВ Report and during interview.

294 **'Hanging over Robson . . . to a wheelchair'**: Cave diving pioneer Jochen Hasenmayer is a hero of Robson's. In the early years of Robson's cave diving career, he

became interested in the German diver and can recite details of his various expeditions. I tried a variety of ways to contact Hasenmayer, but these eventually came to nothing. Therefore, I've had to rely on other sources. Details of Hasenmayer's ill-fated dive featured in an article by Hubert Kaltenbach, 'Beim Auftauchen informierte der Höhenmesser falsch: Hasenmayer war plötzlich gelähmt bis unters Kinn', published by *Südwestumschau* sometime in 1990.

296   'The aircraft touched . . . him in time': Sokolov, the ОПБВ Report, MChS Вестник.

298   'Seven hundred miles . . . about Robson's incident': Shyrokov.

298   'Shyrokov had burst . . . boats and booze': Shyrokov, Robson.

299   'The previous evening . . . see you there': Shyrokov.

301   'At some point . . . to recover from': Informed by Francis and Mitchell, 'Pathophysiology of Decompression Sickness'; and Balestra and Germonpré, *The Science of Diving*, and the book's associated DAN/medical conference in Brussels, December 2014.

301   'Martin Robson remembers . . . out of there': Robson.

302   'The giant IL-76 . . . any other way': Sokolov, the ОПБВ Report.

303   'The machines in . . . move his toes': Robson.

304   'He couldn't wiggle . . . time to move': Robson, Sokolov.

305   'Giant men in . . . into the DART': Robson, Sokolov, Gorpinyuk. Additional information from video shot by

an EMERCOM official, and news reports from NTV, including one posted online at https://www.ntv.ru/ novosti/262934/ and headlined 'Дайверы Мартин Робсон и Андрей Родионов надеялись отыскать дно «бездонного озера». Один погиб, второго увезли на скорой' ('Divers Martin Robson and Andrei Rodionov hoped to find the bottom of the "bottomless lake". One died, the second was taken away by ambulance').

305 'Sardined inside the . . . for the heavens': Robson.

306 'What Robson didn't . . . the other end': Sokolov. Descriptions from video and photographs taken by EMERCOM.

306 'Then the aircraft . . . filled his ears': Robson, Sokolov, Gorpinyuk. Descriptions from video and photographs taken by EMERCOM.

309 'On the other . . . nerve tissue damage': Sokolov, the ОПБВ Report, MChS Вестник.

310 'Vikki Batten's phone . . . I missed it': Batten, Robson.

The Long Soak

311 'The discomfort of . . . patient and attendants': The epigraph is from Donald E. Mackay, Surgeon General, Royal Navy, 'Comments on Therapeutic Recompression', in Christian J. Lambertsen MD and Leon J. Greenbaum Jr MD (eds), *Proceedings of the Second Symposium on Underwater Physiology*, Washington DC, 25–26 February 1963.

311 'The first men . . . alleviating the pain': Triger, 'Mémoire sur un appareil à air comprimé, pour le perce-

ment des puits de mines et autres travaux, sous les eaux et dans les sables submergés'.

311 'Such treatment might . . . men with morphine': Gal, *Des dangers du travail dans l'air comprimé et des moyens de les prévenir*; and Snell, *Compressed Air Illness*.

312 'Sometimes men sought . . . turned to dance': The case was reported in Hill's *Caisson Sickness*.

312 'For the first . . . work, apparently well': Catseras, *Recherches cliniques et expérimentales sur les accidents survenant par l'emploi des scaphandres*.

312 'Nature's efforts, that's . . . kinder than expected': Blick, *British Medical Journal*, December 1909.

312 'Nature's efforts weren't . . . to save him': Description of photograph in S. Zografidi, 'Contribution à l'Etude des Accidents de Decompression chez les Plongeurs a Scaphandre', *Revue de Médecine*, 1907.

313 'Physicians in the . . . following fifteen months': Ernest Moir, 'Tunnelling by Compressed Air', *Journal of the Society of Arts*, May 1896.

314 'The use of . . . for many years': Richard E. Moon and Des F. Gorman, 'The Treatment of Decompression Disorders', in *Bennett and Elliott's Physiology and Medicine of Diving 5th Edition*.

314 'When Gunner George . . . to his bedside': Gunner G. D. Stillson, US Navy, *Report on Deep Diving Tests*, under the direction of the Bureau of Construction and Repair, Navy Department, Washington DC, 1915, held by the Rubicon Foundation.

314 'Another nine years . . . something more efficient':
E. D. Thalmann, 'Principles of US Navy Recompression
Treatments for Decompression Sickness', in Richard E.
Moon and Paul Sheffield (eds), *Treatment of Decompres-
sion Illness: proceedings of the 45th Undersea and Hyper-
baric Medical Society Workshop, Palm Beach, Florida,
June 18–19, 1995*, Undersea and Hyperbaric Medical
Society, Aerospace Medical Association, Kensington, MD
and Alexandria, VA, 1996.

314 'In 1937, a . . . the new protocol': A. R. Behnke and L.
A. Shaw, 'The Use of Oxygen in Compressed Air Illness',
US Navy Medical Bulletin, January 1937.

315 'Behnke continued his . . . long oxygen table':
'Treatment of Decompression Sickness', *BUMED News-
letter*, May 1944.

315 'To divers, long . . . an overnight soak': *Military Diving*,
War Department Technical Manual, September 1944.

315 'The development didn't . . . only six subjects': O. E.
Van der Aue, W. A. White Jr, R. Hayter, E. S. Brinton, R.
J. Kellar, 'Physiologic Factors Underlying the Prevention
and Treatment of Decompression Sickness', NEDU, April
1945, held by the Rubicon Foundation.

315 'These tables, however . . . cases of decompression':
J. C. Rivera, 'Decompression Sickness Among Divers: An
Analysis of 935 cases', NEDU, February 1963, held by
the Rubicon Foundation.

316 'In a report . . . a hundred trials': M. W. Goodman
and R. D. Workman, 'Minimal-Recompression, Oxygen-
Breathing Approach to Treatment of Decompression

Sickness in Divers and Aviators', NEDU, November 1965, held by the Rubicon Foundation.

318 **'Within eight years . . . for decompression sickness'**: T. E. Berghage, J. Vorosmarti Jr and E. E. P. Barnard, 'An Evaluation of Recompression Treatment Tables Used Throughout the World by Government and Industry', Naval Medical Research Unit, Bethesda, Maryland, May 1978.

319 **'Their relative success . . . than pure oxygen'**: Michael H. Bennett, Simon J. Mitchell, Derelle Young and David King, 'The use of deep tables in the treatment of decompression illness: the Hyperbaric Technicians and Nurses Association 2011 Workshop', *Diving and Hyperbaric Medicine*, Vol. 42, No. 3, September 2012.

319 **'Probably the most . . . on his feet'**: A. Rosen, N. Oscarsson, O. Gräbel and G. Sandström, 'COMEX 30 for the treatment of hypotension with neurological symptoms', *Läkartidningen*, February 2017.

320 **'Other doctors reported . . . could be difficult'**: R. W. Smerz, R. K. Overlock and H. Nakayama, 'Hawaiian deep treatments: efficacy and outcomes, 1983–2003', *Undersea and Hyperbaric Medicine*, Vol. 32, No. 5, September–October 2005; and R. K. Overlock, K. A. Tolsma, C. W. Turner and N. Bugelli, 'Deep Treatments and Hawaiian Experience 1988 through 1995', in Moon and Sheffield (eds), *Treatment of Decompression Illness*.

321 **'Doctors expressed other . . . a year later'**: Bennett et al., 'The use of deep tables in the treatment of decompression illness'. Simon Mitchell, an anaesthesiologist

practising at Auckland City Hospital and a diving physician providing on-call diving emergency services to North Shore Hospital, Auckland. He is the Head of the Department of Anaesthesiology at the School of Medicine, University of Auckland. Additional information from Barbara Trytko and Simon Mitchell, 'Case Report Extreme Survival: A Serious Technical Diving Accident', *SPUMS*, Vol. 35, No. 1, March 2005.

322   **'In Russia, physiologists . . . the long soak'**: Historical details of the Russian approach to the treatment of decompression sickness come from two books Sokolov co-authored: Декомпрессионная болезнь (*Decompression Sickness*), Moscow, 2010, Chapter Five: 'лечение' ('Treatment'), and Основы барофизиологии, водолазной медицины, баротерапии и лечения инертными газами (*Fundamentals of Barophysiology, Diving Medicine, Barotherapy, and Inert Gas Treatment*), Moscow, 2008.

324   **'On a makeshift . . . appeared utterly lost'**: Robson. During his treatment, Robson wrote detailed notes for the medical team, describing his body's reaction to the treatment. At the end of the treatment, the notes were collected by Mike Shyrokov and handed to Robson. They are one of the few things he has kept from the ordeal. He shared the notes with me and allowed me to use the contents, with the exception of a few highly personal entries. All descriptions of Robson's body in the pages that follow come from these contemporaneous notes. Robson used the notes to jog his memory during interviews. Hereafter, they are referred to as Robson's Notes.

326 **'He lifted his . . . above Robson's bed'**: Description of the chamber comes from photographs taken shortly after Robson's treatment ended, and an article on the chamber, 'уникальный барокомплекс' ('Unique Baro Complex'), in Russian diving magazine Нептун, June 2012.

326 **'Robson looked across . . . He needed help'**: Robson. Description of Morozov from photographs and video taken by EMERCOM. Robson cannot remember what drugs he was given or what they were administered for. During a research trip to Russia he asked doctors about them and didn't get a complete answer.

328 **'Around 3 p.m. . . . get for you?'** Shyrokov.

330 **'Robson asked for . . . clutched Mikhail's cross'**: Robson, Shyrokov.

331 **'In official terms . . . happening in Sochi'**: Sokolov. The description of the treatment table and the details of how it was designed to work come from the book Sokolov co-authored, Декомпрессионная болезнь (*Decompression Sickness*).

335 **'Seated at a . . . his treatment plan'**: Sokolov, Shyrokov. Taking the treatment table, I was able to build a timeline covering the period that Robson was in the chamber, which corresponded with events as described to me. Descriptions of Sokolov during this time were informed by watching him carry out a deep dry dive chamber run at his Institute in Moscow. I also visited a recompression chamber in the UK and watched the medical team deliver recompression treatment to a diver who was reporting loss of sensation after returning from vacation a few days earlier.

338 'Mikhail Shyrokov helped . . . moments," Mike says': Shyrokov, Sokolov.

339 'Anyone watching Shyrokov . . . friend was saying': Shyrokov, Robson.

340 'When Robson fell . . . his new friend': Shyrokov, Sokolov.

340 'When talk turned . . . for the patient': Sokolov.

340 'Vikki and Martin . . . in one piece?' Batten, Robson.

343 'You can tell . . . cramps," he added': Description from Robson's Notes.

343 'Keeping a record . . . continually disturbed him': Robson.

344 'The note was . . . and Morozov stirred': Shyrokov.

344 'Waking up was . . . of treatment was premature': Robson, Shyrokov, Sokolov, Batten.

346 'There was a . . . coming back stronger': An article by Sochi-based news agency Park Info, 'Известный дайвер Мартин Робсон из Великобритании проходит уникальный курс реабилитации в Сочи' ('Famous diver Martin Robson from the UK undergoes a unique rehabilitation course in Sochi'), at http://parkinfo-tv.ru/news/2012/Jan/world017.html, 23 January 2012.

346 'Except inside the . . . to heal him': Robson, Batten.

347 'At regular intervals . . . at fifty metres': From the treatment table and associated timeline.

347 'As time ticked . . . became shorter, sharper': Robson. Shyrokov describes the sound of Robson and Morozov conversing in the helium atmosphere as like ducks quacking.

349 '02:05 Sharp shooting . . . of the night': Robson's Notes.

349 'The chamber had . . . of the liver': Sokolov with addition information from Chapter Five of Декомпрессионная болезнь (*Decompression Sickness*).

350 'Inside the chamber . . . chamber was leaking': Robson, Shyrokov, Sokolov.

The Iron Doctor

353 'I had considerable . . . and permanent paralysis': The epigraph is from Neil R. Swanberg PhD, 'The View from the Stretcher', in John N. Miller and James L. Parmentier (eds), *Rehabilitation of the Paralyzed Diver: proceedings of a workshop held 8–9 March 1984, Point Clear, Alabama*, 30th Undersea Medical Society Workshop, Undersea Medical Society, Bethesda, MD, 1985.

353 'Everything had been . . . for a moment': Robson, Sokolov, the ОПБВ Report.

355 'Confused, Robson reached . . . ankle very stiff': Robson's Notes.

355 'Under the orange . . . lock transfer system': Sokolov, the ОПБВ Report.

356 'About an hour . . . but is improving': Robson's Notes, Sokolov.

357 'When Mike Shyrokov . . . most complete recovery': Robson, Shyrokov, Sokolov.

358 'Most doctors who . . . it's absolutely heartbreaking': Francis.

359 'Over the years . . . to cure him': Sokolov.

361 'Inside the chamber . . . would be okay': Robson, Shyrokov.

364 'Outside the chamber . . . Just in case': Sokolov, Glukhov.

365 'The headaches began . . . be left alone': Robson, Robson's Notes.

367 'Looking at the . . . return you back': Robson, Shyrokov. Robson kept a copy of Shyrokov's letter, which I was able to read and quote from. Robson's Notes.

369 'The days of . . . lip, he heard': Robson, Robson's Notes. Robson still has a copy of the second letter Shyrokov wrote to him, and the letter he wrote concerning the headaches. I was able to read both and quote from them.

371 'He swallowed the . . . He'd had enough': Robson, Robson's Notes.

373 'Later, when all . . . back to diving': Robson, Sokolov, the ОПБВ Report, MChS Вестник. Robson returned to Russia a few months after the incident to attend the Golden Dolphin Diving Exposition. While there, he met Dr Sokolov and various members of the expedition to thank them personally for their help. During the exposition, Robson met with senior members of Russia's diving community for a round table to discuss the lessons that could be learned from his experience. A report of that meeting was published in MChS Вестник. A more detailed report was published by the tetis.ru diving forum, titled 'Круглый стол' по вопросам безопасности в техническом дайвинге' ('Round Table on Technical Diving Safety Issues'), on 10 July 2012, at http://www.tetis.ru/diving/diving_art/event/446/

376 'At dawn on . . . And they did': Robson, Shyrokov.

379 'As Robson moved . . . of the incident': Sokolov, the ОПБВ Report.

379 'When Robson had . . . developments it con-tained': Description comes from video footage shot by EMERCOM.

380 'After the crowd . . . years of service': Sokolov. His comments to the journalist are drawn from a story published on 29 January 2012 by Sochi-based news agency Park Info, 'Сегодня в 6:40 смк из барокамеры Южного регионального поисково-спасательного отряда МЧС России вышел английский дайвер Мартин Робсон' ('Today at 6:40 a.m. the English diver Martin Robson left the pressure chamber of the Southern Regional Search and Rescue Squad of EMERCOM of Russia').

380 'Robson was told . . . as he could': Robson, Batten, Shyrokov. Sokolov also referred to the incident with the dog in his ОПБВ Report.

382 'Elsewhere in Russia . . . moment to relax': Glukhov.

382 'When the news . . . of the bottle': Khuazhev.

382 'The ambulance took . . . me help you': Robson, Sokolov.

Afterword

385 'The spirit of . . . Hebrides and Italy': Robson, Batten.

386 'For a while . . . Russian destroyer *Tenacious*': Robson, Khuazhev.

387   'The more Martin . . . like a colander': Robson.

387   'New research into . . . a boulder choke': An overview of the project can be found on the website of the Underwater Research Center at https://urc-rgs.ru/en/activity/expedition. Accounts were published in the Kabardino-Balkarian edition of *Pravda* under the headline 'Специалисты Русского географического общества раскрыли тайны Голубого озера' ('Specialists of the Russian Geographical Society have revealed the secrets of the Blue Lake') on 9 February 2017, at http://gazeta.kbpravda.ru/node/15018, and in various other media outlets.

387   'During the summer . . . went off exploring': The description of the events concerning Robson's return to Russia is taken from my personal recollection, notes, photographs and video of my trip to Moscow and Kabardino-Balkaria in August 2018.

A NOTE ON THE AUTHORS

Mark Cowan is a journalist with over two decades' experience in newspapers and television. He spent twelve years as a crime correspondent for tabloid, broadsheet and Sunday titles in Birmingham, and was embedded with the British Army in war-torn Kosovo. He has also worked on crime documentaries for the BBC and ITV, and is a technical and cave diver. To bring Martin Robson's dramatic story to the page, Cowan has drawn on hundreds of documents and dozens of interviews collected over five years of reporting, combined with unprecedented access to the people involved in this true life-or-death thriller.

Martin Robson is one of the world's leading instructors on technical, cave and rebreather diving. A former Royal Marine Commando, he has been cave diving for more than twenty years, leading explorations and tours of systems in Europe and North America. In 2003, he discovered a new passageway in the Durzon cave, France, more than a mile into the cave and one hundred metres underwater. Only a handful of people have ventured there since.

Unbound is the world's first crowdfunding publisher, established in 2011.

We believe that wonderful things can happen when you clear a path for people who share a passion. That's why we've built a platform that brings together readers and authors to crowdfund books they believe in – and give fresh ideas that don't fit the traditional mould the chance they deserve.

This book is in your hands because readers made it possible. Everyone who pledged their support is listed below. Join them by visiting unbound.com and supporting a book today.

Diane and Edward Batten

Vikki Batten

Rikki Battistini

Rob Baxandall

Andreas Beckmann

Odile Bégin

John Belchamber

Elizabeth Bennett

Shane Bennett

Dan Benveniste

Anders Bergman

Colin Bertling

Kieran Bevan

George Birch

Richard Blackburn

Brandi Blasi-Hebbard

Zack Bloom

Brandon Boas

Piers Boileau Goad

Jean-Marc Bouilly-Lila

Julian Bray

Tom Breen

Alison Brinkworth

Terry Brisco

Stephen Brothers

Dan Brown

Michael Büchi

Tanith Bunce

Jeremy Burgum

Tim Burrows

Axel Busch

Cynthia Butler

Lee Butler

Craig Callear

Stacey Cannon

Ashley Carr

Cascade Aviation & Marine Ltd

Melanie Chambers

Astrid Charters

Suzanne Cherry

Rob Chilcott

Mickael Christien

Andy Clarke

David "Jesus" Clarke

Jason Clarke

Trevor Clarke

Patti Clarkson

Jim Coates

Andrew Coleman

Ian Coles

Liz Collier

John Collins

Tony Collins

Joe Cope III

Bill Cornish

Jeff Cornish

Sarah Courbet

Alison Cowan

Lindsey Cowan

Raymond Cowan

Ryan Crawford

Geoff Creighton

Martin Crew

Martin Cridge

Cristian Cristea

Laura Cull

Robert Cullen

Karen Curtis-Vincent

Leon Dabbs

Robert Dagge

Jurg Dahler

Paul Dale

Ben Daniels

Maryse Dare

Mark de Barra

Stefan De Bie

Chris de Putron

Joeri De Wit

Christopher Dean

Kevin Dean

Aina Demirova

Tim Dibben

Douglas Dignall

Rostislav Dimitrov

Caroline & Adam Dingle

Mark Dixon

Anthony Donald

Vasil Doychinov

Jim Driessens

Koen Ds

Mike Duggan

Lenny Dunlap

Guilhem Duprat

Julie Dutil

Mathew Duxbury

Jacek Dyminski

Steve Dyson

Cornelia Elbert

Nick Ellerington

Emma

Rolf Engelsman

James Evans

Matt Evans

Tom Everett

Mark Faas

Mark Fancote

Flavio Fanelli

David Fatzinger

Kris Fearnley

Markus Federmann

Marc Ferraby

Leo Fielding

Alessandra Figari

Maxwell Fisher

Keith Fitzgerald

Kristian Torød Flakstad

Tony Flaris

Steve & Jan Flowers

Sue Ford

Andrew Foster

Michael Fowler

Rob Fowler

Luke Fozard

Dennis Freshwater

Max Fursman

Nicco Garbo

Gibbo

Julie Gibbon

Elisha Gibson

Marc Gibson

Susan Gilbert

Andrew Gillespie

Steve Gore

Dmitri Gorski

Timothy Gort

Jon Gower

Danny Graham

Tom Grain

Annwen Gray

Mike Greathead

Alex Griffin

Stephen Groves

Marcus Gyllemalm

John J. Hache

Manuel Hamel

Richard Hannah

Daniel Hardman

Richard Harpin

Nicholas Harrington

Mick Harris

Paul Harris

Kieran Hatton

Lee Hatton

Chris Haubold

Darren Hector (Dive Academy)

Alastair Hendry

Steve Henshall

Jerad Hewitt

Gerry Hickey

Nobuyuki Higashiura

Takuya Higashiura

Andy Higgie

Philip Hodson

Peter Hogan

Craig Holdstock

Paul Holliday

Pam & Ken Holloway

Scott Holmes

Brad Horn

Andy Horsley

Joshua Hotaling

Catherine Howard-Dobson

Helen Howard-Jones

David Hunter

Moona Huttunen

Riku Ihalainen

Hiroaki Ikarugi

George Illaszewicz

Aleksi Ilmonen

Mat Ireland

Toby Jackson

Heather Jefferies

Kelly Jessop

Brian Johncey

Lori Johnston

Andrew Johnston Ph.D.

Oliver Johnstone

Adrian L. Jones

Ian Jones

Melinda Jones

Michael Jones

Roger Jones

Steve Jones

Abigail Joynes

Firas Jundi

Stefan Kaemmer

Jurek Kamrowski

Marko Kauppinen

Simon Keeble

David Kidger

Dan Kieran

Alex King

Peter King-Lewis

Evgeny Kireev

Mikolaj Kolmer

Simon Koster

Andreas Kouris

Paul La Planche

Tobi Laczkowski

Gabriel Lamarre

Andy Langler

Kirk Langley

Robin Lawrence

Rob Lawton

Ferdy Leemput

Sam LeFlore

Cathy Lesh

Dr. Michael D. Levine

Steve Lewis

Stefan Lidén

Simon Lile

Zeb Lilly

Michael Lindley

Natalia Lindley

George Linnane

Jake Linton

Miranda Litchfield

Christine Loew

Dave Lofting

Jamie Long

Toni Long

Sunny Longordo

Mark Lovatt

Patric Lundevall

Rosemary E Lunn / The
    Underwater Marketing
    Company

Cailin C E Mackenzie

Kathy Mallon

Augusto Marques Ramos

Tony Marsh

Jan Martin

Karen Martin

Brod Mason

Marc Mason

David Mattick

Dr Stephen McCabe

Peter McCamley

Ian McCarthney

Paula McCartney

Megan McCormick

Andy McCowen

Darren McDonagh

Derek McNeill

Tom Melvin

William Messner

Matt Mills

Simon Mills

Chris Minton

John Mitchinson

Chieko Mizuno

J Mohr

Fiona Moncur

Alastair Monk

Michael & Tracy Morgan

Patrick Morgan

Denis Morozov

Clive Morten

Tania Murphy

Douglas Nash

Nautilus UK

Carlo Navato

Carolin Negrin

Jean Nelson

Tom Nelson

Stewart Ness

Mark Nevin

Herbert Newhouse

Tony Nguyen

Colin Nicholls

Mark Nix

Dean Nolan

Ben Norcutt

Thobias Norrbin

Toni Norton

Dan O'Callaghan

John O'Connor

Gorka Otaola

Demetra Papachilleos

Gabriele Paparo

Greg Parker

Janet Parker

Martin Parker

Brett Parry

Ronald Pasic

Ken Paton

Paul

Team Paulsen Glen & Susanne

Edoardo Pavia

Jonas Pavletic

Richard Peck

Simon Perkins

Daniele Petrone

Giancarlo Pfeifer

Bénédicte Philippon

Jon Phillips

Colin Philpot

Olivia Phipps

Mark Piper

Justin Pollard

Paul Porter

Andy Powell

Mark Powell

Ollie Powell

Renee Power

Duncan Price

Andy Procter

Henry Procter

Nadir Quarta

Krstine Rae Olmsted

Franck Raeppel

Wayne Rawle

Tony Regan

Dan Reynolds

Steve Richardson

Poppy & Honeysuckle Robson

Connor Roe

Richard Roethe

Colin Rotheram

Peter Routledge

Jesse Rowell

Benjamin Royal

Toby Royal

Adam Ryan

Piotr Ryjak

Iwona Sadler

Steve Sadler

Jaspal Sahota

Jani Santala

Tatiana Sevortyan

Sebastian Ted Sewter

Lisa Shafe

Umaid Shah

Pete Shaw

Sarah Shaw

Luke Shepherd

Alan Sheward

Jim Sheward

Amy Shores

Phil Short

Karl Shreeves

Mike Shyrokov

Myron Siciak

Jarno Siltamäki

Chris Simmonds

Stefan Sirkiä

Don Six

Gary Smerdon

Barry Smith

Michael Smith

Sam Smith

Richard Somerset

Evan Spaeder

Wendy Staden

Jim Standing

Jenny Staples

Samuel Nicolas Stasaitis

Yana Stashkevich

Yitzi Stern

Chris Sterritt

Jessica Stewart

Tara Strachan

Jorgen Strandquist

Alli Straus

Rob Summers

Suunto UK

Steve Swingler

Zsolt Szabo

Ryan Taylor

Ricardo Ten Kortenaar

John Thixton

Bryan Thomas

Michael Thomas

Brett Thorpe

David Thorsell

Stephen Tierney

Cristina Torrente

Poltsi Törrönen

Todd Toussant

Patrick Trapp

Marie Trisollini

Natalie Trotter-King

Caroline Trumper

Sven van den Heuvel

Joery I-haven't-found-Elvis-
yet Van Doninck

Rudy Van Uytsel

Wes Vancour

George Vandoros

Jeroen Vanhoof

Matthias Vertommen

Mikko Vikkula

Phil Vinter

Charles Waddell

Lee Ann Waggener

Andy Wagner

Clare Wain

Jacqui Wakefield

Ashley Walker

Bryan Wallbridge

Karen Walton

Naomi Watson

Dave Watts

Ueli Werner

Frank Georg West

Sean Wheeles

Tim Whitbread

Daniel Widmann

Janice and Lionel Williams

Linda Williams

Timothy Williams

James Wills

Forrest Wilson

Peter Wilson

Richard Wilson

Simon Wolf

Chris Wolverson

Samantha Wood

Graham Woodcock

Richard Worley

Boris Worrall

Marianna Worthy

Erik Wouters

Mike Wynd

Peter Zaal

Alexis Zebrowski

James Ziemann

Vasilis Zografos

Николай Максимович

Василий Романюк